TO BE AN
ENTREPRENEUR

TO BE AN ENTREPRENEUR

Social Enterprise and Disruptive Development in Bangladesh

Julia Qermezi Huang

CORNELL UNIVERSITY PRESS   ITHACA AND LONDON

First published 2020 by Cornell University Press

Library of Congress Cataloging-in-Publication Data

Names: Huang, Julia, author.
Title: To be an entrepreneur : social enterprise and disruptive development in Bangladesh / Julia Qermezi Huang.
Description: Ithaca : Cornell University Press, 2020. | Includes bibliographical references and index.
Identifiers: LCCN 2019030757 (print) | LCCN 2019030758 (ebook) | ISBN 9781501748271 (hardcover) | ISBN 9781501749551 (paperback) | ISBN 9781501748738 (epub) | ISBN 9781501748745 (pdf)
Subjects: LCSH: Women in development—Bangladesh. | Businesswomen—Bangladesh. | Social entrepreneurship—Bangladesh. | Poor women—Bangladesh. | Ethnology—Bangladesh.
Classification: LCC HQ1240.5.B3 H73 2020 (print) | LCC HQ1240.5.B3 (ebook) | DDC 305.48/2095492—dc23
LC record available at https://lccn.loc.gov/2019030757
LC ebook record available at https://lccn.loc.gov/2019030758

For the iAgents
and their futures

Contents

Figures and Illustrations

Acknowledgments

The research on which this project is based was generously supported by fellowships from the London School of Economics (LSE, 2011–14) and a grant from the Netherlands Organisation for Scientific Research (2014–16, as part of the LSE Innovation and Co-Creation Lab's project on "Productive Employment: Research on Inclusive Development"). Organizing this material into book form was possible through an LSE Fellowship in Economic Anthropology (2016–17), which provided me time, mentorship, and a vibrant intellectual community. I am honored and thankful for the expression of confidence in my work.

I am grateful for the institutional support of the Tata Institute of Social Sciences in Guwahati (Assam, Northeast India) and the BRAC Development Institute at BRAC University in Dhaka (Bangladesh). Geeta Borooah, Rafiul Karim, Anthony Sarker, Prerna Sharma, and Rima Treon helped to prepare me to conduct research in Assamese, Bangla (Bengali), and Hindi while my project sought geographic (and therefore linguistic) roots.

In Dhaka, I am deeply grateful to the Barolo-Rizvi and Awal families. Gowher Uncle, Agnese, Maya, Tafsir, and Tajwar transformed my research trips to the capital into adventurous and reenergizing experiences from the time Maya and I shared a moment of bemused skepticism at a social business conference. The Barolo-Rizvis gave me a home, and they will always have my deep affection.

The London School of Economics provided a dynamic environment for this project to come to life, and many friends and colleagues have sharpened my thinking, commented on my work, and helped to make the writing process a lively one. They are too numerous to mention, but special thanks go to Natalia Buitron Arias, Harry Barkema, Agustin Diz, Andrea Elsik, Matthew Engelke, Katharine Fletcher, David Graeber, Luke Heslop, Yanina Hinrichsen, Tomas Hinrichsen (and of course Bob), Geoffrey Hughes, Deborah James, Naila Kabeer, David Lewis, Meadhbh McIvor, Mary Montgomery, Fuad Musallam, Chloe Nahum-Claudel, Mathijs Pelkmans, Andrea Pia, Fernande Pool, Mitch Sedgwick, and Alice Tilche, as well as Catherine Dolan at SOAS and Bridget Kustin at the University of Oxford. Thank you to all the members of the writing seminars, the economic anthropology seminar, and the Friday research seminar on anthropological theory, who provided thoughtful engagement with this work in progress. Current team members in social anthropology and the international development group at the University of Edinburgh supported me to bring this book project through its final stages and gave me a new and welcoming intellectual home. They are many: Jamie Cross, Andreas Hackl, Ian Harper, Lotte Hoek, Delwar Hussain, Lucy Lowe, Rebecca Marsland, Michaela McCaffrey, Jeevan Sharma, and Alice Street deserve special mention. I could not ask for better new friends and colleagues.

I feel tremendous gratitude to my mentors. Mukulika guided me through the early (India-based) phases, and she continued to support me through key transitions and to provide opportunities for professional development. Katy Gardner joined my project in the writing stage and offered consistently insightful feedback as she pushed me to identify the particularities about this moment of change for Bangladesh. Laura Bear has been a wonderful mentor and source of inspiration for a decade. I always left meetings with her full of ideas and motivated to start the next piece of writing. She often helped me to see arguments I was making before I realized myself what they were. Lois Beck, Jamie Cross, Geert De Neve, David Lewis, Caroline Schuster, and Anke Schwittay deserve special mention for providing deeply engaged and extensive sets of comments on entire drafts of the manuscript that proved fundamental to transforming this project into the book that it is today.

Jim Lance has been the ideal acquisitions editor. Much gratitude goes to him, and to Jennifer Savran Kelly, Julia Cook, and the team at Cornell University Press for taking notice of my work and helping me produce it into a real live book.

A version of chapter 2 was previously published in an article titled "Digital Aspirations: 'Wrong-Number' Mobile-Phone Relationships and Experimental Ethics among Women Entrepreneurs in Rural Bangladesh," which appears in the *Journal of the Royal Anthropological Institute* (24, no.1 [2018]: 107–25). Parts of chapters 4 and 6, here substantially revised, appear in an article titled "The Ambiguous Figures of Social Enterprise: Gendered Flexibility and Relational Work among the iAgents of Bangladesh," published in *American Ethnologist* (44, no. 4 [2017]: 603–16). One scene described in chapter 6 appears in an article titled "Transient Assemblages, Ephemeral Encounters, and the 'Beautiful Story' of a Japanese Social Enterprise in Rural Bangladesh," published in *Critique of Anthropology* (40, no. 3 [2020]). Permission to reprint is gratefully acknowledged.

Many people have contributed to this project over the years, often unwittingly, through their encouragement, friendship, and professional inspiration. Mosharrof Hossain, Kelly Michel, Will Muir, Maria Clara Pinheiro, Ananya Raihan, Pradip Sarmah, Irina Snissar, Vipin Thekkekalathil, Pooja Warier, and everyone in AIESEC anchored me in optimism for the world of social enterprise. From Agustin Diz, Meadhbh McIvor, and Katharine Fletcher flowed an endless supply of irreverent laughs and the knowledge that we were all in this process together. From Erin Finicane, Kenya Lyons, Margaret Kearney, and Pan Pan Fan, some of the strongest women I know, came the inspiration that as our paths branch off, we always come back to one another. To Bridget Taylor, Katrina Rankin, and the team at Tribe Cycle and to Mark Jennings, Reynold Antwi, and the team at Another_Space: This project was fueled by the energy you brought to every single day. A group of people have explored the Scottish Highlands with me, and these trips have been an important part of mental clarity; I am grateful to Ian Harper, Casey High, Elliott Oakley, Jean-Benoit Falisse, and Simon and Joanne Cooper and Luke Brady (Adventure Family!). Luke, you witnessed this writing project unfold from start to end and all over again; thank you for keeping me grounded and energized through our cooking projects, cycling adventures, and appreciation for the here and now.

My parents, Lois Beck and Henry Huang, have always encouraged my international adventures. It was they who instilled in me a deep curiosity to learn how the world works. Mom, thank you for sharing ethnographic worlds (both mine and yours) with me, providing the foundational experiences that drive much of what I do today, and teaching me the craft of writing. Dad, you always encouraged me to look for the bigger picture, the deeper patterns, and the wider significance of things, and that drive has served me well in this project.

Most of all, I thank the social enterprise leaders and workers, the members of partner organizations, and the many individuals who strove in their particular ways to make Bangladesh a better place. Protecting their identities prevents me from mentioning them by name. One person in particular guided me through the intricacies of the social enterprise and laid bare its deepest flaws and his deepest hopes for its improvement. I wish him and his family all the best for their ongoing endeavors. My deepest gratitude is reserved for the dozens of young women entrepreneurs who have shared with me their lives, homes, families, daily trials and tribulations, and dreams for a better future. Their stories populate these pages (although all errors remain mine), and it is my hope that sharing these narratives will lead to better circumstances for young people like them in the future.

Abbreviations

ACRU   Akaas Center for Rural Upliftment
BOP   base/bottom of the pyramid
BRAC   Building Resources Across Communities (formerly Bangladesh Rural
        Advancement Committee)
CSR   corporate social responsibility
DFID   Department for International Development (UK)
GDP   gross domestic product
ICT4D   information and communication technologies for development
MDG   millennium development goal
MLM   multi-level marketing
NGO   non-governmental organization
PMO   prime minister's office
RTI   right to information
TIE   Technological Innovation for Empowerment
SAF   Shabar Adhikar Foundation
SSI   Sustainable Sourcing International
UISC   Union Information Service Center
UNDP   United Nations Development Programme
USAID   United States Agency for International Development
USB   universal serial bus
USD   United States dollar
VGF   vulnerable group feeding

Note on Style

Language: Research was conducted primarily in the Bangla (Bengali) language. I represent Bangla words as transcriptions (to be as phonetically accurate as possible) rather than transliterations, in order to capture more closely the nature of vernacular speech.

Currency: In July 2013, the value of the Bangladeshi taka was approximately 78 BDT for one US dollar.

Names: Key personal, organizational, locational, and other key identifying details have been altered to protect the anonymity of my interlocutors.

Prologue: Digital First Responders

December 2013. iAgent Rahela and I were cooking spiced potatoes for her family's breakfast over the fire pit behind her thatched house when her mobile phone rang. Something had happened near the railway station at the market town, a district official reported, and she should cancel her plans for the day and attend immediately. Rahela handed the wooden spoon to her younger sister and called iAgents Rimi and Brishti to join us. We wheeled our bicycles from her yard to the dirt road.

As the four of us cycled across the fields bordering the train tracks, we saw the upraised rail line, a throng of people, and train cars laying in unnatural positions. The train had derailed, and onlookers informed us that there were many casualties. The engine and the first few cars had shot off the tracks—at the location where the fishplates had been deliberately removed—and rested crumpled on their sides at the bottom of the steep embankment.

The time was one of unprecedented political chaos, at least in Rahela's memory. Opposition parties were boycotting the upcoming national elections because the ruling Awami League did not heed demands that it resign and establish a neutral administration to oversee the polls (M. Chowdhury 2015; Islam 2015). The protests (*hartals*) were forms of mass demonstration that meant the shutdown of workplaces, offices, shops, and roadways sometimes for a week at a time. Shutdowns were often enforced violently by sabotaging railway tracks, felling trees across highways, and throwing firebombs at vehicles daring to travel. Thus far, *hartals* for iAgents had meant that they needed to avoid markets, but the protesters primarily targeted shopkeepers and drivers who supported the ruling party, not girls on bicycles. *Hartal* violence had so far been a distant, nationwide reality, an ever-present danger. Yet this danger existed just beyond the boundaries of the "local," which for the iAgents and me meant the fifteen-kilometer (9.3-mile) radius within which we cycled each day. The national political drama had now entered the intimate and everyday lives of the iAgents.

We left our bicycles at Brishti's aunt's house in a village across the tracks and fought our way through the crowd. A family stood guard over a plot of young rice plants near the embankment and attempted in vain to hold back the multitude of onlookers and interrupted passengers with a length of rope. The train's engine car leaked thick black oil onto another family's tiny agricultural plot. A small boy, squatting in the field, used a piece of bent metal gathered from strewn train parts to spoon the oil into a plastic bottle. Hawkers availed of the concentration of people to sell newspaper-wrapped packets of puffed rice.

We searched for the officer who had telephoned Rahela. We found him in a dense cluster of people pointing their camera phones at the ground. The officer shuttled us to the center, where we encountered three dead bodies. "You have to take their photos so we can identify them," he instructed.

Rimi and Brishti pulled out their Sony cameras, and Rahela held out the tablet she had received as an award for high performance as an iAgent. At no point did the iAgents display emotion or self-consciousness as they shoved men aside to view the bodies and efficiently cover all angles. Rimi and Brishti commented jealously that Rahela had been the one called for the job because she possessed a tablet, which people considered a more professional piece of photography equipment than a point-and-shoot camera. Rahela retorted that they could have won the tablet too if they had decided to work harder. After promising to print copies of the photographs for the officer, the iAgents and I headed back to Brishti's aunt's house. We scrubbed the mud off our feet and trouser hems and then went to the nearby market to buy winter shawls.

The next day, people on the distant river islands where Rahela resumed her normal work discussed the train accident. Rahela interrupted these conversations by asserting that we had been there to witness it firsthand and she launched into a dynamic account of the event and the number of people who had died. Tears in her eyes, she described poignantly how seeing one of the three victims, an old man, made her experience intense suffering (*onek kosto kortechi*). She noted how dirty he looked lying on the hard ground, when he had probably bathed that morning in anticipation of the journey. He and the other victims did not have mobile phones with them, only small plastic bags carrying extra clothing and their tickets. "And they had only one more stop to go!" Rahela lamented, her tears streaming. She commented on the poverty of the three victims, which she interpreted from the quality of their clothing, and said that she had sobbed while looking at the old man. No one had come to claim them even twelve hours after the accident. "They didn't have anyone. Can you imagine how terrible it would be not to have any people?"

I wondered about the seeming disjuncture between Rahela's response at the accident site and her narration of it later. Perhaps she was initially in shock, and the emotion developed more fully in the social context of reliving and retelling. Perhaps also she intuitively knew that firsthand experience of local news was a resource that might connect her to her clients more personally. Perhaps her varying ways of dealing with the events were a means of coming to terms with the intense uncertainties and anxieties of life in rural Bangladesh as an iAgent.

In this book we see how young women occupy the forefront of transformation and ambitious expectation, as Bangladesh undergoes monumental change in its economy and society. They epitomize the liminality, precariousness, and ambiguity that characterize the country's experience with the conflicting registers of speculative growth accompanying developmental "success" and blockaded mobility generated by political chaos.

Two of "the world's busiest laboratories" (M. Chowdhury 2015, 192)—in constitutional democracy and market-driven development models—converge in this scene of young women attending to a sabotaged train in northwestern Bangladesh. The disruptive events and changes provoked by these "social laboratory" experiments in politics and development are summons for alternative and better futures, but they also intensify the already precarious existence of many people. In both cases—as the political elite engages in the destructive politics of violently contested elections and the economic elite marketizes social programs that previously existed as "charity" or "welfare"—it is the poor who are most negatively affected and who experience aggravated inequalities. Interrupted livelihoods, forfeited land, and the fear of not belonging to key social support structures are central to the stories of many families in Bangladesh. The train derailment not only symbolizes the unsettled everyday lives of citizens while political parties act at whatever cost to assert their agendas. It also serves as a metaphor for the ruptures that people face as new types of organizations rearrange social relationships in the name of poverty alleviation and societal betterment—for instance, as new patronage models threaten the ability of old patrons to look after their beneficiaries. Citizens experience these broader events as ethical disjunctures that reference the erosion of social values, which iAgents seek to repair for themselves through various projects.

Broader anxieties about the ways in which social relations are changing in Bangladesh are brought to bear especially on young women who challenge gender norms. This book documents the aspirations and struggles of young women who work as iAgent entrepreneurs as they try to handle the transitions from home-based work to outside work, from philanthropic modes of development organization to dispassionate market-driven ones, and from paternalistic patronage relations to detached ones promising "empowerment." This book traces changes within a social enterprise model in the context of emergent global development priorities, shifting class structures and relations, and gendered constraints and opportunities in the country. As Bangladesh further experiments with governance structures, liberalizes its economy, decentralizes its state functions, and submits its poverty-alleviation plans to local and global markets, young women—as garment workers, health-extension workers, microcredit customers, and iAgents—bear a remarkable burden of emergent and contradictory expectations and new forms of accumulation and aspiration.

TO BE AN
ENTREPRENEUR

DISRUPTIVE DEVELOPMENT IN BANGLADESH

Entrepreneurial Pathways

February 2013. Rahela and Taspia, two iAgents living in different districts in northwestern Bangladesh, set out each morning by bicycle on the hard-packed dirt paths leading out of their villages. The shawl of one and the thick sweater of the other kept the morning chill away and concealed their teal and yellow uniforms. The sun had risen, but only a dim brightening of the thick late-winter fog divulged it. The young women turned onto main roads and slowed to avoid potholes that appeared only moments before their front wheels would tumble over them.

Signs of life began to appear. Taspia saw men clad in *lungis* [cloth sarong] and bent ankle-deep in paddy fields while they thrust individual electric-green young rice shoots into the sodden earth. Rahela nodded to elderly men wrapped in blankets who emerged from thatch houses for morning walks. Pullers of flatbed rickshaw carts sat in clusters while they drank steaming tea and waited for passengers. Few women ventured to the road this early in the morning; they were tending animals and preparing breakfast.

Rahela and Taspia each described how the feeling of flying along the road made them cycle faster, pushing against the wind. Large satchels strapped to rear racks carried the iAgents' tools of the trade—laptops, modems, and digital health equipment. The young women carried the hope that each tomorrow would be slightly different and better than today.

July 2013. Five months later, and nearly every day in between, the two women were again on the road to pursue the day's work. The first of the two, Rahela in Lalpur subdistrict, eagerly took the paved track to the market, where a tailor had just finished her new three-piece outfit (*shalwar, kameez,* and *urna*; a knee-length tunic over loose cotton trousers and a scarf draped over the shoulders) made of embroidered cloth of a design imported from India. Along the way, people waved or shouted a greeting as she passed. Exchanging friendly news with the tailor, she wrapped the bundle of cloth carefully and tucked it away, eager to hear her aunts' exclamations as they inspected the quality of the handiwork. She would change clothing when she arrived at their house so that her new outfit would stay fresh in the humid monsoon heat. It was Ramadan, the month of fasting, and that day Rahela would visit her mother's natal village. She would invite her relatives to celebrate an Eid ul-fitr (end of Ramadan) meal with her parents and younger siblings so that they could see the finished work of her parents' house. Rahela herself had paid for the renovations by using her iAgent earnings and hiring her unemployed cousins to replace the brittle bamboo frame with freshly cut stalks and to exchange the disintegrating thatch walls for fresh tin panels. In the middle of a month in which people were more sedate because of fasting from dawn to dusk, Rahela provided only casual iAgent services and advice, serving the regular customers who visited her house and refraining from holding group sessions and traveling far from home. Her duties managing the shop adjacent to her house had lessened since her father and brother began working there full time. Most days of Ramadan, she sat on a platform in the bamboo thicket opposite her house, enjoyed the breeze, and took one call after another on her mobile phone. "The families who used to criticize me now send me monthly marriage proposals. But I don't want or need any of them!" Rahela laughed.

Meanwhile, the second young woman, Taspia in Amirhat subdistrict, struggled to move her bicycle on interior roads to reach the village of her farmers' group. Her muscles burned as she forced the soft tires to turn on the soggy path, and several times she sank into inches of mud. She found it difficult to pull her bicycle out of the waterlogged earth, and in so doing she dirtied her *shalwar* hems and nearly lost her sandals. Rather than helping her, men hanging out on a roadside bamboo platform spoke hurtful words about the impropriety of girls riding bicycles. Taspia ignored them. She had been too exhausted from a full day of work the previous day to arise for *sehri,* the predawn meal before a day of fasting. Now, in the forty-degree Celsius (104 degrees Fahrenheit) heat with the full humidity of the monsoon, she regretted not having drunk a large glass of water. Sweat stung her eyes, but she had to keep struggling. Her first iAgent loan installment of 2,632 taka (34 USD) was due this month. She had earned less than 800 taka (10 USD) in her first three months as an iAgent, and she would need that money to purchase Eid gifts and food for her parents and sisters. No one else in her family had the financial means to contribute in this way. What would the neighbors say if Taspia and her family were the only people not wearing new clothes on Eid? How shameful it would be if, instead of distributing beef *pulao* (rice cooked in a seasoned broth) to visitors, they would be the ones slipping into their relatives' houses for a meal. Having no brothers to step in when their father injured himself at the jute processing factory where he worked for a pittance, Taspia took it upon herself to play the role. Yet her dream of rescuing her family from poverty seemed ever more elusive, especially when she arrived at her destination to find that none of the farmers had shown up for her session; instead they were napping in the shade of their homes. "I'll never get married," Taspia lamented. "Before it was because we had no money for a dowry. But now it is because this iAgent hawker work is so shameful and forces me to go here and there peddling things people won't buy! My reputation is ruined."

The iAgents of Bangladesh

How did these two individuals—in a place where women were expected to stay at home and computers were absent outside of district centers—come to be riding bicycles and carrying a suite of electronics? Why did Rahela's and Taspia's present circumstances vary so starkly, despite their common social backgrounds, village contexts, and present livelihood? What does it mean to be an entrepreneur in rural Bangladesh?

This book addresses the ascendant place of entrepreneurship in development projects and settings across the globe. It takes place in Bangladesh, a country at the forefront of inventing market-based development models, and in the context of women's empowerment as a continuing key development strategy. This account also identifies the ethos of "disruptive innovation" that signals the increasing influence of Silicon Valley–style cutting-edge managerial-science approaches on international development practice, especially in social entrepreneurship. The concept of "disruption"—which in business circles is understood as the valorized process of displacing established organizations, institutions, and value networks with radically improved business models and offerings—is also a productive and critical analytic device to describe the broader, progressive and regressive actions and effects of market-driven development.

That both young people described above acted outside of women's customary roles in Bangladeshi village society is beyond doubt. Yet the impact of their iAgent work disrupted their lives in profoundly different ways. While the identity of "iAgent" enabled one of the two young women to accrue status within her family and other established relationships, it offered shame and stigma for the other. Rahela seemed to have displaced herself from the prevailing gendered ordering of work outside the home and she managed to reverse some aspects of gendered hierarchy by enlisting her male family members in furthering her projects. Taspia's life was certainly disrupted as well, but in a disempowering way. Instead of an expansion of power and agency, she experienced a contraction of her life's possibilities.

The divergence in the two women's experiences, as I argue throughout this book, is an outcome pattern of poverty capitalism, the set of ideologies and practices that organizes the poor to participate in new forms of accumulation and market activity in the name of poverty alleviation and profit making.[1] The stories of Rahela and Taspia are thus not entirely unique; they represent a pattern of possibilities encountered by thousands of women in districts across Bangladesh and by millions of social enterprise participants across the world. Social enterprise, with its ethics of disruptive innovation, is a key organizational form of poverty capitalism and is the focus of this book. Other market-based movements— such as microfinance, financial inclusion (or, in policy parlance, "banking the unbanked"), and information and communication technologies for development (ICT4D)—are also significant components of the iAgent assemblage. In the following chapters, I explore the ways in which these practices influence people's experiences of agency.

"Disruptive innovation," a term coined by the business consultant and scholar Clayton Christensen (1997), refers to a novel idea, device, or method that creates a new market by providing an alternative set of values that ultimately displaces an existing market with its established values. While it has been applied primarily to Western capitalist markets, the language of disruptive innovation has also been adopted by many social enterprises to refer to the ways in which their development models provide compelling, marketized alternatives to disadvantageous or regressive "traditional" practices. Institutional microfinance, for instance, replaces local moneylenders; smokeless stoves with charcoal briquettes eliminate the need for women to collect firewood and risk carbon monoxide poisoning while cooking; and mobile phones and solar home systems leapfrog over the technologies of landlines and connections to the national electricity grid. The aim of disruptive innovators is not to offer incremental improvements to existing practices and lifestyles of the poor, as many development and aid projects seek to do, but rather to introduce radical, game-changing business models that transform the fundamental ways in which the poor interact with markets and thereby improve their own lives.

The architects behind these initiatives, which include the iAgent model, imagine a positive cycle of disruption, in which the new, the market, and the modern release people from the fetters of inefficient customary social practices and relations. Yet they fail to consider the more pernicious effects of dislocating people from existing webs of dependencies without providing alternative inclusive support structures on which people can rely.

This book therefore explores disruptive development from two perspectives. First, it examines the valorized narratives and exemplars of social enterprise—such as stories the organization tells about iAgent Rahela—in which market access and cutting-edge technologies propel people along a linear path of self-improvement. Second, the book calls attention to the actual experiences of social disruption that occur when already vulnerable people such as Taspia are pushed into circumstances of heightened moral scrutiny and are held personally responsible for market failure.

"Disruption" is also a concept that slices across different scales. At a global level, the environment of competitive market innovation in development practice produces models like the iAgent program and frameworks of authoritative knowledge that vie to be replicated around the world. As innovations gain traction and capture the attention of funders and investors, they disrupt existing development models, capital flows, and infrastructures based on NGOs, aid, and charity. At the local level, as market-driven development practices transform the logics of resource distribution and hierarchies of accountability, they dislocate development actors from existing structures of class and connection and reorder patron-client networks.

Such observations do not imply that older forms of development are best perpetuated or that development actors should not innovate. But they do call upon social enterprise practitioners and commentators to pay close attention to the experiences of beneficiaries and the many ways in which dislocating them from familiar structures can be both liberating and precarious. There are many different kinds of social enterprise, and many different ways to define what a social enterprise is and is not. While I do not enter into definitional debates here, these differences often hinge around the diverse ways to structure the relationship between the market activities and social work aspects of the organization. In this book, I refer specifically to social enterprises where the basis of income generation (and/or profit-making) stems from the labor or the purchasing power of the poor.

The iAgent Social Entrepreneurship Program is a key example of the new ethos of market and social disruption. The program comprised a network of individuals and organizations championing the idea that young Bangladeshi women from poor villages who were trained to serve as information agents, or "iAgents," could transform themselves as well as their communities. Equipped with internet-enabled laptops, digital medical equipment, and multimedia content on topics including family planning, legal rights, agricultural techniques, and hygiene, iAgents traveled by bicycle to provide access to information to marginalized villagers. These young entrepreneurs—Rahela, Taspia, and over one hundred others in 2013—charged a small fee for each service and attempted to generate an income sufficient to support themselves and their families. The overarching aim of the iAgent program's architects was not only to shake women free of patriarchal structures and restrictive norms about women's work being limited to the home but also to revolutionize (and marketize) the ways in which development resources would be distributed throughout rural society, with these women as new market-makers.

The iAgent model was created by Technological Innovation for Empowerment (TIE), a Bangladesh-based non-governmental organization (NGO) based in Dhaka, the country's capital. (Like all key names in this book, the names of the organization, the program, and its personnel have been given pseudonyms to protect the anonymity of my sources.) TIE was founded and comprised by a fully Bangladeshi leadership and membership base. Thus, while it took inspiration from global trends in development, the organization retained a strong national character.

The iAgent model worked through a multitier licensing structure. TIE's private-limited corporate arm, Sustainable Sourcing International (SSI), licensed the iAgent brand through a hub-and-spoke model.[2] Local organizations across the country selected by TIE to act as midtier licensees (iAgent rural information centers, or "centers") in turn recruited young village women to be iAgents and serve in a rural distribution capacity. According to the then-current iteration of the business model, iAgents bore a 75,000 taka (962 USD) loan from a large commercial bank to invest in their training, equipment, and other start-up business costs. As license holders, iAgents had to be formally approved by TIE to operate and they sported the iAgent brand on their uniforms, equipment bags, and signs outside their houses. They were trained in a variety of services that would be performed within a radius of five villages around their own.

This for-profit structure was the second of three iAgent models with which TIE experimented during the research period (April 2013 to July 2014). The market-driven second model was an attempt to scale up rapidly the successful but donor-driven (and hence unsustainable) pilot project. Simultaneously, TIE planned its further iAgent expansion strategy with new partners and experimented with a new open-source model.

To recruit iAgents, TIE and its local NGO centers targeted young women who had completed high school or were enrolled in two-year-degree colleges. iAgents represented the poorer village households that owned little if any land. Their female relatives performed household and microcredit labor, and their male relations engaged in sharecropping and day labor. While pursuing higher education and formal employment (*chakri*) was increasingly accepted and even aspirational for young women, working "in the field" was not. Riding bicycles on tough terrain and selling services for fees and commissions and not for a salary stigmatized iAgents for violating *purdah* (gender seclusion) norms. It cast them as hawkers or as NGO workers exploitatively turning a profit on goods that many people insisted should be provided to the community for free.

In the pilot locations, where iAgents received daily support from TIE and center staff and full subsidies for their start-up costs, some young women were able to cultivate respect for their work and transform their positions within their families and wider communities. Rahela was one of these participants. While these success cases received ample attention, featuring in interviews with national and global media and occupying the glossy pages of TIE's annual reports and Facebook groups, little consideration was paid to the majority of participants, such as Taspia, who experienced a far less empowering process.

This book explores a salient trend in poverty capitalism and disruptive development: the conviction among practitioners that social entrepreneurship, along with cutting-edge information technologies, is sufficient in itself to engender women's empowerment and usher in a digital modernity. These models claim to tackle poverty through market mechanisms, pursuit of profit, and low-cost but advanced technologies in the hands of women entrepreneurs. To understand the effects on the lives of the poor targeted as "clients" of such initiatives, I conducted fifteen months of continuous ethnographic research among the iAgents of Bangladesh from April 2013 to July 2014. This book draws primarily on data from two locations: a donor-driven pilot location at the NGO Atno Bishash in Lalpur *Upazila* (subdistrict), where Rahela worked; and a failed business-model location at the NGO Akaas Center for Rural Upliftment (ACRU) in Amirhat *Upazila*, where Taspia worked. These two sites included the two centers and their forty iAgents in neighboring riverine districts in northwestern Bangladesh. Nine other license-model locations and one other pilot-model location continued to operate during the same period, and they were fraught with many of the same issues encountered by the Lalpur and Amirhat participants.

The Book's Framework: Entrepreneurship as Disruption

This book provides an in-depth ethnographic case study of a social enterprise and the new kinds of women entrepreneurs at the cutting edge of Bangladesh's efforts to become a modern, "digital" nation. It examines the emergent techniques and technologies of development that were used to reformat the social identities and behaviors of young women and configure them as individualized, profit-seeking entrepreneurs. These mechanisms of "reformatting" include the market devices, modes of information transfer, networked models of distribution, and mobile communication technologies used in creating market actors and infrastructures in pursuit of both economic and social outcomes.

The iAgent social enterprise and the larger global shift in development ideology that it exemplified displaced existing NGO-driven development practices with new business models and interrupted the socioeconomic structures on which poor people, and especially women, relied. "Disruptive" development conceptualized in this way brings class, gender, kinship, generation, territory, and labor relations back into debates on what is new and innovative about social enterprise.

What follows is a systematic examination of the disruptive development apparatus (the specific economic processes, innovative managerial-science approaches, modelling logics, and market devices and technologies) that animated the delivery of the social enterprise model and enmeshed the social identities and subjectivities of enterprise actors. The "reformatting" of subjectivities—which are entangled with class, gender, and other identities—is a resonant motif to describe the fundamental ways the technologies and techniques of entrepreneurship were implicated in subject formation and articulated across all levels of the development project. While the Silicon-Valley style of disruptive innovation and radical entrepreneurialism were central to the status- and identity-building projects of the urban development elites, these practices also implicated local development practitioners and their middle-class patronage relationships, which had been created through older NGO structures. Of most crucial importance are the fundamental ways these technologies of entrepreneurship became involved in the subject formation of the women participants and the extent to which these participants negotiated socioeconomic relationships in their attempts to establish and maintain themselves as entrepreneurs.

The chapters in this book identify the many devices, logics, and apparatuses that produced this particular social enterprise and enabled its leaders to make claims on multiple intersecting values of profit, program sustainability, and social benefit. I show how these values were pursued in a lopsided way: the enterprise mobilized village social relations for profit, but it also refused to recognize disruptions to these relations and the value systems they encoded. I reveal the violence perpetrated against actors pushed and pulled by mutually incompatible values. The financial and social risks of mediating these contradictions and multiple bottom lines were offloaded from the social enterprise onto the women entrepreneurs, whose ethical and relational labor underwrote the ability of the social enterprise to function.

Each chapter explores the ways in which women entrepreneurs primarily and development practitioners secondarily worked to resolve the conflicting values and contradictions produced by the enterprise's attempts to shape the women as digital development subjects. I also detail the tactics, compromises, gains, aspirations, and unexpected possibilities that the digital social enterprise opened up and how these diverged from messages put forward by the development organizations that promoted these initiatives. In so doing, I reveal systematically the broader social effects of disruptive development models.

Two central questions motivate the project of this book: What constitutes a social enterprise, and what does it mean to be an entrepreneur of poverty capitalism? These questions are also important beyond the local setting of poor families in Bangladesh. Market-driven poverty entrepreneurship programs proliferate across the world, and temporary and zero-hour contracts, outsourcing, and other forms of casualized and flexible labor increasingly characterize multiple kinds of economic circumstances (e.g. Gershon 2017; Snyder 2016). The relationship between entrepreneurship and empowerment is important in these and in many other contexts where a rhetoric of self-help pressures the poor and unemployed to "enterprise" their way out of precariousness and where other structures of support fall away.

Each of the book's chapters traces the intersections between and among social enterprise logics and the social lives of enterprise participants. What are the specific economic processes, market devices, and innovative managerial techniques that produced the social enterprise? In what ways did they generate contradictions for iAgents and development actors; how did these actors mediate conflicting value regimes; and what were the broader social, economic, and political effects? Six chapters are organized around three arenas of disruptive development: incongruities between social versus enterprise models of success, challenges of converting social relations into economic capital, and struggles within and between socioeconomic classes. The three parts of this book begin with short narratives, written or recorded by iAgent entrepreneurs, that situate the iAgents' experiences within the broader context of their life trajectories.

Chapter 1 examines the models of disruptive development that asserted a singular version of successful womanhood based on entrepreneurial success, one that was expressed through stories of social transformation and the use of both fictional and real-life exemplars. These stories of victory communicated the social enterprise's theory of change and narrative of women's empowerment and thus also formed the basis of the enterprise's claims of being a moral organization that delivered social benefit. Yet these models of behavior thrust upon women participants disrupted their existing livelihoods in a context in which women's work was already a field of cultural struggle and moral anxiety and a site of control over women. The use of exemplars generated the "cruel optimism" (Berlant 2011) of easy, linear empowerment, which the enterprise ultimately was unable to deliver. Participants attempted to ethicize their iAgent work within a socially valorized narrative of "kin work" (Di Leonardo 1987) and family-oriented action to protect themselves from accusations from the village community of inappropriate behavior. iAgents criticized the loss of important social values among the people around them and they cast their own activities as ones defending these values in order to reassert their claims to being ethical persons. Overall, the narrative of positive, innovative change masked the actual disruptions to women's sense of self and social identity, disruptions that were often disempowering.

Chapter 2 provides an in-depth exploration of women's efforts to reconcile tensions and problematic ethical doubts produced by a specific technology, the mobile phone, which exemplifies the new modes of sociality and connectivity required of being a digital entrepreneur. This new connectivity generated moral anxiety surrounding women's propriety and contact with unrelated men and produced further contradictions between the model of individual successful entrepreneurship and the model of successful womanhood. Women's efforts to develop and negotiate new, "digital" identities and innovative subject positions led to empowered ways of thinking about the role of men in women's working and personal lives.

We next follow iAgents as they begin their training and venture out to pursue their entrepreneurial work. Chapter 3 examines the training protocol and its mechanisms of reformatting social identities into digital entrepreneurial ones to produce a female workforce that would serve as both the agents and objects of development for the social enterprise. The asocial entrepreneurial model of behavior, however, proved to be incongruous with everyday social life and generated conflicting socialities, temporalities, and relational obligations. Women in one iAgent location were unable to mediate these incongruities, and the structure of the program meant that they absorbed the negative consequences of the program's failure. This case exemplifies the new model of development that enables NGO resource accumulation while it offloads the financial and social risks of failure onto the "beneficiaries." New managerial-science approaches enabled the social enterprise to control the flow of information and disinformation and to detach itself from negative consequences.

iAgents who managed to persist in the program beyond the training phase encountered a diversified basket of services that they were tasked with delivering to the community. The multiple services—spanning public goods, private consumer products, and development inputs—required different types of provider roles and were driven by clashing transactional logics. In chapter 4, we see how iAgents had to engage in continuous, exhausting switching among multiple types of roles. The ethical labor they undertook to manage these contradictions included enduring community critique, engaging in extreme spending on their families, and entering into unfair alliances. These processes solidified a model in which the hidden but intense and distressing relational work of young women underwrote the capital accumulation of social enterprise owners and investors. They also disempowered those women who could not or refused to mediate between and among all of these conflicting roles and value regimes.

Chapter 5 shifts the focus to the public narrative of radical innovation, which was controlled by the elite leadership of the enterprise. Wikipedia entries, Facebook pages, annual reports, and program websites were outward-facing renditions of the iAgent program that attracted foreign investment and also served as the currency of elite status and recognition. These sites of narrative-building remained inaccessible to lower-level (rural) partners and head office leaders with alternative viewpoints. Conflict over program direction and resentment over the unfair distribution of credit manifested as epistemic struggles among the urban elite leadership. Among the rural staff and implementation partners, new strategic directions destabilized the fundamental nature of their relationships with beneficiaries. Local NGO leaders either refused to exploit the poor and rejected these new models (thereby losing funding) or pursued these new models (and thus broke from the existing system of local patron-client reciprocity). In both cases, emergent models eviscerated the capacity of local organizations to engage in meaningful rural development. These changes heralded a new class dynamic marked by a shift from the "social inequality" characterizing the patronage of NGO leaders providing for rural clients to the "antisocial inequality" that resulted as development networks became delinked from local, preexisting patronage networks. All of these alterations resulted in the diminished ability of the poor to make claims on resources and the curtailed capacity of local patrons to support "their own poor."

Another aspect of controlling the narrative was the deliberately fluid portrayal of the role of the iAgent entrepreneurs, as described in chapter 6. This flexibility enabled enterprise leaders to accommodate the expectations of multiple types of partners and to display the enterprise's commitment to empowering young women as free agents while also dictating the women's everyday activities. Different representations (with underlying implications for the entrepreneur-enterprise relationship) were required for producing (social) value and extracting (economic) value. iAgents encountered a playbook with constantly shifting rules, which guided the relations, responsibilities, and power dynamics between themselves and enterprise managers. While social enterprise staff were able to flip easily and profitably among these different representations, iAgents struggled to defend their own interests and they complied or resisted by emphasizing one or another particular set of rules. These multiple systems in action reveal only a partial transition for the entrepreneurs, from an NGO patronage moral economy to a market-based one. The resulting processes retained the relations of domination of the former while allowing the disavowal of organizational responsibility of the latter. As a result, the poor lost access to crucial protections while still being exploited by the NGO middle classes.

The conclusion ties together the themes of the book, suggests the implications that these market-driven models have for people's experiences of agency, and indicates ways in which development policy and practice might work more productively for the poor.

Bangladesh in Transformation

Between Political Chaos and Development "Success"

The three young rural women in the prologue who were acting in the capacity of iAgents to help identify the latest victims of Bangladesh's political violence exemplify the contradictory effects of political assemblages that simultaneously undermine public infrastructure and increase inequality while also celebrating achievements in industry, development, and women's empowerment.

Since Bangladesh gained state sovereignty in 1971 following a bloody war of independence from Pakistan, citizens have endured ongoing environmental and political turmoil. The country has undergone severe floods and cyclones; mass demonstrations, protests, strikes, and mutiny; executions of political opponents; bomb blasts and infrastructural sabotage; boycotted elections; and politically preventable industrial disasters. These events and incidences resulted in the death, injury, starvation, displacement, and homelessness of hundreds of millions of people.

During political turmoil in 2013–14, three hundred people were killed in violence relating to parliamentary elections when the ruling and opposition parties were unable to compromise. Violent strikes, public protests, and street battles shut down workplaces, interrupted educational processes, and cut off movement in the country. Linked also with the executions of (primarily oppositional) political leaders convicted of war crimes as well as with debates over the place of political Islam in the national democratic system, these events exposed "the level of political volatility at play, the weakening law and order situation in the country, and a virulent strain of political and pseudo-religiosity that is trying to move from the obscure margins to the mainstream" (Dominguez 2015, n.p.). Such is the political environment that created the railway disruption that the iAgents and I witnessed in 2013.[3]

Despite conditions of political instability and continuing high levels of poverty (the country ranked 142nd out of 187 countries on the United Nations Development Program's Human Development Index in 2016), Bangladesh simultaneously gained international attention as a development "success" ("The Path through the Fields" 2012). From being "best known for its poverty and the natural disasters that hit it with depressing regularity" (Wassener 2012, n.p.) and famously derided upon its independence as a "perpetual economic basket case" (a comment often misattributed to United States Secretary of State Henry Kissinger; see Lewis 2011, 36), Bangladesh was increasingly heralded as a progressive testing ground for development innovations (Faaland and Parkinson 1976). Its rapid progress toward achieving the United Nations Millennium Development Goals (MDGs) gained the country respect for reducing poverty by half, attaining gender parity at the primary and secondary education levels, and reducing infant and maternal mortality by the MDGs' target date of 2015 (Bangladesh Planning Commission 2015; UNDP n.d.).

Much of this international attention has centered on the targeting of women in poverty alleviation and economic growth efforts. "Decades of microlending and, more recently, the growing garment industry have underpinned the progress by turning millions of women into breadwinners for their families," an article in the *New York Times* declared (Wassener 2012, n.p.). Following the global spread of institutional microfinance popularized by Dr. Muhammad Yunus in the 1980s in Bangladesh, Yunus and his bank, the Grameen Bank, were awarded the Nobel Peace Prize in 2006 and the Congressional Gold Medal in 2010, the United States' highest civilian award. Since its inception in 1976, the Grameen Bank had garnered seven million borrowers, 97 percent of whom were women, and had disbursed three hundred billion taka (over 3.8 billion USD) to them.

The garment industry accounted for three-quarters of Bangladesh's exports (24.5 billion USD) in fiscal year 2013–14 and constituted 80 percent of all export earnings and 13 percent of gross domestic product, signaling a dramatic structural shift in the economy—from an agrarian one to one of export-oriented manufacturing. A majority of the four million people employed in the country's three thousand textile factories are women from rural areas. Such a shift was encouraged by the World Bank (2016, n.p.): "Increasing female participation in the labor force and boosting private investment are current priorities to maximize growth and help realize the country's goals of becoming a middle income country." The garment industry's targeting of women as low-cost and docile labor mobilized for corporate and national profit (while overemphasizing the benefits enjoyed by the women) typifies the ideology and practice of poverty capitalism.

The dream of "Digital Bangladesh" (part of the political manifesto of the ruling Awami League party) embodies the national modernist philosophy of using digital technology to ensure national growth and the democratic principles of transparency and accountability. Children read about "Digital Bangladesh" in their textbooks; they check their examination results online at state-outsourced union information service centers, where they later participate in online international labor recruitment processes; and they register their parents for NGO-delivered e-services. Through the successful integration of information and communication technologies (ICTs) in education, health, and labor regimes, Bangladesh aspires to reduce poverty and enhance the productivity of its citizens.

This book explores the meanings of new livelihood opportunities, different kinds of economic activity and work for women, and the cultivation of aspirations for digital modernity. These macroeconomic and global stage events offer the context in which the idea of the iAgent—female entrepreneurs who took on loans to build ICT-based businesses in order to lift their families and thus the country out of poverty—took root and secured the backing of powerful actors and institutions.

Structures of Connection in Rural Bangladesh

At the time of my research, families such as those of Rahela and Taspia and the majority of other rural Bangladeshi people lived in small villages of fifty to one hundred households (250–500 individuals) some distance away from towns and market centers. Households typically contained three or four generations, including paternal grandparents, parents, brothers with their wives and children, and unmarried sisters. Marriage was patrilocal (although exceptions were common), and brothers often formed separate households shortly after marriage. The majority (90 percent) of people in Bangladesh were Sunni Muslims, while Hindus constituted 9 percent of the population. This ratio is also reflected in the constitution of iAgents selected across the country.

In the northwestern riverine districts where I conducted research, houses were constructed from bamboo pole frames sunk into a packed-earth platform and lashed as crossbeams to support a corrugated tin roof. Walls and fences were made of bamboo strips and jute woven into mats. Brothers' houses often faced a joint internal fenced-in yard where socializing and primary cooking, washing, and bathing around a tube well occurred. Men and women did not have separate spaces; everyone used the house and yard. Men's daily work took them to the fields for sharecropping, the roads for day labor in construction or driving rickshaws, and the market for daily shopping. Women's work occurred primarily inside the communal yard, but they also visited the market and socialized with other women in the village's open spaces. Few of these households owned land sufficient for cultivation, and the average daily wage that men brought home was 150 taka (1.92 USD), which placed them at (and fluctuating above and below) the national poverty line of 2 USD per day (along with 47 million, or 26 percent, of Bangladeshis in 2010; Bhowmick 2013, n.p.).[4]

The majority of people in rural Bangladesh, over the last three generations, have accessed two main structures of social connection for obtaining resources: inclusion in kinship patronage relationships and participation in NGO programs (another form of patronage). Without enforceable claims to formal entitlements (as offered by the government) such as infrastructure, secure contract employment, social security, healthcare, and education, social connections of access were key to survival and upward mobility (Gardner 2012; Hussain 2013).

Other potential structures of access were not widely available for the poor in many areas. State patronage (such as lifelong and secure salaried contracts, housing, and pensions) was abundant for people who obtained coveted government jobs in administration, bureaucracy, hospitals, and schools. Access to these jobs required education and training, success in passing a rigorous and competitive entry examination, connections to decision-makers within these bodies, and hefty "fees" or bribes.

State social safety net programs, such as the Vulnerable Group Feeding (VGF) program, provided food to low-income families in the wake of natural disasters and for age- or disability-related incapacities to meet basic survival needs. Other programs were meant to help housewives to earn a living through investing in assets such as poultry and fish farms. Despite the fact that up to 2 percent of Bangladesh's gross domestic product was spent on social security, 70 percent of poor people did not receive any support directly from the state (The World Bank 2014). Lower-level state bureaucrats regularly captured the benefits and distributed them among their clients. Rural people often associated the receipt of government safety net benefits with the shame of non-kin charity, which may have been another reason why people did not seek to claim their entitlements (Gardner 1995, 152).

Within Islamic patronage moralities, charitable contributions in the form of *zakat* (compulsory alms-giving) and *lila* (ritual distribution at festivals) were other means of helping the destitute. The charity given as alms to non-kin beggars was distinct from help given to the poor of one's own lineage (Gardner 1995, 152). The act of asking for help from within the lineage carried little shame or stigma, but asking for charity from strangers did. Islamic charity as a source of help was thus irrelevant for most poor people. Only the destitute were recipients and only marginally so, because *zakat* did not provide a means for them to change their circumstances. Poor families were also expected to give *zakat*, usually in the form of rice cakes to visiting beggars during festivals and uncooked rice or other basic commodities on other days. When people lamented that the local rich no longer helped the poor, and I asked about *zakat*, they frequently responded that *zakat* is "for orphans and cripples but not for us."

The following paragraphs offer an overview of the central role that kinship and NGO patronage structures played in the lives of the rural poor in Bangladesh in the absence of other forms of support. They provide context for the changing nature of people's connections.

KINSHIP PATRONAGE

In the literature on rural Bangladesh, class is often noted as difficult to identify or demarcate because of high levels of economic mobility, resulting, for example, from a son securing a wage job, a father giving a daughter's dowry, or flooding causing crop loss (White 1992, 36). Kinship-centered patron-clientage was historically the primary relationship organizing rural Bangladesh. Patronage, in the context of Bangladesh, is "a reciprocity of exchange based on unequal rank," which involves economic exploitation, political domination, and ideological control (Jahangir 1982, 88). Wealthy households exerted power over poor ones, which were dependent on such patronage to survive (Lewis 2011). Thus, kinship served not just as social order but also as safety net (van Schendel 2009, 134), crucial for many stages of life (Devine and White 2013, 136). Patron-clientage was a form of social inequality that featured an imbalance of power but also forms of reciprocity that ensured redistribution of wealth and mutual social recognition.

The division between rich and poor (*bhalamanush* and *chhotomanush*, literally "good people" and "small people"; Gardner 1995, 137) within a *gusthi* (patrilineal descent group) referred to social background, character, and education. Class was rooted historically in land tenure and a family occupying a farmer or a tenant status.[5] Continuing land ownership was central to structuring social interaction through labor relations.

Among *gusthi*s, providing *shahaja* (informal help) was perceived to be the duty of rich kin toward poor kin and was a process by which the status and reputation of the patriline was maintained (Gardner 1995, 152). Forms of help included providing meals, accommodation, loans, dowry support, lending of land, and employment within the households of the wealthy (but in a position socially distinct from that of laborers and servants). Katy Gardner draws on Pierre Bourdieu to explain the social relations of patronage that enabled material access and provided the key safety net for the poor. Bourdieu characterizes social capital as "the aggregate of the actual or potential resources which are linked to possession of a durable network of more or less institutionalized relationships of mutual acquaintance and recognition" (Bourdieu 1983, 249; in Gardner 2012, 41). People used their connections and social capital to maintain their place in the socioeconomic order and to enable the transformation of their standing. For patrons and clients, giving and receiving were social acts that enabled survival, shaped social identity, recreated social hierarchy, and maintained inequality and difference through their connectedness.

Networks of kinship help were intimately linked with the status position of the overall *gusthi*. Thus, a high-status *gusthi* was generous with its support of its "own poor" and, conversely, the poor members of a high-status *gusthi* were expected to avoid bringing shame to the patriline, such as by begging for charity outside the *gusthi* (Gardner 1995). The act of "recognition" was important in the social act of giving and receiving (Appadurai 2004). To deny requests was to fail or refuse to recognize the relational and moral claim underpinning the request. To deny help was to fail as a patron. Patron-clientage was thus at once a system of entitlement (Drèze and Sen 1990), a network of relationships underpinned by moralities of kinship connection, and a form of personalized and patrimonial authority of loyalty (van Schendel 2009, 215).

The idiom of help served partially to hide the inequality, as Gardner notes: "It can thus be seen as a 'myth' . . . , which masks the reality of transactions; clients are dependent upon their patrons, and their exploitation remains hidden" (Gardner 1995, 153). *Gusthi* membership was not strictly defined, and families engaged in the relational work of selectively "remembering" certain, sometimes fictitious, ties and "forgetting" others in order to claim benefits or safeguard resources.[6]

Gender was another marker of inequality within individual *gusthis* and households. In a patrilocal system, descent, ancestry, and connection to status and place were traced through men. Women fell under the patronage of men—first their fathers, then their husbands, and later sometimes their adult sons—and relied on them for their social status. This dependence of women on male guardianship carried "patriarchal risk," which implied the danger of dramatic decline in lifestyle (both economically and socially) in the case of the loss of guardianship due to divorce or abandonment (Cain, Khanam, and Nahar 1979). This risk generated the incentive for women to comply with rather than contest male dominance (Cain et al. 1979, 408). Matrilineal kin were often distant and less easily drawn into regular circuits of help (*shahaja*; Gardner 1995, 152), although the support of women's natal families could be used to enhance their bargaining power within their husband's households.[7]

Patron-client alliances fell along lineage-based status hierarchies. Even if a household was economically poor or landless, if it belonged to a prominent *gusthi*, it enjoyed a better material position and social status than a poor household in a lower-status *gusthi*. Thus, economic position and status classification often operated independently, although these two factors seemed strongly correlated in the context of my fieldwork, where people's relationships were more fragmented. This latter observation implies fundamental changes in the political economy of rural Bangladesh.

People in northwestern Bangladesh also differentiated among *borolok* and *chhotolok* (or *boromanush* and *chhotomanush*, "big people" and "small people") to indicate wealth and class.[8] Yet the importance of lineage groups in structuring patronage relations and conferring status on households was minimal, in contrast with Gardner's finding. The poor infrequently discussed *gusthi* as a contemporary unit of social and status organization.[9] *Gusthi*, iAgents explained to me, was how people *used to live* before sons took up the practice of subdividing soon after marriage and cutting economic relationships with their brothers. Eirik Jansen (1987) predicted that population increase and shrinking landholding would mean that no one would be able to fulfill the role of patron, as surplus households of agricultural landowning fathers were divided into individual but deficit households headed by brothers. This situation was predominantly the case in northwestern Bangladesh, but some families found other income streams to replace the role of landholding, such as international migration (Gardner 1995) and investment in industry. In my research sites, people frequently criticized the rich for no longer helping the poor due to greed and pursuit of personal interests. Tensions built especially among siblings who found themselves in different positions of fortune and held varying notions about their responsibilities for one another.

In addition to inheritance divisions, river erosion and other environmental factors caused endemic landlessness in the northwestern riverine districts, which caused a high degree of forced geographic mobility among the poor. When segments of families relocated, links to their extended family members attenuated. (By contrast, in the areas and periods of Gardner's research, international migration generated considerable wealth for many families that maintained strong connections between members abroad and at home.) The terms *dhoni* (rich) and *gorib* (poor) were also used interchangeably with *boro* and *chhoto* to refer to social and economic status, and they rarely implied a patronage or familial relationship.[10] Landlords lost authority and status as providers when people no longer were tied to working their land and taking loans from them. Younger men increasingly sought education and refused agricultural work, and former kin-dependent agricultural laborers found opportunities as rickshaw drivers or small traders or sold their labor elsewhere. They thus became incorporated in new non-kin patronage relationships, where clients sought patrons' ability to resolve practical everyday problems and paid less attention to patrons' possession of land and status *per se* (Devine and White 2013, 139). The distinctions between the expected kin relations in Gardner's field of study and my own one are not only due to geographic variation but are also temporal. They highlight the rapidity of change in rural society.

Rural middle-class families continuously have had to remake their status through new livelihoods, style of house, possession of assets, and other activities rather than relying on existing prestige acquired from birth and bolstered by bonded labor. One such activity was to act as intermediary in channeling resources intended for development programs from national and international sources to local areas. The following section provides the background of development efforts in Bangladesh and the ways in which they grew in importance for the rural middle classes.

HISTORICAL ROLE OF NGOS IN BANGLADESH

The role that non-governmental organizations played in rural development in Bangladesh evolved over time with changes in global and regional political economies, and thus the current movement toward market-driven development needs to be situated within this broader history. Since before the inception of Bangladesh as a nation-state, foreign-influenced NGO work has been the primary provider of rural social services and has also overlapped significantly with kinship-based patronage structures. A historical perspective also shows Bangladesh's long-standing preoccupation with "model-building," a process by which a combined set of rural development solutions is tested in one location and then scaled up to solve problems on a national level. These models are often associated with a particular named individual, although contestations over ownership also occur.

The roots of Bangladesh's reliance on aid extend to preindependence times. Pakistani policymakers focused on modernization through centralized and authoritarian planning. The government invested almost exclusively in private enterprise, which meant that few people benefitted and only a small proportion of investments went to Bangladesh, then called East Pakistan (van Schendel 2009, 144). In 1955, experimentation with local development models began in Comilla with the Academy for Rural Development. The "Comilla model" was headed by the Pakistani development practitioner and social scientist Dr. Akhter Hameed Khan to pilot cooperative microfinance and rural community development programs (Lewis 2011, 36; van Schendel 1981). Communities were clustered as units for introducing modernization and a scientific blend of expert and local knowledge and were given instruction in family planning, irrigation, electrification, and credit (van Schendel 2009, 146). While the Comilla model did not yield the results Khan had hoped for, it was significant in instilling the idea that local communities in Bangladesh needed to develop "vigorous local institutions" (Khan 1983, 190) because top-down state planning would not offer a sustainable solution.

By the 1960s, East Pakistan saw a six-fold growth in external aid, but these resources were allocated to local patrons, who became the main supporters and vote brokers for politicians (van Schendel 2009, 215). Exchange networks among kin and community continued to constitute the primary base of social welfare for ordinary villagers. Urban and foreign migrants, rather than NGOs or the state, took responsibility for building and maintaining mosques, *madrasas* (educational institutions), and hospitals (Feldman 2003, 6).

The postindependence period of the 1970s and '80s saw the first boom of indigenous NGOs working at the grassroots level and marked their entrenchment as a primary conduit of resources for rural areas (Karim 2001, 98; Feldman 2003, 6). Primarily funded by international aid, these postwar NGOs initially focused on relief and rehabilitation; intermittently channeled disaster aid following the famine in 1974, floods in 1988, and cyclone in 1991 (among other crises); and gradually shifted focus from relief to community and economic development. By the late 1990s, Bangladesh boasted twenty-three thousand registered NGOs with a total of twenty million rural women clients, covering 78 percent of all villages (White 1999, 310) and taking in over twenty US dollars per capita in aid (van Schendel 2009, 220).

NGOs expanded their remit to healthcare, safe drinking water, employment and productivity, better schooling, infrastructure, and protection against natural hazards (van Schendel 2009, 223; Feldman 2003, 8). Following trends among international donors, these organizations adopted an increasing awareness of the role of gender in social inequality. The focus on women shifted from population control and family planning to income generation and skills training (Feldman 2003, 11).

One school of NGO thought, centered on the causes of structural poverty, employed Paulo Freire's ideas about raising the critical consciousness of poor and marginalized groups (Karim 2001). These leftist NGOs (as compared with those that targeted a lack of resources as the cause of poverty and thus provided goods and services) fought against unequal rural power structures and engaged in nonparty politics for grassroots political mobilization. They advocated for reforms such as the distribution of government land to the poor, and they sponsored women in village-level elections. Yet their efforts to empower the poor—referencing historical struggles for social justice and political transformation among oppressed groups against patriarchal and caste- and ethnicity-based hegemonies—were met with resistance by vested interests. As a result of "the depoliticisation and subversion of a process that challenged the deepest structures of social power" (Batliwala 2011, 111), the term "empowerment" entered the mainstream in the 1990s, co-opted by liberal development paradigms (and the emergence of poverty capitalism) that sought to "empower" the poor by enfolding them into capitalist markets. Emptied of its political content through its decontextualized overuse within state and NGO policy, "empowerment" grew to be associated with individualized processes based on the assumption that social and political advancement arises from participation in the competitive marketplace.[11]

In the 1980s, General Hussain Muhammad Ershad supported the growth of service-provision NGOs so that such organizations would compete with the left over the loyalty of the poor, thereby undermining the work of leftist organizations and political parties (Karim 2001, 98). Globally as well, aid increasingly became an instrument of enforcing privatization and liberalization (van Schendel 2009, 220). As the NGO sector became professionalized and bureaucratized, a changing discourse from redistribution and social welfare to individualism, entrepreneurship, self-reliance, and empowerment accompanied the process. Leftist social mobilizers criticized donor policies that displaced state development efforts with NGOs. Some organizations continued to employ principles of critical consciousness in village groups in an effort to mobilize against rural elites and bureaucratic domination, but few organizations that retained these principles still existed in the early twenty-first century.[12]

The 1990s were a decade of global market deregulation, and NGOs became central to processes of privatization, thus reflecting neoliberal shifts in the donors' policies, the collapse of the socialist project, and general disaffection with government as an institution of development (Feldman 2003, 6). The franchising out of the state led to an erosion of accountability mechanisms (Wood 1994, 314), because NGOs did not respond to buyers' preferences (as markets are thought to do) or to citizens' preferences (as democratic governments are thought to do). NGOs instead acted in accordance with donor priorities. Yet "the intention to help the poor often gets entangled in and constrained by market forces, donor markets, state policies, national policies, and local power structures" (Karim 2001, 93), which were often contradictory and not aligned with the actual needs of the poor. Rapidly becoming the "community face of neoliberalism" (Hardt and Negri 2000; Petras 1997), NGOs exerted reforms from the grass roots while international capital pressurized the state from the outside (Karim 2001, 94). Delwar Hussain describes the process by which these non-state actors produced "state-like" effects. "In this way, the state, in its 'multiple incarnations' continues to be a powerful object of encounter even when it cannot be located as a unitary structure" (Hussain 2014, 2, drawing on Aretxaga 2003, 398). In his rich ethnography, Hussain shows how the state was merely one—and not even the most significant—of the actors engaging in governance activities in Bangladesh. He suggests that the rise of NGOs did not generate an erosion of the state because postcolonial states such as Bangladesh had always been characterized by mediated sovereignty, with only the players changing over time. The nature and role of NGOs—as a shadow state—were thus ambiguous and displayed at once the features and behaviors of patronage, governance, and kinship structures.[13]

Microfinance is but one model of market-driven development that emerged from Bangladesh, popularized by Dr. Muhammad Yunus and the Grameen Bank and tapping into emergent ideas about global poverty capitalism.[14] Premised on the idea that the borrower knows best and that prioritizing entrepreneur-led growth is more efficient than investing in the public sector, microfinance is "a popular development strategy that engages market principles to achieve socially progressive goals, such as promoting economic development of marginalised communities and empowering the poor" (Shakya and Rankin 2008, 1214). The Grameen Bank model started in 1976 in opposition to top-down donor-driven development models and the lending principles of mainstream institutions when its founder, Dr. Muhammad Yunus, then a professor at Chittagong University in Bangladesh, issued loans adding up to a mere twenty-seven US dollars in total to forty-two women and their families. Unable to show the requisite collateral to acquire a loan from commercial banks and otherwise subjected to informal lenders with high interest rates, these families had been unable to climb above subsistence level. The families' use of his small loans as start-up money for small businesses "proved" to Yunus that microcredit would work as a viable business model that would also reduce poverty in Bangladesh (Bornstein 1996).

By the late 1990s, Bangladeshi NGOs—many of which now offered microcredit services—were heralded as "one of the most effective agents of change in the 21st century" and Bangladesh itself as the "NGO capital of the world" (World Bank Report 1996, 5, 43; in Karim 2001, 94–96). Bangladesh continued to serve as a testing site for the latest market-driven development models. "Empowerment" efforts sought to "include" the poor in the global market (for example, by bringing them into formal banking) but did not seek to examine the implications of existing structures in the reproduction of poverty. The work of local development NGOs increasingly pursued market-based approaches, following not only foreign donor practices but also high-profile experiments from within Bangladesh (such as the "microfinance revolution" of Muhammad Yunus and, later, his new model of "social business," a more restrictive form of social enterprise). How did these ideological and practical shifts toward poverty capitalism reconfigure the moral economy of NGO patronage?

THE MORAL ECONOMY OF NGO PATRONAGE

James Scott's (1972, 1977) model of the moral economy of peasants in terms of their relationships with land owners is useful for considering the relationship between beneficiaries and NGOs in postindependence Bangladesh. Scott argues that peasants live so close to the subsistence line that they prefer to be embedded in patron-client relations where the wealthy protect the weak rather than to be subjected to the free market. In his model of patron-clientalism, the balance in the exchange of goods and services, while highly unequal, formed the basis of landowner-peasant reciprocity and bolstered the legitimacy of elites in the eyes of peasants. Events of conflict arose as a result of changes in resource flows disfavoring the peasants, sometimes due to external events (crop failure, poor harvest, introduction of market forces) or ones central to the relationship (an exploitative patron). If these flows brought the provisional levels of peasants below acceptable cultural and objective minimums, or if peasants were denied protections and socially reproductive redistributions (such as rituals and festivals), this imbalance constituted a breach in sociality and provided a moral basis for the peasants' critique of elite legitimacy.

Anthropologists have observed similar patterns regarding NGO relations with clients that replicated long-standing patron-clientage in rural areas, including when local elites co-opt development resources (Scherz 2014; Shah 2010). In the moral economy of corporate-community engagement in northeastern Bangladesh, company discourses of empowerment and partnership fell at odds with the local moral economies of Islamic charity and patronage (Gardner 2012, 2015). The corporate value of "sustainability" implied disconnection, while villagers expected relationships of hierarchical connection that endured.

Similarly, NGOs in northwestern Bangladesh occupied patron-like roles through the 2000s, having played a significant part in the provision of goods and services since the country's independence (Lewis 2011, 114). The ways in which such development goods were distributed followed a set of common procedures. Local NGOs received funding to implement specific time-bound projects and began a hiring process to select project staff. Current and former staffers of NGOs were often reselected for new projects, especially if they possessed niche expertise, such as finance and accounting, but other people might be selected as well. The new teams identified beneficiaries who fit into project categories and activities (such as river-island farmers to be taught how to grow squash in sandy soil) or selected households to receive particular infrastructural support (such as slab latrines or tubewells). Such a "development moral economy" existed in the rural countryside, where wealthy, land-owning patrons set up NGOs and attracted funding from Dhaka or abroad and then distributed these resources among their followers. The lower middle classes vied to provide their low-cost labor in order to claim the status of possessing *chakri* (salaried employment), and the poor conformed to the role of development beneficiary in exchange for inclusion in the distribution of project resources. When expectations of villagers were not met—such as when *chakri* was provided but no salary materialized and beneficiaries were increasingly expected to pay for development goods—the organizations and their leaders fell subject to intense critique (Devine and White 2013, 141).[15] The chapters that follow detail the many ways in which new, market-based development practices challenged the moral economy of NGO patronage in rural Bangladesh.

The Consolidation of Poverty Capitalism

As development problems were increasingly defined through a market lens, development solutions concentrated on the concept of "inclusive markets." Practitioners and some scholars adopted a "residual" approach to poverty that assumes that people are poor because of their inability to participate in mainstream capitalist markets (Mosse 2010). Yet "including" the poor in markets often meant taking advantage of their large numbers and relative density as cheap labor or as low-paying but high-volume consumers, and so the real beneficiaries of these processes were likely elsewhere. Encouraging the latter (selling products to the poor) among multinational corporations was a central project of management "guru" C. K. Prahalad in his book, *The Fortune at the Bottom of the Pyramid: Eradicating Poverty Through Profits* (2006). Similar to "disaster capitalism" (Klein 2005), which refers to "national and transnational governmental institutions' instrumental use of catastrophe . . . to promote and empower a range of private, neoliberal capitalist interests" (Schuller and Maldonado 2016, 62), "poverty capitalism" is built on the recognition that profits can be made from processes associated with addressing the problem of poverty, as long as poverty is understood in market terms. As entities (such as states and multinational corporations) beyond the development industry acted on this recognition, poverty capitalism expanded and took root in many new forms. Poverty capital, the money that flowed through these projects and organizations, was thus "a subprime frontier where development capital and finance capital merge and collaborate such that new subjects of development are identified and new territories of investment are opened up and consolidated" (Roy 2010, 30).

Anthropologists describe poverty capitalism as a set of institutional assemblages that seemed to align the objectives of businesses, governments, and development organizations and bring them into new forms of interaction (Ong and Collier 2008; Schwittay 2011a). Many different types of organizations with varying legal structures and business models practiced forms of market-driven development, and anthropologists have conducted ethnographic studies among many of them. These include fair trade (Dolan 2007; Luetchford 2007), corporate social responsibility or CSR (Dolan and Rajak 2016; Gardner 2012, 2015; Rajak 2011a), corporate "base-of-the-pyramid" (BOP) businesses (Cross and Street 2009), social enterprise (Cross 2013 and 2019), microenterprise (Elyachar 2005), and microfinance. Each of these forms carried a tension between the "financialization of development" (in which capitalism attempted to undertake action for poverty alleviation) and the "democratization of capital" (a belief that expanded access to financial services would eradicate poverty) (Schwittay 2011a, 383; Roy 2010). The involvement of business in the process of poverty alleviation was "intrinsic" to the corporate capitalist expansionist model, argues Gardner, rather than being a "'moral bolt on' to offset the harsh realities of neoliberal capitalism" (2012, 165; also Rajak 2011a). Such a blending of social and financial (and sometimes also environmental) objectives, whether by an NGO's adoption of a business model or a company's development of products and services with explicit "social impact," has been heralded as a radically new economy.

According to an industry report from 2009, *The Phoenix Economy: 50 Pioneers in the Business of Social Innovation*, a "new economic order is rising from the ashes" of "the dinosaurs of the old order" and "a new generation of innovators, entrepreneurs and investors is accelerating the changes essential for delivering scalable sustainable solutions to the world" (Elkington, Litovsky, and Love 2009, 1, 4). Even "traditional" multinational banking corporations were on board. J.P. Morgan published a research note asserting that impact investing (which provided debt or equity to mission-driven businesses serving the "base of the pyramid," thereby yielding a financial return while creating positive social impact) constituted a new asset class worth up to 667 billion USD in profit opportunity over the following decade (J.P. Morgan and Rockefeller Foundation 2010). Partially in reaction to the unscrupulous practices highlighted by the 2007–8 global financial crisis, enthusiasm about social business investment grew.

Capitalism's ever-expanding demand for new frontiers of growth and profit has pushed it into consort with agents of development, driven by a misguided assumption that the interests of the poor and those of multinational corporations are compatible (Karim 2011). The political concept of "the forgotten man at the bottom of the pyramid" whom the state has a responsibility to help (Roosevelt 1938) morphed into the economic concept of market potential, or the "fortune at the bottom of the pyramid" (Prahalad 2006). And the shift globally from projects of social wellbeing to profit-making financial intermediation among NGOs will certainly have implications for their relationships with beneficiaries.

What are the disruptive effects (both positive and negative) of such market-driven practices on existing social support structures for the world's poor? What logics and moralities underpin the new kinds of relationships that are asserted under market-driven development and social enterprise, and how do they interact with other dominant relationships? What implications do these new configurations have for women's agency and empowerment, social mobility for the poor, and class relations?

The iAgent social enterprise network is an apt site to explore the effects of poverty capitalism because it includes, simultaneously, many different types of development modalities: NGO project cycle, bilateral aid, government bureaucratic outsourcing, human rights advocacy, political mobilization, corporate social responsibility, corporate "base-of-the-pyramid" business, "financial inclusion" in banking, and public-private partnership. Interactions among these modalities historically reveal the continuous revision of development trends and demonstrate those that capture agenda- and discourse-setting power. Over time, certain development modalities lost purchase, and others became increasingly attractive to a variety of players. Changing trends have important implications for participants at the bottom of the hierarchy, for the ones whose "development" is the primary stated goal.

CHANGES IN STRUCTURES OF ACCESS IN SOUTH ASIA

As new moral economies of poverty capitalism interacted with historical structures of connection (kinship and NGO patronage), they reformatted the relationships and opportunities of the rural poor. I show how the changes in these relational economies impelled the poor to embark on projects of high risk in order to gain viable livelihoods for themselves and their families.

An anthropological study of relational economy involves an investigation of the regimes of social, political, and economic value that underpin relationships between and among people of particular structural positions.[16] It provides an analytic lens for examining economic actors not only in terms of their social situatedness (a core anthropological assumption; all economic acts are social acts) but also in terms of the political and ideological projects that compete to organize relationships among economic actors. Understanding these configurations and the ways in which they change offers a glimpse of the structural and relational features of the broader political economy. An ethnographic approach to relational economy enables a fine-grained examination of the everyday relationships influenced by global capitalist processes, refracted through various modes of market-driven development in local contexts.

The vignette detailing Rahela's and Taspia's experiences suggests some of the relational changes at play. Kinship connections feature centrally; both women were expected to perform certain duties for their families, and they achieved varying degrees of success. The shadow of the development project of which they were a part also appears, the precise relationships of which we do not see directly. The expectations of people in the iAgent hierarchy seemed to affect Rahela less overtly. Her activities as an iAgent seemed to have contributed to her present successes and bolstered her ability to engage in kinship relationships more favorably. By contrast, Taspia seemed to be bound to the demands of the project. The time frame of repaying the loan conflicted with her ability to fulfill kinship and class expectations. Being embedded in both development and kinship relational economies was a gendered project; what successful womanhood meant in the two sets of expectations might have conflicted with or bolstered one another.

Some relational economies may have elective affinity with one another. Max Weber (1930) demonstrates, for example, how the behavioral expectations and relational ethics of Calvinism were conducive for modern capitalism to take root and flourish. Institutional resonance is always contingent, however; in other cases, relational economies might conflict, thus creating intense ambivalence that might result in a failure in the uptake of new models of behavior. Multiple coexisting value systems may also result in the reformatting of existing relational economies, for example if the ends are congruent with existing values even if the means are not.

When Rahela first started iAgent work, she experienced the same social stigmas as did Taspia. Yet when her work proved to be financially successful, and she invested money in relationships congruent with the relational economy of kinship, then her activities (selling products and services outside of the home and interacting with non-related men) were increasingly accepted. Many girls sought to emulate her livelihood trajectory.

In Taspia's case, the relational economy of iAgent work continued to conflict with that of models of appropriate behavior as an unmarried daughter, and she was never able to use the work of the one to fulfill the expectations of the other. New relational economies and subjectivities (such as those of the market) do not steamroll over existing ones, as globalization alarmists might postulate. Transnational models and exchanged ideas are always interpreted locally in the social spheres of kin, work, and community. Thus, the anthropological project here is to explore the ambivalences that are produced when people face expectations to act within the context of multiple relational economies.

The concept of "relational work," developed by economic sociologist Viviana Zelizer (2012), enables an investigation of relational economy to touch down ethnographically. It takes as a unit of analysis the creative efforts people make in initiating, sustaining, negotiating, reworking, and terminating distinct social relations. People seek to define a relationship in ways favorable to them through the distinct social ties between them, the types of transactions they undertake, the media of exchange of those transactions, and the negotiated meanings with which they endow them. Changing one of these aspects has implications for the rest. The transition from salary to piecework, for instance, denotes a new relational configuration in which the responsibility of employership (ensuring workers a living wage regardless of business outcomes) is denied in favor of flexible procurement (making workers responsible for business risk and the costs of their own survival). Such a shift changes the balance of power between workers and owner and the ability of each to make claims on the other. In other cases, people may undertake relational work to disguise the power differential implied by certain types of transactions. For example, live-in domestic help may be paid a wage or room and board to look after children and perform household duties (roles that may traditionally correspond to that of "wife," who performs unpaid domestic labor). Families may try to disguise the economic transactional nature of the relationship, in face of the intimacy of the care work performed, by including domestic labor in circuits of kinship exchange. Considerable experiences of ambiguity can result when multiple representations clash and reveal noncorresponding terms of exchange.

What are the relational economies that inform how people act in the context of contemporary social enterprise programs such as the iAgent model? The iAgent experience shows a case of intense ambivalence in which the local political economy of opportunity increasingly necessitated young women to undertake risky projects of nondomestic labor for the survival of their families. The erosion of strong kinship patronage ties and of kin help—and thus the increasing responsibility of families for their own individual survival—arose from many factors. These factors included the declining landholding of families and the inability to forge an agriculture-based livelihood, increased forced geographic mobility, fragmentation of extended families, and new livelihood opportunities in industry. Simultaneously, global trends in development shifted, from prioritizing NGOs that implemented social projects using foreign donations to market-driven approaches, in which the poor were expected to help themselves, using one-off technical inputs. Below, I detail the theoretical framework I use to apprehend these change processes and multiple relational economies and their social, political, and economic implications.

The Disruptive Development Apparatus

Enfolding previously marginalized people in the ambit of global markets required markets to expand their frontiers, where they found customers and workers who lacked the right "habitus" (Bourdieu 1977). The anthropological literature on poverty capitalism has thus tended to focus on the ways in which market devices (as conceptualized by Muniesa, Millo, and Callon 2007)—such as documents, procedures, and technologies of discipline—were employed to convert the poor into new entrepreneurial subjects in the service of capital accumulation.[17] Yet the market-oriented entrepreneurial subjectivities encouraged by these programs—especially for women—often conflicted with existing social expectations, such as kinship roles and religious and cultural notions of women's propriety. Further, the new rhythms of time established by market devices clashed with the timescales of village life and social reproduction and affected the ways in which people could act. Women entrepreneurs needed to navigate these multiple and competing activities, negotiate their different social roles, and adopt flexible models of behavior. In the process, they appeared to both organizational and community actors as morally ambiguous subjects.

Market devices were implicated in other social and political relationships. Social enterprise techniques encoded the ideologies and assumptions of poverty capitalism and the institutional and personal projects of actors in the social enterprise network. They acted as vehicles for exerting and amplifying existing relations of domination such as those of class and gender. In Bangladesh, where development resources sustained a significant portion of middle-class livelihoods, the shifting ideas about how development should be organized threatened class status. The local development elite worked hard to maintain their access to development resources and their patronage over the local poor. By focusing on these issues, this book offers a political and relational reading of Annelise Riles's (2000) notion of the "network." Showing the significant role that class contentions played, I contribute new insights about the underlying logic of social enterprises and their networks. The contradictory social and business expectations, intense experience of ambiguity generated by entrepreneurial roles, and the political-moral valence of market devices—employed not by abstract actors but by situated persons—meant that these devices generated a network with the relational features of patronage rather than "free" markets.

Market Devices

To understand the processes of change by which social enterprise networks are meant to transform the poor into entrepreneurs, I begin with the concept of "market devices" as a "simple way of referring to the material and discursive assemblages that intervene in the construction of markets" (Muniesa, Millo, and Callon 2007, 2). In the context of a particular institutional model being implemented, in this case the iAgent social enterprise, devices such as administrative measures require people to "conform to the institution's discursive and practical universe" (Escobar 1991, 667). These devices are also meant to calibrate or translate people and objects into calculative or calculable beings, in order to enact particular economic properties or provoke economic behaviors. While the primary beneficiaries of the iAgent model were meant to be villagers in the iAgents' surrounding communities, I focus on the devices applied to iAgents themselves. Market devices are designed to reconfigure what market actors are (ontologically) and what they can do (performatively).

Markets cannot be created by devices as objects or procedures alone. Thus, I focus on the idea of the intermediary charged with the responsibility of transforming villagers into customers, under the motivation of the iAgent's own self-transformation and through the role model that her mobility and knowledge provide for others. Thus, this transformational process is necessarily relational and political. I interpret the ideal iAgents as "market actors" who must be shaped as agents for the construction of markets through a set of market devices. Similar to Kimberly Chong's organizational interlocutor, the iAgent social enterprise "fashions its own organisation and workers as an exemplar of the kinds of organisation and subjectivities which it tries to reproduce amongst its clients" (2012, 24). Thus, what these organizations attempt to do externally can be apprehended through the mirror of what they do internally (Riles 2000). The intended systematic reshaping of iAgents as market actors can be seen as a concentrated (and therefore more ethnographically locatable) form of how TIE sought to reshape the traits of rural Bangladeshi people through these iAgents.[18]

These models of social engineering, through their market devices, reveal central assumptions—held by practitioners—about the linearity of their effects. Models in academia employing the notion of market devices often assume communicative models of transmission. Yet market institutions are fundamentally sociopolitical institutions; they do not operate through a communicative model of information exchange. Rather, market devices and information-carrying artifacts are inflected by the personal projects and class politics of the people participating in market activity.

The entrepreneurial transformational process is thus not steady and teleologically inevitable but is instead contested and may be rejected. Market devices are not isolatable mechanisms to be analyzed along a linear evaluation of "effectiveness" or "causality" (as impact assessments or randomized control trials do). Rather, they are indivisible from the broader assemblage of relationships that TIE forged in the implementation of its social enterprise model. By adopting, performing, or rejecting these practices, iAgents made claims about the nature of their relationships with these powerful external others. These techniques and the iAgents' responses to them were political projects of defining and contesting hierarchical relationships of power.

While market actors and markets were not the dominant outcomes of such processes in this case, the transformations that did take place amplified the internal contradictions of these models, revealing their inability to map impersonal transactional models onto social reality, and instead mirrored existing hierarchical relations of domination.[19]

The Network

The institutions, individuals, and practices that constituted the iAgent project formed a network that projected market logics but operated through patron-client linkages. Networks, Annelise Riles (2000, 3) shows us, "internally generate the effects of their own reality by reflecting on themselves." The iAgent network was effective at drawing together a diversity of actors, not only young women and NGO staff but also partner organizations and resource-givers. The network's devices (such as representations it produced to describe itself) were performative in drawing in new resources aligned to those representations. For Riles, the aesthetic power of the network—instantiated in documents, procedures, and other market devices—drives it and gives it its self-perpetuating form. I borrow these ideas but emphasize aspects such as the class aspirations and self-making projects of the network's members. I explore how the network refracted its constituent relationships and contextual complexities by taking up existing modes of patronage and class relations and then amplifying them through these procedures and documents.

This book shows that the constituting and contextual features of the network (meaning the people and their cultural, class, and socioeconomic positions) affect the ways in which artifacts and knowledge practices materialize. NGO workers in Bangladesh aspired to a neutral, communicative implementation hierarchy driven by procedures and documents. TIE staffers, for instance, invoked an information society in which their model's devices translated linearly into practice. Yet through their actions, practitioners molded the network to existing structures of patronage and domination.

The network took up and mirrored not only the representational and discursive artifacts it produced but also the properties of its members' existing relations. Fundamentally, these models were extensions of people's class positions and efforts of self-making.[20] The conception, negotiation, performance, and rejection of models such as the iAgent social enterprise were all built on the entanglement of social, political, and economic projects. Rural families experimented with new livelihood activities not only for survival but also according to notions of honor and shame. Middle-class struggles for upward mobility strongly inflected the anxieties of the iAgent staff at TIE's local partner NGOs who exerted pressure on iAgents to make more money. The concerns of local staff members were amplified by their own precarious position as middlemen in projects of the political, economic, and NGO elite to strip back welfare services and devolve investment, risk, and responsibility onto the lower classes—making them responsible for their own development—while rulemaking and policy framing processes accrued upward to national and international bodies (Mosse 2011, 3). Far from being external factors that enabled or constrained the efficient functioning of projects and markets, these processes need to be understood as constitutive of such projects. Laura Bear (2015b) shows how many of these practices are invisible in the public domain and in formal procedures even while they centrally form and recreate economic life. Thus, such effects are not immediately discernable and require long-term ethnographic research to apprehend.

Further to Riles's portrayal of the network as a set of activities and artifacts that draws people together, generating a set of personal relations and overcoming differences (Riles 2000, 68), I show how the activities of workers within the iAgent assemblage were also geared toward the maintenance and enhancement of difference: namely, class and power hierarchy. This observation is central to understanding the relational economy of poverty capitalism. Riles's central motif is that the "outside" and the "inside" of the network are the same form, seen twice. In iAgent terms, this insight refers to the relationship between the formal, external-facing representations of the iAgent model and its components, and the informal, personal experiences and narratives of it. One was not a false image of the other's reality; they enabled one another to exist. They were two sides of the same coin, representing different facets, and both illuminated the class projects and relations of power that underpinned them. The process of navigating the disjunctures in representations and experiences of the network formed the core of intense relational work performed by iAgents and other interlocutors and defines the central thrust of this book.

Flexible Entrepreneurial Subjectivities and Ambiguous Subjects

While social enterprise networks exert new organizational authority over entrepreneurs, existing kinship and community expectations also continued to wield influence. The valorization of entrepreneurship in development discourse did not match community understandings of these new roles. Rather than appearing as local heroines, lifting their communities out of poverty one client at a time, the new entrepreneurs of poverty capitalism have been depicted as shadowy, ambiguous figures, in both the community and the organizational perspective—and also in the emerging literature on the anthropology of finance-at-the-margins (Dolan, Huang, and Gordon 2019; Schuster 2015). They defy familiar structures of expectation and provoke moral anxiety. This book traces the ways in which the "flexible" identity of the woman entrepreneur produced by social enterprise programs not only enabled opportunities but also caused her to appear as an economic actor of ambiguous moral and relational quality.

The rendering of time, capital, labor (Chong 2012; Snyder 2016), bodies (Martin 1994), subjectivities (Urciuoli 2008), citizenship (Ong 1999), and family structures (Stacey 1990) as "flexible" is central to contemporary global capitalist orthodoxy (Freeman 2007). The entrepreneur, as neoliberalism's quintessential flexible actor (Bourdieu 1998), is a figure expected to adapt fluidly to multiple economic activities, embody risk-taking subjectivities, and move easily across social and spatial boundaries.

In the development context, Caroline Schuster (2014) identifies the ways in which flexibility and entrepreneurship are particularly gendered. She shows how the institutional practices of establishing creditworthiness in microfinance organizations in Paraguay produced flexible, relational, and feminized borrowers. Because of the need, for instance, to attend microcredit group meetings at short notice and to juggle family obligations with outside economic activities, women accepted precarious and informal work with flexible hours. The cobbling together of multiple economic activities often cast women in ambiguous light. They struggled to offset the negative readings or stigmatized aspects of their activities by engaging in intense "relational work" (Zelizer 2012; applied in this context to the micropolitics of enacting flexibility) to meet gendered structures of expectation regarding women's domestic labor (Cattelino 2010). Carla Freeman's (2007) work shows how women in Barbados experienced entrepreneurial flexibility as offering new opportunities and pathways to upward mobility but also throwing their middle-class aspirations of respectability into question. The new figure of the female entrepreneur—neither lowly hawker nor elite family businesswoman—is an ambiguous character, a "shadowy figure in the cultural imagination" (Freeman 2007, 261).

The growing trend in encouraging entrepreneurship not only among women enrolled in development projects but also among other intermediaries such as loan officers, extension workers, and consultants is increasingly the subject of anthropological investigation. Agents are shown to exert intense physical, emotional, and relational labor to mediate incompatible ethical and business logics as well as to make their own work ethical, all of which is often viewed with suspicion by the community. Sohini Kar (2013) captures the ways in which microcredit collection officers labored to distinguish themselves from both moneylenders and banks, both of which were perceived to be violent and coercive. Often, commission agents and organizational staff members held different mental models of mutuality and economic action, which generated confusion about the nature of the entrepreneurial project (Dolan, Huang, and Gordon 2019). Work on mobile money agents (Maurer, Nelms, and Rea 2013) shows how agents appeared to managers as ambiguous figures because of the shifting nature of their status between intermediaries (an infrastructural role based on existing distribution networks) and mediators (a value-adding role leveraging social relationships and trust). Such doubling of capacities generated anxieties about the appropriate way to expand, monitor, and regulate agents' activities. The figure of the entrepreneur is therefore ambiguous not just in the eyes of family and community members, but also from the perspective of organizations that run projects founded on the idea of a network of enterprising local agents.

This book explores how actors in the iAgent network navigated interpersonal and interorganizational ties in order to advance their own ideas about how kinship and NGO relational economies should perform. In particular, the young, often unmarried iAgents experienced anxiety in negotiating their relationships with clients, neighbors, family members, fellow iAgents, NGO staff, and people from partner organizations. iAgents faced competing models of expectation placed on them and corresponding to their different subject roles in the family and community, where they were simultaneously local kinswomen, traveling salespersons, and NGO representatives.

Ambiguity is thus central to the act of model building. The activities of establishing a rural information and communication technology marketplace through iAgent social entrepreneurs took the form of seemingly communicative acts, such as TIE's training of iAgents in market subjectivities and iAgents' efforts to negotiate the prices of their services with neighbors. Yet the codification of these acts through a standardized and licensed model concealed the social and political projects—between iAgents and their community members and between iAgents and TIE—that infused these relational performances with meaning. An in-depth look at the sociopolitical dynamics behind the activities forming these relationships reveals not the stabilization of particular clear forms but instead a strategic juggling of multiple, simultaneous, and often conflicting forms. The overall effect produced and required by these interactions was ambiguity, which made the project work. The project also produced ambiguity, which was a resource used by project actors in the relational work of negotiating recognition and authority. This book contributes to the anthropology of development by showing how project agency or planning agency is subject to the ability of individuals to navigate temporal incongruities and ambiguous representations in ways that draw in and co-opt the compliance of others.

In academic scholarship emerging from linguistic anthropology and communication theory within the field of organizational behavior, ambiguity is a phenomenon of communicative action that can be used strategically—in spoken and written language—to accomplish goals such as fostering deniability and promoting unified diversity (Black 2004; Eisenberg 1984). Indeed, the ways in which TIE structured information (and misinformation) helped the organization to enlist women participants and later shed responsibility for the program's failure.

Yet I show that ambiguity is productive beyond dyadic communication. iAgents also experienced ambiguity as structural (through their liminal position as unmarried women working outside the home); as existential (while they strove to provide a multiplicity of services that each implied different qualities and identities for them); and as relational (because these identities provoked different relationships). While the concepts of "flexibility" and "relational work" capture the positive (albeit labor-intensive) resources that enable people to assume different mantles and gain advantages, "ambiguity" expresses the morally perilous terrain onto which women entrepreneurs ventured. The following section introduces the contexts in which these ambiguous experiences take place.

Field-Site Experiences of Ambiguity

The iAgent Social Enterprise Program: Transformation of a Model

TIE (Technological Innovation for Empowerment), an organization established in Bangladesh in 2001 that, as of 2013, employed ninety people and operated on a two-million-dollar budget, sought to use a blend of technical and social innovations in the building of sustainable and scalable models that would work toward poverty alleviation as well as wealth generation for all stakeholders. Under this remit, TIE undertook a range of programs that developed or invested in technology for education, healthcare, decentralized governance, e-commerce, and digital publication of national scientific and artistic works. This book focuses only on the iAgent project, which was separate from but in some cases served as a vehicle to implement these other activities. The iAgent and other programs were built on a communicative model of society in which inputs generate knowable outputs. Information and technology were imagined as neutral and apolitical, thus allowing their users to convert them into knowledge and to deploy them in overcoming technical constraints. In the chapters to follow, we also see the many ways in which information and technology are laden with ideology and wielded as tools for asserting class, gender, and other political claims.

Prior to the iAgent model, TIE built a network of rural information centers hosted at local NGOs, where villagers could consult weather reports, check school examination results online, apply for work abroad, print land registry papers, and perform other tasks facilitated by modern information and communications technologies. In most places, information centers heralded the first extension of the internet in those villages. When the team at TIE realized that information centers were not reaching the most "marginalized" people (which it defined as children, women, bonded laborers, and elderly and disabled people, deemed to be the main victims of poverty), the team experimented with a model that would target them directly. TIE hired a young woman living near the information center in Lalpur *Upazila* (hosted by the NGO Atno Bishash) to visit rural people's fields, discover their problems (such as pests attacking their crops), and, using her mobile phone, call a helpline manned by TIE staff to source solutions (such as pesticide use). By having a mobile female extension worker for each information center who brought services directly to villages, the TIE team hoped to expand the impact of the model. In 2007 Intel released the Classmate PC (a low-cost laptop computer), which TIE used to enhance the capacities of the mobile information center agent. This person was renamed "iAgent." In 2009 the first cohort of iAgents, along with TIE and the information center staff dedicated to the iAgent project, began work (figure 1).

The ideal iAgent was meant to provide crucial information, products, and services to rural people in their homes, schools, and communities. To perform this

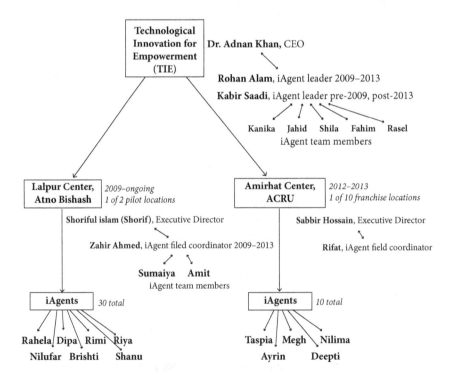

FIGURE 1. Organigram of the iAgent hierarchy with key interlocutors.

way, she needed to bicycle from place to place as she built up a circuit of regular clients and responded to urgent requests. She needed to be proficient in using her suite of ICTs. Her main tool was a laptop computer with an internet connection, with which she showed educational videos, helped people to send emails and talk on Skype with distant relatives, and downloaded school examination results. She also carried digital health equipment—for instance, to test for blood sugar levels, blood pressure, blood group, weight, and pregnancy.

TIE grappled with the question of how this program should be managed structurally. Should iAgents be employees and receive salaries to conduct their work? Should they be NGO workers, paid on a time-bound project basis to implement a sequence of one-off programs defined by other agencies and funders? Or should they be multi-level marketing entrepreneurs who received profit on the sales they generated as well as a commission of the sales of new entrepreneurs they in turn recruited?

The iAgent model was piloted under a grant-based structure through local NGOs. Figure 2 contains a schematic of funding flows in the first pilot model,

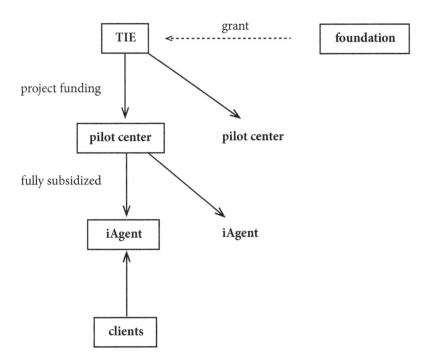

FIGURE 2.   iAgent pilot model: Foundation-funded NGO structure with training costs and equipment for iAgents donated (implemented in Lalpur *Upazila*, at the NGO Atno Bishash and one other location).

with arrows indicating the direction of money transfer. The Dhaka-based Shabar Adhikar ("Rights for All") Foundation (SAF) funded TIE to test the iAgent idea in two locations, one of which was Lalpur subdistrict in partnership with the local NGO, Atno Bishash. (The NGOs serving as iAgent information centers concurrently pursued five to twenty other programs from as many donors.) In each of these two locations, several rounds of ten iAgents were selected, trained, and mentored to begin their work. All expenses for training and equipment for iAgents were covered under the grant scheme. iAgents provided some services (such as educational group sessions to watch multimedia content on the laptop) for free for participants and received an "honorarium" from TIE's partners, and they charged fees for other services (such as blood pressure readings).

With guidelines from TIE, center staff determined the weekly agenda of projects for iAgents to complete. Included in the project budget were salaries for each center to hire a field coordinator and a monitoring officer dedicated to the iAgent project locally. In Lalpur, these two individuals (Zahir Ahmed and Sumaiya Begum) visited several iAgent sessions per day, maintained contact via mobile phone with the other young women, troubleshot their problems, ran monthly meetings, and organized promotional events for iAgents to build up their networks among villagers and local service providers. Rohan Alam, as founder of the iAgent program at TIE and leader during this period, also spent time in the field and on the phone with iAgents and center staff.

When visiting iAgent working areas, Rohan took an interest in the group members and, in exceptional instances, arranged solutions to their problems for free. One group member, for example, had been born without arms but could cook, eat, write, and garden using her dexterous feet, and Rohan arranged typing lessons for her so that she would be skilled enough to gain an NGO or office job and raise her status. Still working out its model of social change, TIE experimented with the services iAgents could provide, and Rohan managed to secure the resources to do so from his outside networks. While iAgents continued to charge villagers for many of their core services, the initial process of testing the business model was subsidized by project funding and fit the interactional schema of other NGOs working in the area. Rounds of grant money were won and disbursed according to a predefined roster of activities. iAgents recalled this period fondly. Brishti recounted, "Before, things were good. We had so much work, but actually it did not feel like it, and we felt good, all ten of us together with Zahir *bhai* [elder brother, a term of respect], Sumaiya *apa* [elder sister], and Rohan *bhai*. But now those three have gone, and there is no more project. It's just a lot of work by ourselves with no enjoyment and very little money, and everyone worries about their own problems."

In late 2012, TIE began the scale-up phase of the iAgent program in ten new locations, one of which was Amirhat subdistrict in partnership with ACRU, a local NGO. Figure 3 shows the ongoing funding flows in the new model, with arrows indicating direction of money transfer. Ten iAgents were selected in each location. In order to make the model scalable and sustainable, TIE did not want to rely on grant money to cover the iAgents' start-up costs. Instead, it established a multitier licensing structure in which each entity had to pay a license fee to the next one upward. iAgents were required to take loans from a commercial bank to cover these fees and equipment costs.

"After three years of piloting . . . the model is self-sustaining and sufficiently income generating," TIE wrote in an application for a prestigious social enterprise award backed by the Asian Development Bank, outlining an ambitious plan going forward: "TIE is currently starting the process of scaling up the model countrywide. The plan is to initiate three hundred iAgents in the field by the end of 2013 and by 2017 inaugurate 11,400 iAgents." What had been demonstrated in the pilot was that young village women *could* ride bicycles and run ICT-based businesses and that rural villagers *were* willing to pay for (some of) these services. Yet the Lalpur pilot model was impossible to replicate at the level of TIE's ambition. Millions of dollars in donations would be

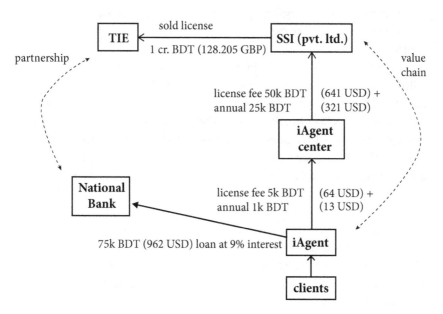

FIGURE 3.   iAgent scale-up model: Multitier commercial licensing structure with formal loan advanced to iAgents (implemented in Amirhat *Upazila*, at the NGO ACRU and nine other locations).

required to prepare iAgents to reach Lalpur's standard. TIE needed to develop a different kind of organizational model to support its activities. Rather than soliciting charitable donations and grants to fund the creation of iAgents (costs of equipment and training), TIE planned for iAgents to take loans from large-scale commercial banks. Rather than allowing iAgents to run their businesses independently and relying on external funding to support its own costs, TIE would claim a cut of iAgent earnings by extracting recurring rents and eventually reach a level such that even TIE staff salaries and overhead could be drawn from this internal revenue source. By creating social business entrepreneurs, TIE itself could become a social business, self-sustaining through its core market offering and not reliant on donations. In addition, the rhetoric of independent entrepreneurship aligned with internationally recognized "best practices" in contemporary development, which increasingly valued principles such as "self-help" and "sustainability" and encouraged microbusinesses fueled by access to formal streams of capital.

At the same time, TIE's support of the notion that these models truly had empowering effects fed into the global hype and contributed to focusing the agenda on these practices. The iAgent model received extensive media coverage by prominent news outlets (such as the BBC and Al Jazeera) and won internationally acclaimed awards for innovation, entrepreneurship, and women's empowerment. In this way, best practices and embellished narratives became codified and institutionalized as new features and programs and spread across the globe.

To achieve its scale-up plan, in 2011 TIE created a new commercial entity called Sustainable Sourcing International Pvt. Ltd. (SSI), of which TIE was the majority shareholder (and whose managing director was the wife of TIE's executive director, Dr. Adnan Khan). SSI would be the replicator of the iAgent concept through a multitiered licensing structure. Yet the team required seed funding to kickstart the business and cover overhead costs. TIE submitted a proposal to their previous funder, SAF. More concerned with women's rights than with the business of making money, SAF wanted the iAgent enterprise to look like a traditional NGO as opposed to a business model. The foundation did not want to support ideas that extended exclusive ownership rights to large organizations rather than to the community. Yet in the end, Rohan explained to me, because SAF's primary funder, DFID (the UK's Department for International Development), pressured SAF to submit proposals quickly, the iAgent business model was sent and accepted.

TIE then sold the license of the iAgent concept to SSI for a one-time price of 1 crore taka (128,205 USD). TIE would continue to perform research and development, monitoring and evaluation, quality assurance, mentorship, and license guideline development roles. SSI would be responsible for all operations, including identifying an information center in each subdistrict in Bangladesh and running selection, training, and supply-chain processes.

In turn, SSI would license the model to local NGOs selected as rural information centers for an initial price of 50,000 taka and a 25,000 taka annual renewal fee (641 and 321 USD, respectively). After selecting up to thirty iAgents, each center would then sell licenses to them for an initial price of 5,000 taka and 1,000 taka for an annual renewal fee (64 and 13 USD, respectively). For the start-up costs of iAgents' businesses, rather than covering them from foundations as it had done previously, TIE negotiated a loan product specifically for iAgents with Bangladesh Bank (the governmental policy-making body) and National Bank Limited (a commercial entity). The deputy managing director of National Bank was a close friend of Adnan Khan from the time when both had lived in Europe studying for their masters' degrees. The loan product did not require any form of material collateral and featured a 9 percent interest rate (as opposed to the normal commercial rate of 19 percent) and a three-month grace period. iAgents would require their fathers or husbands to serve as guarantor, and the center would become the fallback institutional guarantor. A 75,000 taka loan (962 USD) would cover the license fee, training manuals, and basic equipment. Centers could also apply for loans under the iAgent agreement to kickstart their supply-chain businesses and invest in training iAgents.

According to the model, SSI would build the supply chain downward, by selling iAgents their equipment as well as products for them to sell to villagers (such as fertilizers, sanitary hygiene products, and contraceptives). SSI would also establish an upward supply chain, by purchasing agricultural or handicraft products from villagers collected by iAgents and aggregated by centers. In this way SSI was meant to profit from license fees paid upward and its margin of products moving up and down the value chain. Centers would be financially self-sustaining through the products they bought from and sold to the community. iAgents would also receive a margin to enhance their incomes, and villagers would receive products they wanted and would benefit by a better-paying market in which to sell their produce. The ambition of stimulating these integrated market linkages did not materialize in reality, for reasons that this book details. The network and its market devices did not generate impersonal market actors or market relationships. Rather, the network took up and amplified existing patron-client relations among its constituent actors and consolidated power inequalities. In 2014, at the end of my research period, SSI was disbanded, and TIE was experimenting with an open-source and consultative model in which any organization could implement the iAgent model while paying a fee to TIE for its technical expertise.

Ambiguity infused the iAgent project on all levels and scales. Within the project, different "discordant" interpretations of development were used over a short span of time (Gardner 2012). Thus, project relations needed to be constantly reconfigured, and iAgents performed considerable relational work within the villages and in organizational spaces.

Field-Site Selection and Methodology

UNORTHODOX ARRIVALS

My first encounter with the iAgent model was through the paper application to the Asian Development Bank for its global social enterprise award, in which TIE proposed to scale up its for-profit licensing model. I was preparing to travel to Bangladesh for fieldwork with a different social enterprise when I received an email from a friend who worked for Ashoka, a prominent network of social entrepreneurs worldwide. I knew her from the time I had worked in India researching the ways social enterprises and associated industries grew to be so prolific in the South Asia region. My friend's message said that the award committee was experiencing trouble gaining access to the finalist candidate in Bangladesh. The primary interviewer was trapped in Dhaka due to *hartals* (shutdowns and blockades as a form of political protest) and was unable to extend her visa. Knowing about my upcoming trip to Bangladesh, she wondered if I could conduct the interview and site visit, after which I would write a short report. Due to the timeline of the award's selection process, I would need to complete the evaluation within the first week of my arrival in Bangladesh. I agreed, thinking that the task would be a useful opportunity to meet people involved in social entrepreneurship and to visit the countryside.

On my first day in Bangladesh, I visited TIE's offices in Dhaka to meet the founder, Adnan Khan, and his team. I was installed in an empty meeting room and instructed to watch a promotional video about the iAgent social enterprise in which a young woman, sitting in front of a blank screen, introduced herself as "iAgent Mita" and discussed in Bangla (Bengali) with English subtitles what the program meant to her.

> I am iAgent Mita, and I hold an educated village woman's modern profession. I am twenty-six years old and married. Instead of making traditional handicrafts, I am engaged in a larger independent profession, which is called iAgent. As a modern successful woman entrepreneur, I use my laptop, internet modem, and digital camera and give

information consulting to the village's common people. By doing this I earn money, from which I contribute to my family's expenses, and the rest I save. This profession has brought me much respect. In the morning, some children come to me to study. I could have utilized this time in doing something else instead of teaching them. But since I am an educated person, I feel that this is one of my responsibilities toward my society. By now, I have realized that I have become the light of hope for poor people in the village. For example, Rahmat uncle, an elderly person, feels weak most of the time. But he doesn't even know what his problem is. As an iAgent, it's my duty to stand beside him. I must listen to their problems and at the same time provide them with the solution. I do not work under anyone. I work with my own investment, my own hard work, my own expertise and knowledge, my own time. I am not required to share my earning with anyone. Whatever I earn, whether it is more or less, belongs to me. For these reasons I call the profession modern and independent.

Reading from a script, Mita expresses TIE's aspirations for and representations of who and what an iAgent should be: a woman who confronts traditional practices, supports her family, and helps others in her community out of a feeling of duty and responsibility, all enabled by investing in her own business for her own profit. The aspiration is one rapidly entering today's Western business environment: "How can I do well for myself while also doing good for others?"

The day after watching Mita's video, I accompanied Rohan, the leader of the TIE team at that time responsible for the iAgent program, to one of the two original pilot locations of the iAgent social enterprise model in Lalpur subdistrict. Coincidentally, my site visit corresponded with the visit of another foreigner interested in the iAgents of Bangladesh. The primary reason for Rohan's journey to Lalpur was to accompany Hugo, a French documentary filmmaker. Rohan and the staff of the local NGO regaled Hugo, the video camera, and me with heart-warming stories of iAgents' dramatic transformations from shy village girls to confident local leaders and the ways they had visibly influenced community health by teaching about sanitation and reducing the frequency of child marriage. We visited iAgent Brishti, whose father—a librarian at a boys' *madrasa* (religious school)—had started telling families to send their daughters to school after seeing what Brishti was able to do with an education and working as an iAgent. We watched an elderly woman carry out a teary but joyful conversation over Skype with her grandson, a migrant laborer in Muscat, Oman, under the patient guidance of iAgent Rahela. The visit featured live case studies, turning-point narratives, and demonstrations of success. We easily became enamored with the uplifting stories, and we listened with rapt attention as the next "rags-to-riches" (relatively speaking) or "overcoming-all-odds" account unfolded. The project held great allure.

I wondered about the resulting documentary film. What would most catch Hugo's eye to be delivered to French and international audiences? Would it focus on the poverty-alleviating successes of iAgents through entrepreneurship? Or would it point toward women's empowerment, which would in turn enable them to dismantle patriarchy one iAgent at a time? Perhaps the film would feature the digital dream of "appropriate technology," which promised to transform the ways in which people tackled their problems.

Here is an example of the ways in which the iAgent notion appealed to foreign audiences. Five months later, another group of documentary filmmakers, this time from Switzerland, arrived in Lalpur to film the iAgents. They shared with me the prefilming synopsis of the kind of story they hoped to capture, written prior to their arrival in Bangladesh. The following is a condensed version of one scene:

> Gita is a girl of fifteen years with deep eyes and worn hands. Clutching the hem of her blood-red sari, she hesitates before asking iAgent Jasmin, who has just delivered a group session in Gita's village, whether she might use the laptop to register on Facebook. Jasmin agrees and charges Gita 20 taka for the service. Gita has decided to spend her savings on being able to connect to the virtual reality of Facebook, a dream world she heard about at school. Under the gaze of Jasmin, Gita completes the form to create a new profile. Jasmin is surprised to see that all of the information Gita entered is fictitious. In Facebook, Gita has become Mehedi, a fashion model living in Dhaka, who lives from festival to festival wearing this clothing brand and that clothing brand. In reality, Gita works every day in the fields with her family and now uses the little money she succeeds in saving for those fifteen minutes of connection to her dream life. Although the request is unusual, Jasmin agrees to come to Gita's village each week so that Gita can delve into the life of her imaginary character. She knows that the internet is as much a full-fledged virtual world as it is a tremendous source of information, and she is its literal interface.

In this incredible representation, an iAgent is the direct broker between the arduous and insecure world of real-life rural Bangladesh and the fantastical virtual utopia of (what Swiss filmmakers assume to be) the aspirations of village girls. The role of iAgents would be to unlock the freedom enabled by the internet—not only the practical, real-world freedoms that might be assumed to come from knowing market prices, weather forecasts, or the *actual* costs of a government teaching job application, but also the temporary and escapist freedom of inhabiting a virtual world in which a person can fulfill her deepest aspirations.

That first week in Bangladesh was an intensely rich learning experience. First, the way in which my "expertise" and suitability to conduct the enterprise evaluation were unquestioningly accepted by the award committee on the basis of my friend's recommendation alerted me to the degree to which international social enterprise networks were personalized. Second, my friend's organization had a Bangladesh country representative, a young woman raised and educated in Dhaka. She was skipped over for the role of interviewer although she was instructed to accompany me on several visits, thus demonstrating the hierarchies and inequalities of power and knowledge in these networks. Third, the many actors implicated in the iAgent social enterprise network held strong ideas and imaginative assumptions about the iAgent persona and the relationships she was meant to have with the community, the state, and the market. Among many other sets of representations, the application's appeals, Mita's testimonial, Rohan's running commentary, and the angles Hugo chose to capture on film all signaled to me the role of storytelling in the crafting of a social enterprise. They all focused on different aspects, some of which contradicted one another but did not seem to create discordance. Rather, people seemed heavily invested in their own version of the idea of the iAgent and were able to disregard any images or information that did not suit their expectations. The readiness of outsiders to accept claims of emancipatory impact and empowerment by social enterprises fed into building the high level of hype and money ready to be deployed internationally to these ventures. An emergent set of associated industries vied to provide financing, develop social-impact metrics, build best-practice-sharing networks, establish new-idea incubators, form dedicated media outlets, confer awards, and launch university and business school programs centered on social entrepreneurship. Yet they all seemed to interact with social enterprises on the level of their written business models and best-practice stories and they largely ignored the realities of implementation.

Having written an analytical report about the iAgent model, I moved into a slum in the western part of Dhaka where I planned to conduct ethnographic research with a social enterprise that helped urban informal workers, particularly cycle-rickshaw drivers, to own their means of production. I had been in touch with that social enterprise through an introduction from the founder of another social enterprise in Assam, northeastern India, with which I had just conducted six months of ethnographic research before leaving because of political instability in the region. I hoped that the two similar businesses would afford me a cross-border comparison of urban informality and the effects of social enterprise. Yet when I discovered that the rickshaw project in Dhaka did not have any dedicated staff members, and the two implementing entities could not provide the names or contact information for the rickshaw drivers who were supposed participants in the program, I jettisoned the project. The next week, Adnan and Rohan agreed to my research among the iAgents. I had been drawn in by serendipity and by personal relationships and their inequalities inside the network.

SITE SELECTION AND METHODOLOGY

Being interested in social enterprises as key examples of poverty capitalism and the ways market mechanisms are used for development goals, I wanted to conduct research in one of the ten new license-model locations of iAgent. I selected Amirhat because of its position in the poorest region in the country. The area is also proximate to the border with India, and I was told that the dialects there are similar to Assamese, a language I had learned for my previous fieldwork. The Amirhat rural information center, located at ACRU, was about to embark on refresher trainings for its first batch of iAgents. In early April 2013, I arrived on the first day of a five-day training session.

Of the ten iAgents in Amirhat, two (Taspia and Deepti) volunteered to host me for the duration of my fifteen-month research period. The final decision was made by TIE staff, who said that Deepti, being Hindu, lived in a "distant and dangerous" area and insisted that I stay with Taspia's Muslim and more market-proximate family. Over the next six months, I lived with Taspia and spent time with each of the nine other iAgents as they attempted to conduct their work. Through processes that I explain in chapter 3, in late September 2013 the Amirhat iAgents declared their intention to withdraw from the program, for they had been unable to earn sufficiently to repay the bank loans they had been forced to assume. Three officers from TIE visited Amirhat to "resolve" the situation, which included informing me that I should return to Dhaka. They did not want me to witness or influence the aftermath of the project's failure in that location.

My experiences with the ten Amirhat iAgents from the very beginning of their work until the very end bore little resemblance to the emancipatory claims I had heard during my first week with the social enterprise in Lalpur and in its Dhaka offices. I was struck by the extent to which TIE focused energy and attention on one place—Lalpur and the Atno Bishash iAgents—which became the public face of the enterprise. All foreign visitors were sent to Lalpur to be amazed by the program, where iAgents were ready to tell turning-point narratives. When visits to other locations occurred, attention was deftly organized away from individual experiences. Making the most of the forced rupture from Amirhat, I decided to move to Lalpur, to discover the realities behind what I had begun referring to in my field notes as "the origin myth of the iAgent." Adnan and his team were satisfied with my proposal and seemed assured that I would not discover any problems at their one exemplary location. Although Lalpur served as the iAgent exemplar, it did not take many days for me to begin seeing contradictions, discontent, and, above all, acute anxiety and ambiguity surrounding the work of iAgents.

I spent the following nine months in Lalpur, where thirty former and current iAgents worked, and most of my time was spent with eight of them. TIE did not permit me to live in an iAgent home; its directors said that they wanted me to be less involved in the personal lives of iAgents. Instead I stayed in an empty room in the Atno Bishash NGO buildings. In Lalpur, I became well acquainted with the iAgent and other local NGO staff members who worked on different projects. The debacle at Amirhat had highlighted for me the intensely hierarchical and authoritarian nature of the relationships among iAgents, local center staff, and TIE. I thus intensified my focus on the iAgent network and the relationships among actors in the network—that network became my "field site" (rather than a particular village or geographical location). By "studying through," following Janine Wedel, I was able to unite different scalar fields into a single field of analysis and "situate the actors among the interactive levels through which the policy process is diffused. In this way, ethnography brings together different organisational and everyday worlds across time and space. The historical background, actual power structure, intended individual strategy, official documents both contemporary and historical, thus, can be studied through and in the process of seeking the power webs and relational activities between actors" (2004, 169).

In both Amirhat and Lalpur, my primary mode of data collection was participant observation, recorded through notes that I wrote on a daily basis. iAgents, center staff, and others used mobile phones many times per hour to communicate, take photographs, and play music, so I was able easily to record voice memos and type digital notes on my own phone during the day to remember significant details and document people's remarks verbatim. I accompanied Amirhat iAgents as they learned to ride bicycles, faced opposition from parents about their activities, grappled with the training content, established groups and attempted to provide services, and broke down in despair after a hard day's work that yielded no income. I conducted a survey of Taspia's village in order to capture household memberships, lineage connections to Taspia, and the livelihoods and activities of residents there.

I joined Lalpur iAgents as they provided over fifteen different types of services, often by traveling thirty kilometers (18.6 miles) by bicycle (and sometimes by boat in this riverine region) each day to reach distant villages. In the course of iAgents' daily journeys through different areas, I participated in their interactions with farmers, fishermen, schoolchildren, college classmates, frontline workers of other NGOs, lower-level government officials, and relatives. I recorded genealogies and family histories of iAgents. I took part in the activities of everyday life, such as preparing food, visiting relatives, tending animals, joining ritual observances and festivals, commenting on village disputes, and participating in a house-building project from start to finish.

In both locations, I observed activities at the local NGOs, which included administering other donor-driven projects, hosting training and monitoring sessions with iAgents, negotiating the relationship with TIE, and attempting to win other sources of funding to expand their presence in the area and to maintain their patronage roles. On short visits to Dhaka, I visited relatives of iAgents who worked in factories and lived in extraordinarily precarious circumstances. I conducted semistructured and unstructured interviews in Bangla and in English with TIE staff involved in the iAgent project, and I accompanied them on visits to four other iAgent locations in different parts of Bangladesh. I interviewed leaders and staff members of partner entities (government ministries, banks, multinational corporations, NGOs, advocacy groups, and bilateral aid agencies) and accompanied them on their visits to iAgent locations. I attended social business conferences and workshops hosted by Muhammad Yunus and the Grameen Bank.

While living in Bangladesh, I asked many iAgents to write their life stories or to dictate them into their phones. Two iAgents completed their narratives on paper in Bangla before I left the country (these I translated myself), and, with the encouragement of Taspia, eight more women sent me their stories (both in Bangla and also translated into English with support from Rohan Alam) by email over the following years. I am grateful that they have allowed me to share their writings here. Composite narratives (which I have anonymized to protect the identities of individuals) head each of the three parts of this book. While they convey the personal views and life courses of specific iAgents, these accounts are also representative of the experiences of many other women similar to them. The passage of time has enabled many of these writers to think reflectively about the role the iAgent program played in the broader trajectory of their lives. The myriad perspectives these different forms of data embody enabled me to discern the structural and relational attributes of the social enterprise network, which will become clear in the pages to follow.

Part I
DISRUPTING ETHICAL MODELS

iAgent Megh's Story

*I was born in a middle-class family, but now we are poor.
My name is Megh. My father was a farmer. He had a little
amount of land, and he earned his livelihood by cultivating
those lands. Both my parents lead a very simple life. They did
not have any kind of jealousy or arrogance. My father always
dreamed that they would have a son and that he would take
care of the family. But I didn't have any brothers. We were four
sisters. My elder sister got married before my birth.*

*My mother told me that they married off my sister after
selling most of the land we had. My sister's husband was also
a farmer. Their financial condition wasn't good. My sister had
three daughters. In our country, people still think that it's a
curse to have a daughter. They think this because we have to
raise our daughters up and then marry them off, which is very
expensive. "They'll work at other people's homes their whole
lives." People say so many things like this. My sister couldn't
reply to any of these comments. She had to suffer a lot for being
born as a girl.*

*I started to grow up. I had two elder sisters at home, and they
loved me a lot because I was the youngest of all of them. I heard
that my eldest sister didn't get any education. The next two got*

admitted to school. My father was the only earning member in the family. His little income couldn't fulfill all of our needs. He couldn't manage our food, education, and other needs. He worked cultivating other people's lands, and he worked inside other people's houses too. He didn't have any other way.

I got admitted to primary school and went there every day. I loved going to school. I made so many friends there. I studied after coming back home. My friends studied with the help of private tutors, but I never studied with the help of someone from outside. My sisters taught me everything. My parents were not educated, so I learned everything from my sisters. Days passed by like this. Although I could not understand our poverty, my sisters could because they were older. They couldn't buy the clothes they liked or eat the foods they loved. We couldn't do anything about it because this is what happens to a poor middle-class family.

My father kept saying one thing again and again. "If I had a son, would there be so many problems?" The neighbors said, "Get married once again, and then you will have a son." But my father didn't remarry because he thought, "What will happen if I get another girl child!" Father said, "It's all my fate."

When I was only ten, I began to understand everything. I could hear my father saying that he would get his middle two daughters married because he couldn't bear the cost of their study and other expenses. I heard this often. My sisters couldn't hear what our parents said because they slept in a separate room. But I was younger so I heard everything.

My second sister's name is Somita. One day father was telling mother, "Somita grew up. We will get her married after her secondary school exam ends." Mother replied, "Do whatever you think is best." Father said, "We need to sell all the rest of the lands if we want to get her married, because there are so many expenses. We need so much money including dowry and other expenses. Let's tell everyone that I'm going to sell lands."

Then my father told everyone in the village that he would sell his lands. Meanwhile, Apa's [elder sister's] exams began. She did not know about any of this.

One day a man came inside our home to see Somita Apa. Apa didn't realize that he came to see her. Then my father's land got sold, and father accepted the marriage proposal for Apa. Maybe I didn't understand everything then, but now I do. Maybe Apa wanted to study more, or maybe she liked someone else. But she couldn't say anything that day.

It's normal that there will be poverty after a girl from a middle-class family gets married. You need a lot of money for a wedding. Plus, we were four sisters. My father always said, "I'll sell all the lands I have and get my daughters married. Then whatever is in my fate will happen." From that time, I could understand that girls don't have any freedom after getting married in this country. They have to do everything according to their husband's will. Those girls are being deprived of the light of education due to facing such problems. I used to feel really bad when I thought about these things.

In 2003 I was in the eighth grade. I began to understand about people's suffering. My other sister, Mituni Apa, would be attending the secondary-school exam that year. And father arranged her marriage. He didn't want any of his daughters to study much because he knew he'd need a lot of money to do that. He also told my mother, "Megh is also growing up. We have to get her married too."

Mituni Apa cried a lot during her wedding because she didn't want to get married at that time. But she couldn't say anything to father. I cried a lot because all my sisters were gone and I was alone.

Ninth grade finished. Now I was a student in tenth grade. I had to study a lot because it was my turn to attend the secondary-school exams this time. I was so scared in the exams because people told me that if I move during the exam, they're going to take away my answer sheet. So I was scared all of the time. When they published our results, everyone passed, and only I failed. They all started to go to college but I didn't.

Later, I had to retake the exam, and I passed. Then I got admitted to the humanities section at the girls' high school. I met so many girls. Runa was my best friend. We always stayed together. I used to tell my thoughts and secrets to Runa. She used to tell me hers too. Runa told me about her dreams that she wanted to become a schoolteacher after finishing her studies. And I loved that occupation a lot. So I also said that I would become a teacher when I grow up. Runa told me, "It will be great. We will both be teachers."

Suddenly one day we heard that our friend Chameli would get married. She invited all of us. When we were second-year students, almost all of my friends were married. I was really afraid because my father was prepared to get me married. I remembered what happened to my sisters. I saw how their dreams got broken in front of my eyes. Runa told me that she didn't want to get married quickly. But I said, "I can't say this to my father."

When high-school exams were over, I got admitted to a college near my sister Somita's home, and I lived with her. My new life started. I saw new dreams, and I started moving forward. I made a lot of friends in college. My days passed very well. They were so colorful.

Then what I feared the most became real. My father came to my sister's place and said, "Megh, let's go home. Your mother is sick." I asked him, "What happened to mother?" Then father said, "You'll see after you get home." The next day, we went home. My parents and sisters knew everything about my wedding, but I didn't because no one told me about it. After I came home, I saw that mother was okay and nothing had happened to her. I asked her, "What happened to you?" "Why? Nothing happened to me," she replied. Mother said, "I don't know what your father told you!"

I didn't like this. Because I knew my father, I began to suspect him. I asked my sisters, "Tell me, why did father bring me home?" Then my sisters said, "It's your wedding! Don't raise any objection." I just listened to them. I cried a lot because I had thought that maybe my dreams wouldn't break like this. I thought to myself, "I didn't even get the chance to love someone."

My husband's name is Ibrahim Ali. One lakh taka was given at my wedding and two lakh taka was spent, including wedding expenses. I had to move to his house. Everything was new. I'd never seen my husband before marriage. I didn't know him.

The new environment was awkward, but everyone loved me. I started building good relationships with everyone. My mother-in-law took care of me a lot because I'm her eldest son's wife. We became close in a really short time.

My husband was jobless. He didn't do any work. Still, it was a new marriage and a new family. I didn't know what was to happen. They had some land, and my brother-in-law had a business. But he saved all of his money for himself. I told my husband, "You should do something." He said, "Yes, I will!" But he never did any work. I felt very bad sometimes.

My husband spent the one lakh taka that was given by my father for his daily expenses. I was worried about what would happen when all of it was spent. I was very tense about it but I couldn't say anything because I was afraid that he would beat me. Ibrahim Ali just chatted with his friends sitting in the bazaar, eating snacks and drinking tea. The year 2012 passed like this.

Then in 2013, a man from ACRU asked, "Your wife passed high school, right?" Ibrahim Ali said, "Yes, she did. Why?" He learned that ACRU had a new project. He told me everything when he came home at night. He said, "Your father gave so little money, and now it is gone. Here is a chance for you to start earning now." I said, "If you want, then of course I will do the work." He told me, "Try it. We can have a little income from our village through this."

A few days later, our training began. But I couldn't stay through the whole training because I got sick there. After two months of trying to work, I became very weak because I had to do so much hard effort while working outside. I also had to do housework after going back home. My husband said I should try harder. One day, I felt dizzy and began vomiting. Day by day I was becoming weaker. I went back to my father's house. I felt so bad that I couldn't do those works. Then one day I heard that everyone was giving back their machines and tools. It felt a little bad. I didn't think that the work would end before I even started it well.

I went back to my husband's house. After going there, I heard that my friend Runa had gotten a job. She is now a teacher in a primary school. I became glad that her dreams came true. But I couldn't communicate with her because her posting was very far, and I was sick, and family life wasn't going very well. My husband still didn't do anything. The year 2013 ended like this.

In 2014, one day my husband told me that he would take me to Dhaka with him. He said, "I will do a job and you will stay with me" A few days later, we both went to Dhaka. He got jobs for both of us in a company called Epyllion. My job was in the drawstring section. That company made many kinds of shoelaces, blazer laces, and other stuff like this. We worked for eight hours every day. His salary was 8,000 and mine was 6,000. But even with this money, it wasn't possible to live in Dhaka. It was very hard to manage everything. But we were *earning together. This went on until suddenly I became pregnant, and I went back to my in-laws' house to give birth.*

One day in 2016 my father suddenly passed away. He didn't have any sickness. I felt very sad because I never thought he'd suddenly leave us like this. My mother became alone too. I had two uncles; one of them is a teacher and another is a politician. None of them helped my mother. Everyone is selfish. They think only about themselves. We, the four sisters, decided that my mother would go to my elder sister's house.

Before, my father had sixty-six satak [0.66 acres] of land. It was all gone because he sold them to get us married. We could do nothing to help support our mother. Everyone cried a lot. Maybe this wouldn't happen if we had a brother. But what's done is done.

I had a dream, and it was becoming a schoolteacher. I recently attended two tests but didn't get any job. You can't get government jobs without bribing. And after ACRU, I don't want to work at any NGO. But for now I must work on my family and raise my child. Now, my child is one year and five months old. This is my life's story.

WOMEN'S WORK
The Arena of Disruption

While Megh was unable to work long as an iAgent, many of the challenges she experienced in life were precisely the challenges for which Technological Innovation for Empowerment hoped to solve through the iAgent model. TIE delineates the theory of change that it claims to catalyze through participation in the iAgent model in the following statement:

> Challenging the status quo and creating voice was the essence behind the concept of "iAgent." The iAgent model challenges the status quo at two levels—the individual and the social. At the individual level, the model breaks the fear and apprehension of a young village woman, who lives in a low-resource setting and has limited access to knowledge about the world beyond the village. It is a transformation for the woman herself; she rides a bicycle and challenges the status quo in a male-dominated society, where it is perceived that riding a bicycle is a man's business. She takes a profession that embraces the latest information technology, like laptops, Internet, and smart phones. Again, she challenges the stereotype that women cannot deal with technology. Finally, because the young woman earns from the work she performs, her voice is counted both in the family and in the community.

This statement assumes that, by performing paid work outside the home and using technologies typically confined to the male domain, young women will become more equal to men in knowledge, confidence, and skills and will earn respect in their communities. These assertions suggest that acts such as riding bicycles and using computers generate specific, desirable, and predictable social effects. TIE bases its work on a model of "disruptive innovation" for development, where disruption of the status quo leads to empowerment. The objects of disruption, according to this model, are women's mental and physical states, social and gender norms, and perceptions of women and their place in the village. Through disruption, restrictive, discriminatory views transform into appreciation, respect, and inclusion. Fear and ignorance yield to the illuminating effects of technology and money.

While this statement and other material published about the iAgent model did recognize both individual/personal and social/relational factors, they fundamentally misunderstood the content and interplay of those two aspects. The model did not consider why women might or might not want to challenge certain aspects of the status quo. It also did not account for any reactions from families and the wider society that might have resulted from women's defiance of established patterns. Nor did the model take note of possible reasons why targeting women as earners might amplify their exploitation by men at home.

While the iAgent model and many other market-driven development programs celebrated the Silicon-Valley ethos of "disruptive innovation," they did not acknowledge the other types of disruptions these programs caused. Turmoil at home, public shaming, and the undermined value of women's domestic labor were common consequences not anticipated by project designs. Yet the participants, facing family poverty and the prospect of being sent away to work in the disreputable garment industry, were attracted by the rags-to-riches narratives of social enterprise. This chapter explores how these market innovation development processes both became central to and also threatened women's efforts to position themselves as upwardly mobile and ethical persons.

We have already seen that the actual implications of iAgent activities were equivocal and that multiple forms of disruption generated opposing effects for participants. The vignette that began the introductory chapter highlighted the divergent experiences of Rahela and Taspia, iAgents in Lalpur and Amirhat. The trajectories of these two individuals represent particular patterns of outcome in the iAgent network and in the political economy of market-driven development. In their work, Rahela and Taspia gained the confidence to travel on their own through villages and to towns. They both learned to ride a bicycle and operate digital technology. And they both, at least to some extent, earned money from their efforts. Yet "empowerment"—in TIE's definition of gaining mobility, respect, and voice through women's work outside the home—was achieved by only one of the two entrepreneurs, and only after several years of struggle.

Rahela eventually experienced a high degree of mobility, the self-earned purchasing power to elevate her social standing, and the ability to fulfill social obligations on behalf of herself and her family. Taspia, by contrast, experienced harassment from strangers about cycling and from family members about incurring a potentially ruinous 75,000-taka (962 USD) debt for her household. Although she could fulfill some social obligations, such as purchasing Eid gifts, she did not possess the ability to support her family in a substantial way or to change her life circumstances. Her family now faced the risk of losing everything—not only her unpaid-for laptop and bicycle but also the family's house, land, and social standing. The iAgent process enabled the performance of successful ethical personhood for one group of young women but not for the other. Both sets of women experienced "disruption" in their everyday lives and the ways other people related to them, but not in a predictable, uniformly positive way. The iAgent could be seen as either a new kind of female community leader or a new kind of stigmatized female hawker. These divergent experiences and valuations of iAgent work indicate that outside labor, technology entrepreneurship, and disruptive innovation in themselves do not lead to empowering outcomes.

The Silicon Valley–inspired model of disruption has infused the discourse and practice of many social enterprises. This model of change undergirded the iAgent program's raison d'etre and the narrative of women's empowerment, and it formed the basis of the social enterprise's claims of being an ethical organization that provided social benefit. A primary device for accomplishing this result centered on descriptive narratives of the model iAgent—sometimes generalized, as shown earlier; sometimes represented by a fictionalized exemplar named Mita; and sometimes portrayed through stylized depictions of Rahela. Such narratives achieved the dual role of signifying to partners TIE's social impact and generating standards against which real-life young women participants were compared. The achievement of positive disruptive outcomes by pilot-project iAgents such as Rahela—a small minority of the total number—produced a model of aspiration for other young women such as Taspia and served as a device for sustaining the idea of iAgent as embodying successful and ethical personhood. Such devices as models and exemplars generated a "cruel optimism" (Berlant 2011) and framed in stark relief the two types of disruption—the empowerment model and the real-life disturbance—that were operative here.

An ethnographic perspective on the lives of real iAgents reveals that women's work—both within and outside the home—was already a domain of contestation, a field of cultural struggle (Mills 1997), a source of moral anxiety, and a site of control over women. Thus the agenda to disrupt women's existing livelihoods and social interactions, while well-intentioned, was not a neutral exercise. Rather, it compounded the contradictory and often antagonistic experiences women faced in everyday life. The development teleology of "good" disruption clashed with these actual experiences of adverse social turmoil faced by iAgents.

When enterprise-driven views of women's work conflicted with social ones and rendered women's social identities morally questionable, the burden of reconciliation fell on women. Women sought to diffuse these tensions in painstaking ways, and this chapter explores their efforts and the broader social effects of such disruptive transformations.

The self-making projects and emotional labor of young women in rural Bangladesh were therefore centrally implicated in the definition, delivery, and sustainability of the social enterprise. The iAgent business model defined itself by targeting young rural women who, driven by the precarious circumstances of poverty, were willing to risk their personal (and also family) reputations to earn a living. Women's desperation and the ethics of endurance, along with relations of patriarchal dominance within the home and working environments, ensured that the program would always find participants, despite the hardships women experienced. iAgents' feelings of self-responsibility for family betterment were also core to the process of mediating the contradictory expectations generated by

FIGURE 4. An iAgent considers whether or not to visit yet one more village before returning home. Photo by author.

the social enterprise. Such a personal investment helped to enable the program's sustainability. The burden of managing and accepting the consequences of the social disruptions upon which the social enterprise staked its impact claims was offloaded onto women participants. This chapter pays close attention to this unacknowledged and fraught ethical and emotional labor taken on by development's primary beneficiaries.

The following sections explore women's work, both within and outside the home, as a significant site of cultural struggle. As they attempted to reconcile the enterprise-valorized persona of the disruptive entrepreneur with the socially stigmatized role of the impoverished hawker—while also fulfilling their family-oriented duties—women developed new ethical positions that enfolded their outside activities within an ethics of kin work and an ethics of endurance. Yet the broader social effects of these processes militated against genuine empowerment for women. It is within the context of these contestations, ethical fixes, and social consequences that iAgent work must be understood and that programmatic modifications should be considered.

Women's Work as a Site of Cultural Struggle

If a key aim of disruptive development is to "liberate" women from domestic labor and the constraining features of patriarchy, then we must examine the conditions, relations, and values surrounding this "traditional" work environment in order to know if new workplaces provide genuine improvements.

Women in Bangladesh have often framed household work within the context of suffering (*kosto*), which referred particularly to poverty and the long-term efforts and sacrifices that parents put into creating and caring for children (Lamb 2000). Although framed as a complaint, struggle and suffering were cast as a feminine virtue in Islamic moralities, and *kosto* was perceived in vernacular theories of women's agency as a crucial aspect of being a good person and achieving success.[1] Although they remained dependent on family members (especially men), women were aware that kinship was the only reliable and secure support structure available to them. Thus, their family-oriented service work or kin work was a fundamental part of their pursuit of self-interest. The work of kinship was a crucial enabler of their own autonomy and self-construction as virtuous people.

Paid labor outside the home, by contrast, was considered shameful for the majority of women, and it often stifled their autonomy despite the wages they might be able to bring home. Spending time in public places with unrelated men subjected women to increased social scrutiny, and they also experienced intensified patriarchal exploitation in their new workplaces. The double burden of labor fell on the women, who continued to be responsible for domestic work on top of outside jobs, and also on their female kin who remained at home and needed to absorb extra duties. Therefore, despite the hardships and inequalities they faced, many women considered being able to work at home a pragmatic first choice. It meant that they belonged to a family with sufficient means, which did not need to send its women to find menial labor outside. Yet the economic reality of many poor families necessitated extra income. Women from these families struggled especially to reconcile the conviction that they were sacrificing themselves virtuously to support their families with the feeling of shame due to the heightened moral criticism cast upon them. Therefore, for many women, any outside earning activities (combined with the emotional and ethical labor they undertook to defend their honor and that of their families from the shame of these activities) must be considered alongside domestic labor as part of the work of kinship (Di Leonardo 1987).

Women's evolving reflections about ideas of kin work highlight the shifting meanings and valuations, social implications, and transformative potential of different acts of labor. Both domestic labor and outside work (such as iAgent participation) were considered forms of kin work because they ultimately enabled social reproduction, the extension of networks for household welfare, and ethical self-making through supporting the family. These objectives, consistent with women's views of successful personhood, were not always compatible with the iAgent model of a successful entrepreneur, which sought to eject the young woman from her webs of dependencies and refused to recognize the burden of social struggle inherent in change processes.

Yet the motivations for iAgents in joining the enterprise were as much embedded in collective, kinship-centered notions of progress as they were in self-improvement on more personal terms.[2] It is difficult to separate one from the other, for even individual success accrued value by virtue of social recognition, and investment in kin work yielded greater security for women as individuals with agency than did pursuing an independent trajectory. Correspondingly, the failure of individual iAgents to conform to social expectations exposed the whole family and community to shame. Any social intervention that sought to work with individuals and yet failed to consider their embeddedness thus imperiled its participants by passing all social risk onto them. "Empowerment" was not an individual process in Bangladesh but instead was relational due to the need for social connection.

To mediate the contradictions generated by their new economic and social roles, women positioned their iAgent work within their narratives of a kin-centric ethical position, leveled critiques about the erosion of values in society against other community members, and framed their own deviant actions as ones that repaired widely held moral values. Rather than replacing notions of women's primary responsibility for household work with entrepreneurial autonomy and independence, these disruptive processes thus paradoxically required women to escalate their kinship commitments in order to counteract their perceived social deviance. While these processes enabled women to form emergent ideas about agency and aspiration, they also generated considerable moral anxiety.

This context is crucial for understanding the ambivalence with which women embarked on their journeys to become iAgents. New iAgents often used the trope of suffering to describe their service work in the villages, but this type of struggle unsettled their notions about agency and progress. At the end of the day they had few results to show for their efforts, they faced hurtful stigma from neighbors, and they had not contributed to household labor. As will become clear, their attempts to assert the value of their efforts outside the home (to counteract social criticism) often belittled the efforts of their home-bound kin, and these claims joined NGO narratives in further devaluing women's domestic labor. Against stated objectives, the Western development injunction to "liberate" women from the home often relied on and reinforced the continuing need (but also the continuing lack of recognition) for the "traditional" woman and her household labor.

Domestic Work as Virtuous Struggle

The simplistic portrayal of village women prior to their "rescue" by the iAgent program—as being fearful, ignorant, and not productive in terms of valuable work—does injustice to women's daily efforts and the value society placed on them. Women provided the majority of domestic upkeep, care of children and elders, home economic management, and processing of agricultural products.

A typical day of work for Tamanna, an elder sister of iAgent Taspia, is representative of rural women's regular domestic labor patterns. The day began with rising early and preparing breakfast for the family. She washed pots, swept the earthen-floor house and yard, and let out the animals (chickens from covered baskets and cows and goats from their shelters to be tied outside by the haystacks). She hurried to complete these tasks and then rushed to a nearby house to deliver a microloan installment in the medium of well-worn bills in small denominations tucked inside her NGO-issued repayment booklet. Tamanna hoped that she would not miss the collection officer and incur financial penalties. The officer had not yet left, but he chastised Tamanna for her hurried demeanor. After his departure, Tamanna remained behind to exchange news with the other women. Rabia, another credit group member, had fled to her parents' home following yet another beating from her husband. Silpi's son had been fired from his garments job in Dhaka and was now "just sitting" back home. The boy did not have any money, and so Silpi had sent him her month's earnings for him to use for bus fare and food; as a result she missed this week's credit repayment.

Credit work was a particularly gendered part of household labor that exemplifies emergent models of women's domestic responsibility as market-driven development became increasingly naturalized. The basis of microcredit is to collateralize women's labor (as compared with assets) or, more specifically, their future potential for income-generating work that would lead to paying off the loan with interest. Women used these loans primarily to supplement domestic consumption and social-reproduction activities, such as entertaining visiting relatives. When guests arrived, women needed to prepare snacks, tea, and meals and to purchase betel nuts and leaves for chewing, in order to honor the arrivals and to maintain the family's status and social connections. Renewing familial support structures was often a more stable investment for women than was rearing chickens or purchasing a sewing machine. Yet my interlocutors indicated that these notions were beginning to change as families became increasingly fragmented and kin less frequently helped one another.

After returning from the neighbor's house, Tamanna bathed (still clothed) in the house's yard by drawing buckets of water from the manual pump and throwing them over herself. She washed the family's clothes by driving suds through the wet bundles and pounding them against a stone block. She finished in time to help her mother prepare and then serve lunch to her father who was returning from work at the jute factory. If her husband had not taken a job in Dhaka, Tamanna would be living with her in-laws and would be spending much of the day serving them. After sharing the remaining food with her sisters and mother, Tamanna visited a woman in a nearby homestead who had recently been ill. Back home, she made tea; prepared and served dinner; washed up again; watched Hindi dramas on a neighboring house's television; and then unfolded and tucked in the hanging mosquito nets around the family's two shared beds.

During the harvest season, Tamanna and other women assumed additional work, including carrying bundles of threshed rice hay from fields to their settlements; spreading out hay and unhusked rice grains to dry in the sun; and repitching the hay in a pile to cover at night and sweeping the rice into jute sacks. Work related to cultivation was significant even when families did not own agricultural land. Their arrangements with landlords included sharecropping or sharing in the processing work for a portion of the yield. Women completed innumerable other jobs throughout the year or episodically. When leaves fell from the trees in autumn, women collected them in baskets to store for cooking fuel.

Home-based skilled income-generating activities were valued forms of domestic labor, but no one in Tamanna's family possessed such skills. Some neighbors embroidered, to varying degrees of proficiency, designs on saris, *shalwar-kameez*es, and winter blankets. Those families used the finished pieces or sold them in markets and to contract buyers. A profitable deal could be struck if a buyer agreed to order several dozen embroidered blankets for 500 taka (6.41 USD) each. Women sat together in the afternoons when free from other tasks and talked while they worked. If the investment was possible, a woman might buy a sewing machine and supply school uniforms, for a fee, for the village's children. Taspia often praised such skilled work because it allowed the person to support her family by fulfilling domestic duties simultaneously with earning money at home.

While primarily occurring within the homestead, women's "domestic" work also included activities outside the house that strengthened household status and networks. The male domain of the bazaar was not the only market. Women interacted with door-to-door traders, share-tended animals, engaged in sales and moneylending between households, and ran small businesses related to agricultural processing.[3] Women's market engagement included illicit or hidden economic activities (such as saving the cash surplus from the purchase of a sari and lending out accumulated reserves of money), often to hide a husband's shortfalls in providing for the family and to protect him from shame. Such concealment revealed personal autonomy for collective purpose as opposed to resistance against male-dominated patterns of market behavior. It indicated the pursuit of not only personal interest but also household interest, as the two were mutually constituting and were central to women's notions of ethical personhood. Women's economic activities—both domestic and extradomestic, paid and unpaid, and operating along a continuum of locations—were therefore a fundamental part of the broader "kin work" they performed.

Micaela Di Leonardo defines the work of kinship as "the conception, maintenance, and ritual celebration of cross-household . . . kin relations; decisions to neglect or to intensify particular ties; the mental work of reflection about all these activities; and the creation and communication of altering images of family and kin vis-à-vis the images of others" (1987, 442–43).[4] Kin work encompasses the upkeep of familial networks, nonmarket activities of social reproduction, and household generative projects that may include market activity. The kin work concept enables an analytical joining of perspectives on women's work that not only relates to the upkeep of domestic networks, nurturance, and other-orientation but also connects with women's goal-oriented activity as self-making labor. These multiple activities were intertwined in the relational work young Bangladeshi women performed within their families. Wage labor in the public sphere for women may be a necessary move to supplement household income for social reproduction, and maintaining a link with a distant relative may enable access to skills used in market activities or the exchange of household products. Family in Bangladesh is not merely social context; it is "the core institution for the delivery of welfare and social control; for the performance of gender and age-based roles and responsibilities; and stands as a microcosm for the wellbeing of society as a whole" (White 2012, 1431). The family, the only structure of security and support for women, was central to the ways in which they oriented life decisions.

The work of kinship therefore reflects women's dependence on familial relationships as well as providing them with a source of autonomy and stability. Benefits and disadvantages cannot be separated out, as "women's place in man's life cycle has been . . . the weaver of those networks of relationships on which she in turn relies" (Gilligan 1982, 17). The everyday choices women (and also men) made reflect the considerable relational work they performed to situate themselves and their families in favorable ways. Thus, the project of aspiring and acting, for iAgents and other women who contemplated new economic activities, can be read as embedded in the household's welfare.

Outside Work as Shameful Disruption

While many of the activities of a "housewife" or a daughter who performed domestic labor regularly took her outside the home, those mentioned so far (with the exception of iAgent work) were generally regarded as normal and acceptable. Yet forms of women's work occurring primarily outside the home were seen to index poverty and desperation, and thus shame and low social standing. It indicated a last-resort option for families who were forced to prioritize economic necessity over claims to dignity and status.

Women's employment in the 2000s across South Asia was low compared to other world regions. Women who worked outside the home came from the extreme upper and lower ends of the socioeconomic ladder (H. Donner 2008). Middle-class husbands who earned stable incomes tried to prevent wives from working outside because such activity cast doubt on their ability to provide for the family and thus harmed their honor and respectability (S. Grover 2009, 9). When poor women did work, their activities and workplaces—whether occurring in textile factories, brickyards, or the homes of middle-class people—often reproduced rather than diminished the patriarchal social order.

The poorest families, lacking stable jobs or agricultural land, engaged in an impressive combination of livelihoods that pulled both women and men into menial labor outside the home and cast suspicion on women's propriety.

The most shameful act of local, non-household work, performed by the most impoverished women, was begging. Itinerant women, often widowed or abandoned, walked great distances to places where no kin lived, in order not to damage their lineage's reputation.[5] Often in pairs, older women occasionally entered Taspia's homestead wearing faded saris with no blouses and holding rounded baskets. The baskets contained few items, sometimes a handful of raw rice and several folded rotis under a tattered piece of cloth, likely a retired sari. Without any greeting, comment, or inquiry, Taspia and Tamanna's mother, Jorina, would pour a cup of sugar into a fold of their saris, give each of them a roti, or put handfuls of uncooked rice in a bowl made from half a dried coconut. On special days in the Islamic calendar, such as *Shabe barat* when people prayed long into the night, the homestead received a steady stream of beggars throughout the day. Allah is purported to have said that night, "Who wants forgiveness, I will forgive you. Who wants food, I will provide food." Jorina spent the previous day pounding rice into flour and making a stack of rice rotis primarily for distribution to needy visitors. She explained that everyone always performed this task on this particular day, although she was unable to explain why. The practice of *zakat* (compulsory alms-giving) is different from kinship-based patronage, in which a person supported "one's own poor" rather than stranger-beggars. This form of religiously sanctioned and detached giving remained, while the personal ties of lineage seemed to compel people to help one another less frequently. People worried that the claims of strangers might become stronger than the claims of kin.

Hard manual labor was another opportunity for the poorest women. Taspia and I visited a brick factory, an industry that dotted the horizon along national and district highways in Bangladesh. The factory owner purchased red clay to be trucked in and deposited in huge piles and then harvested and carried in round pans on the head for processing by a machine that ran on diesel fuel. The brick workers arrived at dawn and worked late into the evening for a daily wage of 130 taka (1.67 USD). Only after I spoke with some of the workers did I realize that many of them were women. All workers wrapped cloth around their heads and faces, already black with soot and dust. On top of the women's normal clothes (*shalwar kameez*) they wore men's *lungis* and button-up shirts. Shocked and unable to hide the disdain in her voice, Taspia asked them why they dressed this way and pretended to be men. They explained that they protected their clothes from the dust, hid their identities from familiar passers-by, and thus avoided complete impoverishment, but the heat of multiple layers made the full day's work grueling.

Urban migration in Bangladesh offered a highly gendered labor market. For men, the options were work in transport, construction, public works, and informal trade; for women, they were domestic labor in cleaning and cooking and industrial labor. People claimed, "There is money in Dhaka, but none in the village."

The main source of young women's employment in the city was the garment sector, which has experienced rapid growth ever since the 1980s. Shifts at the factories often lasted twelve hours with one-hour lunch breaks and options for late-night overtime. Taspia's second cousins from the same village stitched trousers on sewing machines for 5,000 taka (64 USD) per month, along with 1,500 other workers on their floor and 6,000 in the building. Each hour, floor managers checked their rates of completion, which was stressful when workers suspected that they might fall short.

During Riya's three-month stint in garment work after her secondary school examinations, the former iAgent applicant lived in Dhaka with her brother and sister-in-law and worked in the same factory as they did. Life was difficult; they shared a room with twelve other people from five families and only one cooking pit and bathing area. During periods of heavy orders, in addition to normal twelve-hour shifts, they were required to work overtime, which sometimes lasted until just a few hours before the next shift began the following day. Because of her age and the fact that she was not formally employed, Riya earned only 900 taka (11.54 USD) per month without overtime. Sometimes, as with Taspia's second cousins, garment work was a strategy for the whole family, but often only daughters were sent. The majority of female garment workers at this low level, despite their hopes, did not earn enough money to save or to send home. (The better-paid floor managers and supervisors were predominantly men.) When Taspia's second cousins heard about the Rana Plaza disaster in April 2013, in which over 1,200 garment workers were killed in a single building collapse, one of them said resignedly, "If that is to be my fate [*bhaggo*], it is the will of Allah."

Taspia often rejected garment work as not suitable for a girl with middle-class aspirations such as her, but toward the end of her iAgent work she confessed that perhaps garments would have been better because she could have earned a stable salary for her hard work, unlike in her role as an iAgent. While financial desperation characterized the main reason expressed by these young women for garment employment, as Taspia suggested, poverty alone cannot account for all narratives because of the economic diversity of the female workforce. Differences in their lives and circumstances also affected their perceptions of the nature of the new work. Their attitudes were influenced by whether or not they had worked in manual labor previously, whether they entered employment by active choice as opposed to a distressed sale of their labor, and whether they secured the consensus of other members of their households. Megh did not need to worry about objections to her iAgent and garment work from her in-laws (because both activities were her husband's idea), but when other people criticized her work, it was to Megh and not to her husband.

On a trip to Dhaka, I visited Taspia's first cousins, whose departure for garment work occurred while I was living in their village. Taspia's niece, nine-year-old Sahara, worked in the Matador pen factory across the sludge lake over which her family's housing colony perched. Sahara was the only one in the family to work in a factory, although Taspia and her immediate relatives thought that everyone was engaged in garment work. The two sisters cleaned houses and their husbands were rickshaw pullers, but the relational work of managing pride and shame led them to tell people that they were all garment workers.

Established in 1998, Matador Ball Pen Industries boasts that they are the largest pen manufacturer in Bangladesh. The factory turns out 1.6 million pens per day for domestic orders and international export (Matador n.d.). Sahara understood how the company managed such high levels of output. Alongside many other young girls, Sahara worked twelve hours a day, six days a week, for 3,000 taka (38.46 USD) per month. Her job consisted of putting caps on pens one after the other. If she did not work quickly enough, the floor supervisor beat her. She made *lathi*-strike motions with her hand and then reached tenderly for her back and shoulders as she spoke. When she tried to work more quickly, she stabbed herself with the pen tip, and she showed me the ink-filled puncture wounds on the thumb and index finger of her left hand. She rapidly capped and recapped a Matador pen to demonstrate to me the speed she had to maintain in the single task she performed all day long.

Sahara dropped out of fourth grade when her family moved to Dhaka. She missed her friends who continued their studies and she lacked the time to make new friends in the city. She said that knowing exactly how her life would proceed made her sad. Without an education, she could never study further or obtain a respectable job, and she would never earn enough money to arrange a favorable marriage, one in which she would enjoy the luxury of being a housewife. Comparing the futures of her ex-classmates with her own divergent future, Sahara experienced factory work as a severe contraction of agency and choice.

Women's factory work ultimately did not lead to a renegotiation of domestic roles. "Labor-class" women often endured sexual abuse in the workplace from supervisors, contractors, and business owners (Parry 2014). People rarely blamed this violence on men; the shame of sexual misconduct and accusations of prostitution instead fell on the victims, diminished their marriageability, and forced parents to pay higher dowries. After marriage, many women considered it inappropriate for their husbands to have to perform household work in their absence

(Kabeer 2000, 123). In a majority of cases, taking up wage work caused women's bargaining positions in the household to diminish because of the burden of two full-time jobs (employment and housework).[6]

In many instances, households had to cobble together multiple economic strategies. The family of Riya, a woman who tried to become an iAgent but was unable to make the initial financial investment, exemplifies the stitching together of various activities for survival. Riya's father drove a rickshaw in Dhaka, while she and her brother worked in the garment industry for a short period. Back in the village, they bought young cows and goats to fatten and sell. Her brother sold almonds in the market and began cooking *halim* (a savory stew) at home to sell in the market from a moveable stall. While she studied in school, Riya bought paper and pens and sold them from her house, for a profit of one taka (less than a penny) each. When her father drove a rickshaw again, this time in Sylhet, he did not send money home, and Riya and her mother traveled from house to house begging for rice. Riya later enrolled in various NGO schemes: working on a road-construction team, taking microloans to be repaid in bags of rice, teaching in a school run by the NGO BRAC, and undertaking iAgent work. In optimistic moments, Riya told me that salaried employment (*chakri*) would not be useful for her after all, because the job would mean sitting in one place all day long doing paperwork. By contrast, she preferred some sort of business (*byebsha*) because she could perform many tasks at once and interact with people. Despite these rationalizations, she continuously searched for employment opportunities and the security they would entail. Other families persisted in disparaging her and her family despite their hard work and ingenuity.

Working in a government-service job as a nurse or teacher, as permanent, salaried, and high-status work (*chakri*), was highly coveted and did not incur criticism or shame. Yet for most people such work was nearly unattainable, primarily because of the need for higher education, personal connections with someone on the inside, and a hefty bribe to secure a position. The poor lacked access to such networks and cash. Many NGOs fell prey to similar accusations. Riya tried for months to secure a job teaching at an NGO school in the river-island areas, but someone low down in the NGO hierarchy required a 25,000 taka (321 USD) bribe to pass her application upward. She eventually abandoned the idea because she could not pay the upfront investment, as had also been the case when she sought iAgent work.

In contrast to the negative valuation attributed to women's outside work for non-elite classes in contemporary Bangladesh, Western models of development and women's empowerment continued to valorize work outside the home, assuming that it enabled liberation from the yoke of kinship and tradition. Rachel Heath and A. Mushfiq Mobarak (2014) have suggested that because "attractive manufacturing jobs" required basic literacy and numeracy, expansion of industry would lead to higher school enrollment, employment, and delayed marriage and childbirth for women. "Taken together, our results suggest that education policy in developing countries is closely tied to trade policy or industrial policy, and enrollments strongly respond to the arrival of jobs, especially if these jobs reward education. The manufacturing growth also improves welfare for young women, as they are able to avoid early marriage and childbirth, which have adverse intergenerational consequences" (29). In my research, however, I found that these emancipatory implications applied only to men, who were able to secure jobs in the lowest managerial roles and work their way upward. Women by contrast worked the shop floor in capacities that did not require literacy and numeracy and rarely presented them with opportunities for advancement.

Rather than leading to respect, acceptance, or emancipation for women, the commodification of the characteristics that made women seem more profit-generating at the lowest levels (such as manual dexterity, unlikeliness to cause trouble at work, and willingness to tolerate worse pay) further entrenched the performance of these traits (at workplaces and at home) as well as the feminization of work such as low-level garments jobs. Businesses that targeted young rural women and persuaded them to migrate to urban settings relied on other women's traditional home-based roles of social reproduction. In many parts of the world, young women "provide a highly flexible pool of labor through out-migration while, at the same time, the continuing economic ties between workers and their village homes bear part of the cost of maintaining and reproducing this labor force, thereby allowing urban employers to pay lower wages and offer fewer benefits" (Mills 1997:38).

Even girls' education was not always an indicator of better outcomes for women. Schooling for girls, from many parents' perspectives, was more often a factor for enhancing their position in the marriage market rather than in the job market.[7] Modern education generated symbolic capital for daughters to attract higher-quality husbands, and young men often desired educated wives, not for a career but to raise educated children. While such preferences may have influenced the age of marriage for girls, girls also continued to be situated in a stringently patriarchal ordering of society.

While valued as an essential part of women's emancipation in Western market-driven development assumptions, women's pursuit of jobs and a separate income per se did not index independence from the household or a gain in power for women within it. Women pursued their household's interests and fulfilled family roles, not purely individual ones. When women spent money, it often—by their own choice—served the interests of the household. These activities enabled better negotiations of dependence and were a crucial part of the cultivation of ethical personhood.

Anthropologists have demonstrated that markets inherently reproduce structural inequalities, and so pushing women into market-related activities is not a straightforward avenue to empowerment (Karim 2011).[8] Until gender relations are transformed, women's position in the workforce will remain on unequal terms to that of men, and they will continue to bear the primary responsibility for household labor and child rearing as well.

Larger Arenas of Contestation

Women's work was an active site of contestation not only in their everyday social interactions but also within wider policy debates and development agendas. Anthropologists have considered in many different contexts how gender and women's labor potential are pliable, contested images that can be leveraged to serve nationalist politics and economic interests. Ara Wilson (1999) documents how women direct-sales entrepreneurs in Thailand adopted a livelihood espousing the self-help rhetoric that claimed to give individuals and households the means to extract themselves from the Asian economic crisis, a philosophy that linked individual and household futures to those of the nation. Mary Beth Mills (1997) similarly shows how the identities of female rural-to-urban migrants were bound up with cultural discourses of Thai modernity that assume an easy movement between globalized registers of fashion and friendship and household-based values of deference to traditional cultural forms. In nightshift call-center work across India, Reena Patel (2010) exposes how notions of women's place and mobility were recodified to meet the needs of national and global capitalism.

Power exerted by kin and community on women's bodily discipline and the micropractices of everyday social life, such as *purdah* (gender seclusion) norms, can be analogized as "capillary power" (Foucault 1977, 1980) because it was widely dispersed and anonymous.[9] Yet gender inequalities were implicated as much in broader capitalist processes as in traditional and cultural norms, as Patel argues: "Conceptualizing globalization as a force that liberates women from local traditions is tricky because it can inadvertently be used to disguise and rationalize the exploitation on which this 'liberation' is based" (Patel 2010, 57). Thus, new proposals about "empowering" women through work need to be situated within an analysis of the broader interests served by harnessing the labor power of women without reconfiguring responsibility and gender relations at home.

Sarah White shows how this power over women's bodies was exerted in Bangladesh through multinational aid regimes: "Over gender issues, the Western aid community is openly critical of Bangladeshi society, and is deliberately aiming not only to raise economic standards of living, but also to change basic social relationships," such as bringing women out of the home and mobilizing against *purdah* (1992, 13). Bangladesh, being the client in this development-patronage relationship, routinely had to accept the intervention in gendered expectations of women despite its contradiction with ideals of national cultural and political autonomy. Opportunistically regarding aid as a resource channel for obtaining funds and enhancing political recognition, ruling parties in Bangladesh adopted a "nominal commitment to women's development," which they used instrumentally to advance other agendas (White 1992, 15).

Despite this, the gender commitment of NGOs in past decades has tended to reproduce gender norms and inequalities. For instance, the promotion by development NGOs of income-generating activities such as embroidery or small-livestock rearing that were labor intensive, low-profit, and occurring in the domestic sphere also militated against women working in the public domain (Kabeer 2000; White 1992). "The idea of the [at-home] . . . worker promoted by microcredit programs kept the majority of women inside their home, . . . dependent on their husbands, kin, and NGOs. Thus, we need to analyze carefully the 'arrangements' within which NGO narratives of women's empowerment get produced" (Karim 2011, 130–31).

In recent years, with the contribution of women's textile-factory labor to Bangladesh's economy, development priorities have focused on bringing women out of the house and into the formal labor force (Yardley 2012). The twenty-billion-dollar-per-year export-oriented textile industry is composed of several million female workers, which accounts for 80 percent of the country's manufacturing exports. This realization of women's potential contribution to national and private economic growth has been accompanied by increasingly confident assertions in development policy that outside work and access to markets have empowering outcomes for women. That this positive impact is commonly measured through GDP growth is telling.

Mediating Contradictions: Relational Work and Ethical Fixes

Caught by the need to work but also by the unattainability of government, private, or even NGO *chakri* and by the social stigma attached to manual labor, many young women joined the iAgent program as a seemingly acceptable compromise. This broader context of problematic livelihood opportunities for women also partially explains why many iAgents remained in the program, despite the many challenges they faced. The second half of this chapter explores their attitudes toward their work and the ways in which they sought to recast their activities as projects of ethical personhood, through an ethics of kinship and an ethics of endurance.

Taspia often justified her decision to find outside work as a way to reclaim her family's lost status as a provider within the village community. Her father used to run a food and tea shop in the market. It employed ten people at 150 taka (1.90 USD) per day and secured an average income of 10,000 taka (128 USD) per month for the family (three times his current earnings at the jute factory). When the government renovated the market, it confiscated all land and began taking rent for the newly arranged shop spaces. Taspia's father could not afford the fee (that is, the bribe) for securing a place and paying rent. "Because of corruption," explained Taspia, "we were a middle[-class] family before, but now we are a poor family." Her distinction between these statuses references social and economic registers as well as kinship expectations and the moral economy of patronage. "Middle-class" status came from generosity and the patronage role that was possible when a family was financially stable.[10] Taspia's household had been a gathering place for poorer kinswomen who performed a few hours of work and in turn received food—an arrangement that was "not presented as payment but as 'help'" (Gardner 1995, 153). The ability to provide livelihoods and food to people in need distinguished the family as patrons in the wider kinship network and village. To give payment for these women's efforts would denigrate both parties; it would cast visitors as laborers instead of kinswomen and it would undermine the giver's status. This patronage role had been central to Taspia's sense of herself as she grew up, and although she now identified her family as "poor," and the family no longer actively fulfilled the role of provider, vestiges of prestige from the earlier time remained. The role also stimulated her desire to recreate a respectable livelihood for her father, obtain a decent job for herself, and thereby reinstate a higher status for her family.

Good work for Taspia meant *chakri*, work occurring inside an office with a stable monthly salary. If she acquired such a salary, she would purchase calves to fatten for the annual Islamic festival of Qurbani Eid and sell for a handsome profit, and then she would convert the money upward by building a convenience shop for her father. Having no brothers to support her parents once she married, Taspia said she felt responsible for fulfilling the role herself. She regularly spoke about people who did not help their families and she reflected that people no longer had the "fresh mind" (*mon fres*) that a proper upbringing implies and that stimulates people to fulfill their socially expected roles. Taspia foregrounded the desire to support her parents through her work outside the home, even when the effort was detrimental to her sense of self. She often spoke about reviving the values she perceived to be under threat in contemporary rural society.

The keenly felt pressure among young unmarried women such as Taspia to accept the burden of responsibility for domestic upkeep and social reproduction as well as for income earning and the socioeconomic uplifting of their natal families was new. This novel situation arose from multiple overlapping, interrelating factors: the loss of agricultural livelihoods and means of subsistence; the lack of alternative employment opportunities for men; unprecedented numbers of girls attaining primary and secondary educations and being exposed to alternative life possibilities; rapid expansion of market-driven development programs and mass-production industries targeting women; and the resulting increasing expectation that young women generate their own dowries.

The need to pioneer ways to make their new economic endeavors socially acceptable—on top of the burden of family survival thrust on young women—was particularly widespread within Taspia's generation. Recognition and "having her voice count" did not occur automatically as a result of bringing home earnings, as they appeared to do in TIE's model of change. Rather, women had to struggle to mediate negative social fallout. Taspia's pursuit of outside work, and her retrospective explanation of her decision, reflect the ways in which iAgents and other women in similar positions took on the onus of family poverty alleviation. Subsequently these women had to mediate the social contradictions they encountered as a result of their efforts.

The next section illustrates how this dilemma was a relatively new generational burden for garments workers, microcredit takers, and development entrepreneurs—women whose mothers had confronted only one option, that of being housewives. It explores emergent vernacular theories of aspiration and agency among these women who faced uncharted circumstances, which included explaining differences between themselves and the women who occupied more traditionally feminine roles. Thinking through these divergent trajectories helped iAgents to further frame their choices in a virtuous light. For instance, they emphasized their struggle for and economic investments in their families, criticized a perceived loss of social values among other people, and set themselves apart from those they perceived as having lost these values.

A New Generational Burden

A discussion of the women in Taspia's family provides insight into the models of successful womanhood among which Taspia grew up and also offers an analysis of their trajectories as representative structural positions reflecting generation, gender, and class features.

Women of the generation of Taspia's mother, Jorina, spent most of their lives in their fathers' and husbands' homesteads and were not exposed to ideas about alternative futures. Jorina married in her adolescence and had not experienced any formal schooling. She said she did not understand what was happening to her at the time; she did not know her age or the possibility of other choices. She remembered being frightened about moving to a new place, but when she arrived at her husband's home and saw that his father and mother loved her, her fears eased. Her daily work rhythm remained the same. She reflected that the experience was easy, and she adjusted well because she was young and did not understand. Older women often spoke of their choices in these terms of incomprehension, in part perhaps to defer the responsibility of major decisions to their male guardians. They were also aware of their lack of formal education (synonymized with "understanding" and even "consciousness"), a resource that people among them, including younger women, increasingly possessed.

Jorina's natal and marital families were also related by kinship, which moderated the transition. Her husband's father was from the same village as hers, and her husband's and her paternal grandfathers were cousins. A relative had negotiated the match. When I asked Jorina if she would have chosen any different path for her life, she replied, "I don't know anything else. This is my life. What else could it be?"

Many people like Jorina, especially in poorer villages with few external connections, conceived of the future as similar to the present. Expected changes were life stage–related and observable among older siblings and neighbors.[11] Yet women in the generation of Jorina's three daughters experienced greater uncertainty and a wider scope of opportunity, and their life trajectories varied regionally, among villages, and even within households.

Jorina's second daughter, Tanzila, had married first, at the age of ten, to a tractor driver in a neighboring village. She never considered working outside the home. Jorina's eldest daughter, Tamanna, studied until tenth grade and dreamed of working in an NGO. When she married at the age of eighteen, she knew that her dream would not materialize. Taspia, the youngest daughter, explained that men with sufficient money wanted their wives to stay at home. Tamanna's husband held stable employment in a pharmaceutical company in Dhaka and he forbade his wife from working outside the home. Taspia could not explain why Tamanna had lacked the persistence to realize her dream of NGO work, especially because she herself would not marry a man who did not allow her to work. (Half a generation younger than Taspia, girls in middle and high school often told me boldly that they would study until completing their master's degrees and only then would they think about getting married.) The three girls came from the same parents, upbringing, and social setting, and yet significant differences among their opportunities, preferences, and livelihood trajectories were apparent.

The stories of the three women—Taspia, her sister Tamanna, and her mother Jorina—interwoven in this chapter reveal differences in aspirations and life possibilities between generations and families and also within them. My choice of three different "typical" women aims to emphasize that the capacity to aspire was a gradient across classes and also within them. People within households and during the course of their lives adopted many livelihood strategies, and no single typicality occurred. Yet some trajectories were more socially acceptable than others, and women such as Taspia needed to do more work to justify her choices than did her sisters.

Vernacular Theories of Endurance and Agency

The precarious social positions of iAgents prompted them to reflect critically about differences between people. These differences led to their own decisions to assume the social risks of outside work, whereas other women appeared to them to lack the motivation to do so. In casting moral judgments about these other women, iAgents made claims about their own ethics and the virtue of their (socially controversial) activities.

Arjun Appadurai (2004) describes aspiration as being disproportionately distributed to the wealthy and powerful because they are exposed to a fuller range of choices, resources with which to experiment, and corresponding observed outcomes, which in turn reinforce a deeper horizon of aspirations. Such individuals also endure fewer political, economic, and social constraints.

Taspia keenly understood this principle, but she also recognized that the ability to dream was a function not just of wealth and power but also of education, social values, and another trait residing in the individual: a quality of the mind/heart (*mon*) that affected how the person prioritized among different desires. She explained that a difference between large and small dreams (*svopno* or *ichchha*, "wish") indicated the quality of one's mind/heart. Small dreams were about things a person wished to happen that did not change her circumstances or imply progressive growth. Taspia gestured toward a young woman who had expressed her hope that her husband, returning from work in Dhaka, could bring electricity to their house and buy a rice cooker. Large dreams, by contrast, were about changing a person's situation, which led to more opportunities for improvement. Yet big dreams required education and a good mind. A few young women living in the area attended college, but their shyness and lack of sufficient motivation meant that they would not likely achieve large dreams. While Taspia's sister pursued many years of education and desired NGO work, she did not ardently enough feel the need to help their parents in the long term. She did not prioritize cultivating a good mind, suggested Taspia.

Riya also spoke about differentials in the capacity to dream. She focused on differences in a person's relational situatedness as well as in an internal quality of mind. She encountered a friend who had started work at the iAgent center office.

The two embraced warmly, having attended primary school together. Later, Riya contrasted her friend's salaried office job with her own precarious work in the field. "She wanted less but got more, while I wanted more and got less. We were the same, but she is my 'yes, madam' now." She attributed the status difference to her friend's father, who was their teacher and was connected with more opportunities that his daughter could make use of. Riya's hard work and strong will could not overcome her lack of connections to secure *chakri* for herself. Unlike Appadurai's observations, which place explanatory force on interclass power dynamics, Taspia's and Riya's explanations account for variation within social class, local community, and family.

The examples articulated by Taspia and Riya motivate a distinction between two aspects of the capacity to aspire. The first is the ability to envision (through dreams or wishes, whether large or small) a potentiality or a future different from the present. The second is the intention and capacity to act toward the achievement of that intention or, following Elizabeth Povinelli (2011; 2012), the endurance to bridge the gap between imagined potentiality and being, despite facing structural marginality and hardship.

Povinelli's concept of "endurance" adds a critical dimension to the capacity to aspire in situations of poverty and hardship. She suggests that the capacity to endure is the property that people engage to cope with the gap between potentiality and actualization when the material and political supports needed to pursue projects of aspiration are lacking (Povinelli 2011, 110). The notion of endurance also mirrors vernacular portrayals of women's work as sustained virtuous suffering and struggle (*kosto*). Yet iAgents display endurance and aspiration that is not sequential and teleological. The ethical act of endurance, a virtue in itself, is at its core a project of aspiration and an agentive means of pursuing dreams.

The ways in which the poor, who faced precariousness every day, scraped money together and invested a lump sum in risky projects must be understood in the context of the current political economy of Bangladesh and the lack of steady jobs available to support people. In this new situation of fragmented opportunity, women such as iAgents were engaged in a project of stitching together various possibilities that was creative and generative as well as desperate. Because the household was the only consistent security structure for women, the act of undertaking an unconventional project reflected the pursuit of collective ends and women's fear of the insecurity emerging from individual autonomy. Yet these projects also encoded both endurance and aspiration; women struggled to meet family needs but they also formed new desires and new ways to achieve their intentions. Often, they found themselves caught between and among different dreams and forms of kin work. The ethnography and analysis that follow introduce the projects of endurance and aspiration for iAgents and the tensions between them, situated against those of other women in their communities.

As a young girl, Jorina had few examples around her to indicate that life could be different. She did not envision an alternative future toward which she could strive. She lived by expectations congruent with the singular available model of successful womanhood. Her capacity to aspire to being and doing otherwise was constrained by the sociostructural circumstances in which she grew up. Tamanna, by contrast, observed some of her primary-school classmates obtain further education and jobs in NGOs, and she aspired to emulate that path. These desires conflicted with other aspirations about marrying a well-situated man who could provide an independent *pukka* (brick-and-cement as opposed to thatched or tin) house and secure domestic life, aspirations that corresponded with social expectations. She allowed her dreams of *chakri* to remain as desires held but not acted toward. These desires were also expressed as individual ones, as opposed to means toward collective ends. Taspia often criticized Tamanna and her husband for selfishly not helping the sisters' natal family, and Tamanna would retort that her choices would lead to a more secure and stable life for her son. The temporal orientation of her ethics faced the future, rather than the past generations. Despite Taspia's judgment, Tamanna's choices were no less collective, and she subsumed her own "individual" dreams to them.

Taspia was committed to achieving her dreams of higher education and employment in a way that would provide her with opportunities to fulfill a social role and perform the kin-work values that she saw being eroded. She desired *chakri* as opposed to independent entrepreneurship. She sought incorporation in established structures of hierarchy and dependence, and she planned to employ her earnings in projects of intergenerational-care work for future dependents (elderly parents and children), not to be liberated from them as Western empowerment models often suggested poor women needed. Unlike Jorina, Tamanna and Taspia inhabited nearly the same cultural universe, so the differences in their priorities and values cannot only be attributed to structural position but must also be accounted for in agency, preference, will, ethical substance, and capacity to endure and "be otherwise" (Povinelli 2012).

People's responses to the practical implications of new arrangements of dependence and independence were ambivalent, as illustrated by Ara Wilson (1999). The idea of autonomy from the constraints of kinship was significant in the narratives of direct-sales entrepreneurs with whom she worked, especially because they experienced connection to social worlds beyond kinship and possibilities for self-identification with transnational qualities. At the same time, the direct-sales company's "accessible methods and expansive affiliations provided not so much escape from as respectable leverage within local hierarchical worlds"

(Wilson 1999, 410). Similarly, iAgents simultaneously pursued the fulfillment of social obligations as well as expanded their range of personal aspirations through participation in the program.

Did being an iAgent generate in people a cultural capacity to aspire and find pathways for their realization? Or was being an iAgent primarily a means by which already-aspiring young women pursued their alternative visions of the future? White encounters this dilemma among women running successful small businesses who gained status and recognition: "It is difficult to distinguish cause and effect in this: it could be that more enterprising women take up businesses, and their centrality in the household derives more from their personalities than their business activities as such. The truth is probably that it is both more enterprising women who undertake such work and that they grow in confidence and recognition as their activities prove successful" (1992, 77). Women who successfully converted microcredit into income-generating businesses were those who typically already displayed autonomy in household decisions (as opposed to autonomy being a result of participation in microcredit per se) (Karim 2011, 80). This observation affects development interventions, as they may never reach their intended targets of women with the lowest resources and the highest constraints on their autonomy. Additionally, the idea that possessing aspiration and embarking in enterprise is linearly causative indexes an uncomfortable teleology that does not match empirical evidence. Many desperate people take on enterprising but non-aspirational projects as a way to endure, while others endure existing hardships as a means to fulfill an aspirational future. Neither case necessarily correlates with empowerment.

Another factor may be that the normatively biased assumptions about the meaning of "empowerment" in Western notions of development enabled iAgents to extend their horizon of articulated aspirations while simultaneously narrowing the set of aspirations upon which they were able to act. To a large extent, the preexisting aspirations of iAgents—which were rooted in kin work and social relations, collective values, and religious practice—became delegitimized as incompatible with Western notions of modernity and progress. The iAgent case can thus shed light on the political economy of aspirations within development contexts. This book leaves open the psychological question of the origin of different people's ability to form aspirations; instead it focuses ethnographically on the limits the Western values of the iAgent program imposed on aspirational capacities. Empowerment in Bangladesh was not individual but relational due to people's need for social connection. Misunderstandings of this fundamental matter within market-driven development projects rendered them unable to live up to their discourses of achieving empowerment through individual entrepreneurialism.

Retrospective Ethical Work and Projects of Legitimacy

Young women often spoke about differences not only among other people but also between their present selves and their lives prior to beginning iAgent work. In many of their narratives, they desired simultaneously to escape from their family's poverty and to help the family to overcome its difficulties. Being retrospective reflections, these accounts are revealing as political projects of justification and self-crafting. Although women often rationalized being an iAgent as allowing them options in life, few iAgents had actively sought out the iAgent project. They desired office jobs (*chakri*) instead. They learned about the iAgent opportunity and reacted to it without much understanding of what it entailed, which turned out to be a radical departure from their existing ways of working, being, and interacting.

The penchant among Western visitors (who were usually affiliated with the media or NGO) for rags-to-riches turning-point stories as the dominant (Protestant-inspired) ethic of proving worthiness significantly affected the ways in which some iAgents narrated their life stories. Their accounts became political projects angled toward legitimizing their decisions in the eyes of their families and gaining resources and opportunities brought by these powerful others.

Rahela described her pre-iAgent self in consistent ways to multiple visiting groups:

> Initially I suffered from poverty in my family, and I was not independent. If I went to school, I was allowed only if someone accompanied me. Otherwise my father did not permit me to leave home alone. While facing this struggle, I wanted to be independent and do something on my own, to walk with my own feet. During the process of joining iAgent, I faced many challenges from my family when they did not allow me to begin some training. Those days I stayed at my aunt's house and went to the training sessions from there. I felt that in order to become independent I have to struggle, so if I am experiencing struggle, then that's the right thing.

Struggle (*kosto*) and overcoming it featured prominently in iAgents' narratives about their past and referred not only to domestic housework but also to their efforts to pursue outside opportunities such as schooling and employment. Riya's father did not allow her to continue her education because of the cost. She managed to convince the teachers to lend her secondhand books and waive the enrollment and examination fees, but when she entered grade six, the new teacher beat her. She learned to wait until he left the room before entering and reading from her friends' books. Before examinations, she bought a stack of discarded paper (usually purchased by itinerant hawkers to sell rolled-up cones of roasted peanuts) and copied information from the textbooks. By struggling through adversity, she managed to earn satisfactory results and pass middle school.

Seeking to escape family poverty through self-initiative and a measure of independence, these young women also desired to use their new positions to help family members. Taspia oriented her life trajectory toward what would have the least negative impact (delayed marriage and therefore delayed dowry payment) and provide the most help to her family (earning money to build her father a shop). Rahela hoped that her siblings would never be lacking because their elder sister supported them. As soon as she paid back the money she had borrowed from relatives to invest in her iAgent business, she increasingly used her income for household expenses and items for family members, who became dependent on her.

Projects for family improvement initiated by iAgents were not always successful. Dipa used her large savings from successful iAgent activities to help her brother seek work abroad, but in the end he was cheated out of all the money (2.5 lakh taka; 3,205 USD), which he gave to a middleman purportedly for his passport, visa, plane ticket, company fee, middleman fee, and bribes.[12] Each of the women spoke about iAgent work not as an aspirational end in itself but as an instrument for accumulation that might be converted upward to more socially acceptable and economically profitable work, such as NGO *chakri*, a family cattle-rearing business, a shop, or international labor migration. Only the first of these desired endeavors entailed independent work for the woman herself; the others were improvements in livelihood from the perspective of the household. By enduring and overcoming hardship, women situated themselves in structures of dependence as providers, thus ensuring that those dependent on them would not need to face similar struggles. Thus, understanding the meaning of women's work requires contextualizing these activities in broader projects for the family.

These brief cases illustrate the clarity with which iAgents were able to narrate their pathways, early aspirations, and capacity for persistence before assuming iAgent roles. They also show the centrality of kin work in projects of aspiration, which were possible only once iAgents were able to overcome significant difficulties.

Ethical Judgments and Acts of Repair

As livelihood strategies for families grew increasingly varied and new opportunities became available to individuals, greater economic and class differences grew between and within families in the same villages, and people confronted these new distinctions in various ways. Households became sites of contested authority and overlapping interests, and any particular livelihood choice, especially for women, was rooted in household tensions and collective strategies.[13] Conflict within households centered not only on choices of particular livelihoods but also on the ways in which available wealth (in money, assets, connections, knowledge, or skills) was or was not distributed.

Exploring these conflicts in household decision-making can help make sense of the aspirations, anxieties, and hierarchies that underpinned issues of consensus and discord. Bangladeshis worried about social fragmentation and people becoming more individualistic and selfish (Devine and White 2013, 137). Conflict over wealth distribution arose most poignantly because of increasingly unmet expectations that sons and sons-in-law would support their parents and parents-in-law. People often commented in scandalized tones that someone's son left to find work in Dhaka but selfishly never sent money home.[14] With the increasing incidence of love marriages, parents feared that their sons would forget them and focus all of their attention on their wives (Lamb 2000, 76).[15]

I was often a party to exchanges such as this one: Tamanna, entering the yard where Taspia and I sat, said she had spoken with her husband in Dhaka. She announced with a smile that he now held five lakh taka (6,410 USD) in his bank account. I asked if he ever helped her family, and Taspia jumped in, shouting, "No! He doesn't help! He never has!" Tamanna's phone rang again, and we listened as she asked her husband for money. Taspia instructed her to request three thousand taka this month. Tamanna used the tactic of listing the medicines and foods that their baby had required because he was ill, and she added that they needed to buy grass for the cow so that the animal would produce better milk for the child. Entering the courtyard and having heard these remarks, Taspia's mother remarked that her son-in-law would not give any money because he used it only for his own purposes. When he had visited the previous month, he had not contributed any amount, even for the food he ate from their cooking pots.

When people became more wealthy, they suddenly grew selfish (*shartopor*) and greedy (*lobhi*), according to Taspia. By contrast, their sister Tanzila's husband, a considerably less wealthy tractor driver, possessed a "good mind/heart" (*mon bhalo*) and always helped the family when necessary. When Taspia's father was injured in a bicycle accident, Tanzila's husband provided all the money for doctors. He gave Taspia several hundred taka here and there without expecting any return, while Tamanna's husband had never given Taspia any sum. Of the money Tamanna occasionally received from her husband, she sometimes offered her father only part of it, whereas Taspia said she always handed over all of her own income to her father. I later asked why she thought some people assisted their families and others did not. She replied simply that she, Tamanna, and Tanzila all thought differently, and so did their husbands.

Later, Taspia presented a different, more nuanced theory. Girls sometimes still desired to help their parents, more so than did boys. Yet girls usually did not have access to cash income, and their educations made them clever and vocal. When they married, this capacity translated into selfish behavior, and they told their husbands to keep all the money for themselves and their children rather than supporting the husband's parents. Not so long ago, Taspia continued, all girls were *chhotomanush* ("small people," in this context meaning uneducated) and were uninformed, and they left all decisions to their fathers and husbands. In her view, if women were educated and worked hard, then their families would have two incomes and be able to support their parents as well as their children. Yet education needed to become normalized as a social model of ethical womanhood, an endeavor Taspia sought to embody. She wanted education and an outside job as a means of (rather than as a detriment to) upholding her ethics of kin work and endurance.

Sarah Lamb (2000) documents how the Bengali concept of modernity since the 1980s and '90s has invoked the notion of broken-down social obligations, such as the decline of the joint family and the decreased desire to care for the elderly. People often blamed the ills of modernization on urbanization and the Western individualist education system. "The old people's words are not mixing with the young people's anymore. Now the young people's intelligence has become very [or 'too,' *besi*] great" (Lamb 2000, 91). Resonating with Taspia's explanation, Lamb adds that daughters-in-law specifically are better educated and able to assert their own interests as separate from serving their parents-in-law, and they often desire to live apart from them.

The trend of families becoming increasingly nucleated also presented itself in land inheritance and usage patterns. In the past, as sons married, they occupied a section of the parents' house, and the new couple continued to remain part of the same homestead (defined commonly as "eating rice from the same pot," Lamb 2000, 36). Brothers jointly owned the land. Now, brothers and their brides preferred to split from the parental homestead (*bari*), often by erecting walls on their piece of land, managing the household independently, and cooking at different hearths. Taspia and her mother agreed that having a separate house was better, and the initial request to divide now often came from the new bride and was opposed by her father-in-law. When Jorina married, her husband and his three brothers all lived together, and their properties were still one. I asked her if being separate was now better. She leaned close, lowered her voice, and grinned: "Yes, because now when we all quarrel, we can go home for some peace. Otherwise there were too many people, too many children, and too much fighting."

Even with separate homesteads, brothers might spend years arguing. Rahela's father and his brother, whose house was directly adjacent, were not speaking to one another. The quarrel concerned the division of land between the two, particularly the space now occupied by the concrete shop that Rahela had built from her iAgent savings. Rahela clarified that the ownership of the physical space was uncontested. Rather, the quarrel was rooted in the envy felt by her uncle because of the impressive income Rahela's shop continually brought to her nuclear family.

Ultimately, according to iAgents and members of their families, these inter-relational problems came from greed (*lobh*), the state of being selfish (*shartopor*), and envy (*hingsha*). They attached these qualities to specific types of people in specific times and places; they were not general human traits. Wealthy people in general, but especially the newly wealthy, were perceived as selfish and easily susceptible to envy. Once they started earning money, they thought only about money and how to accumulate it. They stopped being generous and helping others. This characteristic seemed to be a recent trend in society. Taspia said that when her family had previously earned money from their market shop, they regularly gave food, employment, and assistance to people who needed it, and other wealthy people behaved similarly. Now, none of the rich people in the village offered anything or helped anyone. As Taspia pointed out, of the approximately thirty extended families (many of which were branches of the same lineage) in this village, five were rich. She detailed their circumstances—type of house, type of employment, and extent of land ownership—which sat in stark contrast to the economic situations of everyone else. Yet despite the fact that nearly all the families in the village were blood-related to at least one of these wealthier households, none of them received any assistance. The wealthy "are thinking only of their own benefits and costs! They think, only they can become wealthy, and no one else," criticized Taspia.[16] Her complaints were weak claims, but claims nonetheless, to the fortunes of her wealthier relatives. They can be read as broader contestations against the declining state of kinship-based patron-clientalism and the erosion of personal ethics that accompanied it.

"A Fresh Mind": An iAgent Vernacular Model of Everyday Ethical Agency

The way to avoid the downfall of greed, envy, and selfishness was to cultivate a good mind/heart (*mon bhalo*), which was central and deliberate in the approach taken by iAgents such as Rahela and Taspia in conducting their work and seeking to cultivate ethical personhood. These two iAgents often collaborated with others, for example, by accompanying another iAgent on her visits to clients and handing over the results of the combined effort to the other iAgent. When I questioned them about their seemingly non-self-interested behavior, they usually referenced *mon bhalo* or *mon fres* by way of explanation. Rahela invited other iAgents to fill in forms together for the Aponjon service (for pregnant women to receive health information via text message), because they often needed to travel longer distances and stay away all day. At the end of the day, she gave all the forms to the other iAgent to help her meet her targets set each month by TIE. She explained that she was already fulfilling her own targets so the forms and associated income were not important to her and that her mind became fresh (*amar mon fres hoye gelo*) by visiting new villages and working companionably. As Taspia explained, "With iAgents, there is no envy. I think it is important for all the iAgents to have income."

Shanu was an iAgent who dropped out when she married, had a baby, and wanted to continue studying for her degree. She reported that many people in her village still visited her for advice even though she had stopped working as an iAgent and had returned her equipment to the NGO center. Enjoying playing this role in the community, she added that possibly the greatest impact of the iAgent program was when the iAgent "returned" to society. Because she retained her knowledge and position of authority (but not the uniform or technologies), she continued to help people without charging fees for her advice, which Shanu said was important for her mind/heart. Assisting others restored her to the position of being able to help people rather than hawking services for money.

A good and fresh mind/heart came from education, respectable parents, keeping Allah in one's mind, hard work, and generosity. Taspia's father influenced her by the positive role model he set; he used his shop to provide employment and free food to needy people. This work generated prestige for the family, a quality that endured longer than the shop itself. She also learned in school and from reading Islamic texts about how to have a good mind/heart. Women often sat together for an hour in the afternoon to read Islamic books aloud while others performed stitching work. Faith, along with diligent work, was often referenced as the anchor for successful personhood. According to Taspia, without either sincere work or faith, a person would lack a good mind/heart and would not succeed in life. Prayer and keeping Allah in her mind caused her wishes to become realized (*ichchha puron hoy*) through hard work (*porisrom*) and struggle (*kosto*). Rahela explained that she worked intensely and sincerely, which was the reason why Allah had chosen to help her. Without hard work, prayer alone would not be effective; without prayer, hard work would result in nothing.

Women's models of agency included maintaining faith in and daily mindfulness of Allah. Retrospective accounts of events revealed when and how notions of divine fate played a more significant role than individual choice and action. Being and acting as an ethical person was a precondition to receiving Allah's help. Although Allah's intentions were not known, people speculated that unmet hopes resulted from a lack of patience or from an unethical act committed in the past. When people perceived events to be fully out of their control (such as a factory disaster that kills many people), and immediate ethical action could not have played a part, people explained them as "fate" (*bhaggo*).

Explanations of the entanglement of agency with fate could also be projected into the future in cases concerning the ethical or unethical choices of individuals and the influences such behavior had on one's fate. For example, I wondered about people who prayed but did not work hard and about successful people who were greedy and selfish. Taspia pointed out that both kinds of people lacked a good mind/heart. As a result, the former remained poor, and the latter were currently successful, but their present and past actions would destroy their futures. As proof, she referenced Sabbir Hossain, the Amirhat center director, and how he had suffered a stroke and incurred catastrophic financial loss as a result of cheating the iAgents. In a series of events described in chapter 3, the iAgent center in Amirhat had just collapsed as a result of Sabbir and his employees treating the iAgents as a source of personal income for themselves.[17]

Riya stated that Allah fulfilled people's wishes over time. Because Bangladeshis were not patient and did not want to wait, they took shortcuts (such as intimidation and bribes) and thus ruined their chances for their wishes being fulfilled. Explanations offered by iAgents can be read as local theories of agency and help to clarify their decisions and actions. By judging others, they attempted to redefine the substance of ethical personhood in contexts of rapid change and unstable relationships.

Obstructed Solidarity

The social effects of disruptive development and the ethical fixes of women of Taspia's generation in the long term remain to be seen. Perhaps the pioneering role of this generation will provide real-life exemplars for younger women, realistic ones that do not instill false hope in frictionless success. In the short term, however, the presence of TIE's exemplars continues to generate a narrow aspirational pathway to success based on individual entrepreneurialism and lures young women into socially perilous roles. Women's ethical fixes—while helping them to justify their own actions and carve out respectability, when successful—also have the effect of degrading and devaluing other women's domestic labor and creating divisions among women.

Ideas of economic growth that necessitate removing women from the home do not come exclusively from Western development personnel. iAgents themselves, echoing comments they heard from TIE staff during training, increasingly criticized the current low status of women because, they reasoned, the role of the housewife encouraged women to be lazy, unproductively quarrelsome, and perpetually dependent. After visiting a poor village for a group session, Rahela explained that areas such as that one remained "remote" (meaning underprivileged and unconnected) because the agricultural land belonged to a few educated people, and everyone else was very poor. "In Bengali culture, people are lazy [alosh]. When they are uneducated, they remain that way. They do not work, especially girls, who remain dependent on their parents until they become dependent on their husbands." Rahela added that she was able to act independently only because she was working self-sufficiently as an iAgent—a role that came about through her own choice and action—and was studying for her college degree. Without one or the other, she too would be dependent. iAgents often explained that they possessed traits different from other women. They said they held a quality of mind/heart and ethical personhood that enabled the pursuit of dreams larger than merely following the paths laid out for them. Otherwise, they would be unable to fulfill kin-work expectations. They warned me not to visit remote villages alone, because residents there were untrustworthy, "unconscious" (or "unsensitized," oshosheton), and lacked good mind/hearts because they did not work intensively to support their families.

Often, noises of a fight in the village erupted, perhaps because someone's cow ate someone else's store of hay or two brothers argued over land division, and everyone ran to spectate. Taspia criticized this feature of village life as unproductive and a symptom of the lack of other opportunities. "In Bangladesh, there is no work, no employment; there is only sitting and quarreling." A trenchant recrimination about the role of daughter-in-law especially was that "she is doing nothing; she is just sitting." Nilufar, an iAgent in Lalpur, explained that a primary motivation for becoming an iAgent was to escape from a life of sitting in the homestead with her quarrelsome mother-in-law. "If I hadn't become an iAgent, I wouldn't be able to move around outside. If I would have stayed in this family all the time, there wouldn't be any improvement for me. The day would be wasted in arguments. My mother-in-law is that type, as you know. Now, if there is any problem or crisis at home, I can go to the office or to meetings in the field." Many iAgents considered a positive feature of their outside work to be their opportunities to flee from confrontations and some responsibilities at home.

Yet iAgents weren't able to escape the demands of housework. In some cases, the ability of iAgents to do their work relied on the labor power of kinswomen engaged in more traditional domestic labor. For these iAgents, working outside seemed to exempt them from domestic work, and other women were relied upon to take over the additional burden. When women married or assumed a female head-of-household role, in the rare cases that they could continue with their iAgent work, they were expected to participate fully in both the public and private domains.

Unmarried iAgents were often swept into domestic work because they were perceived as a flexible labor pool on the home front as well. Rimi, stirring chicken curry over a fire on a river island one day, commented with chagrin about how her boat trip across the river to register women for the Aponjon program was hijacked by her married sister's insistence that she and I eat lunch with them, thus leaving Rimi to cook the meal while the sister completed other work. Rimi laughingly called herself an "all-rounder" (English word), using a term with a usually positive connotation but delivered in an ironic tone of voice and a dismissive gesture that suggested otherwise. Far from achieving women's empowerment, schemes for women to work outside the home do not often change gender relations. Instead, women's domestic labor continues to be treated as a way to subsidize (men's) "productive" labor and now also subsidizes NGO processes of accumulating resources.

This chapter takes a closer look at how the activities historically perceived as low-class labor (such as the door-to-door selling now associated with the rural sales force of multinational and national corporations) were gendered as female and recast in market-driven development models as aspirational entrepreneurialism. Skill was thus "an ideological category imposed on certain kinds of work by virtue of gender" (S. Sen 1999, 105). The fictitious character filmed for TIE's promotional and training purposes, iAgent Mita, explained a facet of this gendered skill: "I feel that this profession is only for females, because a woman can easily mix with many people. It is rather difficult for a man to associate with people of a different profession or class." Her comments reflect an intriguing recasting of gendered seclusion. They also reflect the program's assignment of responsibility for bridging gender and class divisions to women alone, rather than expecting men also to take up new kinds of work and amend gender and class inequalities.

Disruptive development in Bangladesh dislocated women from established social roles and placed them in a new kind of gendered work that occupied a position of deviance from social norms. Needing to prove the value of their new activities, women positioned their supposedly individual, entrepreneurial work within this existing model of successful womanhood, focused on service to the family. Thus, rather than freeing women from these "traditional" norms, such market-driven models forced the burden of social reconciliation on women, who needed to escalate their commitment to these models of behavior in order not to lose the security of family and kinship, the only reliable support structure for them.

As women attempted to reconcile the ethical contradictions arising from their participation as iAgents, the narratives they told themselves and their families played a crucial role in the relational work of redefining the moral boundaries of women's public and private activities. This emotional and social effort shows women to be active agents in navigating precarious circumstances, but it also underwrote the social enterprise's ability to continue functioning without recognizing or addressing these internal contradictions.

iAgents possessed a strong vernacular for expressing modern ideas of work and kinship. These ideas reflected their notions of agency and ethical action, which were bound up in models of being a good relational person (through generosity and performing intergenerational kin work) and working diligently for a desired future. These reflections did not arise spontaneously; they were part of the ways in which iAgents sought to reconcile the negative impact of choosing work that was socially stigmatizing for young unmarried women. Women's notions of proper work outside the home were influenced by their ability to act virtuously and were informed by existing forms of exploitative female livelihoods, such as begging, hawking, or factory work in Dhaka. Stories of oppression and shame served as counternarratives to aspiration.

The act of taking on iAgent work was a risky endeavor, embarked upon and situated in a generative but ambivalent kin-work project and within a broader set of aspirations. The notion of a desirable future, held by iAgents who were recently commencing their work, were influenced by multiple factors. The conditions of poverty in which these women and their families lived provided motivation to seek pathways out, and TIE targeted desperation as an internal quality of young women to ensure their commitment to working hard. Thus, I consider the iAgent program to be a project of endurance, which constitutes a central part of aspiration. For these young women, the components of endurance were engaging in hard work (*porisrom*), accepting the attendant struggle ("suffering," *kosto*, valorized in Islamic models of feminine labor), cultivating patience and a good mind (*mon bhalo/fres*), and accepting divine judgment ("fate," *bhaggo*). These qualities were central to the iAgents' discourses of agency and success.

For iAgents, this model of behavior permeated everyday choices, such as assisting other iAgents and persevering through challenges. Their ethical action engaged a long time frame through the intention to follow values perceived to be otherwise deteriorating in contemporary society. These perceived responsibilities have shifted generationally in rapid and profound ways. For many, the iAgent work was also an effort to seek incorporation in established institutions (secure NGO employment and a kinship network), rather than independence from them. In situations of poverty and inequality as faced by iAgents, "individuality as a way of social being is extremely precarious" (Khilnani 1997, 26). Through the process of being pushed into risky, non-traditional opportunities as generative kin-work projects, iAgents also encountered new self-making potential. If they became successful in their endeavors, they were able to incorporate themselves more deeply in structures of dependence in a giving rather than a receiving role.[18]

These narratives demonstrate the intense ambiguity, struggle, and burden of the work of kinship not captured by outside analysts in existing models of aspiration (Appadurai 2004) and relational work (Zelizer 2012). Myriad constraints and models of expectation surrounded women, women's work, and women's social interactions in rural Bangladesh, and each new opportunity carried its own set of expectations that might or might not have corresponded with women's existing circumstances. The ways in which women understood their capacity to act with regard to their notions of ethical personhood provide crucial insights for projects seeking to empower women.

Nationalist and development projects involving women celebrated the contribution women could make to domestic (in both senses of national and household) economies, and entrepreneurship discourse, inspired by the Protestant ethic, resonated in particular ways with the vernacular, Islamic moral valorization of hard work for women. The success stories of first-generation and fictional iAgents served as exemplars and positive models of aspiration for later-generation ones. Yet, as the following chapters show, new iAgents encountered aspiration as a problem when their personal experiences did not match those of their role models. In this way, fictional figures and other models can play a crucial role in sustaining systems of inequality.

Subsequent chapters handle the less emancipatory implications of iAgents who engaged in the for-profit license model of the social enterprise. In Amirhat, when iAgent work impinged on the ability of young women to be good persons in the world, they quit to avoid "future damage" to themselves. There, iAgent participation did not translate into mobility capital, and iAgents were not able to work on terms that enabled them to improve their families' quality of life. They suffered physically and often complained about becoming thin and charred by working all day in the sun. As Sabina Faiz Rashid reminds us, "the body is not merely a site of suffering but the space and medium through which one can articulate the experience of the self" (2007, 120, drawing on Kielmann 2002). The women's comments invoked the punishing and unequal circumstances that depleted their bodies of vitality and power.

The extractive work of the organization took physical, mental, and financial tolls on iAgents and it also began to instill in the women the negative values they sought to act against from the beginning. Caught in desperation mode, they began quarreling among themselves, which aroused feelings of jealousy and self-serving behavior. Spending entire days working futilely at their jobs, they missed out on their college educations. Not yet having reached social acceptance of their activities (riding bicycles, traveling alone outside the village, and being perceived as hawkers), they were unhappy about others who judged them unfairly. Not yet having reached financial success, they failed to contribute income to their families, and they did not participate (sufficiently) in household work.

Worst of all, if iAgents could not repay their bank loans, a burden equivalent to an extra dowry payment would fall on their parents, likely causing the family's ruination. What they experienced as a result of the iAgent program was severe disconnection, not connection or empowerment. Unlike successful iAgents, whose initial experiences of ambivalence were partially resolved by their enhanced ability to fulfill kin-work expectations, the competing subjectivities of Amirhat iAgents began to rend their social worlds apart. When Taspia finally decided to resign from her iAgent work, she resolutely stated, "I know well that if I stay I will be destroyed by such a little laptop. I cannot spoil my life because of this laptop. I cannot leave my future to be ruined."

DIGITAL TECHNOLOGY

The Problems of (and Solutions to) Connectivity

Riding her bicycle one-handed for many kilometers as she returned to her village after a long day's work in a neighboring district, twenty-one-year-old Rahela accepted one call after another on her mobile phone. She shouted in mild exasperation at a final caller and terminated the conversation as we approached her house. "I switch SIM cards in the evenings when I come home. It's part of the struggle of being *digital*. During the day, men are afraid of me when they ask my advice as an iAgent, but in the evenings, they all want to marry me," Rahela laughed.

Rahela's light tone masked the ambivalence of the "struggle" she mentioned of "being *digital*" and keeping her personal and work relations in order. This chapter deepens our discussion of the ways in which social enterprises used models of disruptive innovation that were intended to "liberate" women from gender and culture norms but instead brought them under heightened scrutiny. Technology—and the specific case of the mobile phone—introduced new, often problematic forms of connectivity and sociality.

The expected entrepreneurial availability and 24/7 doorstep service of its young female workforce was a significant part of the social enterprise's claim that it provided social impact. These expectations, however, generated moral anxiety surrounding women's propriety and appropriate levels of interaction with unrelated men. Women's struggles in handling mobile phone use exemplify the ways in which they needed to navigate, on their own, the contradictions between the social enterprise model of successful entrepreneurialism and social models of virtuous womanhood.

Yet this chapter also aims to strike an optimistic tone by highlighting instances of positive unintended consequences of market- and technology-driven development. It demonstrates the ways in which young women in Bangladesh developed new ethical sensibilities, renegotiated *purdah* and gender norms, and emphasized their *digital* identities through mobile-phone interactions with young men. The local notion of *digital* (an English word repurposed in the Bangla language) stands for modernity, awareness, and education, and yet the term does not necessarily imply the opposite or rejection of "traditional" values such as purdah and women's propriety norms, arranged marriages, and dowries. *Digital* thus references ambivalence and struggle over the meanings of women's new activities and socioeconomic roles.

This chapter details the ways in which women negotiated ethical positions in the context of new forms of interaction—through their unconventional work outside the home and through mobile phone conversations with non-kin men. The phone was not merely a communicative device to facilitate market exchanges between iAgent providers and villager consumers. Sometimes, the phone sparked new relationships when young men dialed random numbers hoping to hear a young woman's voice. By focusing on the fearful excitement and ambivalence experienced by young women who engaged in these mobile phone–enabled "wrong-number" relationships with young men, we can understand how phones and other digital communication technologies were embroiled in contemporary discourses of moral anxiety regarding male-female interactions and in the ongoing efforts of women entrepreneurs to fashion themselves as ethical subjects.

While mobile phones and the connectivity they implied cast young unmarried women onto perilous terrain, they also provided an arena for women to exercise the critical resources of ethical reflection, cultural critique, and "the capacity to aspire" (Appadurai 2004). As risky adventures that might lead to reversals of fortune for poor women, these relationships stimulated the imagination and helped to shape women's understandings of the kind of husbands they wanted. Yet the intense fear of social stigma led most young women to drop phone relationships before they escalated and to value matchmaking by kin. Even so, their new critical resources assisted them in negotiating better positions during the process of arranging their marriages.

Mobile-phone relationships, in addition to women's work and livelihoods, thus constitute another significant "field of cultural struggle" (Mills 1997; Ong 1991) for young Bangladeshi women. This case allows us to deepen our understanding of what cultural struggle means on concrete, personal terms. I suggest that cultural struggle involves 1) an ambivalent mixture of fear and excitement elicited by new opportunities; 2) intense ethical boundary work that includes the evaluation of peers and the differentiation of one's own virtue (a reason why cultural struggle is fragmentary and rarely leads to broader class or gender struggles; Ong 1991); 3) cultural critique and recognition of social alternatives, which may provide space to challenge hegemonic ideas; and 4) the expansion of aspirations. These processes are vernacularized in women's notions of "being *digital*," an analysis that captures the opportunities and contradictions facing educated but poor working women in contemporary Bangladesh. Digital relationships serve as a lens for observing the ways in which young entrepreneurs experimented with the boundaries of freedom and enjoyment, negotiated purdah and propriety, and imagined futures in which fathers need not be ruined by the expense of dowries and husbands might support their wives' careers.

This ethnographic case engages the anthropological literature about the creative ways through which people engage in ethical self-fashioning. Paying attention to the importance of the senses in ethical reasoning reveals how media affect the awareness, emotions, and receptivity of users and provokes reflection about the complexities of cultivating an ethical life (Hirschkind 2006). People find resources from within religion and kinship to become virtuous actors (Mahmood 2005). Women's autonomy and self-actualization are not exclusively found in resistance to patriarchal norms and institutions (as development programs such as the iAgent program often assumed), and their aspirations and sense of ethical self are thus not necessarily split between traditional expectations and new ideas brought about through contact with the modes of entrepreneurial individualism espoused by market-driven development programs. As we saw also in the previous chapter, the embodiment of religious and ethical values affords women deeper forays into their entrepreneurial worlds and more active engagement in processes such as marriage arrangements. Saba Mahmood (2005, 115) calls these emergent situations "the modernity of traditional practices," an evaluation that exposes the ways in which binary contrasts (in both scholarly analysis and popular discourse) obscure emergent social phenomena (Lipset 2013).

Where this analysis departs from the literature on ethical self-fashioning is in confronting the idea that people form themselves (only or primarily) in relation to strong existing ethical systems. The iAgents conceived novel ethical orientations and established original expectations about marital life and public engagement by drawing on a range of norms concerning virtuous comportment, kinship obligations, entrepreneurial practice, and their own critical imaginings of the future.

This chapter also provides a further nuanced reading of Arjun Appadurai's (2004) evocative but flawed concept of the capacity to aspire, the idea that aspirations derive from larger cultural norms that structurally constrain poor people from being exposed to new experiences and therefore prevent them from building a navigational capacity to widen their horizon of ambitions. By contrast, through their active participation in phone relationships (which were inflected by the phone's relational and material affordances; Juris 2012, 275), iAgents extended their aspirations by accessing ethical and navigational repertoires within kinship, Islam, and their own critical reflection and cultural critique.

After situating the practice of mobile-phone relationships in the broader anthropological literature on new media and relationships and in the context of the literature on marriage in South Asia and Bangladesh, I explore how the idea of "being *digital*" is a Bangladeshi vernacular analysis of the struggle of handling the complexities of navigating these new ethical positions in contemporary society. Two case studies show how, through the local notion of *digital*, young women in different villages in northwestern Bangladesh experimented with mobile-phone relationships and sought to craft themselves as ethical and upwardly mobile persons. First, I examine iAgent Rahela's conviction that only a mobile phone–originated love marriage would secure her the husband (and therefore the life) that she aspired to have. Second, I demonstrate how iAgent Taspia experimented with but eventually rejected phone (and love) marriages in favor of an arranged marriage, which she viewed as an integral part of being a modern woman. While these judgments about phone relationships diverged, they were both part of the struggle of "being *digital*." In the two cases, the phone and the relationships it enabled played a pivotal role in the self-reflection of these young women regarding marriage, dowry, purdah, and the shaping of their aspirations. The vernacular term *digital* frustrates attempts to distinguish between "traditional" and "modern," as Taspia's seemingly paradoxical ideas indicate.

The Anthropology of New Media and Relationships

In recent decades, Bangladeshi people have begun to experience the changing forms of family structures and intergender interaction that became possible through women's increased mobility (in attending coeducational colleges and working in programs such as iAgent), migration (to urban factories), and technology (via the internet and mobile phones since the late 2000s).[1] As access to cheap mobile phones and data plans proliferated in Bangladesh (and globally), so too did popular and professional musings on the social effects of these and other new communication technologies. Public discourses of moral panic emerged on a wide scale and incited responses such as the police crackdown in India on predatory men ("phone Romeos") who used phones to harass women (Barry 2017). These dystopic analyses are balanced by the development industry's confidence in the progress to be achieved—in, for instance, e-governance, mobile banking, and telemedicine—through the spread of mobile phones (Dobush 2015).

Anthropological studies provide nuanced, ambivalent accounts, revealing neither social nor technological determinism (Mazzarella 2010) and neither regressive nor modernist social trajectories (Lipset 2013). The literature on India echoes some of the moral panic discourse by analyzing how phones unsettle inside and outside spaces but also mirror dominant social arrangements by accentuating gender hierarchies (Tenhunen 2008, 530). Young women in North India were forced to relinquish their phones when they married, and further access to phones followed household seniority and gender patterns (Doron 2012, 422–25). In these cases, the phone becomes an instrument of surveillance by male relatives seeking to control women's movements (Patel 2010), thus enacting what Richard Seyler Ling (2008, 14) calls a "digital leash."

Mobile phones are also shown to enable new kinds of access for women by facilitating natal ties (Doron 2012, 423), increasing women's role in marriage negotiations (Tenhunen 2008, 524), and transcending male oversight (Archambault 2013, 93). Phones can support survival strategies for impoverished women to maintain networks and summon resources (Horst and Miller 2005). People manufacture new encounters and search for connection via these new technologies.

Earlier work on literacy and letter-writing offers insights about how new notions of companionate marriage and self-development arise from novel forms of communication. Laura Ahearn (2003) draws a link between female literacy and renegotiated gender relations through the form of illicit love letters. The act of writing encourages reflection on the concept of love, expectations, and self-development. It allows for a deliberation not always possible in person, but which is desirable for the self-mastery that is linked with notions of honor (Constable 2009; Johnson-Hanks 2007, 654). Yet this form of engagement leaves behind material traces that differentially harm men and women and reproduce gender inequalities.

The topic of gendered imbalance and ambivalent experience is pertinent to the context of wrong-number relationships, which have been explored from men's perspectives in Hong Kong (Lin 2005) and Morocco (Carey 2012) and from women's perspectives in Papua New Guinea (Andersen 2013).[2] These relationships evoke the mixed emotions of excitement, fear, amusement, and outrage. They generate concerns about morally appropriate forms of exchange while also providing women with an arena to experiment in the male domain of verbal play. Yet women are sometimes tricked by men's manipulations, and stories of dissimulation serve as warnings to other women (Andersen 2013, 321). Building on this literature, I extend the analysis of ambivalence in women's experiences with mobile-mediated relationships while embedding these struggles in societal and cultural context.[3]

New Marriage Possibilities

The classical literature on South Asia focuses on basic social and cultural institutions and formal structures of kinship and gender (including marriage, caste, lineage, and gift-giving). Both the older body of literature and more recent literature are consistent in their attention to the ways in which women's lives are circumscribed by men: "In facing the day-to-day trials of marriage, a woman's key concern is economic security. The contours of her life are shaped by her relationships with men—her husband, father, brothers and sons—who are supposed to provide for her" (Hartmann and Boyce 1983, 93). This chapter shows how women also acted with agency within these constraints and sought the ethical resources to reshape their situations.

In the literature on Bangladesh, little focus is placed on marriage as an everyday, embodied experience and lived practice, and even less attention is paid to young women's perspectives on the marriage-negotiation process.[4] Customarily, young women did not discuss their marriages, which were negotiated by parents and professional intermediaries. The bride often saw the groom for the first time on her wedding day. Her detachment during negotiations and her expressions of grief during the celebration, while often genuine, illustrated feminine notions of honor (Gardner 1995, 187).

Love marriages in the past were uncommon and scandalous (Hartmann and Boyce 1983, 83). In recent decades, new avenues (such as the rising rates of female enrollment in school and industrial work) have become available for forging male-female non-kin relationships, which have continued to provoke social commentary and moral anxiety (White 2012, 1443). Once discovered, love relationships could be dismantled by parents—for instance, by promising rewards to a son if he desisted. Boys faced incentives while girls found their reputations to be damaged irrevocably (White 1992, 100). Love marriages grew more accepted among women and men working in garment factories (Rashid 2007, 116) because, parents reasoned, their daughters could continue working under the supervision of their husbands. As women increasingly obtained new forms of work alongside unrelated men, such as in the development industry, they needed to reconcile the excitement of new adventures with the desire to protect their reputations.

The earliest study of women working in development projects in Bangladesh occurred in the 1960s, when women accepted work as village-level organizers because of their destitution and loss of male guardianship (McCarthy 1977, 368). While some accounts show that purdah is no longer a determining constraint on women's employment choices (Goetz 2001, 107), others reveal negative attitudes when women work in their own communities, such as in the case of iAgents. Yet women can reconfigure notions of purdah in illuminating ways. Female workers in Chittagong, for instance, "steer the narrow path between innovation and outrage" through deliberate attention to extra-virtuous deportment and professionalism (Simmons, Mita, and Koenig 1992, 98).

The dream in rural Bangladesh of upward mobility through new connections—forged for instance through livelihood opportunities in garment factories and development and through acts of reaching out via the mobile phone—added power to the possibilities of wrong-number encounters. In the past, the prevalence of stories in which a reversal of fortune comes about through international labor migration or mystic-induced miracles (Gardner 1995) shaped people's hopes and encouraged them to undertake new opportunities, despite economic and social risks. These precedents for rapid movement out of poverty and transformation of circumstances may help to explain why phone relationships were so compelling for the youth. Young women experienced the feeling of being open to adventure while also seeking disciplined self-cultivation. They experienced the ambivalence of the thrill of passion and the security of kinship, and they desired a safe level of intimacy, explored further in the vernacular concept of "being *digital*."

"Being *digital*": A Field of Cultural Struggle and Ethical Reflection

Discourses of "being *digital*" were not only localized among rural women entrepreneurs who used mobile phones and other digital technologies. The dream of "Digital Bangladesh" was part of the political manifesto of the ruling Awami League party and embodied the national modernist philosophy of using digital technology to ensure national growth and democratic principles of transparency and accountability. Also not merely an abstract vision, aspects of Digital Bangladesh were increasingly integral to the everyday lives of citizens. Children answered school-examination questions about Digital Bangladesh; they checked their examination results online at internet service centers; and their parents received work postings by text message. Since 1997, commercial mobile services had been available in rural areas, alongside the Grameenphone Village Phone Program, through which microcredit customers could purchase mobile phones and rent them out for profit. This early access to mobile telephony enabled more widespread coverage than that found in neighboring countries. Mobile phone ownership among adults rose to over 50 percent (GSMA Intelligence 2014, 8), with a subscription rate of up to 76 percent (BTRC 2016).[5] Through the successful integration of technology in education, health, and labor regimes, Bangladesh aspired to reduce poverty and enhance the productivity of its citizens.[6]

The ideas (and ideals) of Digital Bangladesh as a political vision and set of state-led practices filtered through levels of bureaucracy and took on new meanings. A Bangladesh Bank officer in charge of a small-enterprise loan program noted, "Giving information is the best way of empowerment. Poor entrepreneurs are not conscious. They don't have access to information about financial policy, but if you make them conscious, digital entrepreneurs, they cannot be stopped." The language of digitizing records for the purposes of transparency and accountability was conflated with ideas about digitizing entrepreneurs in order to empower them with information.

The concept that people (and not just information) can be digital entered the language of rural women entrepreneurs such as Rahela. She and other iAgents used digital health equipment such as blood-pressure cuffs and glucometers. They differentiated themselves from the government-sponsored community clinic staff who used manual equipment. "Because the villagers have become *digital*, we need to serve them using *digital* things," explained one iAgent. "In this respect, we are superior to the government health workers." iAgents served as extension workers for a program called Aponjon that sent health information to pregnant women via text message. They often travelled to remote, off-grid locations where, they assumed, poverty correlated with higher birth rates. Yet when they found few pregnant women to register in such places, they complained, "Even these people have become *digital*." They employed the term synonymously with "educated," "conscious," and "aware," notions parallel to the bank official's meaning of "empowered though the acquisition of information."

In contrast to studies about North India, where mothers-in-law controlled the household phone and supervised the phone use of daughters-in-law (while men carried personal phones), in rural Bangladesh mobiles were primarily used by young people. Older women often could not operate a phone. They referenced their lack of formal education (synonymized with a lack of awareness and understanding), a resource that younger, *digital* women now possessed. They also occasionally used the term *digital* as a critique of the ways in which young people have become "selfish" and uninterested in helping their elders.

"Being *digital*" was thus a particularly Bangladeshi concept that indexed ideas about exposure to new possibilities. Yet aspiration does not arrive without conflict. The young women whose views I discuss here emphasized the ambivalence encoded in the condition of "being *digital*" in a way that the rhetoric of the state and of development organizations concealed. In the teleology of Digital Bangladesh and other models of the information society, access to information straightforwardly "empowered" citizens to improve their situations. Such narratives did not account for the relations of power within which marginalized people accessed new resources, experimented with new possibilities, and faced the disciplinary scrutiny of social superiors. Yet in contrast with Appadurai's (2004) notion of aspiration as a capacity underdeveloped among the poor, in Bangladesh cultural struggle was a process through which marginalized people creatively engaged existing cultural resources to develop new imagined possibilities.

"Being *digital*" for iAgent entrepreneurs did not mean being modern merely by possessing access to fancy technologies and the knowledge of how to wield them. It also meant engaging with existing social expectations and striving to meet them in more explicit ways than their non-*digital* peers did, whom they accused of not fulfilling kinship roles or of inviting shame by talking too long on the phone with unrelated men. "Being *digital*" exemplifies processes of "cultural struggle," a term introduced by Aihwa Ong (1991) in the context of the emergence of flexible labor regimes that rely on migrant female workforces. While women in new work contexts struggled over cultural meanings and values, their efforts were based on individual strategies and covert actions rather than a broader class or gender struggle (Ong 1991, 280). The literature on women's factory labor that followed Ong's conceptual path (e.g., Mills 1997) extends ideas about how new experiences generated cultural struggle through the development of new aspirations (such as consumption practices). Yet these studies often oppose "traditional" kinship-based identities with modern, cosmopolitan ones, which result in accounts of divided or conflicted personhood among women. Experiments with wrong-number relationships instead demonstrate ideas of cultural struggle as part of women's production of new ethical positions that did not map onto typical binaries of tradition and modernity.

Women engaged in processes of ethical reflection to navigate the tensions between emergent aspiration and intensified moral scrutiny. As Michael Lambek (2010) notes, while "ordinary ethics" lies in tacit practice, ethics becomes explicit in respect to its breaches, contestations, and renewals. Actions that elicit social critique about models of behavior enable us to investigate the forms of ethical conduct that guide narratives of respectable personhood. For iAgents seeking to cast themselves in a virtuous light, negotiation over ethical boundaries occurred through evaluations of other people's behavior and actions, and women experimented with the potentialities and boundaries of their own ethical, digital selves.

Rahela's Love Marriage

At first glance, Rahela's comments about switching SIM cards when she arrived home appear to concern the boundaries of public and private, outside and inside, and work relations and intimate ones. Popular discourse invoked these binaries when people discussed appropriate and inappropriate contact with kin and non-kin men. In her remarks, Rahela set up and then traversed the boundary between these opposite spaces through the material affordances of the phone. She physically switched between two designated SIM cards when she traveled across the spatial boundary from the wider outside world into the inside domestic space and when she crossed the temporal boundary from daylight into nighttime.

Yet in practice, Rahela's SIM-card switching did not achieve this clear division. She used one SIM card for communication, regardless of her location or the time of day, and she switched among seven other SIM cards for providing specific services such as topping up mobile-phone credits. Clients often visited her home to access regular services, such as conducting mobile-money transfers, monitoring blood pressure, and signing up for NGO trainings online. Neighbors summoned her in the middle of the night to their homes to respond to urgent health problems. Her home and work lives were not separate. She mobilized her home entrepreneurially—for instance, by instructing her brother to attend the shop she built adjacent to their house—and she earned income through her business enterprise that supported personal and household projects. At home, she used her phone to coordinate client visits for the next day, and while cycling on the road, she conversed with her mobile-phone friends. The boundaries between public and private were not as sharp as they may seem, and Rahela possessed less of a divided identity (between the public-facing sociable entrepreneur and the private demure individual) than her comments indicated.

Precisely because of this lack of clear boundaries, Rahela inhabited a morally perilous terrain that needed ongoing negotiation. Her comments about the differentiated SIM cards can be interpreted not as a physical reification of a defined boundary but as a metaphor for the continuous effort she undertook to cast herself in virtuous light despite her unconventional activities. The materiality of her phone helped her to conceptualize and communicate this ethical labor to other people. Her words referenced her internal struggle over the actions and dispositions that constituted an ethical position and the defense of respectability.

A growing arena of expanding aspirations for young rural women such as Rahela lay in experimentations with the boundaries of ethical relationships with men, mediated by the mobile phone. These links worked as harmless

FIGURE 5.   An iAgent speaks with a "wrong-number" friend while waiting for participants to join her group session. Photo by author.

flings for passing time, as new venues for matchmaking, and as a domain for exploring one's own morality and judging that of other people. Here, aspirations were formed and new possibilities were summoned through the act of typing digits on a phone and conjuring the immediate and very real presence of distant persons. The extensiveness of mobile-phone relationships compels an exploration of how women attached meaning to mobile ties, conceived of new *digital* aspirations, and assessed the potentials, limits, and dangers of these connections.

Wrong-Number Relationships

Mobile phone wrong-number relationships were initiated primarily by young men who dialed random numbers until they heard a young woman answer. After pretending to have dialed incorrectly an acquaintance's number, they attempted to strike up a conversation, usually by opening with a barrage of questions about the recipient's name, age, location, family situation, and activities. Unlike Matthew Carey's (2012) Moroccan protagonists, who provided the least amount of information possible so they did not risk terminating the exchange before its full potential could be understood, young women in rural Bangladesh were (remarkably) forthcoming. They offered their real names and life situations. While men were careful not to provide their precise whereabouts, Rahela explained, some ignorant, "unconscious" girls made the mistake of divulging their own locations. She, by contrast, was *digital* ("conscious" or aware) and knew how to speak with these young men in a morally safe way.

Rahela and other iAgents spent hours every day on the phone for non-work-related purposes while they chatted about random topics with various phone friends. Usually the young men initiated repeat conversations, although sometimes young women sent "missed calls" (allowing the phone to ring once before hanging up) as a signal for the recipient to call back, thus passing the airtime costs to the men.[7] I often asked young women with whom they had been speaking. Was it a boyfriend? A school friend? From where did they know him? They often replied, "Just a friend. No big deal." Or "A nothing friend." (For other types of calls, they gave a name or precise relationship.) They often added, "Wrong number . . . just to pass the time." Craig Jeffrey (2010) documents the concept of "timepass" among educated unemployed youths in North India who found alternative means of performing ideals of successful masculinity. While driven by a different set of circumstances and while occurring in seemingly unproductive, dead time, timepass for these young men and for iAgents sparked a new kind of future-oriented self-reflection. Timepass enabled them to productively explore the possibility of different futures and self-identities.

Among young women such as the iAgents, mobile-phone relationships mostly remained confined to gaps of empty time during the day, but sometimes digital friends agreed to meet if they happened to live nearby. I accompanied Rahela on several of these adventures when we travelled to the district center under the cover of visiting an NGO. Usually Rahela did not find the boy to be handsome, or he turned out to be married, or he had exaggerated his profession; she then blocked his number. Bringing me to meetings, she could use the excuse that I did not approve of him to end the relationship. Flirting over the phone and sharing one's dreams with a disembodied voice was surprisingly easy and exciting, explained Rahela, but meeting in public places a real man with worldly attachments provided a rude shock that transformed young women's newfound boldness into shyness and disappointment.

Beyond meetings, mobile-phone connections were used occasionally in matchmaking. Rahela often responded to wrong-number calls until she discovered that the man was uneducated or she grew bored with his conversation. She sometimes passed along the numbers of other young women in her village

FIGURE 6. Long journeys between villages for iAgent work provide ample time away from the gaze (and earshot) of relatives. Photo by author.

whom she thought might provide a suitable match. These onward connections expanded the network potential of these previously random and dyadic links and generated possibilities for generationally horizontal matchmaking. Parents rarely participated in these attempted matches, for they usually knew nothing about them. Most often, phone relationships faded out, but occasionally girls enlisted their mothers' help in formalizing the union, and mothers might pretend that they had found the boy through their own natal kinship connections.[8]

Exploring a Digital Relationship

Rahela engaged in one steady phone relationship for years. The link had been forged through the Skype application on her laptop. Rahela had finished helping a client speak with her son (a migrant worker in Saudi Arabia) when a chat window opened from a Bangladeshi boy who had been searching random accounts according to names he found attractive. They exchanged phone numbers, spoke daily for months, and met twice in Dhaka (always in the presence of Rahela's female cousin who worked in a garments factory). Rahela explained that the young man, Titu, understood her iAgent enterprise because he worked in an NGO near Dhaka. Unlike most boys who did not want their wives to work for an income, Titu approved of the idea. Meeting this boy gave Rahela confidence that she could continue to work and possibly find a husband who supported her.

Rahela often said that she wanted a love marriage with a boy like Titu, from a distant village who was not involved in her village's politics and she not in his. Yet her father pressured her to marry a local boy, which she was unwilling to do before finishing her degree, and no local boys held a similar educational level or secure employment. She also resisted by referencing a local woman whose arranged husband divorced her because he felt no affection for her. Divorce would damage her reputation, and so Rahela resolved to marry only according to her own choice, to ensure compatibility.

Still, Rahela's family pressured her to marry quickly because her brother wanted to marry a girl from a different district, with whom he had a phone relationship. The brother, nineteen-year-old Rajib, was younger than Rahela and due to custom he could not marry before she did. Rahela said that her brother had no business getting married now. "He uses a smartphone and therefore thinks he's *digital*, but he has no idea what responsibility means," Rahela argued. He had not finished his degree and he had no income and no house for his intended wife. How would he feed her? Rahela was not keen to support them from her own income. She had already funded her household for four years. All the objects in the house and the construction materials for it were bought with her money. She needed one more year for her college degree and planned further study before marrying. Rahela's idea of a love marriage would ensure her continued ability to study, work, and support her family. Her brother's plans, by contrast, were selfish and would only further burden the family, she complained. Yet his status as a son privileged Rajib's desires over hers. Their father did not object to Rajib's relationship, and he would be furious about Rahela's if he had known about it.

Such tensions and discrepancies within the family discouraged Rahela further when her father continued to draw down the balance in her iAgent bank account to invest in his stall at the local market. She had been saving money for her dowry, precisely so that her parents would not be thrust back into poverty upon her marriage. More immediately, when Rahela needed money to pay her examination fees, it was not her parents (or her own income) who financed it, but Titu, who regularly sent her "gift" money via mobile-money transfers. Rahela remarked on the irony that she worked hard, earned well, grew financially independent, and supported her family, and yet she *still* relied on a man to cover some of her everyday costs. She often spoke about marrying Titu but also expressed ambivalence. When Titu called one day to say that he would be posted to an NGO on the other side of the country, Rahela told me that she was relieved because the relationship would remain comfortably over the phone, where she could continue it privately without inviting the commentary of other people.[9] She could enjoy male companionship without physical proximity and the fear of social stigma that might result.

Taspia's Arranged Marriage

"I want an arranged marriage so that I can be a modern woman." Taspia and I sat late into the evening and watched Bollywood music videos on her laptop. The videos were provocative love stories performed by scantily clad singers and dancers, and the village girls had watched them repeatedly as they sang the Hindi lyrics with Bengali modifications. This evening we were alone, and I jokingly asked Taspia if these romantic love stories were the kind she wanted for herself.

Taspia objected immediately; she wanted her family to choose her husband, because love marriages dissolve into quarrelling and divorce. An incompatible marital situation would disrupt her work and hinder her ability to provide for her parents and future children. Bangladeshi men are selfish, she noted, and they spend money frivolously instead of supporting their parents. She added that she did not want to start any relationships before marriage, although she did not lack for opportunities.

A man working in a mobile-money-transfer business in Dhaka phoned Taspia one day, having dialed random numbers until he reached her phone. He insisted that he knew her number because she had been his customer. Taspia had never been to Dhaka, she knew that he was lying, and she blocked his number. Another Bangladeshi man's initial wrong-number call from Italy turned into regular hour-long conversations. She indulged this friend's companionship for a year while she dreamed of being brought to Italy and sending money home to her parents, until he sent a picture of himself. (Taspia did not have a smartphone that could receive the image, but she had a laptop and email account.) She deleted his number. Now she rationalized that she had discontinued the connection because relationships before marriage were wrong for her.

> Listen. Love marriage and relationships are bad because young people start them, but they cannot control their emotions, and so they have to get married. But usually the boy is unemployed, so there are money problems, and then there is a baby, but there is no love remaining in the relationship, only fighting. I will not make any relationship. I want to finish my degree, get a good job, and support my parents. How can I do that if my life is only fighting and my husband prohibits me from working? No. I want an arranged marriage so that I can be a modern woman and my children will grow up well. I am a *digital* person, after all.

Taspia's words revealed her anxieties about the erosion of ethical behavior and her pragmatic determination to live virtuously. Current trends in international development valued higher education for girls and privileged the entry of women into market-oriented livelihoods. Yet these development models also assumed that the creation of so-called empowered women implied releasing them from the fetters of so-called traditional practices such as arranged marriages and the tyranny of kinship. Taspia asserted a vision of modern womanhood (a goal-oriented future enabled by an arranged marriage and work outside the home) and ethical personhood (a focus on intergenerational care work) that the architects of women's empowerment programs such as the iAgent model did not acknowledge. The line between "traditional" (arranged) and "modern" (love) marriages was not as sharp as popular discourse assumed it to be, and practices surrounding marriage indexed a wide set of aspirations for a good life that could not be bifurcated into a traditional/modern binary. In Taspia's terms, being *digital* encompassed this entrepreneurial ethical position.

Taspia's ultimate rejection of the idea of a love marriage was influenced by her experiences with wrong-number friends, and yet it also expressed ambivalence. The men whose digital company she kept had encouraged her dreams of upward mobility. Several of them valued her work and claimed that they were not interested in taking a dowry from a girl's family if she would be earning income throughout her married life. For Taspia, this idea was revolutionary. She had never known a marriage to occur without a dowry or a man to respect a woman's career. Prior to these conversations, she often resolved not to marry at all precisely because of the dowry requirements that would be imposed on her family. Being the youngest of three daughters whose parents lacked a son to care for them in their old age, Taspia also assumed the moral burden of solving this problem. "When a girl gets married, all her family gets damaged. It is a huge loss for them."

Taspia's mother Jorina had lacked a dowry; she explained that dowry was not practiced back then. The custom had been important for Hindu families in Bangladesh, but Muslims there only adopted it when fathers of sons saw that they could extract money from the transaction.[10] The father-in-law of Taspia's eldest sister, Tamanna, had required a dowry of 60,000 taka (769 USD) a decade previously, but Jorina's family could pay only half of it. Several of Taspia's friends had recently married, and their in-laws had required dowries of one or two lakh taka (1,282–2,564 USD), a massive inflation in a short time. Parents were often unable to pay that amount without selling land and assets. When families demanded a dowry that the girls' families lacked, the girls often needed to migrate to Dhaka to work in garment factories. Yet there they would not be able to save money, and their moral purity would be questioned, which might result in the dissolution of the marriage agreement. Families also sent their daughters to borrow from microcredit institutions to fulfill the dowry requirements. The responsibility for marriage expenses thus often devolved downward from the families of girls onto the girls themselves.[11] Taspia worked diligently as an iAgent to earn money, and she borrowed from two microcredit schemes, but she wanted to invest her money in a family shop, rather than to lose it all (and her family's house and land) in a dowry payment.

Stories of Stigma and Shame

While Taspia experimented with wrong-number relationships, she also observed her friends having mixed experiences with them. In hushed tones, they related stories of stigma and shame that befell young women who were not careful (those whom Rahela described as "unaware"). While phone connections provided a novel means for young people to interact and imagine different futures, less emancipatory consequences for women also emerged. iAgents said that they felt ambivalent about the meaning of these relationships, the lack of clarity over their boundaries, and the judgments made by other people. They too participated in evaluating their peers' actions and, in so doing, sought further to differentiate themselves as ethical actors.

Neighbors commented regularly that girls who were often on the phone engaged in many relationships and therefore did not possess good character.

Taspia and other iAgents observed their classmates spending time with multiple boys and accepting gifts from them, and they avoided association with such behavior. Each village seemed to have a tragedy that served as a warning against illicit relationships, such as when a girl's unrequited love for a wrong-number friend led to his denial of responsibility and her damaged future possibilities. Women warned one another not to speak with wrong-number friends for so long that the phone grew hot against the ear. Again, the materiality of the phone (and the heat it produced when overused) became a metaphor for or an indicator of immoral and risky behavior. Because their entrepreneurial work often subjected them to moral criticism, these judgments of their peers and warnings to one another formed part of the work of reasserting their own ethical identities.

Occasionally, girls found strategies through the mobile phone for fleeing unwanted marriages and negotiating alternative ones. Taspia's second cousin Rima married, divorced, and remarried again in the space of ten months. The original boy was found via a professional matchmaker. Rima never saw him before the wedding, where she decided she disliked his appearance. After the festivities, she refused to go home with him to consummate the marriage, and subsequently she initiated the divorce process. She then began a wrong-number phone relationship with a young man who was uneducated but charming, and she married him secretly to avoid people's comments. Some women said that Rima had erred in jeopardizing the support of her parents, but they still admired her for extracting herself from an undesirable situation by using her ingenuity and her mobile phone.

Due to these risks of social stigma, which circulated in stories and acted as warnings to young women, Taspia ultimately resolved to have an arranged marriage, although according to her own parameters. The young man needed to be well-educated, approve of her work, and agree to support her parents by living in her natal homestead. The strong tradition of virilocality in Bangladesh placed the primary responsibility of elder care in the hands of sons and their wives. Daughters were expected to live outside of the patrilineal group upon marriage and were typically removed from the long-term cycle of debt repayments to parents (Lamb 2000). If no sons existed, a daughter might support her parents, but the obligation was not hers. Despite Taspia's multiple and ongoing tactics to make money to provide for her parents, Jorina often expressed plaintively—in the rising and falling singsong tone employed by Bangladeshi women in specific circumstances to describe their endless suffering—that she lacked sons to care for her in her old age.[12] Lamb explains this contradiction through the loss of respect that parents suffered by living with married daughters, who had already been given away to another household and become "other," no longer their "own"

(2000, 85). Relying on a daughter was not the same as relying on a son. Rather, it indicated the failure to produce a son to fulfill this role.

In some cases, a son-in-law moved to the wife's home (and was called *ghar jamai*, "house husband"). In repayment he stood to inherit the house and land. This solution occurred primarily when the boy originated in a poor family or was the youngest of many sons in a family with insufficient land for all of them.[13] Often no dowry was required. "Here the *jamai* becomes in some ways like a wife: he shifts from house to house and is contained in the house of another, rather than practicing the more prestigious male pattern of developing and refining himself in a continuous, straight line, in the home and on the land of his fathers' fathers. . . . Daughters were sometimes embarrassed to marry such a feminine-seeming man" (Lamb 2000, 57). In the past that stigma might have been significant, but Taspia did not seem embarrassed to declare that she would marry a man who would live in her natal house to ensure that her parents would be well looked after. Perhaps the lack of shame attached to the concept of a *ghar jamai* came from the precedent of her grandfather. Jorina's husband's father came from the same village as she did. When he (Taspia's father's father) married, his family had lacked sufficient land for him to inherit, so he moved to the land of his bride's father, which he later passed to his sons.

If any boy forbade her from working, Taspia would reject him regardless of his other qualifications. A separate source of money would help her to remain independent from her husband.

Digital Purdah and Cultural Critique

Although they arrived at different conclusions, Rahela and Taspia underwent similar processes of ethical self-reflection. They critiqued the failure of others to uphold the social norms of the intergenerational care work they cherished and they evaluated the kind of men who might be compatible with their expanding set of aspirations. Their home situations (including male opinion) and the constraints they experienced there informed their conclusions. New forms of interactions required setting new ethical boundaries and created ambivalences for iAgent entrepreneurs, expressed through the *digital* purdah they sought to embody as they balanced entrepreneurial availability with female propriety.

Purdah, Reimagined

The notion of *purdah* (an Islamic and Bengali term referring to the seclusion of women) was traditionally grounded in ideas of family honor and shame.

The danger of losing honor, according to orthodox views, required control over women and their confinement to the domestic sphere to ensure that no shame befell the family. Yet the ideal of purdah and the separation of "inside" and "outside" realms (which are a continuum of locations) were often figurative and not totalizing instruments of control (Kabeer 2001, 69). In rural areas, complete purdah was a reality for only a small proportion of elite households that could afford domestic staff, thus removing the need for women to leave the homestead (to process agricultural products, for example). Patricia Jeffery (1979) discusses purdah as a "negotiated privilege" that was associated with urban elites and a symbol of prestige forcefully defended by women of high class. Wearing a burqa (head-to-toe cloth covering) signaled a woman's (comparatively high) status and her economic security (Callan 2008, 407).

The ethnographic record shows that women's views of purdah are complex and ambivalent, neither fully internalized as natural nor fully rejected as a symbol of oppression, especially among women who work outside the home. Naila Kabeer (2000) explores the multiple understandings of purdah among female garment workers. Few of them adopted the orthodox view that they morally transgressed purdah norms when they engaged in extradomestic activities. Most workers saw their actions as an infringement of norms but a pragmatically necessary one. Some women in Bangladesh understood purdah as a state of mind and argued that a virtuous person is virtuous in all contexts through her behavior and purity of intention. These women reinterpreted the value's core idea to arrive at a more "authentic" and practical notion of moral behavior while simultaneously expanding their agency, opportunity, and movement. Similarly, for iAgent entrepreneurs, the logic of purdah became a resource for women to justify their work choices.

iAgents explained that they used to follow stricter rules of purdah. Some used to wear burqas whenever they left home. Several had never been outside of their homestead alone, a stark difference from their current lifestyles. Once iAgents gained more confidence and experience in their work, they reflected on the contemporary relevance of strict notions of purdah. Modern interpretations of purdah by iAgents and its implications for their ability to perform outside work illustrate their negotiations of moral boundaries to assert the integrity of their behavior.

To iAgents, who did not stay secluded at home and few of whom covered their heads outside, purdah meant having "a fresh mind/heart" (*mon fres*), rather than merely displaying physical modesty. Taspia did not consider that covering was necessary for her since she was not greedy and worked hard. The Prophet Muhammad had decreed a long time ago that purdah meant a curtain or covering separating women from male strangers, and any practices that remained important today related to the metaphorical protection of the mind/heart and resulting modesty of behavior. A burqa was unnecessary if one's interior state was pure. Rahela agreed that she upheld purdah by not behaving improperly, by helping people, and by being modest and hard working. In performing her work outside, on a bicycle and with unrelated persons, she actively defended her family's honor by lifting its socioeconomic status and preventing its members from falling into poverty.

Modesty in the physical sense, Taspia elaborated, meant nothing in the context of young women possessing mobile phones. In the past, restricting a girl's mobility under purdah norms could have prevented the crystallization of male-female relationships, but now young people could develop them from home. When digital communication technologies could penetrate house walls and render burqas irrelevant, how did one cultivate a *digital* purdah? Taspia questioned, "What is the point of purdah and staying indoors when the phone call enters our homestead and goes straight into our ears, regardless of what we are wearing?" In Rahela's and Taspia's accounts of moral action regarding phone use, maintaining a *digital,* internal purdah meant cultivating an awareness of the appropriate boundaries of phone interaction with non-kin men. Rahela's metaphor of differentiated SIM cards illustrates the importance of knowing how to manage this boundary. Allowing the phone to grow hot against one's ear, by contrast, indicates that a young woman has spoken too long and too intimately with a young man and has let her *digital* purdah slip.

The Role of Men, Reimagined

Experiments with mobile-phone relationships enabled Rahela, Taspia, and other young women to gain alternative views on marriage and the roles of men and women in the family. Rahela experienced the contradictions of supporting her male kin financially while also being exploited and criticized by them for her seemingly non-feminine activities. By contrast, her male phone friend, who approved of her work and sent her gift money to cover her daily needs, seeded alternative ideas about relationships with men. Taspia sought to spare her father the shame of being unable to provide for his family and pay her dowry. She was astonished to learn, through interactions with unrelated men, that the possibility of not paying a dowry and still being respected for her work might coexist. In both cases, mobile-phone relationships enabled the young women to imagine alternative futures with novel notions of the supportive role of men in their lives. While the phone-friend experience did not necessarily serve the end purpose of developing an enduring relationship with that particular person, it still provided a means of exploration and self-knowledge. Rahela and Taspia gained fresh ideas about purdah that were based on their own internalized understandings of virtue rather than on externally imposed rules about dress and modesty. They were able to negotiate the legitimacy of their spatial mobility by finding validation in the approval of outside and unknown men, versus relying primarily on the opinions of family men. By discerning alternative patriarchal positions and formulating a cultural critique, women were better able to recognize male dominance as arbitrary and thus negotiable.

The mobility that accompanied additional years of education, work, and communication technologies thus enabled contact with young men but also presented new sets of aspirations in which goals other than marriage were foregrounded. The pursuit of education and work for many girls was a primary strategy of upward mobility that hedged against future problems, including the fickleness and unfaithfulness of men. Departing from social assumptions that marriage would detract from the bride's natal familial security and restrict the new wife's agency, unmarried iAgents imagined future husbands whose role would be to support the women's own work and life projects. In this way, husbands moved from a place of centrality in the imagined lives of these women to a more instrumental role, assisting the entrepreneurial and kinship projects of these women. Although new opportunities to meet young men enabled women to experience the freedom of selecting their own partner, these women also recognized the dangers implicit in shifting practices of marital choice. In arranged marriages, parents were answerable to the outcomes of these matches and were thus expected to offer help in case of difficulties. By engaging in love marriages, women as individuals took on risk and stood to lose the support of their natal kin.

Yet regardless of women's ultimate decisions to pursue a love marriage or an arranged one, in the process of responding to "wrong-number" calls, women's experiential and aspirational horizons expanded. The narratives above illustrate how mobile phone–mediated encounters created space for the cultural critique of social norms that work against young women, the realization of social alternatives, and the contestation of hegemonic forms. Whether or not they developed their mobile-phone relationships beyond timepass, many young women discovered the ability to cultivate new ethical positions (for instance, regarding purdah), marriage expectations, and aspirations for the future. Although often "untutored in ideologies" of social change and feminist empowerment, Ong argues, women "are capable of making alternative interpretations based on their own visceral experiences and cultural traditions. By thus challenging dominant discourse, they expand the space of political struggle in their everyday lives" (Ong 1991, 298). While such struggles in Bangladesh resulted in different outcomes and desires and were fragmentary, limited, and ambivalent, the very recognition of breaks between dominant cultural meanings and lived experience "provide[d] subordinate groups with crucial openings to contest hegemonic forms and generate alternative understandings" (Mills 1997, 41). Such observations open up the potential for future research to track the ways in which young *digital* women and men are able to parlay their new understandings into fundamental changes in gender relations in the postmarital household and in the next generations.

This chapter has explored the ways that young women in rural Bangladesh formed new ethical positions through their active participation in mobile-phone wrong-number relationships. As an unintended effect of the social disruptions of technology entrepreneurship, women were able to empower themselves through their experimentation with new mobile-phone connectivity. Because the social enterprise required iAgents to be "on call" for their village clients in ways that violated women's sense of appropriate contact and unsettled people's image of them, iAgents were forced to come up with ways to negotiate their new *digital* identities. In the process, they generated innovative ethical subject positions. These new ethical judgments concerned their ideas regarding relationships, marriage, careers, and virtuous comportment, which were vitally inflected by the social content as well as by the sensory experience of phone relationships. Through daily calls, women and men experimented with novel ideas, tested boundaries, and gained instant feedback in a bond that was intimate while also being safely distant and detachable. The material affordances of the phone made physically present new forms of relationships and rendered women's experiences and judgments more effable. The phone's disregard of purdah's materiality provoked reflection about purdah as a behavioral expression of virtue beyond the veil. Dealing with the complexities of navigating these new ethical positions was the continuous work of being and becoming *digital*, a uniquely Bangladeshi manifestation of cultural struggle and a vernacular aspirational ideal that related to many issues: national dreams of modernity and progress; development convictions about the progressive use of information and communications technologies; cultural norms regarding propriety and gender relations; and local ideas about education, awareness, and knowledge.

These cases also allow us to extend the literature on ethical self-formation (Hirschkind 2006; Mahmood 2005) and aspirational capacity (Appadurai 2004) by showing how people were able to cultivate innovative ethical possibilities and imagine unorthodox futures beyond those promulgated by powerful religious and ethical systems. They were able to respond in this way not only as a result of exposure to "outside" experiences but also by accessing cultural resources from within cultural, kinship, and religious practice in a way that was phenomenologically new because of the phone's material and relational affordances. In the formation and cultivation of these relationships, women were not merely projecting kinship and traditional relationships onto phone interactions; nor was the experience with new technology a wholly emancipatory one that enabled women to escape the constraints of patriarchy and traditional marriage practice. Being *digital* did not imply a radical modernist rejection of custom and it did not entail aspirations for a future of economic and gender relations premised on individual choice and self-determination. Rather, a *digital* identity was a subject position centered on consciousness, responsibility, relational embeddedness, empowerment, and entrepreneurial openness. Cultivating a *digital* self meant an often-conflicting range of desires and experiences and required constant ethical labor on the part of young women.

At the time of research, while mobile-phone use among young people proliferated, computer and internet access was not widespread. Yet the work of iAgents—as well as the information service centers now in every market town because of the efforts of the government's Digital Bangladesh initiative—increasingly familiarized people with new means of accessing digital information and communication. As growing numbers of people and younger generations "become *digital*," further research is required to understand the complex ways in which the strategies of media users to reach out and connect will fundamentally change both social and technological practices.

Part II

UNSETTLING ENTREPRENEURSHIP

iAgent Deepti's Story

I am Deepti Roy. I was born in a Hindu family. We are two brothers and two sisters, and I am the youngest of the sisters. I have been thinking for a long time that I will write about my life. Today, I have the opportunity. So I'm writing about my life today. Our house is in Joykrishnapur village in Amirhat Upazila (district). Our house is below the dam. It is on the edge of the river. There are no Muslim families in the neighborhood we live in. Everyone is Hindu.

When my father got married, my grandfather had a joint family. My father had three brothers and two sisters. They had a big family. Father said my grandfather had a lot of land, about 648 satak [6.48 acres]. When all of my uncles were married, my grandfather distributed the lands among all of his sons. Everyone got almost 162 satak of land. My uncles were farmers. They sometimes used to fish in the river and sell the fish in the market. My father cultivated many crops: rice, tobacco, maize, potato, garlic, onion, chili, and turmeric. He sold these at the market. The river is beside our house. Most of our land is gone now, under the river, slowly, slowly because of river-bank erosion. So my father and my uncles lost many of their lands.

I had a happy childhood. I talked to everyone all the time. But slowly, I began to learn things about life. Here's one story. I went to school one day and saw that my best friend, Radha, had not come to school. I went to school the next day and saw that Radha still had not come. I went to her house and found that her marriage was fixed. She was going to get married in the next year. Radha said to me that her father did not let her go to school anymore. He said, "From today, you can't go to school. You'll get married and go to your husband's house." Radha was an eighth-grade student. Did she even understand what marriage is? I was upset and came back home. When I came home, my mother asked me, "Deepti, what happened to you? Why are you upset?" I told my mother, "Mother, Radha is getting married. But Radha told me that she does not want to get married. She wants to study. But there's nothing to do because her father is forcing her to get married. Radha can't do anything." Mother said, "This is for Radha's own good. Child marriage is regular in our country. No matter how old or young the girl is, she can understand everything after marriage." But that day I couldn't understand the meaning of my mother's words. Radha got married. Her in-laws' house was far from here. So I couldn't contact her anymore.

I passed grade eight. When I was in grade nine, I made four friends. I was too calm then, and I didn't talk to anyone. Everyone told me, "Deepti, you were such a loud girl before. How did you become so quiet now?" I didn't answer them. I just listened. When the classes were finished in school, we all sat in the school field and chatted. I would say, "Who knows when one of us gets lost? Any of us may have to get married at any time."

After some months, my eldest brother's wife gave birth to her second daughter. Now my parents were upset because it wasn't a boy. In our society, boys are given more importance.

Girls are neglected at every step. Mother always said, "We have such bad luck! We couldn't see the face of a grandson." I just listened.

When I studied in class ten, my parents decided that they would get my second brother married. They started looking for a bride. Within a few months, my brother got married, and the new bride came home. After some days, my mother advised my new sister-in-law that she shouldn't take any family-planning system so that she would have a child soon. My sister-in-law did so. She didn't take any family-planning method. I was fourteen, I understood it all now.

I used to go to school every day. Radha was not with us. We all missed her a lot. We discussed together what we wanted to be when we grew up. We got to know each other's dreams. Rajani said she wanted to become a college teacher. Kalpana said, "I would like to grow up and work permanently in a good NGO, such as in health programs." And I said, "I want to do a good government job." But I do not know whether any of us will be able to do any job at all.

My new sister-in-law had a girl child. My mother yelled at her. What I'm saying is not any random story. Such superstitions have been going on in our society for ages. The people of this country just think that boys can do all things but girls can't. Girls will need much money for their weddings. People say that it is not necessary for women to study because in the end they have to cook in the kitchen anyway. So society has a problem with girls. I understand these things now. If a man and a woman do the same work all day, the man gets more wages than the woman does, even though they have done the same amount of work. There is so much discrimination between men and women. I have seen a number of things myself in this country. If my eldest sister ever comes to our house with her son, my parents become so happy. Good food is cooked. My mother would allow her grandson to eat everything. Yet she gives less food to my brothers' daughters. If I tell my mother that they should get the same amount of food, she would say, "What do you know? Boys need to eat more."

When I was still in class ten, my friends Kalpana and Rajani got married. Their dreams were broken. They were not ready to get married, but their parents forced them. I became very upset, and now my friend Keya and I were alone.

I did not have a mobile phone then. I knew that I could talk on a mobile but I didn't know how to use it. I really wanted to have a phone. So I thought if I got a good result on my exams, then I would ask for a phone from my father. Keya told me, "If we get good grades, we'll go to college together." After some days our results came out. We were both admitted to a college. One day I went there and saw that Keya had a mobile phone. Seeing that, I became upset. I came home and said to my father, "All of my friends have mobile phones, but I don't. Will you please buy me a phone?" Then one afternoon father bought me a mobile. I was very happy. My father was quite educated. He taught me how to use it. I called Keya and said, "This is my number. From now on we can share everything on the phone."

In 2013, Rifat bhai from the ACRU NGO came to our village. I knew him from before because his in-laws' house was beside our house. I saw him a lot. The people of my family knew him well. One day he came to my house and asked, "Deepti, how are you?" We chatted for some time. Rifat told me, "We have a new work project. Do you want to work with us?" I asked, "What kind of work?" He explained some things to me. The work is about Information Technology, Education, Health, and so forth. It's a good job, and if I want, I can do it. My parents weren't sure about it, but in the end they trusted Rifat because we were neighbors with his relatives.

The next day, I went to the NGO place. I met Sabbir, the leader there, who explained everything to me. But he didn't tell me anything about a loan. That was why I agreed to do the job. If I knew that I had to take a loan to do it, I wouldn't agree. It was not possible for me to repay the loan all by myself. The following day, my brother came to hear for himself, because he did not think I should work. But Sabbir explained everything to my brother, and he added that I'd be paid more for the first six months. And after that, anything I earned would be mine. After listening to everything, my brother agreed. He said, "Deepti, you can learn a lot if you do this work. Will you do it?" He encouraged me a lot. I decided to do this job. I thought, maybe if I am doing this work and bringing something home, I won't have to get married yet. But my father did not agree because he understood there might be something wrong with the work. I didn't understand that then but now I know that Sabbir and his colleagues lied to all the girls. Rifat just said, "You don't have to do anything. Just start working. We're from your area. Why would we want to harm any of you?"

Now let's talk about the job. We got a training first where we got to learn a lot of things. I learned about computers, the uses of computers, camera, how to check blood pressure, how to measure weight, how to check blood group, how to do check-up for pregnant women, taking pictures, printing, and so forth. I also learned trading, producing, group formation, and how to talk to the people of my groups. There were many girls with me. The training went on for many days. After that, I started to work. And then I got to know that I had to take a loan to start working.

I became very tense. They hadn't told me about the loans before. I would never have taken part in the training if I knew about the loan. I said, "I won't work." Rifat uncle asked me, "Why won't you? They have lied. You don't have to take a loan. The loan will be in your name, but you don't have to concern yourself with how the loan will be paid." I didn't realize I was being betrayed. I believed in the people of ACRU. They told the same thing to my father. So I started to work.

From the next day, I started working. I had to work in three areas. They were very far from each other. Beside my house, there was a river. Those places were very dangerous. I formed groups in every area. Then I started working with the groups. I loved it the most when I went to the group of old people. I felt good to think that I can serve these old people. I checked their blood pressure, I measured their weight. I gave them neces-sary suggestions if their pressure was high. Those who had low blood pressure, I told them to eat more vegetables.

I was supposed to get five to ten taka for doing these tasks. Most people didn't give me money. They were all old, so I couldn't ask for money from everyone. Where would they get money, when it is hard for them to live a good life already?

Then I went to my women's group. I talked about different health issues with the women: for example, what problems will be caused if they have children frequently; or, girl or boy, no matter what, only two children is enough. I also said that they would get pregnancy-testing kits from me. Furthermore, I told them about the necessity for breastfeeding right after the baby is born. It will keep the child healthy. I made the women aware of their health because many women in our country don't know what to do after childbirth. Many mothers are supersti-tious, so they give their baby cow milk or honey after birth.

Then I went to the farmers' group and said, "If your crop is attacked by any bug, you should send a picture to me. Then I can tell you about the remedy." Then I went to the adoles-cent group and said, "I can fill up the online admissions form. If you ever need anything, come to me. For example, taking pictures, loading phone balance, and collecting songs on your memory card."

Even though I wasn't earning any money, I thought of myself as a self-reliant woman. But often I felt bad because people wouldn't pay. Here's another story. One day I went to an area where many women wanted to check their blood pressure. I checked all of their blood pressures while sitting in one person's house. At the end, they said, "Sister, can you wait? We will go home and bring back the money." I waited. But no one came back with the money. Only the woman whose house I was sitting in gave me five taka. I felt very bad that day. I thought, "Did I just spend my whole day here for only five taka?" People have lost their humanity. They often did such a thing to me.

Another day I went to a school. I told the headmaster that I have a camera. Many of the children at this school received stipends. For that, they needed passport-sized pictures. I can take their photos. The headmaster agreed. I took pictures of about a hundred children. I couldn't edit the pictures because I didn't learn that well from the training. When I went to ACRU for help, Sabbir told me, "There's a good shop in the market. You go there." That guy told me, "I will do the job but the profit share will be equal." What else was there to do? I was forced to obey the condition.

If we faced any problem while working, Sabbir would never solve it. He yelled at us. He said, "Why can't you work properly? Why can't you make people understand?" Then he used to say, "In Lalpur, these works have been going on for three years. If the girls of Lalpur can do it, why can't you?" Later I found out that the girls of Lalpur didn't have any loans to repay.

Then we were told to sell some products such as oil, soap, face creams, and pens. We had to buy them from ACRU and sell them at different houses. I took the products home. It was like a little shop. But the people of my village didn't like it. They started to say things like, "What shameful thing has Deepti started to do?" To be honest, I didn't like selling products either. But there was nothing I could do. I had to take the products and sell them. Some people from my village bought some stuff from me. But I had to give all the money to the ACRU office.

After almost three months of working, one day Sabbir told me, "You have to pay loan installments." I was very worried. I haven't even earned that much money yet. How am I going to pay the installments?

I was speechless. Sabbir asked us, "What are you going to do?" I said, "You said before that we don't have to pay the installments. TIE will pay the loans with our six-month salaries. So why are we talking about this now?" Then I realized that they've lied to us. We didn't get any salary and we had to pay the installments. Sabbir said, "It's your loan, so only you can know how you are going to repay it. Why are you talking to me?" I didn't know what to do. My father thought that I didn't have any loans. Now, if he gets to know that I am in debt, I don't know what's going to happen!

But we couldn't do anything. Because our families couldn't pay the installments, we were all forced to leave the job. I gave back all the machines and tools. I was sad to give them back. I thought maybe I can't ever do anything well. My neighbors said, "Deepti started to do something, but she couldn't even continue it." I felt very bad.

After those days, I took a training in education for two months from the government. We got 3,000 taka for the training. Next, I want to complete my studies. Then, I want to do a good job. For example, a job in a school. And it must be permanent. The jobs I've done have all been temporary. So I want a permanent job. But in our country, it's hard to get a job even after completing studies. Thousands of people are unemployed here. There is no work. Actually, I think everyone has the desire to work, but what if you do not get a job? I have a strong desire to work, but I don't know if I can find work.

It takes eight to nine lakh taka to get a government job. This is not possible for most families. So most of us complete studies and then sit idle. It's different in NGOs. Those who have relatives or known people in NGOs get a job.

Yes, I admit that I'm old enough to get married, but marriage also needs a lot of money. Some days ago, I got a proposal for marriage. The boy is good and his family is also good. But they demanded a motorcycle and ten lakhs taka as dowry. My father would not be able to pay this. And I didn't earn anything from my work. So the proposal has been denied. I hate this life. Without money, girls can't get married. But if we don't get married, society talks many bad things behind our backs.

I feel bad all the time. I think, "Why was I born? Now I am suffering so much." Sometimes I think that being born as a girl is a sin. Parents are so upset that they have to spend so much money to get their daughter married. If I had a good job and got a good salary, I could help my parents. But that didn't happen in my life. Well, this my life. I don't know how much more I will have to suffer.

THE MAKING AND UNMAKING OF ENTREPRENEURS

The scene opens with an aerial shot of a green-painted tin-roofed house in a rural Bangladeshi village. A woman in a uniform—a long teal tunic, mustard-colored trousers and scarf, and a white broad-billed cap—wheels a bicycle from the house's courtyard and moves off the screen. In the next shot, she is cycling on village roads bordered by lush green banana and jackfruit trees, tin-and-thatch houses, ponds and paddy fields. She passes women in saris with the long ends pulled over their heads, a man in a *lungi* alongside a cow tethered to a rope, and a cycle-rickshaw driver pulling a cart laden with passengers. The woman in her bright colors and iAgent-branded outfit presents a vivid contrast to the people around her who wear the muted colors of many-times-washed garments. Against the background of a stringed instrument playing repetitive and melancholy notes, a Bangla-speaking voice narrates: "For an iAgent to carry out her activities successfully within the timeline, it is very important that she prepares a correct daily plan. By following the appropriate plan, an iAgent can increase her earning. Now we will see iAgent Mita's everyday activities and daily work plan." The dynamic scene fades to a black title page announcing "iAgent's Calendar."

We return to iAgent Mita's house, where two small girls with backpacks approach her doorstep. In the bottom left corner of the screen is a cartoon analog alarm clock with a wedge of time shaded in green. The narrator tells us, "Today is Sunday, the first week of the month. 7am–8am: A few students come to study with

Mita." We see Mita feeding the fire to boil rice and then approaching the porch to play cartoons on her laptop for the children.

A fade out, and Mita is cycling near a pond. "8:45am-10am: Mita *apa* [elder sister, a term of respect] is headed toward Baragach village, where she will visit a few houses to provide assistance and sell some products." In this way, we are brought through one- to two-hour increments of Mita's day, helpfully illustrated by the shifting green wedge on the cartoon clock. Mita conducts a women's information session about the government stipend women can claim during pregnancy, sells detergent sachets to her group members, tests a weekly customer's blood-sugar level, brings two of her women's group members to the Union Parishad (the smallest rural-administration and local-government unit) to inquire about their stipends, and conducts a farmer's session to discuss crop problems and sell them seeds. Back home, from 7pm, she plays Bengali television serials for her neighbors and prepares printed passport photographs ordered by customers for her brother-in-law to deliver the next day. With her husband, she records the entire day's income. Then she prepares her sessions for the following day and packs her bag with the relevant equipment so that she can go to bed, precisely at midnight, prepared for the next morning.

As if we do not already feel exhausted by watching "the daily activities of Mita *apa*'s life," we now see "Mita's work plan" on a yellow-lined piece of paper with four columns drawn down the page. We are instructed: "She has identified four planning elements: When it will happen, Who will do it, What needs to be done, and Where it will be done." These titles are written as column headings. The filled-in sheet lists the time periods narrated in the video, with descriptions of her activities. "This is how an iAgent can plan the daily activities for the entire week. As an iAgent, you should schedule your daily activities in this way."

The video rolls credits. The facilitator pauses it and, fumbling, minimizes the screen. He turns to the group of ten young women who slouch in their chairs with wide-eyed looks, pens in hand but nothing written in their pristine notebooks. "What could you understand from this video?"

Market Devices

This chapter explores the market devices employed in the creation of microentrepreneurs who were targeted as both objects and agents of economic development. It details the work of "practical mechanisms, devices and apparatuses through which the authorities of various types seek to shape and instrumentalize human conduct" (Inda 2005, 2) and to install the aesthetics and rationalities of the iAgent network. The iAgent training protocol included devices such as exemplars, models of scientific management, debt contracts, awards and incentives, tests, and surveillance apparatuses designed to reformat women's behavior to resemble that of fictional iAgent Mita. Real iAgents subjected to this regimen found this model of behavior to be incongruous with the imperatives of everyday social life and ethical self-identity, and they were ultimately unable to mediate the disjuncture between the competing sets of expectations.

The iAgent for-profit scale-up model, implemented at the Akaas Center for Rural Upliftment (ACRU) NGO in Amirhat subdistrict and in nine other locations in Bangladesh, comprised a number of players organized in a multitier license structure. TIE's private-limited corporate arm, Sustainable Sourcing International (SSI), licensed the iAgent brand through a hub-and-spoke model. Local organizations across the country (serving as TIE's Rural Information Centers) recruited young village women to be licensed as iAgents and to serve in a rural distribution capacity. iAgents were required to assume a 75,000 taka (962 USD) loan from the National Bank to invest in their training, equipment, and other start-up business costs. The for-profit license structure was the second of three iAgent models with which TIE experimented during the research period (April 2013 to July 2014). This market-driven second model was an attempt to scale up rapidly the "successful" donor-driven pilot project, which was initiated by Rohan Alam, the iAgent founder and team leader, and was taken forward by Rohan's TIE colleagues.

This chapter draws primarily on data from Amirhat subdistrict, where the for-profit model failed, affecting one center and its ten licensee iAgents. Because they rendered important social and political contexts invisible while manipulating economic and technical procedures as devices of detachment, market-based development models were unable to achieve the empowerment objectives they claimed. Further, such development models did enable the extension of sociotechnical practices that were not markets but were instead patron-clientalist relations. The ambiguities that these disjunctures produced enabled the model to sustain its outward image of adopting market logics and achieving success. Thus, a development model "should be analyzed not in terms of the reality it represents (or fails to represent), but in terms of the arrangements and exclusions it helps to produce" (Mitchell 2007, 244). This chapter demonstrates how market-driven development models produce exclusions and inequalities (rather than inclusive economies) not only through their market devices but also through the personalized politics of the people who constitute the model's network.

Examining a case of accelerated failure yields insights into the mechanisms by which key social effects occur and foregrounds processes of exclusion in sharp relief. The nine other license-model and two pilot-model locations continued to operate (at least until 2015), fraught with many of the issues encountered by the Amirhat participants. Simultaneously, TIE planned its further iAgent expansion strategy with new partners and tested new models. It joined a host of other experiments in poverty capitalism that brought market orthodoxy to the center of development and administrative practice.

While previous anthropological engagements with market-driven projects focus on how products reshape consumer practices (e.g., Errington, Fujikura, and Gewertz 2012), Catherine Dolan (2014) shifts attention to how management techniques render objects and people legible to corporate capitalism. By "studying up and through" (Wedel 2004), meaning among the elite and middle-level management people participating in these businesses, Dolan encourages us to look at the mechanisms that enact and produce new forms of economic and moral action among them. While legibility and disciplinary control form the superficial intent of such mechanisms, I argue that the cultivation of ambiguity, detachment, and ignorance (as ways to block the flow of information) also frames moral action and allows these models to work. Through a close examination of the market devices used in the making and unmaking of iAgent entrepreneurs, three themes emerge.

First, models do not translate communicatively into social reality. To enact the model's prescribed behavior would be to deny central aspects of human sociality such as engaging in the relational work of renewing noneconomic ties. Investing in social ties, for instance, often meant waiting for delayed payment for services, which was incompatible with the timeline of loan-repayment. The prescribed times of debt schedules, income generation, and social reproduction did not mesh productively. The success of these models is thus underwritten by poor people's struggles to mediate the disjunctures between project imperatives and everyday lived realities.

Second, market devices, as accelerants in this social enterprise network, are also vehicles for people to enact class, status, and gender politics. Documents are only as powerful as their wielders, and acts of training can be read as political and ideological projects of dominance. As an anthropological object, training can be apprehended as an artifact that conceals the contradictions of the project while appearing transparent (Chong 2012). Modeled as a market device of conversion to a transactional and impersonal relational economy, the training involved here amplifies class difference. This focus on interpreting economic activities in terms of the social and political claims people make on one another draws on a reading of relational work. It avoids reifying a boundary between TIE and iAgents that is mediated through devices that reformat subjectivity to varying degrees. Rather, these techniques and iAgents' responses to them are political projects of defining and contesting hierarchical relationships of power. Thus, following Annelise

Riles (2000), if training is an artifact that perpetuates the network by allowing it to reflect on itself, then considering the class and gender features of network actors is essential for understanding the network's particular aesthetic and the types of relational forms it produces.

Third, market devices used in installing transactional relational economies perform the work of breaking as well as creating relationships. Misinformation and misrepresentation play an important role in building market relations, especially when different social values and moral economies characterize each side of the exchange. Devices of detachment (Cross 2011) are responsible for disavowing former affective patronage relations (and thus violating the moral economy of NGO development in rural Bangladesh) and denying accountability for negative outcomes. This chapter adds to the literature on market devices by accentuating their embeddedness in sociopolitical projects of class, gender, and labor hierarchy.

The Making of iAgents: "The Entrepreneurial Conversion"

Anthropologists have explored the transformative effects of interventions in the contexts of corporate-social responsibility, ethical governance, codes of conduct, and labor standards, "yet few scholars have questioned what such codes and standards 'do' to the companies and workers on whom they are imposed. What sorts of work regimes and industrial disciplines do they produce and what sorts of 'values,' 'workers' and 'persons' do they seek to engender?" (De Neve 2014, 186).[1]

In representations of "fully trained" iAgents found on TIE's website and in popular media outlets such as the BBC, Al Jazeera, and European documentary films, we are moved by stories of empowerment and personal transformation that are primarily sociopolitical in nature. They describe the familial resistance, social stigma, and cliental dismissal of their "knowledge" that fledgling iAgents supposedly overcame. By contrast, the visual representations of iAgents in the training videos show a more mundane and technocratic process of becoming. Each iAgent must undergo a personal behavioral transformation, after which she becomes "charged with the responsibility of bringing about a second order of moral transformation, that is, serving the wider societal project of 'good growth,' a double moral injunction for the 'poor to help themselves [*in order* to help] the economy'" (Dolan 2014, 12, drawing on Elyachar 2002, 500).

The four-minute video described above is part of a series featuring Mita and her constellation of family members, neighbors, clients, and center staff, filmed for the purpose of training newly selected iAgents in the habits, dispositions, practices, and bodily routines of their new work. The dozens of other videos in the set covered topics such as "Group Formation and Session Conduction," "Promotional Activities," "Income Generating Plan," "Doorstep Sale of Goods and Services," and "Daily Accounting and Savings." Separate from the training for the actual services that the iAgent would provide (such as how to operate her laptop and modem to initiate a Skype call, conduct a blood-grouping test, and advise farmers about fertilizers), these topics covered the ways in which she should provide those services. These ways included both the outward presentation of herself to clients and external others and her internal habits and practices. They comprised a continuous set of idioms, procedures, and artifacts for inculcating self-responsibility and maintaining time management and financial and documentary discipline with which she should align herself to the ideal of the iAgent, exemplified by Mita.

The fact that iAgents participated in training was not unusual in itself.[2] The young women and their parents had undergone similar training sessions offered

FIGURE 7.   New iAgents learn how to operate cameras. Photo by author.

FIGURE 8.   New iAgents are instructed on how to stand and what to say while taking people's photographs. Photo by author.

by NGOs over the years. The skills they learned differed; rather than how to rear ducks or how properly to wash their hands, as they learned in NGO training camps, iAgents became proficient in using information and communication technologies (ICTs). Yet this new set of training was striking in that the women also had to learn *how to be*—how, for instance, to approach clients with professionalism and how to plan their words before raising their hands to speak in a meeting.

Despite their initial reluctance to discuss the video in the local NGO classroom setting, the iAgents commented extensively about it after the trainers left the room:

> "How can these be 'the daily activities of Mita *apa*'s life'? Having this busy schedule, how will she fit in bathing, eating, resting, and visiting her parents' home?"
>
> "When will she find time to wash her uniform if she must wear it every day?"
>
> "Won't her mother-in-law slap her for being out of the house all day long?"

"Working from morning to midnight . . . even garment workers don't labor for so many hours, and at least they are not turning black in the sun!"

Taspia interjected, "We know this is only *cinema* anyway. *No one* in the village behaves like that." Indeed, in each shot of Mita conducting group sessions, her members sit in orderly rows, backs straight, with fixed half-smiles and a forced concentration *not* to look at the camera, as they no doubt had just been instructed. In this performance, the participants acted as stylized versions of themselves, all sociality and personality stripped away in this rendering. As Taspia correctly identified, the cinematic representation enacted a model, with the messiness of life redacted. The ideal version of Mita succeeded because she inhabited a model version of the world. The exemplar might have fooled the foreigners being wooed for resources, but the recently selected iAgents were fully aware that life does not work in the way depicted, and Mita would fail in her endeavors if she ignored all aspects of reality. Fed up, Taspia summarily dismissed the topic by using a pun to call Mita "false" (or "a lie"; *mitha*) and an "animation character like Meena," and she stormed out of the room.[3]

Yet while they rejected the authenticity of Mita's representation of her work, iAgents remained intrigued about how she and the pilot-stage iAgents had managed to become so successful, and they were determined to learn the real secret behind Mita's prosperity. The model did not need accurately to portray reality to stimulate new behavior and action. A few days later, the iAgents were back in the classroom, where they learned how to write weekly plans. While "markets contain devices that aim at rendering things more 'economic' or, more precisely, at enacting particular versions of what it is to be 'economic'" (Muniesa, Millo, and Callon 2007, 4), iAgents engaged with devices like weekly planning templates not as ways to transform their own daily habits but as ways to appear cooperative and strengthen their relationship with the organization. This orientation was lost on TIE and ACRU staff. A key aspect of endorsing these Mita-inspired models of being "more economic"—with time, movements, and relationships—was the assumption of a disembedded apolitical social field in which these new entrepreneurs were to begin their work.

Paradoxically, these interventions were framed as solving a set of socioeconomic inequalities (albeit externally defined). They implicitly relied on the sociopolitical embeddedness of the entrepreneurs, who were selected and molded for their ability to "parlay their social relations into hard currency" and to "mobilize affective ties and social collectivities as a source of economic value" (Dolan 2012, 6). Just as Mita as an exemplar is detached from the social reality around her, "through the allure of wealth, these techniques 'detach' women [in entrepreneurship programs in Bangladesh and South Africa] from the constrained world of their present, enabling them to envisage a self and a future full of possibility" (2012, 7). While exercises in imagining future success may simulate this effect, an entrepreneur does not ever actually become "detached" from social fields, and especially not from the constrained patriarchal social worlds of village life and class-based NGO training sessions. Rather, the process of treating the iAgent as operating in a sterile social milieu in itself performs multiple dimensions of relational work. It obscures the actual relationships that mediate her activities, it denies the social labor that goes into producing economic value for the institutional assemblage, and it disregards the notion that other models of expectation are operative on her. Described in another way, the idealized model the iAgent is meant to follow becomes abstracted or disembedded—"not exactly 'from society'—because abstraction is in itself a social operation—but from other *agencements* [assemblages] which were probably less economic" (Muniesa, Millo, and Callon 2007, 4). The model served to render women's social worlds invisible.

Yet the iAgent acted in a social world in which the trainers themselves exerted their class and gender ideologies through the devices of training and disciplining, and thus the actual rendering of these subjectivities was more complex. The training was a process of reinscribing her relationships as pure economic potential (thus concealing sociopolitical qualities) to extract value from them and also to eschew responsibility for the conflicts in which her new positioning might place her. It is a device that allowed people to see only some kinds of information and to ignore others. The ways in which TIE and center members analyzed the challenges of iAgents as merely technical and internal is a recurring theme that ultimately resulted in the institutional denial of responsibility. Below I examine specific market devices, the entrepreneurial subjectivities they were meant to inculcate, and the relationships of inequality through which the devices were mobilized.

Financial Self-Discipline, Ethical Personhood, and the Moral Injunction of Hard Work

The objections of iAgents to Mita revealed their notions of a fulfilling life and of being a successful person and showed how these notions differed from TIE's model of successful entrepreneurialism. Yet the focus here is on the processes by which TIE attempted to reshape young women in Mita's image, or rather in the particular economic dispositions and performances embodied by Mita. These processes meant an attempt to colonize the subjectivities of the women who became iAgents in order to outsource to them not only their own development but also that of their communities. They were meant to be (but they never fully became) "actively converted into entrepreneurial subjects through a set of ideological and material practices that aim to produce and hone the requisite traits of industry, market discipline, and entrepreneurial distinction to succeed in global business. It is through this process of subject-making that business brings into being the new development entrepreneurs" (Dolan 2012, 3).[4] Entrepreneurial ethical traits were most centrally characterized by the virtuous subjectivities of embracing responsibility, competition, and risk. They involved the discursive practices of self-transformation and cultivating the capacity to aspire, namely to envision a future and engage in forward planning (Appadurai 2004).

While the intended self-transformation often referred to the specific material and social dreams of the entrepreneur (material wealth, status, and prestige), to achieve them also required an internal and moral transformation and a set of daily embodied practices and dispositions. This second set of transformations conflated "a Protestant work ethic with a neoliberal emphasis on the self-regulating subject" (Dolan 2014, 11). While market-driven development was rooted in values inspired by the Protestant ethic, the history of NGO "training" in Bangladesh since before independence also indexed the ideological projects of class. The refusal of subjects to be converted can be read as resistance to such exercises of power. In addition, female subjectivities have been shaped in previous eras by various institutions such as nationalism, Islam, and gendered domestic industry (such as manufacturing garments) (Jeffery and Basu 1998). The entrepreneurial imperative of newer entrepreneurship models, delivered through Silicon Valley–inspired technologies of disruptive innovation, was but one of many influences on notions of successful personhood.

The techniques and devices of intended "entrepreneurial conversion" (Dolan 2014, 8) described here included taking on financial and work discipline, business and management logics, and, crucially, debt. I begin with the processes—from recruitment and selection to training and disciplining—that were used to inculcate these characteristics. According to Mita in her introductory video, "Without being trained, this work cannot be possible." Some of these techniques (such as recruitment procedures) were continuous through pilot and for-profit stages of the iAgent program, while others (such as formal-sector debt) were newly introduced for iAgents recruited after 2012 in the scale-up locations.

Recruitment and Selection

Despite TIE's stated focus on the role of information in empowerment and poverty alleviation, little accurate information was provided to iAgents at any stage of their work process, especially when they first joined. According to Rohan Alam,

TIE defined a formal recruitment and selection process for attracting the kind of girls who could most easily be constructed into new iAgents. To advertise the iAgent position, the local center hired cycle-pulled carts to travel through villages announcing a prerecorded promotional message over loudspeakers. Staff built rapport with women's colleges. In promotional material and verbal explanations, TIE specified that it was recruiting young women who were currently enrolled in or had already passed high school or college. They should display quick learning ability, patience, confidence, understanding of the community's problems, basic business sense, and support from their families. Most important, they should be sufficiently stressed economically so that they would remain committed to working hard in the program.

In the selection procedure for both pilot and license models, Dr. Adnan Khan boasted a scientific and objective process by which applicants would be evaluated by a range of "stakeholders" (TIE staff, center staff, local government officials, and local NGO leaders) based on seventeen scored criteria about family and personality traits, knowledge, and the outcome of tests and tasks. (For instance, the ability to fold an origami bird after watching a video of someone doing it once displayed "quick learning ability.") TIE leaders asserted that the long recruitment process helped iAgents to know exactly the type of work they were agreeing to perform. In license-model locations, TIE staffers claimed that iAgents were aware that they would need to invest their own money from the beginning, and the program promised them training sufficient to grow their businesses and recover their investments.

TIE legitimized its activities through this semblance of technical and scientific process, from its initial problem-defining research and theory of change (lack of access to information being the key driver of and therefore solution to poverty) to the codified checklist of desired iAgent characteristics and intricate scoring rubrics. These procedural devices performed the relational work of hiding dynamics such as power imbalances between interviewers and interviewees. Young women became reduced to an aggregate set of numerically additive characteristics (although in the actual selection processes, the subjective feelings of panel members played a significant role). Information, when provided to iAgents, came packaged in forms incomprehensible to them (such as legal documents). These forms enabled TIE staff members to claim that technically it had provided full disclosure. While such models of scientific management generated the appearance of transparency and neutrality, TIE relied on obscuring and manipulating information flowing to iAgents in order to shape the women's behavior in ways beneficial to the organization.

iAgents' stories about the techniques used to recruit them varied from the official narrative. Women first learned about the project from recruitment campaigns conducted by the information center, through the center's other NGO activities, or through a relative or neighbor who was an iAgent client. iAgents who learned through formal recruitment strategies were all pilot-model iAgents, but they were the applicants who had the least amount of correct information (and the most misinformation) about the project by the time they joined. They thought they were applying for salaried office jobs (*chakri*) at the local NGO. Most iAgents under the license model were not aware that they needed to make a financial investment at the beginning of their work, and some accordingly were forced to drop out.

The Amirhat center told future iAgents under the license model that they would receive loans of 1.5 lakh taka (1,923 USD) in their name from National Bank (a commercial entity), but that the office would repay these using grant money. Taspia recounted how center staff members visited her village to recruit young women. They said that, using the loan money, iAgents would purchase equipment with which to educate villagers. Soon Taspia and other girls were called to the center to receive training about computers. The sessions were free, and no further explanation about the iAgent program was offered there. "My family could not afford the costs [of transportation to the training sessions], but I went after all. I truly thought that they would give me this much money, and then I could give it to my father and tell him to build a good business with 1.5 lakh taka." Only after the iAgents were finally selected and indebted to the commercial institution did the staff tell them that they would need to redirect their new incomes to pay back the loans.

Other iAgents learned about the opportunity after visiting the information center for different work. One woman's relative had been a leader of a women's savings group that the Lalpur center had formed, and she advised the woman to visit the office for a job. The center's executive director, Shorif, instructed her to first learn how to use a computer at their training center. "They said, let's see after a month which job you can do. After a month he told me I could be an iAgent. I told my husband that I'll do it, but I don't have any interest in this job. I still want an office job because I don't like doing outside work. But because of my family's financial crisis, I must." Another woman participated in a teacher-training workshop at the center, where the staff told her to apply to be an iAgent. Yet because she had not been part of any standard recruitment process, she never received information about the program until after joining and meeting other iAgents.

The misrepresentations (what economists at TIE called inevitable "information asymmetries") cultivated by TIE and the centers formed a central part of their recruitment strategies. By providing less clarity at the beginning, the project staff was able to attract women through their need-based aspirations and assumptions about the intended work. Once the women were invested in the process, often after passing many hurdles (trainings, examinations, interviews), only then did the project staff specify the procedure. The reliance on ambiguity and misunderstanding was a device that helped enfold women in a process they did not initially understand, until a relationship was cultivated, time and aspiration were invested, and the women were rendered more malleable to different ideas and work modalities. Full information disclosure might have prevented the program from operating; misunderstanding and uncertainty performed the relational work of drawing participants together. This cultivation of ambiguity, in ways productive for building the project but relying on inequalities in knowledge and power, is an example of how this analysis differs from communicative models of market formation.

Debt Contracts

The debt contract was the main market device operative in the construction of the new iAgent. Mita hints at the way this process works in her introductory video, yet her description conceals the binding relationship of debt and instead focuses on her supposed independence. "By my own investment of money, I buy the equipment and work at the field level. I do not work under anyone. I rely on my own knowledge, time, and hard work. I am not required to share my earning with anyone. Whatever I earn, whether less or more, it belongs to me. And for these reasons I call the profession modern and independent." Mita highlights a central tenet of poverty capitalism—self-exploiting labor responsible for its own reproduction and the success or failure of development outcomes. More practically, the financial investment of which she speaks was not precisely her own but was borrowed from kin and from the bank. Of the 1.5 lakh taka she required upfront to become an iAgent, a small portion came from her husband's savings, and the remainder she took from the National Bank. While the business may have been hers, the real iAgent acting as Mita was still subjected to the social and legal obligations of return encoded in the relationship of debt. Her earnings were not fully her own, because the bank and her husband also had claims over them.

Anthropological accounts of the moral economy of credit and debt show that not only official financial indicators but also culturally constructed, nonmaterial criteria are used to assess households' creditworthiness (Kar 2018; Schuster 2015). In this case, desperation was an important factor in selecting iAgents to receive loans, as was their unfamiliarity with legal documents and their dependence on male guardians such as fathers, brothers, and husbands. In other contexts, these characteristics might speak against credit worthiness, but TIE staff members were confident that these qualities would contribute to young women's malleability to be enfolded in the program and to accept TIE's direction.

Mita describes how she earned only 2,000 taka (26 USD) in the first month because people did not want to give their time to receive her services. The center employees instructed her husband to help, and, after that, her income increased over the year to 15,000 taka (192 USD) per month. Mita glosses over the problematic period in the first four to six months when she might make as little as 2,000 taka and need to pay loan installments of more than that. How would she cope in that situation? In the real world of the scale-up-stage iAgents, the process of entering into the loan agreement with National Bank was highly problematic, procedural but lacking in substance and comprehension. The process was dominated by documents, the mere presence of which was assumed to be sufficient for the young women to make an informed choice about signing.

The candidates initially completed two forms, a "Start-Up Costs" form and a "Projected Income/Expense Statement" for the first twelve months. This paperwork was done arbitrarily, and all iAgents produced identical documents by copying one another's forms. Having no experience with this type of work, how could anyone know how much she would earn from blood-grouping tests in month eight or how much she would spend on transportation in month eleven? These documents, required by the loan contract, were signed by the iAgent, the TIE chief executive officer, the center executive director, and the SSI managing director. They provided legal proof that iAgents were "investment-ready."

The temporalities demanded by the loan and its legal framework clashed with the temporalities of actual life, particularly for women.[5] iAgents faced competing obligations—such as agricultural and school cycles, ritual activities, everyday expenses, women's kin-work duties, and customer availability—that fell in different time frames. The temporalities of everyday life determined earnings, rather than the time logics of spreadsheets and "income-generation plans." iAgents seeking to establish farmers' group sessions, for instance, were told to return after sunset when men came home from the fields, which iAgents could not do without violating *purdah* norms and their sense of security. iAgents needed to invest time and relational work to build trust and gain validation in the community before exercises in market transactions could be successful, and the loan-repayment schedule did not take these timescales into consideration (despite the supposedly generous three-month grace period).

At the signing of the loan contract, Sabbir Hossain, the center's executive director, requested that one iAgent read the agreement aloud while the others followed along on paper. He inquired if the women had questions or objections and then instructed them to sign. When they received their National Bank checkbooks, linked to their personal accounts where the loan money was deposited, Sabbir told them to sign all of the checks (leaving other fields blank) and tear them out; he then placed the signed checks in envelopes identified by the women's names. iAgents never saw these checks again. Sabbir assured me that this procedure was standard practice for such types of programs.

The device of the loan contract enacts several operations, primarily related to shifting the relationship between the institution and the recipients from social and affective to functional and technocratic. The debt contract is the quintessential device in poverty capitalism used to disrupt reciprocity relations embedded in social life as well as in long-standing development arrangements.

The financial-legal document severed prior and expected patronage relations between TIE and the iAgents. This act of institutionalized detachment violated people's expectations under a broader moral economy of NGO-driven development in which this project was situated. In the donor-subsidized pilot model, TIE had supported iAgents economically by providing them with assets and supported them socially through ongoing troubleshooting and helping to negotiate culturally and politically their transition into the new role. The more recent iAgents, by way of debt to a commercial financial institution, purchased those assets as well as a fixed number of days of "training and capacity building" from TIE. Having appeared on those days and having "received content" in a standardized and routinized way, iAgents were considered to be "trained." Whether or not each iAgent could apply that training to the service of building her business successfully was treated as a function of the iAgent's individual ability. Being in service to the loan-repayment period bound iAgents to this precarious work for a minimum of three years. Although this model was heralded as enabling women's empowerment and independence, in fact debt institutions created new forms of dependence and bonded labor and facilitated the exploitation of these women.

Rituals of Readiness

Training occurred over five days and consisted of video demonstrations, explanations by TIE staff, and some practice with the technologies. It included tutorials on how to use the equipment (modems, cameras, software such as Adobe Photoshop, printers, first-aid kits), how to deliver services, and how to operate the health equipment (blood-grouping kits, blood-glucose tests, blood-pressure monitors, pregnancy test strips, weight scales) and advise people accordingly. In theory, iAgents were meant to receive a fifteen-day training workshop in which all of these items were covered, followed by periodic "refresher trainings" on specific topics, ad hoc workshops on locally demanded topics (often with government and NGO extension workers), and "cross-learning" visits in which they would travel to other iAgent locations to share "best practices."

In reality, due to TIE's budget corner-cutting, the initial training was halved, refresher trainings were equally brief, and no workshops or cross-learning visits occurred for the new iAgents. The training sessions in which I participated struck me as highly procedural and lacking in substantive learning. iAgents were shown how to make soap, for instance, in turn to teach villagers and thus "increase clients' income-generating activity." According to iAgent Ayrin, "It didn't work. Shila *apa* taught us to make soap but the whole kitchen was spoiled by the chemicals. Was it not a loss for us? We put our money there. We can't even earn money from it. Yet every girl had to pay eighty taka. Did they collect that money gently? No, they argued with us to collect that money."

Other times, the iAgents were instructed to role-play a group session with one playing the iAgent and the others playing the clients. In the session the group members heckled the iAgent with the questions and comments they all had faced in their fieldwork thus far. "Why are you not married?" "You are receiving an NGO salary, so why are you asking us to pay a fee in addition?" "You're supposed to give us food. Why didn't you bring food?" The "iAgent" tried to address these interruptions to what, in theory, was supposed to be a precisely timed and streamlined conveyance of information. No one helped the women to navigate the difficult relational aspects that emerged in their actual sessions in the field.

Another training session introduced the concept of budgeting and cash-flow accounting using Microsoft Excel. The TIE representative passed around a USB stick with an .xls template file for the iAgents to copy onto their laptops. Some iAgents managed to insert the USB into the correct port, but they could not find the file; others copied it but did not know where it was stored on their computers. The trainer gave up on digital formats and drew a grid on the whiteboard to simulate a budgeting spreadsheet. He demonstrated how they should log their expenditures and incomes, which involved several columns for each transaction including iAgent ID number, date, working area, type of customer, item sold, number of units, and cash received. Yet the iAgents registered no comprehension and were unable to interpret the spreadsheets. What was drawn on the board looked nothing like what was on the screens in front of them. iAgent Nilima opened hers on 3-percent zoom and could not see any cells in which to add information. The trainer warned that they should make an effort to learn, because they would be required to send their income and expense spreadsheets to TIE on a daily basis.

At the end of the training regimen, iAgents faced written examinations. The center staff members lamented that everyone performed poorly. They agreed to allow iAgents to retake their failed subjects. A center employee explained that on the "Social Mobilization" exam, "they all scored very low, below fifty-one points. So they have to take it again and again and again. If they score above fifty one, then they understand iAgent, more or less. But if less than fifty two, they are a failure." In this regime of arbitrary numbers, a mere one-point differential carved sharply the line that Dolan (2014) describes between the idle undeserving poor and the future entrepreneurial value creators.

Monitoring and Surveilling

The processes of inscribing business characteristics and market disciplines involve the forward thinking of the "capacity to aspire" (Appadurai 2004), conceptualized by program architects in a way that corresponded to individual wants that could be fulfilled by the economic rewards of business. Yet the capacity to aspire was a relational property embedded in the work of kinship for women in Bangladesh, not in individual material accumulation and rational economic calculation. These change processes also meant forward thinking about the day-to-day activities an entrepreneur must complete to meet certain (primarily economic) goals. Here, time discipline, along with the patience needed for delayed-return investment, required proficiency in short-term task completion. We saw Mita's plans, meticulously documented between ruler-straight lines, for her day, week, and month and implemented according to a day divided into time-rationalized increments and completed accurately to the minute. The explicit goal of these advanced-preparation exercises and practices was the pursuit of increased earning and little else. iAgents were expected to colonize every waking moment of their day for activities that were expected to generate them (and their licensors) the most profit.[6] They were unable to do so because, among other factors, this particular time rationality failed to incorporate existing time rhythms of everyday life.

Shortly after completing training, iAgents were each issued a thick spiral-bound logbook to complete their weekly planning, à la Mita, and to record notes about each session after it was completed. TIE staff members imbued these documents with so much authority (but not so much as to be immune to manipulation by the center staff) that the staff considered that iAgents' sessions had taken place only if they were recorded properly in the logbook. Only after the center verified the records would TIE release the money that iAgents were meant to receive as payment per session conducted. Rather than "empowering" iAgents, such practices delegitimized their word as compared with the official scripts of the center employees, who used this power to their financial advantage.

During the pilot stage of the iAgent program (implemented in two districts), TIE's monitoring regimes centered on the concept of mentorship. To help fledgling iAgents become established, Rohan argued, he needed to follow their activities virtually. He recounted how iAgents overreported their activities and said that they had run their scheduled sessions when they had not. He began conducting "sudden surveys" in which he called an individual iAgent just before a scheduled session and asked if she had arrived yet. She was usually not there, and so he asked how much time she required to cycle from her home to that village, and then he called her again to talk her through the process of setting up the session. Over time, the need for these calls diminished. Rohan described how this process became increasingly technocratic as compared with his original aims:

> I pushed my team members, first of all to ask each one about her well-being and then about her earnings. Stay with her and try to understand her. What is she doing? What sort of problems is she facing? Try to solve them over the phone. Do some sort of mentoring virtually. But what the office staff love to do is just some sort of policing. "Hey, why didn't you earn such money? Why didn't you conduct such group sessions?" Mentoring is not such a thing that you will ask the "why." You should *realize* the "why." You should uncover the reason *behind* the something not happening.

The center in Amirhat applied similar technocratic monitoring procedures. When iAgents grew disillusioned with the program because of their lack of earnings, center employees decided to increase surveillance over their activities, and they proclaimed that iAgents would be required to send daily text messages detailing their incomes, expenditures, and field movements. The difference between the center's style of monitoring and Rohan's style lies in the overtness or covertness of the expression of power. In the former, staff members applied direct force and their hierarchical position to compel the actions of others. In the latter, Rohan employed softer power, in which he created the conditions under which iAgents felt compelled to act. His strategy was more impactful in reorienting the subjectivities of iAgents as self-disciplining workers. In discussing their relationships with TIE employees, iAgents often said of Rohan, "He helped me to remember what I had to do, and he was there to encourage me when I felt bad." Of other TIE employees, to varying degrees, "They ask only how much I earned today, and when I say I didn't earn anything, they shout at me. But they don't understand the field and the challenges that are there." The support and coaching elements fell away, leaving only blatant surveillance. Real-time monitoring over the phone became associated with the other digital forms of monitoring, such as income and expense reports, plans, and session descriptions.

Stimulating horizontal peer-to-peer and self-monitoring complemented top-down surveillance. The techniques employed were verbal praise, exemplar-making, and awards. TIE or center employees often commented to iAgents about how hardworking and successful a particular one had been, thus provoking jealousy and competition in the others. iAgents began comparing how much they earned but doubting one another's word and criticizing one another's skills. Awards became a feature of the program to "motivate" iAgents but often provoked envy and hostility among them. Amirhat iAgents said that they disliked these new socialities because they hindered their ability to cultivate a good mind/heart (*mon bhalo*), which entailed generosity and mutual help. The valorization of the pursuit of financial profit exposed TIE's priorities and the nature of the subjectivities that TIE attempted to inculcate in the women.

When new iAgents consistently failed to earn money month after month, the center called a meeting with them, ostensibly to "solve their problems" but filled instead with technical analysis. In one instance, Sabbir stalked around the room asking each girl how much she made per day, which averaged 15 taka (0.19 USD). Their loan's grace period ended that month, and they needed to start paying monthly installments of 2,832 taka (36 USD), so tensions ran high about the gap between income and projected expenditure. The executive director shouted at the iAgents for "underperforming." He yelled that he was also on the line, because "your business is my business." His position depended on his ability to extract resources from those lower than and dependent on him. Rather than seeking to understand why iAgents struggled to earn, he listed arbitrary numbers representing what they should be earning per service in order to exceed their loan-payment amounts. Such behavior could be interpreted as, and actually was, bad practice in implementation rather than design. Yet this chapter shows that market-based development models were generally unable to achieve the empowerment objectives they claimed when they sought to render sociopolitical contexts invisible (while amplifying their inequalities) and to privilege economic and technical indicators.

Digital forms of monitoring served other relational work besides surveillance. They provided the bait for attracting powerful external others. Performance metrics employ numbers in statistical form to assert comparability and objectivity. Numbers are not disinterested forms of knowledge; they convey authority and expertise (Anders 2008, 2015; Dolan 2014). They mask the sociopolitical maneuvers undertaken to define the categories and units of measure and they reveal the bottom-line concerns of the measurers. The obsession with daily iAgent income—as opposed to the support of her networks, her feeling of well-being, her range of choices, or her level of prestige within her community—reveals TIE's agitation about financial progress. An optimistic interpretation would be that TIE held a simplistic notion of "empowerment" (as its stated goal) that was reduced to financial improvement, despite its claims about the emancipatory role of access to information, which remained unmeasured. A more cynical explanation might be that TIE leaders were primarily concerned with their own profits because the success of licensees directly affected the success of the licensor.

TIE coupled the financial data of iAgents with case studies to attract external, often foreign, partners. These case studies can be read as the selling of iAgents' selves and "success" narratives. Early on, iAgents in the pilot locations learned about the marketability of stories of self-transformation, which they recounted when placed in formal interview settings with foreign documentary teams, journalists, and award evaluators. TIE employed various devices for sustaining these representations through fabricated reports, curated field visits (in which TIE directed attention toward iAgents and clients who were known to be able to speak effectively about the program), emphasis on the idealized model rather than on real events, and the use of past-recorded documentaries as "evidence" of success.

This section reviews the devices employed in the creation of iAgent subjectivities, namely financial, temporal, and bodily discipline and the rule of documents and legal formalities, as well as formulaic training, deliberate ambiguity, and the withholding of information. These procedures were meant to capture the wider and relational aspirations of young women and fit them into a narrow and individualized definition of being. Some devices were blatant top-down and technocratic means of control, such as the session logbooks and income/expense reporting, and these seemed to create friction among and overt resistance from iAgents. Other techniques, such as the patronage relational modes and the capture of external resources from partners, seemed to align the interests of iAgents with those of TIE and may have been successful in co-opting their acquiescence in the program. While the iAgent model and other ventures of "inclusive business" are designed "to bring those below the poverty line above it, the 'line' is reified and reinforced through a range of discursive and strategic practices that actively construct and embed distinctions between the past and the future, valuable and valueless, and the idle and productive" (Dolan 2014, 4). Instead of enfolding the poor in broader systems of inclusion, such projects transform some people (but not securely) and reinforce the line between individualized "bootstrap capitalists" and generic redundant peasantry (Dolan 2014, 20). Most important, debt contracts are technologies that deny social relationships while simultaneously installing functional and technocratic ones. These contracts thus disavow the affective and protective aspects of patronage relationships while retaining the power and dependency in the relationship. In the section that follows, I show how this maneuver plays out in situations of failure. Class and gender inequalities become amplified through the enactment of these devices by individuals already situated in a hierarchy.

The Unmaking of iAgents

In the end, the inconsistencies between narrative and practice differed so wildly that the system collapsed. Several of the same devices that were purportedly meant to create and empower iAgents were used to unmake and disempower them.

On the evening after watching Mita's daily-schedule video, Taspia voiced her deeper concerns. "Mita *apa* lives in a *pukka ghar* [brick-and-mortar house]. All the villagers agreed with her about her services, but you've seen our villagers. They are *digital* people, they are too smart, living so closely to hospitals and markets. And if *apa* can't do her work, her father-in-law will pay her loan for her. Her husband and brother-in-law help, so she won't have any problems. The center supported her too." She reflected a moment as she picked at the manufacturer's label on her laptop. "But me? We are only three daughters living in a *kacha ghar* [raw or "deficient" house, in this context meaning made of impermanent materials such as mud and thatch], and our father is getting old. Juli *apu* [elder sister], you've seen how the center people here are useless and concerned only with their own benefit. So, who will help me?" She pointed out that, among the ten newly selected iAgents, only two were married, and all of them were poorer than Mita.

The exemplar of Mita as a market device was successful in making Taspia compare herself to a higher ideal, but the critiques Taspia made were *not* about her own internal deficiencies regarding her character, skill set, and ability to perform. They were about the structural and class differences between her circumstance and Mita's, in which the failings of the iAgent supportive infrastructures (including the center) played a key role. The familial support structure—which Mita identified as the turning point between her failure and her success—and the compliance of her community, neither of which came about through the training and disciplining of iAgent subjectivities, were also important. The Amirhat crisis situation was not an instance of the "unworthy" rural poor failing to work hard, as TIE would have liked others to believe; rather, it was the structural institutional mechanisms that put those participants firmly on the wrong side of the line. TIE attributed problems to the iAgents' own internal lack of capacity and motivation. Its leaders asserted that iAgents had "freely" entered into the agreement and thereby assumed all risk, and the program hid behind documents and legally defined responsibilities as a mechanism of detachment.

After several months of difficulties in setting up group sessions and earning money, iAgents brought their concerns to the center. Each time, center staff listed problems on the whiteboard. Sabbir, rather than acting to solve difficulties (such as assigning a staff member to accompany iAgents in their fieldwork, for which TIE had provided a stipend for this round of iAgents), tried to convince the iAgents that each issue was not a problem. Hearing the challenge of insufficient earning, he mimicked a woman's voice by saying, "'I have no income, so I'm not going to do anything.' This is wrong thinking. You must earn income; you have to pay your loan. Instead of sitting at home, you have to go to the field. Clear?" iAgents began to call TIE members about their problems, and Rohan proposed a one-month visit to Amirhat to provide support. When another TIE member arrived, she conducted a week of training sessions inside the center classroom and set foot only once in the iAgents' working areas.

When the second loan repayments were nearly due and problems had not been solved, iAgents began to speak of quitting. To solve this crisis, the TIE team "redesigned" the program, which entailed adding new services for iAgents to sell. The new strategy was also supposed to "remotivate" them. The major tactic was using telephone calls (a method they called "psychotherapy," as if the problem lay in the mindset of the iAgents and not in the exploitative nature of the program). The head of the iAgent team in TIE, who assumed the role when Rohan resigned and whose outlook reflected the new direction the program was taking, expressed with personal satisfaction in a call with me that he had just spent forty minutes in discussion with Taspia and solved all of her problems. When he said "forty minutes," I heard his teammate exclaim in the background, "forty-*one* minutes!" He assured me that "now everything is all fine," a comment that made Taspia laugh bitterly when I recounted it.

TIE presented financial self-discipline, particularly savings and investment, as a morally infused process, and the failure of iAgents to save indicated their inability to adopt the correct subjectivities. Kanika, arriving from the TIE head office, instructed a group of iAgents, "Visit the bank often, and whatever you earn, after deducting personal expenditure, try to save that in the bank. Having money in the bank is also a marker of respectability; wearing good garments is not enough. Do you understand?" Financial saving as an aspect of ethical personhood (as much as being well dressed) is a core theme in market-driven development. Yet because such savings did not benefit TIE directly, they were not monitored or documented.

As Appadurai observes with regard to the Mumbai Alliance in India, savings are exhorted as a discipline that "builds a certain kind of political fortitude and commitment to the collective good and creates persons who can manage their affairs in many other ways as well" (2004, 74). Savings, which demonstrate how people are thought to take on new qualities through certain disciplining practices, are seen as part of a larger causal chain linking these new individually practiced qualities to political empowerment at the level of the community. Without savings, "there is no way for the poor to drive changes themselves in the arrangements that disempower them. Thus, the act of savings is an ethical principle which forms the practical and moral core of the politics of patience, since it does not generate large resources quickly. It is also a moral discipline which produces persons who can raise the political force and material commitments most valued by the federation" (Appadurai 2004, 74). Yet remaining unclear, for both the Mumbai Alliance and iAgents, are the precise mechanisms that are meant to translate savings into political voice.

This "politics of patience" with savings (or, in the iAgents' case, debt) at its core meant other aspects of mental discipline, including hard work, self-reliance, and emotional control. Kabir, the TIE head of the iAgent program after Rohan left, visited iAgent Nilima's house with his team member Kanika and scolded Nilima's mother for Nilima's lack of success: "*Caci* [aunt, also a term of respect for an unrelated older woman], today you are here because you have worked very hard, right? Otherwise, you could not have arrived at where you are today, so your daughter should also work hard. You needed to have given her ideas, suggestions, and courage." Yet, the degree to which entrepreneurs could depend on other people for support was limited, as Kanika explained to Nilima. "We don't have any medicine to provide you that will solve all your problems. We will not give you any solution. As your intellect matures, you will realize that even your parents will not be able to extract you from the problems you have in your life if you don't want to solve them for yourself." The centrality of patience while working strenuously for the benefits of investment to arrive (even if they never do) appears again, for example through local agricultural metaphors Kanika employed to explain to Nilima's family: "Don't you cultivate? Does a plant start giving you fruits immediately after you plant it? This [iAgent business] is also a land but a different type of land. . . . You had to give it time to work." The knowledge that Nilima's meager income *now* could not repay the monthly installment of her bank loan, or even begin to cover costs of living, was relevant to TIE people only to point out that her lack of earning was due to her lack of patience, effort, and problem-solving initiative.

TIE represented and addressed problems with the implementation of the iAgent model in Amirhat by blaming the iAgents for their personal characteristics, such as their mindsets, work ethics, logical capabilities, and intelligence. Despite TIE's description of societal and institutional factors (such as gender discrimination and marginalization of the poor) that stimulated the demand for this intervention, TIE located ongoing problems within poor people's subjectivities that needed to be fixed, as opposed to hierarchical relations with the nonpoor that could be addressed and handled.[7] If the iAgents failed, then failure must have resulted from their inability to absorb the learning as opposed to structural programmatic failure or wider sociopolitical barriers.[8]

TIE representatives explained that iAgents did not work earnestly. Development workers assigned a level of moral value to intense work, hardship, and struggle. The women did as well, seeing a feminine virtue in them. (Yet from their perspective, they *had* worked hard and struggled and were frustrated by the lack of results.) These development workers behaved as if the poor should not be able easily to improve their situations, that improvement would be inauthentic unless the poor faced severe challenges, which were spun and lauded in the success narratives sold to potential partners to attract financial resources. The poor were not simply entitled to a better, more secure, less vulnerable life that they could take for granted; rather, unlike the privileged classes, they must work hard to earn it.

When TIE and the center's staff visited a few iAgent homes on the eve of the women's exit from the program, a center employee chastised Nilima's mother: "In the last two months, how many groups did your daughter actually visit? Will Allah provide you any wealth if you stay at home and do nothing?" The irony that he was paid a salary to attend all iAgents' sessions but actually attended none did not seem to register with him. The moral economy of divine reward for hard work sincerely undertaken, in vernacular theories of agency, resonated here with the ideology of market-driven development, inspired by the Protestant ethic. Yet the young women were doubly confounded by a new logic of poverty capitalism that infused this project. While iAgents worked arduously for zero gain, the center and TIE staff accrued income by performing no work at all.

Devolving risk and responsibility onto the poor for their own development (or failure) was a key mechanism of the iAgent social enterprise and of poverty capitalism more generally. In the heightened crisis days preceding the iAgents' loan default and resignation, TIE staff frequently threatened the women about the consequences of not paying their loans and brought the weight of the national legal system against them for not behaving in the properly disciplined manner that the trainings and other market devices were meant to instill. This maneuver was no longer soft power exerted to mold their subjectivities; it was overt threat of violence against them and their families. At Nilima's house, I witnessed the following exchange:

> Nilima's mother to Kanika: Take away all your equipment!
> Kanika, the TIE employee: We have nothing to do with those equipment, and we have no way to take them back.
> Nilima's mother: Then I will have to sell my land.
> Kanika: You are being angry and emotional. I have come here so that such a bad situation will not take place. Now if you get angry at me,

then will it be possible for me to find a solution? If there will be any such damage, who will suffer? It will be you. I will leave for Dhaka, and I will not come back here to see your situation. The loan is not in my name but in your daughter's name. The bank people will search for your daughter. Let's see how many people from the bank will look for me. You have bought rice from the store, so will the rice go to my house or will it go to your house?

Regardless of the causes, failure to participate correctly in these projects of "inclusive business" meant, for the poor, being locked into exclusion for good. As Kanika explained to all iAgents together, "In life there is failure and success. If you fail you'll have many problems in life." She told them the consequences of not paying their loans. The bank would inform other institutions, "This girl does not pay back loans so don't give her one and don't invite her to participate in your programs!" When accused by iAgents of running a scheme to cheat the poor, TIE leveled arguments of free will and said that iAgents joined using their own agency. The organization would refuse to recognize any responsibility of its own. Kanika elaborated, "It was your own decisions that led to this situation today. You had your own interest in this work, but for different reasons there was not enough effort to make it successful. Perhaps you are as talented as I had assumed you were [at the point of selection], but you didn't show your talent in the field."

TIE and the center mobilized formal bureaucratic processes and hid behind documents to shed responsibility for the harm done to iAgents during and as a result of participating in the program and for the default on their loans. When Taspia, in a group meeting at the center, brought up the topic of how center staff had lured them into the program initially by saying that they would not need to repay their loans, Sabbir did not deny it but shouted at her, "When all of you accepted the agreement, there was no objection from you then! Now my hands are tied, and you must pay your loan yourselves."

The National Bank loan product for "iAgent Social Entrepreneurs" stipulated that iAgent fathers and husbands would be personal guarantors and that the local center would be the corporate guarantor. Sabbir might have been keen to have iAgents pay their loans so that the responsibility would not fall on him if they defaulted. I soon discovered that this outcome was not possible. The National Bank officer in Amirhat requested that TIE finalize the corporate-guarantor documents because the bank faced an upcoming audit. TIE explained that the local center was the appropriate guarantor. Sabbir also visited the bank for an institutional loan and requested that TIE guarantee it. TIE refused on the basis that the center had dodged responsibility as the corporate guarantor of the iAgent loans and instructed Sabbir to complete those documents first. By the time the iAgents withdrew from the program, these processes still had not taken place, and so the center was never made legally responsible for the iAgents' loans.

Rohan, despite being assigned now to a different project, tried to find a solution that would help the iAgents in Amirhat. He was unable to do so because neither TIE nor SSI would commit the resources. One party was responsible for mentorship and the other for implementation, and they could not agree under which domain the problem of the loan fell. A core feature of the license model seemed to be what Jamie Cross (2011) calls the "ethics of detachment." Each party claimed no responsibility or passed off responsibility to another party, and ultimately no one was called to account for actual events. No one bothered to learn what happened at the lowest level of the hierarchy (among the people TIE was supposedly "empowering"), and this lack of knowledge granted free license for the lack of action by the organization to mitigate damages.

David Mosse encourages a research perspective on "documents [in development] as sets of social relations" and suggests that researchers describe "the social production of numbers, which are privileged in translocal development planning because of their capacity to strip out context" (2013, 233). Documents are not pieces of authority in themselves but are embedded in sociopolitical fields. They carry "hidden relational baggage" and should not be "analysed as dead artifacts; they are alive with the social processes that produced them and they have a 'performative quality' and social effects, even though the salience of policy ideas that they convey summarize and hide this 'politics of interaction'" (Mosse 2011, 7). The hierarchical ordering or authority of documents falls according to their owners' or writers' position in the social hierarchy. Even when documents are "official" in the eyes of the law, they endow more power to the users who have the cultural capital to read, interpret, dodge, find loopholes in, and understand the consequences of them, and to write them in the first instance in language that preserves and asserts their own interests. The loan contract and agreement signed by TIE, SSI, the center, and iAgents is a case in point. Even when responsibility was legally required to be taken, such as loan guarantorship, the related organizations managed to exempt themselves through calculated deferral to another organization along the chain. While nonpayment of the loan resulted in bank officials pursuing iAgent families, those project staff members who did not deliver promised support and services to iAgents faced no consequences. iAgents lacked any channels to make claims against the participating entities.

A Social Gamble

The purpose of this chapter is to illustrate how market devices, deployed as part of market- and social-enterprise-making projects, act on and are mediated by individuals, relationships, and societies, but not in ways resembling the intended models. These models seem to exacerbate the inequality and precariousness of people through the very technologies meant to alleviate these problems. Through the political tactics of detachment, ambiguity, and misunderstanding, these projects are able to elide responsibility for the negative social consequences of their actions while organizing attention toward their "success cases" in order to attract additional resources.

This chapter contributes to academic readings of market devices as technologies for building markets. While market creation may be the intended purpose of market devices, most markets are not built in abstract planes. Rather, they inhabit sociopolitical landscapes. I do not examine what market devices are meant to do; instead, I attend to the parallel social effects that are produced. The market devices employed here act as technologies of denying responsibility and dodging accountability for actors who already possess power in unequal relationships. Devices allow their implementers to disavow existing affective relations and eschew the type of ethics of care that underpins rural Bangladesh's moral economy of NGO patronage.

The ambiguities produced by disjunctures between models and realities are not merely unfortunate and unintended by-products of the processes of abstraction and simplification. Following Michel Callon (1998) and Timothy Mitchell (2007), I show that such representations enable the production of the very exclusions upon which market formation relies. Market mechanisms reinforce lines of power between the NGO middle classes and the poor. For the middle classes, development projects are the means to win resources to bolster their positions as well as to assert their dominant class, gender, and status over clients. Devices that sustain such power imbalances instead of ameliorating them are documents (which are legible to and serve the interests of their wielders) and numbers (which are normative and nonneutral). The will to misrepresent illustrated here provides a direct counterpoint to a communicative understanding of building markets and implementing projects and also shows the inequalities embedded in seemingly transparent processes. The next chapter adds layers to this observation by revealing the work of structural and relational ambiguities in enabling the model to function.

Was the decline and ultimate failure of the iAgent program in Amirhat inevitable? Perhaps, but my argument is not one of the hegemony of market devices in reformatting iAgents in ways that serve the interests of capital. These devices largely failed in the first instance to induce new individual subjectivities because of their social impossibility. According to the model as explained by TIE's executive director, Adnan Khan, failure might just be structurally inevitable. When Adnan was discussing with a global agricultural research organization how the latest model iteration would be different for its newly recruited iAgents in southern Bangladesh in June 2014, a representative from the organization wondered about protection mechanisms for iAgents in case an Amirhat-like situation happened again. Adnan replied, "A lot has changed, and I am confident that risk management is in place legally and business-wise." Not only did he remain vague about what had actually changed, but he also mentioned other modifications in subsequent days that seemed to indicate that new elements of the TIE-iAgent contract were in place to protect TIE alone from risk (such as removing the organization's guarantorship of loans). Adnan added, before changing the subject, "When dealing with human beings, you have to gamble. Social change itself is a gamble. If we have ten thousand iAgents and a 90-percent success rate, that is really good, isn't it? You can't get much better than that." The empowerment model itself assumed and accepted this level of risk, but it denied responsibility for the negative effects of risk as a form of structural violence, the violence of exclusion inflicted by the model.

Riles (2010) describes failure as internal to the aesthetics of transnational institutional practice. Failure emerges in processes of generalization, which lose important aspects of social reality that show up only in complexity. An aesthetics of failure is instantiated in these self-aware gaps (such as the one Adnan identified), which are endemic and pointed to systematically in the network form of organization. Alice Street (2015) attributes the acceptance of failure to the difference between a bureaucratic ethics of care (espousing a "let die" logic, Li 2009) and a humanitarian ethics of care (defending compassion for all). Adnan's framing of the issue as "gambling" and his use of "impressive" statistics seemed to be a mechanism of detachment from the actual lives involved. It organized concern away from the 10 percent (one thousand iAgents similar to Taspia) who inevitably, according to the "success" rate objectives of the model, were destined to fall out of the system with debilitating loans on their backs. Thus the cycle continued.

4

A DIVERSIFIED BASKET OF SERVICES

Arriving to deliver a healthcare information session for housewives hosted by her aunt in a nearby village, the iAgent enters the homestead in the role of a niece, inferior in social status but welcomed. While she and the others there exchange news about relatives, someone gives her a plate of the cold rice and vegetables that the family had eaten for lunch. As the session begins, she inhabits the coveted position of NGO worker and bearer of knowledge and expertise. Someone thus presents her with biscuits and tea, the offering made to high-status guests. Participants soon complain that she has not brought any items to give them. As the session ends and she tries to convince people to buy health services or consumer products, she slips into a hawker or vendor status by pushing her wares and having to explain repeatedly why they must pay for these items. People including hordes of children push and shove to take turns standing on her digital weight scale and make such a clamor that she cannot possibly require them to pay for the privilege. As she packs up her equipment and rides away, men comment on the indecency of a woman on a bicycle.

The Work of Social Ambiguity

Who, or what, is an iAgent: a close relative, a respected NGO extension worker, a lowly hawker, or a deviant female? This snapshot, a common scene in the everyday lives of iAgents, touches on the intense ambiguity central to the experience of becoming and being one. The overall project of iAgent was congruous with young women's efforts to pursue existing modes of aspirational womanhood in changing socioeconomic conditions, but the day-to-day requirements also meant engaging in activities that ran counter to their sense of identity.

A diversified basket of services was the primary means by which the social enterprise made a steady flow of income, claimed it achieved social impact, and accommodated the demands of numerous resource-providing partners. Yet this multiplicity of roles also framed the iAgent locally as an ambiguous and ethically suspect figure. iAgents had to undertake the work of continuous switching among different positions, justifying each of them socially and cultivating the overall appearance of virtue. Doing so was emotionally and financially exhausting. Only through extreme spending on their families, entering into unfair and unequal alliances, enduring regular criticism, and allowing themselves to be exploited by community members did these women find ways of absorbing and managing all the contradictions inherent in their work with the social enterprise. Once again, we see how women's unpaid relational labor is what underwrites capital accumulation for the social enterprise and how such a program actively disempowers women who are unable to mediate between and among all of these conflicting roles and value regimes.

While their stories of joining the program featured the desires of fulfilling relational and kin obligations as well as accessing new individual opportunities, their actions were often interpreted by family members and TIE staff—for different reasons—as inappropriate or irrational. Because their social identities were thrown into ambiguity as a result of taking up iAgent work and switching among many different social roles and activities, young women worked hard to situate themselves within known registers of identity and relationality. Yet feelings of ambivalence permeated their enactment of multiple roles as they moved through their social worlds and tried to mobilize them entrepreneurially.

In this and the following chapter, I focus on the ambivalent position of iAgents as acting within a blurred and overlapping double interface (Arce and Long 2002) and thus serving simultaneously as agents and objects of both socioeconomic change and the establishment (or failure) of rural ICT-based markets. This interface was constituted first by these young women in their position as field workers representing the wider iAgent enterprise and distributing services on its behalf among rural villagers. Second, it was constituted through their identity as young village women negotiating a vertical relationship with TIE and the other organizational actors it engaged. As "market makers," women are targeted to play the role of "interpretation and interface between [the] capitalist economy and local moral economies" (Guérin 2017, 4). The ways in which these multiple and often contradictory subject positions also changed contextually and temporally had implications for notions of empowerment and the stabilization (or not) of digni-fied livelihoods for women. As iAgents learned and performed the subjectivities expected of them by the enterprise, how did they navigate competing models of expectation placed on them by their communities? How did they reconcile the meaning of being a successful relational person when they were meant to emulate the stripped-back social model of the self-maximizing entrepreneur?

A relational and processual analysis of iAgent work illuminates the specific social and political projects that underpinned the diverse economic transactions that defined the women's everyday work. "Processual ethnography" (Moore 1987) is an actor-based method and mode of analysis focusing on the individual-as-decision-maker through a series of changes taking place over time and in relation to other people and institutions. In this case, it incorporates the tempo-ralities of the iAgent livelihood as young women moved from activity to activity and from interaction to interaction, enabling analysis of the embodied experi-ence and lived practice of the iAgent work.

This chapter explores the series of mismatches found among the contradic-tory transactional and temporal logics that the different project modalities had with one another. It also shows the tensions between the types of economic transactions institutionally demanded by particular iAgent services and the ones socially understood by family members and neighbors, the potential "clients" of those services. iAgents especially needed to navigate cases where the social rela-tionships implied by certain new transactional logics were detrimental to their aspirational sense of self. For instance, in this chapter's opening vignette, how might the iAgent stabilize a favorable representation of herself while also setting the conditions to earn a viable income? How was she meant to use her "social capital" to extend her business when doing so undermined the model of appro-priate sociality of her relationships?

Descriptions of the many types of products and services that these women provided, which contained within them contradictory relational logics and caused iAgent-client relationships to be fraught with ambiguity, illustrate the complexity of iAgent work. iAgents attempted to assert favorable interpretations of their role, to counter more recognizable but less advantageous readings of their work such as that of the hawker (who were paid for their services but occu-pied low status) and that of the NGO worker (whose aspirational status as a salaried employee meant that they could not take fees from beneficiaries). This chapter also sheds light on the changing relationships within families by focus-ing on the attitudes of relatives toward iAgent work, shifting financial flows, and turning-point narratives of gaining acceptance. Yet iAgents' efforts to cast their work in a particular vein were never complete. Situations of dramatic change required not the stabilization of activities and relations but rather their continual multiplicity. Ambiguity was what made the project "work." The project also produced ambiguity, which was a resource used by project actors in the negotiation of recognition and authority.

iAgent Services and Negotiations

TIE designed eighty-five income-generating services for iAgents to sell, which covered topics in health, education, literacy, agriculture, livelihood, law, technology, and communication. Each of these services entailed a different set of activities, rationalities, and income streams, thus necessitating a different set of subject positions for iAgents vis-à-vis their "clients" and therefore requiring continuous relational work. But first, clients had to be crafted out of family members, neighbors, and inhabitants of nearby villages. The techniques of "customer segmentation" and group formation, which was one of the topics of training received by iAgents when they joined, were the primary instruments. People in villages needed to be rationalized and rendered legible according to the products or services they might purchase and then to be clustered accordingly. The classification and quantification of "customer segments" was intended as a stabilizing device; "Establishing metrics for the description and the assessment of products [and services and consumers] is a crucial ingredient of the performative processes that shape markets" (Muniesa, Millo, and Callon 2007, 9).[1]

Yet instead of stability, the implementation of this composite model produced continuous flux and negotiation. In the ethnographic descriptions that follow, we see how villagers defied definition as consumers in the ways that the iAgent model attempted to construct them. I track the partial and differential construction of iAgents through the products and services they peddled and through the often conflicting relational positions these implied. According to the type of product or service, the exchange modality in which it was offered, and the way in which the client/beneficiary/consumer/member was classified, relational configurations emerged with different implications for the social and economic position of the iAgent.

iAgents were tasked with forming two of each of the following groups for weekly meetings: children, adolescent girls, housewives, farmers, unemployed laborers, and dependent citizens (defined as disabled, elderly, widowed, divorced, and abandoned people). TIE identified these six "types" of people because they represented the most "vulnerable," "disadvantaged," and "downtrodden" of the rural population and suffered from lack of access to information-based services that their development supposedly required. These groups were considered to be internally homogeneous, defined by the problems they were imagined collectively to experience and the information TIE believed to be crucial for their empower-ment. Examples include maternal health and HIV/AIDS information for house-wives and livelihood and livestock information for farmers. Topical information, similar to the rural villagers themselves, was thus gendered and segmented and then delivered to its directed audience via offline audio-visual material stored on iAgents' laptops. Four types of services an iAgent might provide in the course of a day—and sometimes in the course of a single session—included education of the group members through digital multimedia, fast-moving consumer goods sales, health diagnostics checks, and Right to Information Act advocacy. To tease apart their underlying, often conflicting sociofinancial logics, the concept of relational work is again useful.

For all economic activities or transactions, Viviana Zelizer identifies four ele-ments, the negotiation of which constitutes relational work. These are: distinct social connections among the actors in the activity, transactions of goods or ser-vices, tokens that serve as media for those transactions, and negotiated meanings with which actors endow the transaction and relationship (Zelizer 2012, 151). To account more ethnographically for power and the directionality of exchange, I consider the structural features of the relationship through models of kinship- and NGO-patronage relational economies and draw on the Bangladesh develop-ment and patron-clientage literature.[2]

iAgent Brishti's Typical Service Day

After cooking a breakfast of fried potatoes for her family, Brishti packed up her bag of equipment, hauled her bicycle up the steep embankment to the dirt road, and cycled toward her morning information session for farmers. In this weekly event, she showed digital multimedia to "build awareness" about planting and harvesting cycles and selecting the right fertilizers and pesticides. Her group con-tained twenty men, including several uncles, whom she had invited from proxi-mate villages. These one-hour sessions were meant to follow a predefined flow, but she usually ditched the formalities. As a young woman with no direct experi-ence in farming, she said she felt uncomfortable lecturing to older men who had farmed their whole lives. She skipped straight to the video, thus allowing the technology to do the talking.

Brishti's members did not need to pay to receive information in group sessions, which were often also attended by nonmembers attracted by the entertainment. Instead, Brishti received an "honorarium" of 70 taka (0.90 USD) per session from TIE's foundation partners. As iAgent project founder Rohan explained, while iAgents were entrepreneurs, they should not be providing income-generating services exclusively. They also needed to offer awareness and education to the villagers, which was the primary activity upon which TIE based its social-impact claims. TIE eventually realized that it needed to give a financial incentive to iAgents for these sessions.

Group meetings were a modality familiar to many villagers; for the past several decades NGOs had commonly offered them. Brishti in this context was understood to be a type of NGO worker, which implied a hierarchical connection over members despite her inferior social position. Within the NGO moral economy in Bangladesh, patrons were expected to distribute resources or gifts to clients in an ongoing relationship. Indeed, Brishti experienced difficulty when she established regular group sessions because, although she gave the "gift" of free information, other NGO workers and state officials had previously provided free meals, clothing, and other material objects that beneficiaries had come to demand as forms of "help" (*shahaja*). Informational videos were entertaining, but people did not consider that they benefited from them in the same way that they would by a new towel or a chicken. Instead, iAgent gifts resembled the "development gift" (Stirrat and Henkel 1997) that, instead of strengthening social hierarchical ties, was structured ultimately to sever those ties for the purpose of "sustainability."

FIGURE 9. An iAgent sets up an information session about breastfeeding for housewives. Young boys join in, attracted by the spectacle. Photo by author.

During a particularly cold winter, TIE organized warm clothing and blankets for iAgents to distribute to their group members. During subsequent winters members repeatedly complained that iAgents now "gave them nothing." The ties that Brishti and her group members tried to stabilize were incompatible with one another. Group members understood that their social ties with Brishti should be one of NGO worker and beneficiary, in which gifts were given regularly in exchange for compliance. Members often rebelled against Brishti because of her repeated failure to uphold the moral economy of the relationship. They refused to show up for sessions, disrupted the flow of meetings, and demanded food and gifts. They refused to behave like "proper beneficiaries"; the failure of expected transactions violated their sense of how the relationship should work.

After playing a video about a technique for threshing dried rice plants, Brishti tried to sell some consumer products to the farmers' wives. Because of the perceived barrier between rural people (particularly women) and markets, iAgents were commissioned as arms of direct distribution to people in their villages and homes. Organized by TIE, iAgents assumed the identity of *Aparajitas* (meaning, in Bangla, "women who cannot be defeated"), part of a rural sales program developed by CARE, an international NGO, and by the Bangladesh subsidiary of Unilever, a multinational corporation. The Aparajita program, a strategy for expanding the markets of Unilever, BATA, Square, and other multinational and national corporations farther into the "unreached" rural areas of Bangladesh, was cloaked as a program of empowerment. Villagers could purchase a basket of "impactful products" (Rashid 2014), and destitute women could transform their lives by becoming sales agents and earning a living (Dolan 2012). Products included Vim washing powder, Fair & Lovely skin-whitening cream, and Sunsilk shampoo, all in the single-use sachets iconic of C. K. Prahalad's "fortune at the bottom of the pyramid" corporate social-business models (Prahalad 2006). The program operated within a hub-and-spoke setup, with TIE and its local NGO partners receiving commissions as the franchising bodies, and iAgents/Aparajitas capturing a marginal profit. Aparajitas, of which four thousand existed in the country in 2015 (Jita Bangladesh n.d.), enabled the extension of the corporation through this "inclusive business" model, but the women remained excluded from the benefits of corporate employeeship.

Brishti had been trained that her role was to engage in simple market exchange, in which she would supply her fellow villagers with products for their standardized retail value in cash. The relationship was modeled to be equal and transactional, with debts canceled out as soon as cash was given and products were handed over. Yet TIE simultaneously expected that larger markets could be reached by leveraging the social networks of iAgents as a client pool.[3] While markets for companies' products were readily available using a distribution agent's village networks and "social capital," her relationships with persons not otherwise operating under a market logic with her meant that intimates often deferred payment. In Bangladesh, the vendor-customer relationship was often built around credit and delayed payment, rather than immediate cancellation of debts. The iAgent work schedule was incompatible with the mode of economic sociality in rural Bangladesh; the temporality of the loans iAgents were obliged to take to purchase their products conflicted with the temporalities of these customer payments. Gender relations also inhibited Brishti. Men especially took products from her bag while saying that they would pay later, which they often never did.

Brishti and fellow iAgents had resisted product sales in the beginning because its closest local analog was the lowly status of a hawker or peddler (*feriwala*), rather than the high status of an NGO worker. People commented that such work of buying and selling in public spaces was unsuitable for girls because it lowered the social status of their families and created difficulties in finding marriage partners for them.

As a strategy to overcome these obstacles, Brishti set up a shop next to her house. Sitting on a platform raised above the road, surrounded by an inventory of goods on display, she was perceived, if not as a shopkeeper herself, as a sister or daughter of one, and customers were more likely to respect the transaction. Later, as her shop turned over higher volumes of goods, Brishti employed her father and brothers, individuals whom people could more easily embrace in their mental model of a vendor-vendee relationship.[4]

To overcome the stigma of being perceived as a hawker, Brishti also used her group sessions to sell products. The exchange of products and sales of goods between and among households by women had precedence in the village.[5] Thus iAgent sales practices could be enfolded in these commonly understood systems of meaning. iAgents were less likely to be stigmatized as hawkers within the intimate circle of women sitting together.

The farmers' wives did not want to buy any products that week, but several of them requested that Brishti check their blood pressures. A third type of service she provided was health-related diagnostics via digital equipment such as a blood-pressure cuff, glucometer for diabetes testing, blood-type reagent kit, weight scale, and thermometer. As with product sales, these tests required clients to pay a fee per service. Unlike product sales, health services were one of the most lucrative for Brishti. After recovering the initial investment in purchasing her equipment, she retained nearly all the profit with only marginal recurring costs (such as recharging batteries and purchasing test strips and slides for blood work). Initially, Brishti promoted her health services at group sessions until people became familiar with them. After several months, she was able to build up a customer base for regular check-ups, which provided a constant stream of income.

The digital equipment used, and the training she acquired, elevated Brishti's status. Providing health services likened her to an esteemed professional in government community clinics and hospitals and in health-related NGOs. These professionals received salaries, so Brishti faced initial difficulty in convincing customers to pay the fee; she asserted that she was an entrepreneur who purchased the equipment herself. She asked customers how much money they would lose in transportation by rickshaw to a clinic and in forfeit of wages, and she demonstrated that the fee for her iAgent service was smaller and the provision at home more convenient.

In this health domain, iAgents created a new market for bioconsumerism; they generated a "need" that they then fulfilled. In turn, people were classified as biodata to be read so that their lifestyle habits could be governed (Foucault 1980). Brishti became effective at convincing people of the necessity for knowing one's blood type and regularly checking one's blood pressure. The appeal of health technology (especially with digital equipment, which was more "modern" than the manual technology the clinics used) helped further to attract customers,

FIGURE 10. An iAgent measures a woman's blood pressure with a digital monitor. Photo by author.

FIGURE 11. An iAgent's tutoring session is interrupted by a man requesting his weight be measured. Photo by author.

even though Brishti was not a health worker, possessed only technical and not medical training, and often provided misleading advice (she recommended to people with high blood pressure that the affliction resulted from stress and "tension" and that they needed to eat less rice and more meat and spend more time resting). Brishti's connection with people in this context was that of expert and client, with bioinformation and advice exchanged for cash. The allure of the type of knowledge and the material props employed meant that the status of the provider was incremented upward with each transaction. Relationships were often long term and affective, and Brishti was called to take temperatures and measure blood pressures each time someone in her village or nearby ones fell ill, any time of the day or night.

Brishti rested for lunch at her cousin's house in the same village. She had brought her meal, but her cousin provided a plate, extra rice, and some vegetable curry. Two boys, also cousins, entered the house while the women were eating. They used Brishti's laptop to download music videos onto their phones. She grumbled that they were costing her bandwidth and battery strength and that she would normally charge for the service. She did not attempt to collect the money, and the boys did not acknowledge her comments.

After lunch, Brishti cycled to a distant village to provide Right to Information (RTI) Act services. Considered by TIE to be the social work of good-governance advocacy, this service was to ensure people's right to obtain information (understood as documentary material in any form, including paper, audio, video, and digital) from state officials and organizations owned, controlled by, or substantially funded by the state. The idea behind RTI is that information is not a favor to be meted out by the state at its discretion but is instead a public good. The specific service Brishti provided to villagers was to identify people who were entitled to receive state subsidies (such as old-age pensions and disability grants) but who were unaware of their entitlements or whose claims to receive them had been denied by local-level officials.

The work entailed submitting a request for information in the form of a question, such as, "For how many people are VGF cards available in Lalpur subdistrict in 2013, how many remain to be distributed this year, and what are the requirements for getting one?" VGF (Vulnerable Group Feeding) cards are part of Bangladesh's food assistance safety net program, distributed to the "extreme poor" for food rations in regions affected by disaster. If a family qualified for receiving a card and had been turned away by the local government office, the family could return to the office with the written response to the iAgent's question to show that cards were still available for claim, that the family had fulfilled all the criteria to obtain one, and that it would not need to pay a "fee" (that is, a bribe) to the officer for the benefit.

In the RTI program, people were classified not by homogenous livelihood- or lifestage-based profiles as in the group sessions but as citizens "excluded" from the state who needed the weight and authority of documents to make claims to their rights. RTI was not an official venue for pressing claims (people asked questions rather than petitioned for entitlements), but through iAgents the act was used as a tool to enhance the voice of citizens against the informal and personal systems of local officials who distributed state benefits. Information might become a form of social capital, one required for making claims to the state. In this sense, RTI indirectly strengthened local governance and rights by creating a sort of market for documents that wielded power in their ability to extract state resources. In their role as conjurers and bearers of these pieces of paper, iAgents were key actors in the creation of information as a public good, a form of social capital, and a market with its own supply and demand dynamics. As TIE officers explained, the role of the iAgent as intermediary was to stimulate the demand side as a market signal for supply to follow. (TIE aspired, in a future project, to render these pieces of paper digital so that the market for information in any village in Bangladesh would be visible in Dhaka and anywhere in the world.)

RTI services were provided through TIE's partnership with a Bangladesh-based human-rights foundation supported by foreign aid. Villagers did not pay; Brishti received an honorarium of thirty taka (0.38 USD) for each form submitted, disbursed by TIE from the foundation's project budget.

Although the RTI "awareness-building" session followed the same format as the regular group session Brishti had just conducted and it took place in a village where Brishti had previously run groups for housewives and adolescent girls, Brishti was viewed as an extension of the state or at least a broker for it. People made demands on her to bring them handouts and complained about infrastructure (such as village roads and latrines) that had been promised by members of parliament and local officials but had not been built. These demands were made tentatively, and people nodded sheepishly each time Brishti explained with exasperation that she did not provide those services, which they already knew because of three years of experience with her. Yet this fact did not stop them from making similar claims on her each time she visited in the capacity of RTI work. If she was going to assume the role of intermediary for government services, they in turn saw fit to make the counterperformance of supplicant to the state.

People understood their relationship with iAgents who provided RTI services as citizen to state-extension agent. Such a relationship invoked a sharp hierarchy, deep distrust of the value of promises made by the agent, accusations of corruption, and belligerent demands. iAgents struggled to enlist people to ask questions and visit government offices because villagers evaluated iAgents through the lens of what the state had not delivered and through the lens of villagers' previous failures to secure these same entitlements. The RTI program proved to be so problematic that Brishti and other iAgents revolted against it and informed TIE that they refused to participate any longer, a process I detail in chapter 6.

On other days, Brishti sold ICT-based services such as topping up mobile phone credits (as a commission agent of cellular service providers), downloading songs and music videos to people's phones, opening email and Facebook accounts, producing passport photographs, and setting up Skype conversations with migrant relatives. These services operated on a pay-per-use model and usually targeted young customers, especially boys. They conveyed special status to Brishti as a wielder of technology and an enabler of connections (such as to kinsmen working abroad), which other service providers did not offer.

Brishti served as a bilateral program extension worker for a program called Aponjon of USAID and the Bangladesh government, which sent health information to expecting and new mothers via text message. She cycled distances far beyond her usual working area to register women in the program, which meant filling out painstakingly long forms that were thrown out by the Aponjon staff if a single mistake was evident. Aponjon paid iAgents 10 taka per correct form and a bonus if they exceeded their targets (such as five hundred forms per month).

iAgents did not take fees from women they registered, but Aponjon deducted 2 taka per text message from the mobile phone accounts of the clients. Because iAgents were often soliciting registrations in villages where they lacked prior social connection, they operated in an information-extraction and assembly-line mode. They encountered pregnant women and demanded information from them without explaining the program. They represented themselves as NGO employees and extrapolated data to fill in parts of the form at a later point. They competed to surpass the targets TIE set for them so that they might win awards.

TIE negotiated with the national birth and death registration office to outsource this government function to iAgents. iAgents entered details on a form online, which citizens then needed to get printed as a certificate at a local office. They were not paid for this entry service by the state or the citizens, but they charged for internet time used and for printing confirmation pages at the time of entry, thus disaggregating the meaning of this act to its component logistical and technical parts.

Brishti and other iAgents conducted market research for Yamada, a major Japanese multinational electronics firm (Huang 2020). A team of executives from Yamada visited Lalpur three times during my residence there. They tasked iAgents with filling out multipage questionnaires with off-grid households regarding their daily and monthly energy usage as well as their willingness to pay for Yamada products. Yamada conducted a pilot project for a "base-of-the-pyramid" social business installing solar panels on the center's roof in Lalpur and using iAgents as marketers and distributors of photovoltaic batteries to off-grid and riverine areas. iAgents were paid fifty taka per questionnaire correctly completed and were left on their own to determine price points for battery rental to households.

FIGURE 12. Women often do not know their mobile phone numbers by recall (while men, who more regularly share their contact details, seem to take pride in rattling off their numbers from memory). This woman shows an iAgent her number (written on the inside cover of a torn schoolbook) so that she can be registered for Aponjon. Photo by author.

Conflicting Relational Forms

How did iAgents such as Brishti reconcile the relational schematics of the multiple services with the varying self-images and external perceptions they provoked? How did they devise strategies to differentiate themselves from less aspirational livelihood identities and draw connections to those that wielded a higher status?

The challenges of being an iAgent exist within the realm of work outside the home and are also tied to personal relationships. Rahela, as she narrates below, experienced intense ambiguity and ambivalence when she first learned about the iAgent opportunity.

> Having been kicked out of the house by my father as a result of accepting the iAgent position, I passed my days at the home of a distant relative. Every dawn, I would take my bicycle out on the path. People said, "You call us to these group sessions because you work for an NGO. So why are you charging us?" People whispered that I was running a scam to take their money and run away. In the village, some people worked abroad. Using the laptop and modem, I started using Skype so relatives could talk with them. I enjoyed watching the migrant's surprised mother, father, wife, and children when they saw the moving faces of their loved ones on the screen. Now, whenever they wanted, they could speak face-to-face, all for paying just 200 taka per hour! Before, I wouldn't have hesitated to let an aunty from next door use my phone to call her son in Dhaka. But now, they told me in the TIE training that I have to be entrepreneurial and earn money from this equipment. Otherwise, how would I repay TIE for all the things they gave me?

Rahela's narrative conveys the ambivalence that characterized a young woman's transition into iAgent work. Facing opposition from family members, converting affective ties into commercialized ones, and being subjected to social stigma accompanied the optimism of a new opportunity and the pressure of fulfilling contractual obligations with the social enterprise.

Rahela provided communication services for a fee, whereas previously such a transaction would have been approached in the form of help (*shahaja*) and reciprocity important to the moral economy of kinship and patronage. Such an act of commodification "refers to the process of assigning market value to goods or services that previously existed outside of the market" (Constable 2009, 50). While market exchanges regularly transpired in village settings, even among kin and neighbors, a young woman would be unlikely to offer any goods or services for purchase. For most people, interactions such as borrowing mobile phones still existed outside the market. Tensions arose for iAgents who were obligated to assign market value to non-market exchanges and convince people why this transformation was necessary. They needed to justify that charging for such forms of "help" was not due to selfish or other negative behaviors.

iAgents often went out of their way to help others outside of their work to demonstrate that they had not lost the values of reciprocity. This "help" included assisting in food preparation and house mending, opening savings accounts and negotiating purchases, and making their personal bank accounts accessible to their fathers. Thus, the iAgent model achieved a third order of exploitation. First, it extracted the labor power of young women without compensating them for the full value of their labor. Second, the young women needed to self-exploit as entrepreneurs in order to earn a living and deliver payments to the bank and the licensing body. And third, their new skills, networks, and access to opportunities became susceptible to their kin who made claims on them, and they allowed themselves to be exploited by these relatives by acting congruently with the moral economy of kinship and notions of ethical personhood.

At the same time, the "meanings and importance of commodities are transformed in relation to particular local understandings of modernity as related to subjectivity and intimate relationships" (Constable 2009, 55). Some activities, in their relative ability to bring social value by creating favorable subjectivities or spaces of social intimacy, were more easily commodified than others. The laptop-modem-iAgent service assemblage as "commodity" gained importance (and raised the esteem of the iAgent) when Skype enabled people to communicate with distant loved ones.

The daily schedule of Mita, the exemplary but fictitious iAgent who appeared in TIE's promotional and training videos, is relevant here. Mita worked day and night to prepare for, deliver, and follow up on services she provided to her customers. In the seamless stream of Mita's presented life, the fact that the different activities possessed different rationalities and income streams behind them was entirely obscured. Such activities necessitated different subject positions and relational modes that iAgents continuously had to adopt and switch between. Pulling apart the sociofinancial logics of multiple services, I focus on the often-conflicting expectations they evoked in real life. By contrast, in the stylized life of Mita, villagers transitioned among being relatives, beneficiaries, patients, citizens, customers, beneficiaries, and supplicants as smoothly as Mita shifted among the roles of daughter-in-law, teacher, NGO worker, broker, peddler, patron, and housewife. While people routinely related with one another in different ways across contexts and regularly turned one another into fictive kin (a custom in Bangladesh), the social expectations invoked by iAgents' multiple positionalities in this case often contradicted one another. How did "relational work" actually work when simultaneous relational forms clashed?

Rather than seeking to stabilize a particular relational position, iAgents benefited by flexibly leveraging different ones when it suited their purposes. When introducing themselves to new people, iAgents often described themselves as "coming from Atno Bishash," the NGO that hosted the iAgent center with which many people were already familiar because of its long history in the region. In this instance, ambiguity in the nature of the relationship was desired as opposed to well-defined boundary-making. In outward-facing representations (for example, to funders, banks, and foreign visitors), iAgents were independent and financially self-sustaining entrepreneurs, as opposed to salaried employees. In their self-representations with villagers, they often emphasized their alliance with the center NGO to establish credibility. They kept up the appearance of being NGO employees as long as they provided services for which beneficiaries did not need to pay directly (such as Aponjon registration, group sessions, and RTI). Yet as soon as people wanted their blood pressure checked, or iAgents realized that aspiring migrants needed passport photos, they began to assert their status as independent entrepreneurs who took fees for the convenience provided. When discussing the fee structure of their services, they stressed that they were independent businesswomen who did not receive a salary and who relied on the income from fees.

To the extent that iAgents could determine how they spent their time, they gravitated toward activities that generated the most profit and encoded status markers such as the use of digital equipment or connection to foreigners and powerful others. Had iAgents been fully autonomous, they might have focused entirely on activities that both enabled them to engage with people on terms that increased their status and sense of aspirational self and earned them a decent living. The ways in which TIE attempted to control their use of time, activities undertaken, and services provided are discussed later. Yet I note here that iAgents were forced to perform all the services TIE instructed them to do, which resulted in the relational contradictions discussed above and therefore necessitated extraordinary relational work.

Transforming Social Relations in the Community

This chapter so far has explored the difficulties iAgents experienced in navigating social relationships with their clients due to the mismatch of transactional logics and the meanings underpinning the services they provided. Rahela's narrative shows us that the idea of women's paid work outside the home, regardless of the type, was a central source of conflict between young women and their families.[6]

The prevalence of women in NGO work, as participants in income-generating schemes and as frontline workers and project staff members (and, rarely, as managers and leaders), provided a key avenue for easing the process of social acceptance of women's roles outside the home. Training by NGOs in topics such as health and nutrition, agriculture, and social work conferred upon recipients a mark of experience and status as those who carried a respected type of knowledge. The lifestyle changes of women working in NGOs slowly began to index status, including their increased but still limited practical freedoms through mobility, income to use at their personal discretion, and confidence in interactions with non-kin men (Karim 2011).

Once a woman held a coveted NGO position, she would likely be able to obtain another NGO role subsequently. Village-level NGO workers often held long track records with an assortment of acronymed organizations in their work histories. In a village in Lalpur, Rahela liaised with a particular woman to mobilize group sessions and call people to meetings. Three times in six months we arrived to discover that this woman had switched jobs and was the village extension worker for yet another NGO. Regardless of the new project, her role in it only incremented her status as a locus of activity and externally procured resources.

iAgents flaunted their multiple roles and associations in different ways according to whom they wanted to impress. Rahela carried a small box containing the official SIM cards she owned and happily explained each of them when low-level, particularly female office workers in the NGO Atno Bishash commented on how many she had. "Listen, I'll tell you. . . . This one is for Aponjon, these ones are for Grameenphone and Robi flexiload [to top up phone credits], this one is from the program where the member of parliament talks to villagers through Skype on my computer, these three . . ." The regularity and context with which Rahela engaged in these assertions implied a desire to assert authority over the less-experienced but higher-status and salaried NGO employees.

The physical appearance and behavior of iAgents performed the work of making the women seem similar to NGO workers (as compared to hawkers) even though they were not employed by any NGO. For women in Bangladesh (as elsewhere), clothing was a marker of age, level of education, status, financial standing, social connectedness, modesty, religious beliefs, and type of work performed. Appropriate dress was an issue of concern for iAgents, who faced resistance from family members and local religious authorities when they left their homes to render services. Local imams initially disapproved of the program on the grounds that these women were violating *purdah* norms, but TIE explained how the women's dress and behavior were compatible with *purdah*. Appearance (a uniform, branded paraphernalia, particular styles of grooming) and deportment (long strides, head held high, smiling) are also "material signifiers of belonging," and they styled these individuals as upwardly mobile professionals, distinguishable from lowly hawkers (Dolan 2012, 6). For these women, *purdah* was less a matter of their bodily modesty (for they believed they were virtuous actors in their intentions and behaviors) and more about emphasizing symbols of professional legitimacy.

In TIE's iAgent model, the iAgent's house is the "service center," and her working area is the surrounding five-village radius. To overcome the stigma of cycling and working, iAgents avoided their own and proximate villages when they began the job and walked with their bicycles until they were sufficiently far away. Then they started providing services in places where they possessed fewer personal connections and where they were more likely to be interpreted as experienced NGO workers. This behavior resembled that of destitute women who begged or sought domestic or agricultural labor by traveling to distant places where they would not be recognized. It also contradicted common development assumptions that one's "social capital" was a desirable resource to use in the beginning stages of entrepreneurial work.

Working in conjunction with NGOs was not entirely unproblematic. It was often associated with the microcredit sector, especially when local NGOs increasingly succumbed to foreign donors' preferences for funding programs that were "self-sufficient" and financially "sustainable." A distrust of loan collectors prevailed after people witnessed the destruction that microfinance could wreak on social relationships. The intentions of NGOs were scrutinized. Villagers feared that visiting foreigners wanted to kidnap Bangladeshi children and sell them abroad.[7] People in some villages who treated iAgents with suspicion said that these individuals took money from a Christian NGO and would attempt to convert them. Stories abounded of savings and insurance programs that collected money from people for years before suddenly disappearing. Being cheated was an experience with which all poor families were familiar, and new schemes brought by unknown others were met with distrust.

As Rahela's story indicates, iAgents faced harsh opposition from their immediate family members when they joined. Riding bicycles was socially stigmatizing for women, and new iAgents faced unpleasant comments by villagers as they cycled past. Some people proclaimed that the physical activity harmed the women's virginity and fertility, and others said that it violated *purdah* norms, both of which diminished the women's future marriage prospects.

Rahela narrated different versions of the following story for TIE's promotional material, to visiting journalists, and to me when I first met her. The extent to which the story was embellished is unclear. Its significance for this chapter lies in the framing of her experience as a turning-point story. It was told through the narrative arc of intense hardship and suffering overcome through perseverance

and hard work. This form of storytelling and self-representation carried resonance both with local idioms of lament and the virtue of struggle and with
international-development evaluations of authenticity and reliance on the Protestant work ethic as a dominant moral principle. It thus carried weight with
multiple types of audiences.

For many years, Rahela's father had opposed her activities outside the house,
such as her formal education. He said that if she had been a boy, her behavior
might have been acceptable, but "for an adult female to study and for a beggar to
keep an elephant, it is equally senseless!" He shouted angrily when he caught her
using kerosene to study at night by lamplight. He ran a small trading business by
sitting on a mat in the village market with low-cost goods spread out around him,
most of which he sold on credit. He knew that a household could not run on such
a meager cash flow, and the cost of kerosene was increasing. When Rahela used
government scholarship money to pay the registration fee (900 taka; 12 USD)
for her secondary-school examination, her father grew irate and shouted that he
could have expanded his business with the money. When she proudly announced
that she had scored an A-, hoping for validation, he replied, "It's good news about
your mark. But girls studying will yield no benefit, so now it's time for your wedding. I will start looking for a boy."

When Rahela became an iAgent instead, her father did not allow her to return
home. She stayed those early days with a distant aunt near the Atno Bishash
office. The already-grueling process of training and beginning the first work was
made more difficult by having to endure the emotional stress of temporary ostra-
cization from her parents' home. But despite her father's disapproval, her mother
gave her 12,000 taka (154 USD) from her women's savings group for the security
deposit for TIE (another common way that the iAgent program was sustained by
women's kinship ties and gendered access to poverty capital). Three months later,
when Rahela received her first honorarium from TIE for conducting a round
of group sessions, and she placed the money in her father's hands, he began to
change his opinion about her work. With her subsequent income, she repaid her
mother's loan and interest payments and then built a shop next to their house to
sell consumer goods. Thereafter, she continued to be the primary income earner
in the family.

The freedom of movement and choice in matters of study, work, and future
marriage were contingent on Rahela's continuous positioning of herself as the
main provider for the family. Rather than a constraint, the new kinship role
was consistent with her earlier desires to help her family rise out of precariousness, and it was her mother who had made this work possible for her. The
ways in which she and other iAgents (ones who had achieved a relative degree
of economic success in the pilot-model locations) spent their incomes were not

necessarily indicative of an eager consumerism within a rising, rural, lower-middle class. Rather, they indexed the aspirational images and roles iAgents wished to construct for themselves in the context of the changing relationships they experienced in their families.

The primary expenditures of iAgents, aside from the costs of maintaining and expanding their businesses and contributing to regular household consumption needs, featured items that might be read as consumerist. They bought new clothing for themselves, including elaborately sequined *shalwar kameez* sets that indicated their newly achieved distance from hard manual labor. They renovated their parents' houses by using corrugated tin panels instead of thatched bamboo. They bought furniture for their houses, supported siblings' school fees, and purchased requisite gifts and food items for celebrations such as Eid ul-fitr.[8]

Paying attention to "the complex agency underlying consumption practices, beliefs, and motivations can help avoid reductionist views of social and cultural transformation and may provide a richer and more complete understanding of local experiences of change" (Mills 1997, 55). While TIE's model expected iAgents to advance their independent positions by investing earnings in their businesses and personal consumption practices, iAgents said that the best way to improve their social standing was to fulfill and then exceed the social expectations placed upon them, which featured investing in family and household improvements. The social value that iAgents placed on wealth was generated in its relational properties, rather than in its individual accumulation. In this way, the consumption aspirations and practices of iAgents can also be examined as a field of cultural struggle, as an aspect of the relational work they undertook to make claims about their new social and relational positions and prove the value of their work.

In Rahela's story of transformation, she said that sometimes at night while sleeping, she realized that her father was brushing her hair and uttering the words, "I was wrong, my dear daughter. I should not have discriminated between a boy and a girl." Yet despite being the main income-earner supporting her natal family of six and having gained a measure of freedom of choice about everyday matters, as a son might have enjoyed, Rahela was also expected to fulfill the role of daughter. That expectation implied that she would continue to behave in ways that would secure her a good marriage when and in the way her parents expected and, after marriage, to perform all the duties expected of a good wife in addition to her outside work. Depending on the circumstance, one or another of these roles would be salient and necessitate different behaviors and subjectivities at different moments.[9]

In sum, all of these efforts at self-positioning needed to be continuously reinforced. This constant relational work is due to the myriad (and sometimes contradictory) relational logics that inhere in the simultaneous positioning of iAgents as daughters, sisters, and potential future wives; and as NGO representatives, independent entrepreneurs, and market service providers. The concluding discussion complicates the linear model of social stigma turning into social acceptance (shown in the turning-point narratives advanced by TIE) by demonstrating how ambiguity and blurred relational modes continued to be fundamental to relationships long after iAgent work gained some social acceptance.

The Burden of Flexibility

This chapter demonstrates that the multiple types of relationships that characterized iAgents' interactions with customers and family members shifted according to context, service, and other people's social expectations. Rather than efforts to stabilize a particular relationship, the act of flexibly switching *between* different contrasting relational arrangements was itself a strategy for negotiating transactions.

The case of iAgent Taspia (in the failed Amirhat location), who tried to convince her uncle to help her sell consumer goods, illustrates this point. Separate from the agreement with Unilever in the Aparajita project to sell fast-moving products in Lalpur, the Amirhat center contracted with Square Consumer Products, a Bangladeshi company. The Amirhat center's executive director, Sabbir Hossain, invested his own money in purchasing a bulk quantity of Square products (soap, shampoo, washing powder, sunscreen, skin-whitening cream, talcum powder, and baby food) at trade price. He forced all iAgents to take home several boxes of these products to sell within two weeks and then deliver to him the full income, after which he would compensate them with some marginal benefit (less than one percent commission). iAgents would have to pay him for the full cost of the products after two weeks even if they did not manage to sell them, which provoked anxiety. "If I sell you soap, you will not buy soap again until you finish the first bar. Two weeks is impossible," reasoned Taspia, highlighting the temporal incongruities between the expected sales regime and the rhythms of actual life. Trying to overcome this problem, several days before Sabbir expected his profits, Taspia called on her mother's brother (*mama*) to help her sell the products from his shop in the bazaar near his village. Agreeing, he visited Taspia's house. First she employed a business-transaction logic with him. "Look at the range of products I have," she began, carefully enumerating their variety and qualities. "But where is Lifebuoy and Lux?" he interrupted as he pawed through the box. "What are these brands? They're more expensive. People don't know them, so they won't buy them." Withdrawing his offer, he explained that his shop would do better if he sold familiar brands.

Realizing that the position of market transactor was failing her, Taspia switched to one of a subordinate affective familial role. In Bangladesh and elsewhere in Asia, the role of mother's brother implies a relationship of indulgence, and *mamas* are supposed to fulfill their nieces' and nephews' requests (Gardner 1995, 29; Lamb 2000, 27). Taspia began by telling her uncle about the "tension" she was experiencing by having to sell these products and how unfairly the center was treating her. She mentioned the suffering her mother (his sister) endured because she lacked sons, hence the pressure on Taspia to support the family. She appealed to him for his help rather than his business partnership. The tone of her voice changed to that of supplicant, by using the kind of complaint or lament expressed by a person in a position of marginality or inequality to make claims on a superior. She brought him a chair and hollered to her mother to bring tea and biscuits. After hesitating, Taspia's uncle agreed to take the products from her if he could purchase them at trade price. Yet Taspia would have to pay the market price to Sabbir (at the center), and she would wind up with a loss. In the end, not taking her uncle's offer, Taspia tried to sell the products on her own by traveling house to house like a hawker.

This example highlights the partial nature of relational stability, because people continue to occupy other structural positions even while they take on new ones. This observation is magnified if the new role, such as that of iAgent, does not yet have a defined or commonly understood set of rules and meanings that other people might understand.

Money circulated unevenly within iAgent families. Taspia and Rahela had invested their labor, savings, and connections in rebuilding their houses and in building shops in which their male family members could work. Of the monthly income Taspia made by working for a hybrid-seed company (after having resigned from being an iAgent), she gave it all to her father. Rahela's earnings as an iAgent were similarly available to her father who made claims on them; he asked her to withdraw sums from her bank account for his use and did not repay them. Yet this relationship was not mutual or reciprocal. If Rahela needed cash from her parents, they expected her to borrow according to a strict timeline for repayment.

Taspia subsidized the cost of living of her elder sister and nephew because they lived in her natal home eleven months of the year while the husband and father worked in Dhaka. Yet if Taspia needed cash to register for her examinations, her brother-in-law (who earned a handsome salary in corporate employment [*chakri*]), if he helped at all, loaned money to her with interest. Her income became collective property in the household, while her access to family resources needed to be qualified and followed a commercial logic of return. Taspia's identity as entrepreneur and her identity as daughter/sister/sister-in-law were differently evoked in ways that did not always result favorably for her. We can understand how relational work actually works out (that is, what the outcomes are) if we emphasize the dynamics of power and inequality in relational work and add the role of ambiguity. If both parties have different understandings of or interests in how the relationship should be organized, then the power imbalance between them is significant to the outcome.

The women were suspended between the expectations of the iAgent assemblage and longer-standing social values, which added further complexity to these issues. Poor women were constrained by poverty as well as by hierarchies of gender and kinship. Lamia Karim (2011) documents how NGOs, targeting existing vulnerabilities, asserted themselves in these relationships such that breaches in contract (such as non-payment of microloan installments) implied breaches in the collective good of the community. "One can see a shift toward a very important transformation: the making of market subjects who are caught between market principles and existing social expectations," Karim writes (2011, 130). This tension was especially significant in the case of iAgents, whose structural position (as poor young women) allowed them to be easily exploited. If an uncle refused to pay for a service provided by an iAgent, she lacked any means of enforcing the completion of the transaction. Many iAgents were uncomfortable about taking money from people, since doing so was not previously a component of most of their relationships.

As a last effort to make the iAgent project beneficial for her, after being unable to sell her services on her own in villages, Taspia began taking her digital medical equipment to a private clinic in the nearby market. She struck an agreement with the doctor there that she would serve his clients (his technology not being digital and commanding less authority) by using the blood-glucose monitor, blood-grouping kit, blood-pressure cuff, weight scale, and thermometer. Clients paid the doctor, and he and Taspia split the fee evenly. While he retained part of her usual profit, they charged more per service, and she gained access to a steady stream of clients. She hoped that his high-status position would mean a timely payment for services.

Often she and I sat late at night in his clinic, long after clients had stopped visiting, and waited for him to hand over her cut of the income. Taspia said that this arrangement was her best chance at earning money, and so she did not want to antagonize the relationship by asking for the payment directly. Although on the surface Taspia and the doctor entered into an agreement on an equal, reciprocal footing, in reality gender, age, and professional inequalities still played a role. Sometimes he did not pay her the correct amount, and other times he asked to "borrow" the equipment to use himself (presumably to retain the full profit).

She found it increasingly difficult to protest against these practices. Yet her social position of vulnerability (he could cut her out of the deal at any moment) meant that aligning herself with the clinic and being exploited by the doctor was better than being exploited by clients who did not pay at all.

The ethnography in this chapter shows the uncomfortable ambiguities involved in iAgent work, especially in contexts of social inequality and socioeconomic change. As a heuristic device, the relational work concept helps to elucidate the ways in which the actual work of being an iAgent contained within it a multiplicity of social, political, and transactional logics that iAgents needed to switch between flexibly. The achievement of the results of "women's empowerment" through entrepreneurship models was thus contingent on multiple structural and relational factors, all class- and gender-inflected, and all in flux. A processual, diachronic methodology and analysis yields insight into the contours of these processes in ways that the synchronic snapshot-style approaches often used by development practitioners and nonethnographic research disciplines cannot. Ambiguity is what allows the project to work, through the creative efforts of the participants to manage multiple and often conflicting roles and relations. The project also produces ambiguity, necessary for its ability to appeal to a diverse body of resource-givers.

An analysis of the tensions between the expectations of community members and TIE employees concerning iAgents and between different service modalities has shown that ambiguity inheres in situations where it is not possible or desirable to define and fix the hard boundaries of a relationship. Transformations, far from complete and final, are instead partial, continuous, and often internally contradictory, especially when the relational work of several transacting individuals is irreconcilable. In times and places of dramatic change, people find themselves occupying subject positions that lack precedent.

Finally, given the insecure position of iAgents as the more vulnerable parties in most transactions, these ambiguities and relational multiplicities did not often play out in the iAgents' favor. The women labored at the bottom of the hierarchy in both directions of this multifaceted interface, among family and clients and in negotiation with TIE and the wider iAgent network of players. The work of iAgents never took place in impersonal marketplaces; rather, it took up the properties of existing social relationships and expectations. In the final two chapters, I detail the relational work TIE performed to both implement its model—a process that favored misrepresentation and ambiguity—and attempt to reconcile the enterprise's central contradictions.

Part III

RECONFIGURING CLASS RELATIONS

iAgent Ayrin's Story

My name is Ayrin, and this is my life story. We are two sisters and four brothers and have a very big family. The things I'm saying right now are what I've learned from my sisters. My father's house was on the banks of a river. Not everyone knows about life on the banks of a river. Lives on the riverbank get built up and then destroyed. The same thing happened to our lives too. At first, my father's financial condition was good. There was no poverty. Everything was okay. My parents were nice people and kind hearted. My brothers were older so when they grew up they started managing the family. My father was improving financially. But one day our house and lands drowned under flood water. We lost everything. This is how it is.

Father decided that we won't live on the riverbank anymore. Mother said I was seven months old when we came to this new place. It's been almost seventeen years that we've been here. I know there's aspirations and hardship in everyone's life. But we suffered after coming here. It was hard to start everything from nothing again in a new place. I heard from my sister that they had gone through a lot of hardship during that time. Even my brothers had to quit school and work in other people's houses. But gradually it got a little better.

My sister also didn't study much. Her marriage was a sudden event. No one knows what the future holds for us. It took two lakhs taka for her marriage, including a dowry of one lakh taka. Every parent wants their child to live a happy life. That's why my father didn't think about the rest of the family and instead spent so much money on dowry to get my sister married. The same thing happened to me. I didn't know that my life would become full of sorrows. Today I will write everything.

I won't talk about my school life. I wasn't a good student, but I tried my best. I wanted to go to police college and become a policewoman. But a different thing happened to me.

It was 2013. My brother had a friend named Farid. Farid worked at ACRU. One day my brother met him in the market. Farid asked my brother, "Do you have any sisters?" My brother said, "Yes, I do. But why?" Farid asked, "What does she do?" My brother told him that I had passed high school that year. Then Farid said, "ACRU is starting a new project. It's a very good one. Your sister could work there." The next day, my brother met Farid again, and Farid explained everything about the work. After listening to everything, my brother said, "Okay, I will talk to Ayrin about this when I go home." He said to me, "There's a new project at ACRU named iAgent. They're taking many girls there." I said, "If you think it's good, then I can try."

The next day, my brother took me to ACRU. I met Sabbir there and he took my interview. He asked me many questions. He said, "The work you'll be doing here is one kind of business." I asked, "How can I do business? I've never done it before." He said, "We will show you how to earn. But it's mandatory to learn computers for this work." There were many computers in ACRU. I asked, "Can I learn here?" Sabbir said, "These computers are used only for official purposes. You have to learn outside."

I was admitted to a computer-training course in the market. It cost almost 6,000 taka. I went to every single class. Then I went back to ACRU. There were nine other girls there selected for the next trainings. I was very happy because I would meet new friends. For the training, we stayed in the old office of ACRU. We had so much fun. I could make everyone laugh. The next morning our training started. They showed us many things, but I don't remember them.

Sabbir then told us, "You will start work now. Talk to Rifat brother [an ACRU employee] about your work. He will visit your groups." But I didn't take Rifat with me because whenever he went, I had to spend for him too—transport because he didn't want to ride a bicycle, snacks because he grew tired quickly, and so on. But finally I formed my groups.

I faced many problems during field work. Most of the people of Bangladesh are very poor. When I made the groups and wrote people's names, they thought I was there to help them. I told them, "I can't help you." But they didn't believe me and I felt very bad. But I did fieldwork every day. I was very busy and tired. I had to work very hard. People would say a lot of bad things to me. Still I did not give up; I kept working. One month passed but I couldn't earn. One day they discussed in ACRU how to earn from the groups. The next day I earned 300 taka. But I couldn't do anything for myself with that money. I had to buy necessary equipment if I'd used them up. Even then, I did not mind too much because I thought, "I will earn again tomorrow."

Another month was spent. If I faced any problem, there were no qualified or skilled people who would solve the problem. If I told Sabbir, he would say, "Can't you solve this by yourself?" He'd always talk like this.

We had a health training one day. I liked so much that I could give people suggestions about health. I thought of myself as a nurse. After that, I started working in the groups again.

And then everyone began to know that I could provide different types of services. People took my services, but they did not want to pay any money. Even if they did, they wouldn't pay the full money. They thought that I worked in an NGO and that I got paid there. I told them many times that I do not get any wages. The income I get from here is my salary. The situation was getting worse day by day.

Almost three months passed. Then one day Sabbir called us and said, "You have to pay your loan. And from this month you will have to pay the installment. Be ready for all the installments." Then I said, "I have no income. So how will I pay?" Sabbir told me, "How can I know?" I said again that I had no income and could not pay any money. I said, "You told me that if there is no income, then it can be given later by ACRU. So you take care of it now." Saying this, I went back home. Many days passed. I talked to the other girls and found they were ready to quit. They asked me whether I am quitting or not. I said, "I don't know yet."

After some days I learned that they would all be submitting their equipment and quitting. Kanika and Kabir and someone else from TIE came from Dhaka to visit us. They asked why we don't want to work. They asked me many things, but I didn't tell them anything. I asked the girls, "Are you really not going to work?" They said, "How can we work like this? There is no income. Even if there is, we can't pay the installments with that amount." I didn't say anything. I just listened to them. When the people of TIE asked us if we wanted to work or not, everyone said they wouldn't. But I sat there silently. They all gave back their equipment.

I went home and told everyone, "I will work, and I will see the end of it." I believed that if I didn't give the equipment back, nothing would happen. So I didn't return them. The next day, Kanika and Kabir from TIE came to our house and said,

"Look, all of your colleagues have quit. How are you going to work alone?" I asked, "Why not? ACRU will help me, and Sabbir will pay my loan. Sabbir said he would take care of it if I don't have any income. So now Sabbir will do whatever needs to be done. I am not giving anything back." Kanika and Kabir left. One day Sabbir called me and said, "Ayrin, give them back." After some days, he came to my house and asked for the equipment. But TIE telephoned me and said, "Sabbir has not paid your loan, so if anyone from ACRU comes, do not give them your equipment. Instead, send them to TIE." But Sabbir gave me repeated threats. He said, "If you don't submit these, bad things will happen." For many days, Sabbir kept threatening me. I stopped doing field work. I didn't do any work at all. I used to serve people if someone came to my house, but I stopped that too.

Many days passed. Then in 2014 I fell in love with a man named Sagar. His house was on the other side of the river. I met Sagar through a wrong number. We fell in love. Then there was talk of marriage. Sagar brought the marriage proposal to my house. He pretended that a middleman had told him about me. Our marriage was fixed. Sagar's parents demanded a lot of money from us as dowry. It was about three lakhs taka but my parents made it one and a half lakhs. There were expenses for jewelry, food, and other things, which cost almost two lakhs taka. Even then my parents and brothers agreed.

After the marriage, I moved to my husband's house. Everything there was new. I felt bad. After staying there for a week, I visited my father's house. Then I saw that Sabbir had brought many people to our house. About fifteen people were there. They were important people of the village. They said, "Ayrin, return your equipment. If not, it will not be good." My in-laws were there so I didn't say anything. Then my husband lied to them by saying, "The equipment is in our house." After hearing this, all the people left. Then I went back to my husband's house. After marriage, the husband's house becomes everything for a girl. I decided to take the equipment to my husband's house. The income can help the family.

I thought, this is a riverside area. There's nothing much to do here for a living, and there are no services. So I thought my income might increase there. So one day, I came home to my father's house and took all the equipment to my husband's house. My brother forbade me. But I didn't listen to him. How could I have known that this was waiting for me? Then I earned a lot in my husband's area. My husband often took the equipment and earned money with them too.

Many days passed. I always noticed that my mother-in-law didn't like me. Day by day Sagar started to change. He tortured me. I was a victim. But what could I do? I married the person I liked. I took all the hardships. Then suddenly Sagar began to beat me a lot. One day I left everything and went to my father's house. After seeing my condition, my parents were very sad. They took me to the doctor. My in-laws said they would not accept me anymore. Sagar always valued his mother's opinion more, so he agreed.

When I met Sagar for the last time, I told him that I wanted all of my equipment back. He said he wouldn't give them back. I did not bring anything to my father's house. I even left the jewelry in my husband's house. I was in that family for only six months. Now my life is ruined. I do not know if Sagar will give those things back. When the people whom you love leave you, nothing feels good. So I decided that I would divorce Sagar. I'm still in my father's house. But I did not accept defeat.

I was admitted to school again. I've decided to complete my studies, but I won't marry again. If I marry, then my family has to spend five lakhs taka once more. If you want to have a government job in Bangladesh, then you have to pay five or six lakhs taka for a bribe. There is no job without a bribe.

I want to spend five or six lakhs taka for a bribe to get a government job. And I want to spend the rest of my life this way. But I don't have any way of earning money anymore. My brother is not friends with his friend Farid anymore, and he blames me. My father says we will not have any dealings with any NGO ever again. People don't know about the future. If they did, life wouldn't be so hard. I am only twenty-three years old now. I don't know how much more sorrow is waiting for me.

MIDDLE-CLASS PROJECTS AND THE DEVELOPMENT MORAL ECONOMY

Some people think that the network of UISCs [union information service centers] came from Grameen [Bank]. This is not true. It came from the iAgent model. When we piloted the rural information center as the nucleus of iAgent activity, one of our founding members took the idea and left, and he piloted two centers under UNDP [United Nations Development Programme] funding. Later, he brought the idea to the PMO [prime minister's office], which rolled out 4,500 UISCs. We lost our recognition because of the personal politics of our ex-colleague against me.

—Dr. Adnan Khan, CEO of TIE, Dhaka

People call me "The Father of iAgent." Actually, iAgent is not the brainchild of any single person but of thousands. Service recipients, iAgents, and local organizations provided suggestions that we have taken on board. But sometimes people highlight me. I *can* say that I took the full pain of building the iAgent model, whether it is my brainchild or not. It was my sweat out there in the field, mentoring every iAgent and recruiting every partner. But to say that *Adnan bhai* is the founder. . . . Can you believe that he listed himself as founder of iAgent on the Wikipedia page?

—Rohan Alam, former iAgent team leader in TIE, Dhaka

TIE is our donor, yes, but iAgent is not just their project. We jointly created the model, but TIE provided the blueprints to ten other NGOs around the country. Then they sold it to SSI [Sustainable Sourcing International] without calling us to share their plans. In all the literature, it is only TIE and iAgents, they don't ever say it's a joint project. [*He gestured aggressively as he showed me a glossy brochure with a picture of an iAgent helping an elderly woman conduct a Skype video call.*] But this is *our* girl, and this is cheating. When the scale-up model was started with SSI, they said,

"You have to take a license to be a center, to have iAgents." But *we*
are the creator!

—Shoriful (Shorif) Islam, executive director of Atno Bishash, Lalpur Upazila,
northwestern Bangladesh

Shorif *bhai* takes credit for all Atno Bishash projects and all of our
NGO resources, especially iAgent. But he exploits them as NGO
workers instead of treating them as entrepreneurs. He knows
nothing about how it works. He just sucks up to TIE, saying *"Ji sir,
ji sir* ['yes sir']" to everything Rohan *bhai* and his team says. These
NGO executive directors are all really executive dictators, talking
about democracy and empowerment but never relinquishing any
power and using all the resources for their personal benefit. But
who was out there making the iAgent project work? It was me, not
Shorif *bhai*.

—Zahir Ahmed, former iAgent team leader at Atno Bishash, Lalpur Upazila

Who can claim responsibility for the iAgent model? Aside from demonstrating
the contested nature of ownership between and within all layers in the hierarchy
of people involved, this question yields no straightforward answer. So far we have
explored the hidden, invisible, and unacknowledged efforts of iAgents, whose
physical, ethical, and relational labor underwrote the program's "success" and
profits. Meanwhile, other more powerful groups vied to assert control over and
gain credit for the social enterprise model. While acknowledgment and rewards
for success—as well as the power of the ownership claim made—accrue upward
in the chain of influence, practical risk and responsibility for failure transfer
downward.[1] The observation that there is an uneven balance of power when it
comes to acts of claims-making both in the chain between donors and development organizations and within these entities is not new.[2] Contributing to the
literature on development networks, this chapter adds a nuanced account of
the ways in which social enterprises—and contestations over them at different
levels—are embedded in people's projects of self-making and class aspirations
of upward mobility.

The competitive drive to lead the cutting edge of development practice has
long characterized the NGO scene in Bangladesh. This ambition was compounded by the expectation of profit-making now enabled through the new
disruptive-innovation zeitgeist and tantalizingly displayed by the monumental
flows of cash being generated through Muhammad Yunus' model of microcredit.
The latest innovative development model thus became the currency of status

among upper-middle-class development professionals. Not only did a shiny new model enable new forms of capital accumulation through its grassroots operations and attract foreign investment but it also generated a reputation for its designer. Yet as we shall see, the iterative growth and the achievement of viability of these models relied not just on women beneficiaries but also on the creative labor of lower-level partners and staff, who were excluded from recognition in political acts of claims-making.

Among the educated urban elite founders, designers, and managers of social enterprises, these contestations manifested as epistemic struggles between embedded, sociological models of social change and economics-derived ones in which technology (and technology-derived metaphors for human behavior) was an appropriate solution to social and political problems.

The more profound violence, however, occurred at the rural sites of these projects, where profit-oriented disruptive development generated contradictions within the long-standing moral economy of NGO-driven development. Development became delinked from existing patron-client relations, local NGOs had to answer more to funders than to beneficiaries, and the poor experienced a diminished ability to make claims to key resources. Thus, the devices of disruptive development, as they produced the social enterprise, interrupted not only the lives of their supposed beneficiaries, as seen in previous chapters, but also the fundamental class dynamics along the entire development value chain. This process was characterized by an antisocial inequality, which supplanted the social inequality and reciprocal relationship of patron-clientalism.

What follows is an ethnographic treatment of different class positions and the ambiguous relationship between policy and practice, conceptualized and implemented in air-conditioned Dhaka offices, in NGO bungalows in villages, and in "the field" where project "impact" supposedly takes place.[3] Showing the significant role that class relations play in the policy-practice relationship builds on Annelise Riles's (2000) notion of the "network" as driven by the power of its aesthetic, instantiated in documents and procedures. Observations about NGO middle-class insecurities and projects of status contribute new insights about the particular aesthetic of contemporary development networks. "Social enterprise" is revealed to be not only a set of business practices but also an ethical discourse and project of ethical self-making among implementers and not just beneficiaries.

Drawing from anthropological understandings of class structures in Bangladesh and ethnographic observations of these changes-in-motion, this chapter focuses on the relational work that the middle classes undertook in order to embark on generative projects to stabilize their social and economic positions. The middle classes in Bangladesh were heavily dependent on NGO employment and funding from global development patrons in order to maintain their socioeconomic status. Their narratives and representations of events (captured in annual reports, Wikipedia pages, human-interest news articles, and interviews with a visiting anthropologist) served as their currency for claiming and maintaining access to these crucial sources of employment and funding.

The NGO middle classes display a changing repertoire of status. In addition to traditional methods of registering social position through accumulation and consumption, the ability to make one's own name through the ownership or authorship of new development models and activities is a crucial aspect of status production. We will see how Rohan Alam at TIE was attracted to the notion of model building via the public fame and heroism of past development-model builders in rural Bangladesh. On a smaller scale, Shorif at the NGO Atno Bishash pursued social work as an ethics of community leadership, which was connected to building his name through what he deemed to be responsible models of NGO patronage.

This chapter also documents a historical process of the changing moral economy of NGO patronage in Bangladesh as international development priorities were redefined to conflict with villagers' expectations of the role NGOs should play in the community.[4] As rural NGO leaders became increasingly compressed between the demands of funders and the petitions of villagers, their middle-class status and economic position grew precarious. The new time cycles of corporate and financial markets, as they drove the routines of poverty capitalism, conflicted with the time of middle-class social reproduction. Generating livelihood security contradicted their ability to fulfill patronage obligations, and they faced accusations of predatory sociality and corruption.

Development orthodoxy is a continuously shifting set of ideas, as are the ways in which local communities have engaged with different types of international resources. Yet at the level of grassroots implementation, donor models of NGO work had a greater "elective affinity" (Weber 1930) with the relational economy of patronage in rural Bangladesh than did newer enterprise models, which disconnected the poor from durable resources for survival, rather than linking them to these resources (Gardner 2012).[5] This process of delinking the distribution of development goods from rural middle-class patron-clientage relations with the poor had profound implications for class inequality and the ability of the poor to make "declarations of dependence" (Ferguson 2013).

This chapter explores the class aspirations and self-making projects of two groups of people centrally implicated in the iAgent social enterprise. These groups are, first, senior- and middle-level management personnel in TIE responsible for designing the iAgent model; and second, leadership and staff members of two NGOs selected as rural information centers to manage a cluster of local iAgents.

Literature on class and the policy-practice relationship in development offers a framework for interpreting the ethnography of the main tiers of NGO workers in the iAgent social enterprise. The events here span the three phases of the iAgent business model described in the introduction: the initial pilot stage operating under a donor-funded NGO structure (experienced by iAgents in Lalpur), a scale-up social enterprise stage employing a multitier commercial license structure (experienced by iAgents in Amirhat), and a social enterprise replication stage using a combined open-source and consulting structure (experienced by iAgents who were being selected just before I left Bangladesh). The relationships among participants and their involvement in and critical commentary on these phases show the particular ways in which models were explained, enforced, critiqued, and undermined by TIE, centers, and iAgents.

Class Projects among the NGO Elite

The New NGO Elite in Context

The book's introduction outlines the particular kinship-oriented patron-clientage that historically organized rural society and class structure in Bangladesh. Yet the old lineage and agricultural patrons were no longer as significant in relationships due to changes in the rural political economy in northwestern Bangladesh. One aspect was the high degree of geographic mobility due to land erosion, inheritance-based subdivision of property, and labor migration for the pursuit of fortunes elsewhere. Another aspect was the increasingly unstable link between landowners and their agricultural laborers, who became casually hired per season in a one-off relationship. Thus, creating status for oneself no longer rested on lineage name or landholding position per se and needed to come from other activities.

Throughout South Asia, a large portion of the middle class did not hail from the traditional elites, who were typically government employee families (H. Donner 2012, 129). These "traditional" elites in Bangladesh were what Rounaq Jahan (1972) calls the "vernacular elite," a cosmopolitan, secular, and educated class that emerged in the independence period from lower-middle-class provincial families who were able to dominate the bureaucracy and gain a foothold in business. By contrast, newer middle-class groups were less educated and more involved in religious and patronage politics. They increasingly included rich farmers and urban petit bourgeoisie, the poorly paid salariat, and families undertaking a combination of livelihoods in construction, pharmaceuticals, textiles, and other industries.[6]

Chakri (salaried white-collar employment) was the coveted livelihood of the middle classes in South Asia. Elite employment used to refer primarily to government service work. Then, more recently, opportunities for *chakri* emerged from business and industry, which "propelled sections of the local middle classes into prosperity by providing jobs and access to resources" (Hussain 2014, 2).[7] Many local rich families in the areas where I conducted fieldwork became relatively wealthy within the last generation on the basis of these opportunities.

Of the different middle-class groups and factions that emerged and expanded in Bangladesh's postindependence period, few have received attention from researchers (Lewis 2011, 15–17). Anthropologists have emphasized the need for studies that offer a repoliticized understanding of class relations and accumulation and examine middle-class formation relationally with the poor (Jeffrey 2008; Pattenden 2011). A significant avenue of upward mobility was employment in NGOs (Feldman 2003, 17) and other activities strongly linked with foreign-aid flows (Lewis 2011, 17), which generated a new class of social climbers ever since the rise of relief organizations in rural prominence after independence (Karim 2001, 96). As local elites diversified their livelihoods, establishing new NGOs was a major activity, a new source of income, and another way that newly wealthy families extended their sphere of patronage (Lewis and Hossain 2008; Hilhorst 2003). They did not lack for ready participants: "For the poor, there remain rather few alternatives to forming dependent bonds with the wealthy in order to secure access to employment or land, or to the official programmes offering relief or off-farm employment" (Bode and Howes 2002, xv).

New interactions between the village and outside institutions reworked ties between dominant and laboring classes. Rather than dissolving patron-client relations, links with external resources such as state and NGO antipoverty programs allowed the dominant classes to exert dispersed forms of subtle control over the poor and to accelerate accumulation (Chibber 2003, 250). Jonathan Pattenden refers to this process as "gatekeeping," which is "the act of channelling formal and informal resources between [usually] the state [but also NGOs] and society for private economic and political gain" (2011, 164). With the decline of lineage patronage and other forms of kinship help, rural people increasingly looked to new patrons for access to resources. My interlocutors counted among many rural people who were desperate to attach themselves, however adversely, to NGO patrons.

The status claims of the new NGO middle classes and elites did not rest only on classic co-optation of development rewards and accumulation through gatekeeping. This chapter shows that a significant aspect of NGO middle-class status was built on projects of personhood and making one's own name through the creation and promotion of new and compelling development models that would attract international funding, national recognition, and local followers.

In Dhaka, "for those who belonged to a small, intellectual, urban élite, discussions [for instance about the country's challenges and opportunities for action] were often held among extended family members who included policy makers, academics, and members of the international aid community" (Feldman 2003, 10), thus partially enfolding this new arena of upward mobility into older structures of political and economic dominance in the capital. Their common cosmopolitan identity was based on a lifestyle that was "emblematic of the new consumption that had accompanied the explosion of expatriate aid workers, embassy staff, and UN officials" (Riles 2000, 58). This group enjoyed the benefits of secure employment. They often possessed shared cultural capital and networks with donors, which allowed them to adopt and influence broader development models. This trend was especially the case in Bangladesh, which was heralded as the world's NGO capital (World Bank Report 1996). Development work offered not only an elite lifestyle but also transnational connections and the appealingly nationalistic claim of helping the poor of one's own nation by constructing models that might one day be associated with one's own name (such as Akhter Hameed Khan's Comilla Model, Muhammad Yunus' Grameen Bank microcredit model, and, according to Wikipedia, Dr. Adnan Khan's iAgent Model).

At the bottom rungs of the NGO elite in rural areas, social status was more unstable. Similar to the old *gusthi* (patrilineal) patrons, the ability to redistribute still formed the basis of these individuals' status. Yet unlike *gusthi* patrons, these resources were not locally held but were dependent on the vagaries of larger, distant development patrons who did not occupy a shared cultural space. The new rural NGO patrons relied on a steady supply of project funding (and the ability to divert resources from development activities initiated by central government ministries) to hold on to their positions (Lewis 2011, 38). Maintaining this resource flow was relatively easy in a development era of "partnership," when international development actors were desperate to find local organizations to legitimize their funding applications.

People who were granted employment in these NGOs gained status in part by wielding symbols of modernity—new ideas, technologies, capital, *pukka* (brick-and-mortar) buildings, motorcycles, electricity, and running water (Karim 2011, 79). NGOs thus cushioned a new kind of rural middle-class lifestyle, which was a factor in accusations of profiteering motives. "Not all these organisations balanced private action with public spiritedness in equal measure. There were also many NGOs that were started by less scrupulous individuals who saw relatively easy opportunities for the accumulation of foreign funding"

(Lewis 2011, 114), an example of which is detailed in this chapter. This new class of people, particularly the local patrons (NGO executive directors), may have overlapped significantly with older high-status families. Being built on new sources of accumulation and encoding new relationships of patronage, this group is also a distinct class.[8]

The development-resource class even at the rural level was characterized by a stark social distance between NGO staff and "the poor" and a closed, parochial manner. Scholars write about "entrepreneurs who have taken advantage of nation-building projects, economic restructuring, and projects of international development to separate themselves from the poor" (Jeffrey 2008, 518).[9] Aid elites were often committed to moral universals, such as equal rights and women's empowerment, in discursive acts of "moral selving" but they withdrew from the local when the messiness of practice confronted their moral narrative (Mosse 2011, 12). They often maintained an attitude of distrust of the poor and took a morally superior stance: "Fear and stereotypes intermingle with feelings of superiority and the burden of responsibility to 'civilize and develop' the unfortunate" (Hussain 2014, 10).

Yet unlike the *gusthi* patrons with their "own poor" (Gardner 1995), the new NGO patrons were more concerned with high-level moral narratives and the impersonal numbers of people "reached." Means became ends in themselves. Activities such as networking (similar to information exchange and capital accumulation) came to be seen as a good in their own right, rather than as instrumental for another pursuit (Riles 2000, 50). In this way, "development" entered the habitus of people as everyday process (Mosse 2013, 230) and reinforced class divisions through a new set of vocabularies and knowledge about the "developed" and "undeveloped." Within the latter, the "deserving" and "undeserving" poor (Dolan 2014, 13) were differentiated not by membership in lineages or personal relations but by the ability to conform to the projects' definitions of the ideal beneficiary. The shift from the old donor-driven funders to new ones advocating forms of poverty capitalism also deepened the divisions between the local elites and the poor and exacerbated the precariousness of both positions.

Sarah White (1992) encourages scholars to approach class by focusing on the relations that reproduce and reformat socioeconomic inequalities and on the material, human, and social resources that people use to advance their interests. The NGO apparatus offered the allure of one such set of resources for people of different socioeconomic backgrounds to pursue various projects. The urban business elite accessed the NGO as a means to tap into rural markets; rural and urban middle classes sought a source of employment; and the poor searched for a way to secure cheap credit or material resources for daily survival.

The relationships that underpinned these paths of engagement—for instance, in building a poorly paid rural women's salesforce, in working on unstable footing on project-based contracts, or in submitting to disciplinary technologies during loan repayment—were generative of new forms of socioeconomic inequality. The reformatting of vertical ties of dependence and inequality among classes through personal projects significantly mediated the translation of policy into practice.

Policy Models, Practice, and Personal Projects

Middle-class social mobility through NGO ownership and employment was dependent on the relational features of development networks. The success or failure of NGO workers was connected not only to their capacity to implement projects that adhered to the goals of their funders but also to their skill in representing themselves in a way that produced conformity. As much as they tried to mold villagers into ideal beneficiaries, they also needed to adopt the "right" subjectivities themselves to retain the confidence of their superiors and funders, who claimed to advocate notions of transparency, accountability, and professionalism. Simultaneously, they needed to maintain authoritative distance from the people they managed and deny bids for sociality from inferiors. The ability of NGO workers to produce project alignment was significantly mediated by factors beyond their control, such as changes in priority within the field of international aid from donor- to market-driven models.

Actual operational control was limited: "What is usually more urgent and more practical is control over the *interpretation* of events. . . . Power lies in the narratives that maintain the organization's definition of the problem" (Mosse 2004, 646). To stabilize particular policy ideas required relational work. These representations and narratives were thus the primary currency with which workers could continue to secure resources (jobs, connections, funding, and recognition) from potential patrons (government officials, mass media, and donors) in order to pursue their personal projects and maintain their class positions.

Paying attention to these middle-level manager-implementers in projects— and their challenging role of brokering increasingly divergent expectations and representations—enables us to shed light on the obscured relationship between policy models and their intended practices and outcomes. The formulation and achievement of operational goals was tied to practical pressures faced by implementers—whether these were personal ambitions to gain promotion, work targets delivered from above, imperatives to meet the agendas of partner organizations, or the adoption of new "buzzwords" (Cornwall 2007) and buzz-models by the international development community. As a representational device, the model "gives the impression that policy is the result of discrete, voluntaristic acts, not the process of coming to terms with conflicting interests and worldviews in the course of which choices are made and exclusions effected" (Escobar 1991, 667). Such exclusions, involving the erasure of entire groups of people and their ideas and versions of events in official success narratives, were a form of relational work that took place within organizations and among colleagues.

Development and NGO policy legitimated (rather than oriented) practice as a political project, crucial for the assemblage it drew together (and hid), and acted as a vehicle for vastly varying, often contradictory issues. Yet such policy was also an imposition of moral ideas (such as poverty capitalism) exerted by NGO classes to pursue their own projects. The top layers of NGO elites—the visionaries, model-builders, leaders, and managers—often operated in the domain of crafting policy and outward-looking representations that encoded their particular class politics. Random events, chance meetings, webs of personal relationships, and unintended consequences were also drivers of models-in-practice, the effects of which must be systematically ignored or rationalized and incorporated into outward-facing representations.

Failure did not mean the inability to implement policy according to its own design, but rather the inability to perform the relational work of securing a wider network of support and validation, both within an office and among donors. Project failure was a failure of interpretation, affecting most strongly the actors whose narratives and representations did not manage to attract an audience (Mosse 2004, 658). The ability to broker diverse expectations and representations was thus a key skill for an upwardly mobile employee.

Yet the key observation here is not that policy models and practice differ (or that people have different representations of events) per se, but that narrative devices—such as embellished reports and curated field visits—were a crucial part of the relational work performed by NGO workers to weave an appearance (and therefore also an effect) of stability. My contribution to this body of literature is to show how these efforts were embedded in positions of class structure and projects of personhood. People staked their personal identities and professional personas to these development models, and, conversely, models and practice were shaped by personhood and class projects. This dialectic relationship meant that significant changes within one domain (e.g. development fads) can profoundly reshape the other (e.g., class structures).

Thus, it is necessary to pay ethnographic attention to the choices and challenges of people located at different subject positions in order to understand the forms of relationships produced by a social enterprise. What might be read on a surface level as ill intentions, outright exploitation of people lower in the chain, or poorly formulated policy models can also be read in the context of these people's own unstable class positions and the nonlinear nature of the policy-practice relationship. Such a focus enables analytic empathy with groups of people heretofore portrayed as antagonists. This chapter considers how to take seriously the pursuit of a "social good" and how to address the ways that people understand the market as a mechanism for "doing good" even as their attempts to make markets work for the poor (and for themselves) reproduce structural relationships of power and inequality.

The ethnography that follows demonstrates the ways in which the model itself, as well as notions about the appropriate means of implementing it, was contested. These contestations in turn affect the aesthetics of the iAgent network and indicate how network devices and artifacts (such as documents and representations) were tools for asserting and defending people's status positions.

Model-Building and Conflicts over Ownership

This section focuses on two individuals at TIE and the ways in which they represented their roles in the creation of and changes within the iAgent model. Rohan Alam was the iAgent team leader during the pilot and scale-up phases of the program, and Adnan Khan was TIE's CEO. The following descriptions are based on the retrospective accounts of these two men and others' comments about them. Their statements reflect the particular timing of interviews, which occurred on dozens of occasions during the period between April 2013 and July 2014. TIE was in the initial stages of transitioning from the pilot to the scale-up phase when I first met these individuals, and TIE had abandoned the model in favor of a third one by the end. Rohan Alam's interviews spanned the periods prior to, during, and after his departure from TIE, which stimulated his intense reflection about models and the personal politics of implementing them. I follow their accounts with a discussion of the symbolic and relational work they performed.

Personal Narratives as Relational Work

What were Rohan Alam's and Adnan Khan's accounts of the circumstances of their involvement in the iAgent model in its past and later incarnations? When read not for the factuality of their content per se, people's narratives may be apprehended in terms of the relational work they perform in attempting to position the speaker in particular ways. Michael Jackson (2005) suggests approaching storytelling as an act of the present appropriating the past, thus offering insight into how people evaluate and negotiate strategies for social and ethical action in the future. The statements that headed this chapter demonstrate conflicting representations and complaints about other actors' (mis) representations of events and can be read as political claims made by those whose voices have been marginalized. David Lewis, Dennis Rogers, and Michael Woolcock (2008) urge us to consider what constitutes valid knowledge forms and to understand all forms of development knowledge as "stories" that are inextricable from the subjective worldviews of the tellers. Hence, this chapter considers the stories of NGO workers from the perspective that "all knowledge of reality is unavoidably subjective but also that it is inevitably mediated by the representative forms which describe it, and that different modes of representation therefore impart different visions of the world" (Lewis et al. 2008, 199, drawing on Benjamin 1989).

Narratives of a Model-Builder

Rohan came from a village in Noakhali in southeastern Bangladesh and was first introduced to the idea of "model building" in the eleventh grade when his teacher spoke about the work of Akhter Hameed Khan, the founder of the Comilla Model of rural development. For his undergraduate degree in sociology, Rohan was assigned an exercise in which he had to build a hypothetical development model. The process inspired him to dedicate his life to building the next major model for bringing rural Bangladeshis out of poverty. By doing so, he would create a name for himself, although Rohan explained that this motivation was not his primary one. Model building meant first having a sound idea based on an in-depth sociological understanding of a problem and then engaging in rigorous prototyping, documentation, and modification, with deliberate learning at each stage of growth to know how to customize the model to different times and locations. Many people strove to build models, but they usually reached only the first stage of pilot-project implementation and never arrived at a truly replicable state. "I used to think that the iAgent model would be the one for me," Rohan opined, "before I was forced out of TIE."

Rohan had joined TIE after watching a television interview with Adnan. Adnan spoke compellingly about the potential role of information and technology in rural development, which Rohan himself had long considered. When he decided to leave his permanent, well-paying, prestigious job with benefits in the Ministry of Land to work in a then-unknown NGO, many people, especially his family members, questioned his decision. Yet knowing his passion and conviction to exert an impact on Bangladesh society and the plodding bureaucracy within which new ideas lost momentum in the public sector, his closest colleagues and superiors at the ministry (according to Rohan) encouraged him to make the transition.

Rohan was a man driven by a passion for new ideas and their pursuit at all cost, and his personal relationships often struggled. During the most intense period of piloting the iAgent model, he relocated his family to the pilot village so that he could continue to work and also spend time with his wife and children. In other years, he was so engaged in fieldwork that he forgot to return to the city for Eid ul-fitr (a holiday marking the end of Ramadan), which he enjoyed "with his grassroots family rather than his real family." In comparing the leadership styles of Rohan with Kabir (the iAgent team leader who both preceded and followed Rohan in the role), Zahir Ahmed from the Atno Bishash center remarked, "Kabir is a very formal man. He will do nothing without black and white documents. But Rohan is a crazy man. When he thinks of a new idea, he says, 'Let's do it! Directly!' This type of craziness is needed for this work. Kabir would have stayed with the project proposal, and the project would never work out." Zahir's comments credit the departure from—versus adherence to—policy models as the key factor in enabling a project to work in practice.

Rohan's new boss, Adnan, came from a more privileged and internationally connected family. Having grown up in Dhaka, he was sent abroad for his education by his wealthy parents. He studied economics, business management, and information technology at a university in Eastern Europe, an experience that planted the seeds for founding TIE when he returned to Bangladesh with his doctoral degree. Subsequently, he attended many conferences and workshops around the world on the topics of social enterprise and impact investing, which crystalized his ideas about how development should work. The many programs he floated under the TIE banner, including the iAgent model, were built on an information-innovation model of society in which carefully formulated policy translates directly into practice, which in turn generates linear and predictable outcomes for participants. Convinced that the key driver of poverty was the poor's lack of access to information, Adnan was sure that information-inclusion projects that could be locally run and self-sustaining would help marginalized communities to participate in the social and economic mainstream. He spent little time in rural Bangladesh. His colleagues referred to him as a "one-man show" for his propensity to monopolize the limelight when TIE's activities gained national and international attention.

Internal Conflict

Rohan asserted that, despite his fundamental leadership role in designing the iAgent model, he was eventually pushed out of TIE because of philosophical differences and political struggles with Adnan. What they created was neither a charity nor a business, he maintained, but a social model, which required a combination of both elements. Thus any model needed considerable customization. For example, varying developmental needs characterized different areas of Bangladesh, and TIE needed to train iAgents to deliver services accordingly. Yet Adnan said that any successful model, by definition, needed to operate through "plug and play" and require minimal external intervention. Rohan commented, exasperated:

> What are we producing, USB drives? Mouse? That you simply plug in and install and they immediately start operating at full capacity? No, this is a social model. If you give a loan immediately to a village girl, she will say, "I cannot repay this, so I will commit suicide." But Rahela and Dipa in Lalpur [from the pilot model] would not say this, because they are experienced. The loan model is appropriate only when iAgents reach that level of confidence. For some it may take six months and for others one year. It should be customized.

For Adnan, the dominant aesthetic of a social enterprise model was one of disconnection after initial investment and then of big-data-driven governance from afar. His basic assumption was that people would apply training and material resources to help themselves out of poverty, and TIE's role as network node was to aggregate numerical data about their income and expense patterns. He cited the Silicon Valley wisdom that it was better to get an imperfect product out on the market today than a perfect one tomorrow. Doing so, amplified by the data collected about the program's performance, would enable faster and more frequent iterations of development progress.

Rohan, by contrast, focused on the social and structural constraints that contributed to people's poverty and viewed the network through an ethics of social work. Where Adnan saw data points and technical fixes, Rohan saw vulnerable individuals and political impediments. Where Adnan sought to make a name for himself among an international network of development peers, Rohan aspired to become known locally through his role in supporting grassroots people. These different understandings and projects of personhood led to contradictory notions about relationships within social enterprise networks. The divergence between a social model of support and a technocratic model with "the social" organized out of the frame of visibility was profound.

The difference in approach between the high-touch and the hands-off method of engagement with iAgents and centers became a personal criticism that Adnan and his followers leveled against Rohan. Adnan prided himself on having the ability to build a model "as much as possible dispassionately, to allow critical reasoning and the market to play their roles." In a leadership team meeting, a senior colleague remarked that Rohan, by contrast, was "70 percent emotional and only 30 percent rational," which suggested in a condescending manner that he was too personally involved.[10] Rohan suspected that he was being sidelined due to the external recognition that he personally had received for his role in the project.

Conflicts over credit due for the iAgent social enterprise, once it achieved international success in award competitions and visibility in global media, were an additional wedge driven between Rohan and Adnan. Rohan lamented that in Bangladesh in general, inventors and innovators "suffer from no recognition." They advance their ideas to near completion, but then a "muscleman" (figurative and also perhaps literal) takes all the papers and ideas and brings the project to a close while claiming all credit. For example, Ibrahim Sobhan built an education model that made formal schooling attractive to the very poor and their parents by incorporating earning activities along with in-school homework support. According to Rohan, the government grabbed this model and did not recognize Sobhan for his role. Rohan said that this "culture of grabbing" was so pervasive that it occurred in all sectors, including literature.

> We have some renowned writers. When someone new brings a good piece of work to a publisher, the publisher says, "Here is some money, and you won't claim that these are your writings. We will paint it by the name of Humayun Ahmed [a Bangladeshi author of over two hundred best-selling fiction and non-fiction books]." I am damn sure that lots of novels carry the name of Humayun Ahmed but he never wrote many of them. It's another sort of violence and aggression.

Rohan said that this violence was exerted against him.

> It happens as you can observe in a political procession. After some distance the political group achieves some small thing, and a while later the full achievement is demonstrated. The leader initially keeps himself behind the team to encourage its members. "You are the future leader, go further, make this procession happen, do everything." When a small achievement is made, then the leader moves closer to the would-be leaders. At the demonstration of some major achievement, he will slide ahead of everyone, saying, "Look what I achieved!"

After being removed from TIE's iAgent team and placed on a separate project, Rohan handed in his resignation and set off to establish another model. He had failed to organize in his favor the set of representations about the iAgent model. Rohan's story is significant because he placed this failure in the wider context of intra-middle-class politics, which emphasized his position among other inventors and visionaries whose ideas and projects were stolen by the politically more powerful. A broader social critique—of how the greed of the elites hijacked genuine interest in social justice—was embedded in his narrative. By positioning himself as the fallen hero, Rohan was able to cast his failure to control the narrative of the iAgent program as a stumbling block along the road of sustained engagement with women's empowerment and poverty alleviation.

Class Projects and Attitudes toward the Poor

What kinds of personal projects were such efforts for NGO elites? Despite the fame that Muhammad Yunus received around the world for popularizing microcredit and, more recently, social-business concepts, many people in Bangladesh argue that social entrepreneurship was not a dominant part of the national identity. According to the director of one of TIE's supporting partners, rural people took development for granted. NGOs have been present throughout their lifetimes and were central to their ability to survive. Urban middle-class people were unaware of these efforts. In Bangladeshi mentality, the director continued, being a business entrepreneur was a nonaspirational activity pursued when a person could not secure a real job. "So imagine people's attitudes about a *social* entrepreneur. When Yunus was awarded the Congressional Medal of Honor in the US, it didn't even make news here! And men such as Adnan Khan simply do not exist in people's imagination of role models and success cases." What kind of project was it to work in the social sector as an entrepreneur? For these practitioners, what was the meaning of social enterprise?

Adnan stated that the tension between selfish tendencies and the pursuit of social work inhibited many organizations from growing successfully. "It is human nature that we all run after glory, but as a social worker it is crucial to be honest with yourself and put yourself second." Rohan criticized NGO leaders for having a "beggar mentality," for being so eager to benefit from resources freely offered that they routinely failed. He gave the example of the partnership with National Bank to finance the iAgent model. The bank launched the project because its leaders were personally connected with Adnan, and the idea happened to align with the bank's policy of financial inclusion targeting the "industrious poor." The bank's governor declared an allocation of ten crore taka (1.3 million USD) and challenged TIE, as quickly as it could, to scale up to the level of handling that kind of money. By way of an analogy, Rohan explained what happened next:

> In the village, *jomidars* [landowners] keep raw rice in clay jars with narrow lips that widen out again. When beggars come along, they offer them rice but tell them, "You'll take only once." In their one grab, beggars try to take as much as possible. In the beginning they wrap their widespread fingers around a pile of rice, but as they draw out their hand, rice passes through the spaces between their fingers. If they had tightly cupped their hand, they would have ended up with more. TIE is like that beggar. National Bank offers large resources, but TIE doesn't have the capacity to grab as much as it tries to, and it ends up falling short.

The major problem facing TIE's lack of capacity to run the iAgent model, Rohan explained, was the gap between management and the grass roots. Most of his senior colleagues were born in Dhaka and were educated there or in the West. Because they were unaware of the rural context, the TIE staff did not understand simple matters such as the fact that "iAgents are severely limited in their absorptive abilities," by which Rohan meant their capacity to learn new skills. Any training module needed to be repeated over many occasions and over a long duration, rather than all at once as the new TIE team planned.

Despite his close relationship and genuine respect for village people in the areas in which he worked, Rohan exhibited a patronizing attitude toward the poor that was magnified more starkly among his colleagues. While explaining to me how iAgents learned to hawk their services, he said, "I encourage iAgents to think of villagers as if they are one-month-old babies. When a baby is cold, it doesn't know it needs a blanket, and it doesn't know how to ask for it. So that is the role of the mother to provide without being asked. Similarly, villagers won't know to ask for things they need, so you have to push them for some services."

The poor-as-children metaphor was common but less widespread than the poor-as-"unconscious" or "uncivilized" rhetoric. A WaterAid officer told me not to go near villages (not knowing that I lived in one) because the poor still practiced open defecation. His NGO operated a project that "works to get wealthier villagers to motivate the most poor to aspire to a higher state of being civilized."[11] Information and awareness building were the commonly posed solutions. According to a Bangladesh Bank officer, "Giving information is the best way of empowerment. Poor entrepreneurs are not conscious. They don't have access to information about financial facilities and policy, but if you make them conscious, digital entrepreneurs, they cannot be stopped." Apparently, the poor have an innate entrepreneurial tendency, but this capacity must be unlocked by the wealthy who benevolently open their eyes.[12] If entrepreneurs fail after having received this information, they have not been mentally prepared and have not yet discovered that they want to become developed. Kabir, the TIE iAgent team leader who replaced Rohan, used an allegory to explain why the iAgents in Amirhat were not performing well. They needed not only technical training but also mental preparation. "Say there is a canal in front of you. If you don't want to cross this canal, then no assistance will help you to cross it. At first, you have to be mentally prepared and to realize, 'Yes, I will cross the canal.' Only then will it be worth training you about different ways to cross."

Urban elites regarded the poor as easy to cheat, and they exchanged humorous stories. A junior TIE engineer assigned to assist the Yamada team during its multiple visits from Japan to install photovoltaic batteries for off-grid households to rent related one account. When he arrived in Lalpur to meet the truck of solar panels delivered from Chittagong Port, he enlisted laborers to unload the heavy wooden crates. The process took an hour. He announced, "I paid them with one boiled egg each. Giving them money would be expensive, and they would always come back for more paid work. But those eggs in total cost less than one hundred taka! The workers were so happy to sit eating an egg that they didn't realize their loss."

Despite the actual pervasiveness of the rich cheating the poor, NGO elites expressed indignation when the poor asked for a fair wage, and they accused the poor of cheating the rich. When the iAgents of Amirhat said that they would continue to work if they received a salary because otherwise they would not be able to survive and pay off their loans at the same time, Kanika from TIE exclaimed, "They are blackmailing us! They are nowhere educated enough to be paid like our TIE staff! I cannot believe I am subjected to this behavior."

These narratives of urban elite TIE staff members were part of the representational culture of the NGO and the relational work it performed. They served as interpretive accounts of reformatting the past according to claims made in the present, as justifications for future action within a project, and as instruments for pursuing personal and class politics vis-à-vis other groups of people. NGO workers in their representations sought to distance themselves morally from "exploitative" non-NGO elites and also from the "devious" poor, whose welfare they purportedly served. The model itself was an extension of their middle-class personhood as much as it was an instrument of improving the capacities of its beneficiaries.

Another way in which class politics oriented NGO policy and action was through the personal relationships and networks of the staff. These links enabled the organization to function and open new types of opportunities, but their personal nature remained hidden beneath the official discourse of rationally planned models. Personal matters surfaced when a political contestation emerged, such as in accusations of someone bringing emotions into work to discredit a colleague or someone else stealing recognition for the work of others for one's own glory. The relationships that underpinned everyday organizational activity and also recriminations against colleagues reflected people's class positions and the relational work they undertook to defend their power and status.

We now turn to the relational economy of development projects at the level of the rural middle classes and focus on their unsteady position between the demands of their urban elite superiors and the expectations of the rural poor whom they served.

The Declining Patronage of Rural NGOs

The Development Moral Economy

Two organizations—the iAgent rural information centers in Lalpur and Amirhat subdistricts—exemplify the changing nature of relationships between NGOs and their clients.

In Lalpur, despite its long-standing reputation and desire to be the main driver of development for the area, the NGO Atno Bishash fell from its previously important position because of its refusal to comply with new development trends it perceived would be harmful to its beneficiaries. It could no longer attract significant aid funding and thus failed to provide the employment and resource distribution that villagers had come to expect. As a result, former clients accused Atno Bishash's leader of corruption, a charge that corresponded more to their dissatisfaction about resources not being distributed than to the personal use per se of NGO supplies by the executive director.

In Amirhat, the executive director of the NGO ACRU founded the organization after observing how other people (at organizations such as SKS and Grameen) benefitted from brokering between foreign wealth and local poverty. From a starting point of turning the social work of poverty alleviation into the business of self-enrichment, this executive director failed to adhere to the development moral economy that villagers and new iAgents expected from all NGOs, and he ran the iAgent program through practices of blatant exploitation. In Amirhat, ACRU bore a reputation of corruption and greed, and commentators often warned iAgents not to get involved in the organization's projects.[13] Yet because rural relations in general had shifted away from meeting the basic needs of poor families through patrilineal patronage ties, people were pushed into pursuing these risky opportunities.

Case One: Patronage and the Decline of Atno Bishash in Lalpur

Atno Bishash was an NGO in Lalpur *Upazila* (subdistrict), situated in northwestern Bangladesh on the Jamuna River between two close tributaries. Similar to many NGOs in the country, Atno Bishash was founded and grew up in the postindependence period of the 1970s and 1980s to focus on relief and rehabilitation and later on community economic development. The thirty-five-year-old NGO was based on the familiar model of social inequality that characterized patron-clientalism. The wealthy and the poor shared an uneven balance of power but one that was based on reciprocal relations and social recognition.

When Shoriful (Shorif) Islam spoke with me about the founding of Atno Bishash, this NGO was experiencing a rapid decline in active projects. In narrating his story, he justified the decisions he made, which he thinks led directly to Atno Bishash's downturn. He was a secondary-school student in 1979 when he began voluntary work; he organized his friends to participate and he received training from the Village Education Resource Center. Although none of the major events of the Independence War in 1971 had taken place in Lalpur, he remembered the period vividly. (It seemed that no significant events or developments, other than annual flooding and seasonal crop shortages, occurred in Lalpur at all because of its "remoteness.") Little infrastructure had existed, and he and his siblings traveled a long distance to reach the nearest school. The boys were permitted to continue, but his sisters were not. In 1986, with foreign funding (64,000 taka, 821 USD) from a development organization in West Germany, he set up an adult literacy project. With this experience, he attracted funding for other projects, such as disaster response from Oxfam GB, safe drinking water from NGO Forum, and healthcare expansion from Voluntary Health Service Society. On his family land, and mindful of his sisters' lost education, Shorif portioned off several hectares behind his house and built a girls' secondary school. He employed the surrounding villagers as construction workers and teachers and he continued farm work on the existing agricultural land by hiring local laborers. He bought a plot of land near the main north-south road passing through Lalpur and established what became the main site of the Atno Bishash NGO. Within the following decade, he established a women's health clinic and a women's degree college adjacent to the NGO.

Shorif described himself as different from his peers, educated sons of landowning families in the area who were mostly absentee landlords earning handsome profits in Dhaka and Chittagong as factory owners and private-clinic doctors. Rather than improving their natal area, they extracted wealth from poor families in the surrounding villages by paying them so little for casual labor that they were gradually forced to sell their homestead land.[14] Shorif was proud of what he had built; rather than taking money from the land to fund the building of apartments in Dhaka, he brought substantial foreign funds into the area. At the peak of Atno Bishash's activity, twenty projects operated simultaneously, including river-erosion mitigation, primary education for ultra-poor children, and skills training for local elected officials. Project budgets, funded by entities such as the European Commission, IDE/Japan, and Christian Aid, ranged from four lakh to ten crore taka (5,128–1.3 million USD) and employed two hundred people.

While we sat in the Atno Bishash courtyard one humid evening, a senior project leader recalled the disastrous flood of 1988. He indicated on the wall of the building where the water level had reached two meters. Homes were submerged, and residents of the area lived in the railway station and on the upraised tracks for a month. The project leader had just married, and he joked that while he hauled food to hungry families, he most worried about losing his bride in the disaster. General Ershad was in power at the time, and the army and local government offices organized relief work. Atno Bishash was the other major player in the local effort. So much was destroyed—homes gone, roads (none paved at the time) washed away, agricultural land covered in sand, and crops spoiled—and many families fell into poverty. Although many now numbered among the newly poor, Atno Bishash's staffers were the ones who continued to coordinate supplies long after Ershad's military and aid forces retreated. The widespread destruction meant that relief materials had to be brought in by foot, with men slogging through water and holding bundles overhead. Despite Atno Bishash's later decline in activity, distant villagers remembered that the NGO had helped during the floods nearly three decades previously. When iAgents traveled outside the immediate area to enroll women in a fee-for-service mobile-phone health program, villagers commented to one another confidently, "They are registering us so that in the flood season we will get food." iAgents did not bother to correct them.

In addition to providing employment and directing projects that brought resources to people, Atno Bishash's local patronage role extended to hosting festivals and other events open to the community. Many activities took place every year on the NGO's campus: a Bengali new year festival, an anniversary celebration of the founding of Atno Bishash, an education fair, a rally for women's participation in politics, Begum Rokeya day (a Muslim feminist who worked for gender equality and established the first school for Muslim girls in

1909), an award ceremony for women leaders in NGOs, a Victory Day celebration, and an Independence Day performance. For each event, Atno Bishash
threw itself into a frenzy of preparatory activities. The staff decorated the
courtyard, sank bamboo poles into the ground for banners, and constructed a
huge *pandal* [marquee] with an elaborate bamboo skeleton and colorful panels
of cloth to enclose a stage upon which people would give speeches and perform
songs and dances. *Singaras* (Bangladesh-style samosas) and *pitha* (steamed rice
cakes) circulated as snacks during speeches, and a generous meal was served.
For smaller crowds, mutton biryani was dished out on plates with boiled eggs
fried in turmeric and cucumber and tomato salad. When hundreds of people
were expected, the woman who worked in the Atno Bishash kitchen was joined
by several other hired women, the groundskeeper, and the guard. Together they
dug a fire pit outside, over which they suspended multiple gigantic pots for
cooking biryani.

Atno Bishash continued to hold these events for the community during the
time of my fieldwork, even though the number of projects dropped from twenty
to three and the employees dropped from the hundreds to the teens. Why did
the NGO decline so much in recent history? Shorif and other Atno Bishash
senior project managers explained that the NGO's conscious rejection of microfinance was the primary reason. Theirs, Shorif declared, was the only NGO that
had not fallen into the corrupting trap of microfinance in this area; they continued to pursue only pure social work. An organization that ran a credit program clearly indicated that social goals were not primary in its operation. Most
Bangladesh NGOs at the time pursued profitable work as social enterprises.[15]
Shorif gestured around the room. "See, we have simple furniture, no car, and
only our original one-story building. I am a full volunteer in this project. If there
is a meeting in Dhaka with funders, I bear all lodging, food, and transport costs
myself." By contrast, other prominent NGOs in the area were extravagant. "You
see what they can do because of microcredit!" exclaimed Rasel from TIE, as he
assessed which iAgent center would be best for hosting Yamada's pilot project.
Three brightly painted stories boasted forty guestrooms with televisions, private
bathrooms, and air conditioning. "You think this is fancy?" Rasel continued.
"Wait until you visit BRAC or Grameen. They are doing very well with their
profiting." Zahir concurred that "microfinance is a mechanism of exploitation,
not a mechanism of development." Amit described more evocatively (while pretending to bite into his forearm) that "microcredit is like sucking the blood of
the poor."

The cost of maintaining Atno Bishash's ethics of not exploiting the poor was
a decline in the ability to look after the poor at all. Donors now prioritized the
values that microfinance espoused: financial sustainability and profit for the

organization, and self-help and income-generating activities for the beneficiaries. "All NGOs have a crisis of funding," explained Zahir. "It's do microcredit
or die." A former project leader of Atno Bishash who now taught at a technical
college explained donors' reasoning. When the base of an NGO is microcredit,
then money invested will remain circulating, which will attract other programs.
"Because there is cash, they can be more established. They have a better management system and give better salaries. Most projects don't yield any benefits, but
credit programs give good interest, so that is why donors like it." Although he
lost his job at Atno Bishash as a result, this man approved of Shorif's reasons for
rejecting microfinance. He said that people already took too many loans that they
could not repay, which forced them to sell their houses and flee to Dhaka.

Despite his positive reputation from roles he had played in the past, Shorif
faced increasing critical commentary among former and present staff. In the
past, when projects reached a conclusion, employees were reassigned to a new
project. Now, with few new projects available, people were caught in limbo, not
sure if they should apply for jobs at different organizations or wait for a successful funding application. Gradually, after months of not being paid salaries,
most left. I met a man who had worked at Atno Bishash for fourteen years. He
complained that Shorif had cheated employees. He asserted that of five months
of project salaries, Shorif had commandeered three months' worth for upgrading
buildings. A current staffer criticized Shorif's habit of ordering the NGO cook to
prepare him frequent snacks. "His bazaar is the Atno Bishash office, free for him.
But our own salaries don't get paid each month."

When I asked why people in the subdistrict still seemed to respect Atno
Bishash and say that Shorif was a good man, iAgents explained, "He did good
work in the community, while also doing *durneti* [corruption]. This corruption
is nothing new. He has always done it like that. But now he is not doing good
work for the community anymore." People seemed not to mind the wealth-
accumulating practices of patrons as long as these patrons also redistributed
resources.[16] In this era of a changing development relational economy, the rural
NGO middle classes faced the disintegration of the basis of their social capital
(connections to foreign resources) or at least a restructuring on terms that did
not allow them to be locally recognized as patrons. Their middle-class status
became increasingly tenuous, and new development trends (in "sustainability"
and "self-help") required severing patronage relations with the poor rather than
strengthening them.

In this context of a shifting NGO ability to attract donors while also maintaining a desired standard of relationship with beneficiaries, Atno Bishash served
as one of two pilot locations to test the addition of iAgents to the rural information center model. Zahir Ahmed was hired as head of the iAgent project.

He had previously worked at a pharmaceutical company in two regional cities as a medical promotion officer, after which he received his master's degree at a private university and hoped for a career advancement. When his father died, he said he felt obligated to return home to the village and care for his mother and sister, and he searched for jobs. Everyone else in his family had aspirational forms of employment. His father had been an engineer with the local government, his brother had a high-end retail business in the regional capital, and his wife enjoyed a teaching job. At Atno Bishash, Zahir's salary grew steadily, from 4,000 taka (which was too embarrassing to tell his wife) to 30,000, "although I have to say twenty-eight because everyone in the office is required to 'donate' several thousand to our executive director for his own use. This is compulsory." He said that he continuously had to prove himself, and he aimed to build a revolutionary new model for the iAgents, an action more meaningful than working in profit-oriented companies.

As the quotations from Shorif and Zahir that headed this chapter show, credit for the iAgent model was as contested at the local-level centers as it was within TIE's headquarters in Dhaka. The absence of Atno Bishash's role in organizational literature was a sore spot for Shorif and Zahir, but they could do little if TIE wished to erase them from the official narrative. The matter came to a head when financial implications emerged. Because the two men had co-pioneered the concept with TIE, they said, the Atno Bishash team refused to pay a license fee when the iAgent program transitioned to the for-profit model. TIE insisted that all centers had to pay; otherwise other NGOs would complain about unfair treatment. The result was a standoff. Atno Bishash did not pay for a license, and its newly recruited iAgents did not receive approval from TIE to be issued National Bank loans.

Zahir spoke critically of the for-profit model because of the perceived injustice against Atno Bishash and also because he did not expect the model to work. iAgents of the pilot group had established themselves after a long, challenging process of overcoming social stigma for riding bicycles and working outside the home, convincing villagers to pay for services they expected for free from NGOs, and earning the respect of family members and community leaders. In the for-profit model, TIE expected the new iAgents to endure these challenges without center support and burdened by a 75,000 taka loan to repay. In the pilot they were successful because they had customized the program for each iAgent. Zahir offered an example:

> Brishti's house is next to the market, so what kind of service can she provide that shops, clinics, and NGO offices cannot provide? We helped her to start a computer-training center at her house, and she gave other

services in more remote areas on a part-time basis. But Rahela's house is already in a remote area, so all services and products were needed there. Staff members have to find out these matters with iAgents and their families. TIE didn't even know the level of customization we did to the model here.

When Zahir joined Atno Bishash at the inception of the iAgent model, he told the newly recruited young women that they needed to help one another and work as a group. When they approached him with problems, he first instructed them to ask the others for support. Gradually, they began to bypass Zahir to solve problems. "They built a strong unity. This kind of unity is needed for their own belief and confidence. If one girl said that she could not continue, the other girls would help her until the crisis passed. When I found that unity, I wanted to make them an association." Zahir related this idea to TIE, that if iAgents formed a cooperative or association, they would not need the center NGO as intermediary. "We always say that they are independent entrepreneurs, but we never give them freedom. When the NGO hosts an event and needs extra hands, we always call them and don't think about whether they are busy or not," Zahir explained. "This would be a way to free them from the NGO structure." TIE ignored the proposal. Zahir speculated that TIE could not in principle disagree; doing so would violate its stated impact objectives. Yet TIE could not implement the proposal either because, if the iAgents were truly independent, then TIE, SSI, and the centers would be separated from them. The pilot iAgents counted nine thousand members in their group, "and this is also now an asset of the NGOs. If iAgents are an association separately, then the NGOs will lose that resource for gaining foreign funding."

Case Two: Exploitation and Failed Patronage in ACRU in Amirhat

Fifty kilometers down the river was Amirhat *Upazila*, the home of Akaas Center for Rural Upliftment (ACRU). Established in 2006, ACRU was not among the group of NGOs that emerged in reaction to the destruction of life and land in the postindependence period. Sabbir Hossain, the founder and executive director of ACRU, by his own admission "invested so much money into this NGO and the iAgent program because helping the poor in the villages is good for getting a good reputation in the area, and now it can be profitable also." This NGO was based on a new form of antisocial inequality in which the labor and loyalty of the poor was not reciprocated with protection and social recognition by the wealthy.

Sabbir's wife was a head nurse at the local Medical College Hospital. The family owned no land, and they and their teenage daughter lived in the wife's run-down, cramped, but free quarters on the hospital campus. Sabbir took a long-term lease on the land where his NGO was built. His classmates from the district college were factory owners, advocates, businessmen, and doctors. His English-speaking daughter held high ambitions of becoming an engineer. If he did not find a way to become wealthy quickly, how could he support her to become as successful as the children of his peers?

When TIE began recruiting NGOs to serve as rural information centers under the newly designed for-profit model, Sabbir saw his opportunity. Rohan warned TIE that he did not trust Sabbir, but so few other NGOs matched the set of selection criteria for the program that Rohan was pressured into accepting ACRU to fulfill TIE's targets for the first round. Applicant NGOs had to be locally registered and run by local management teams and have the financial strength to invest in iAgents, and they could not be non-profits. They needed to have preexisting entrepreneurial programs. In addition to the usual NGO project cycles from donors, ACRU had experimented with commissioning local women to produce handicrafts. The NGO purchased the products at a low price and sold them in Dhaka street markets through a broker Sabbir knew from school.

Zahir predicted that the ACRU iAgent center would fail. Because it was an NGO, it was used to receiving money for time-bound projects and spending it immediately. Sabbir would extract money for himself from the beginning. TIE forged ahead, though, assuming that the center's investment would be sufficient incentive for the center to take responsibility and function without constant support from TIE.

When the ACRU iAgent center did fail, Sabbir lamented the loss of his large personal investment and the great hopes he had held in the program. He blamed TIE's mismanagement and empty promises as well as the iAgents' deficiencies. His words revealed his lack of understanding of the business nature of the iAgent program, even though the profit potential had attracted him. "All projects have a Title, Subject, Aims, Activities, and Duration, but TIE's iAgent project does not have a Subject, Aims, Activities, or Duration. . . . TIE only sometimes gave us a gift, but they left the center to sustain itself. So I am fully helpless." Because he understood the iAgent program in terms of NGO project cycles, with their influxes of free cash to spend on items budgeted for predefined and time-bound activities similar to his other projects, Sabbir complained that he was being mistreated by TIE. Even as he tried to adapt to the business model at TIE's encouragement, which needed him to invest in the program for it to be successful, TIE was slow to make the necessary arrangements for him to secure an iAgent center loan. "We do not have 100 percent help from TIE. The people there do not fulfill [their obligations], they just take their time. We paid 50,000 taka [641 USD] against our license but we still do not have a loan." According to the licensing guidelines, in order for a center loan to be approved, Sabbir needed to have already completed all paperwork as the guarantor of the iAgents' loans, which he had not done.

Meanwhile, Sabbir and his few staff members continued to treat iAgents as exploitable resources to make money for themselves. ACRU received a small budget from TIE for iAgent training sessions, but Sabbir charged iAgents for the meals on those days. iAgent Megh objected, "After trainings they provided us with something to eat, so we ate, but we did not know that he would charge us. He wrote down all of these amounts, and after a month he claimed that each of us had to pay our bill of 8,000 taka. How many months of loan installments could we repay with that money?" Not only did Sabbir receive double payments for the food cooked on site, but he also violated expected norms of hosting. In Bangladesh, the convener of any meeting, training, or seminar is expected to provide food for attendees. In commenting about such events, people often focus on the meager token snack or the delicious and elaborate feast and not on the content of the meeting. While trying to establish groups to run information sessions in the villages, iAgents faced a major struggle when villagers refused to attend after they learned that food would not be provided.

Staff members of ACRU also availed themselves of the iAgents' services, especially by recharging their mobile-phone credits, without paying the iAgents. Megh lamented that several employees had recharged their phones at her expense and that of other iAgents, and some of them had disappeared without paying. Rifat, still working at ACRU with the iAgents, defended himself with a logic of entitlement. "We have arranged this service for the iAgents to provide. So why should we not benefit from it?"

iAgents were due to receive an "honorarium" for educational sessions conducted with villagers. Instead of the attendees paying, the fee was covered by the Shabar Adhikar Foundation (SAF) in order to reduce the entry barrier for poor villagers to access information and to incentivize iAgents to continue conducting the sessions. This money was transferred from TIE to the centers to be distributed to iAgents according to the number of sessions each of them had conducted. Yet Sabbir devised a different plan. He had previously purchased a truckload of soap and cosmetics from Square Consumer Products, thereby cleverly attaining a bulk discount. Then he distributed boxes of the products among reluctant iAgents, who already knew that such brands would be impossible to sell in their villages because they were more expensive than what people paid at any corner shop. Then, rather than distributing the money TIE sent to the iAgents for conducting sessions, Sabbir kept it for himself. He treated the sum as money owed to the iAgents, who owed him for the cost of the products now in their possession. He was being "efficient" by repaying himself in the first instance. Thus he treated iAgents as cheap distribution channels and also arranged for himself immediate profit from unsold goods by repurposing the money due to the iAgents. In addition, ACRU staff members were paid an honorarium to assist iAgents in running educational sessions with villagers. Beyond the first week, I did not see any staff members attending any iAgent session. The iAgents handed in their session logs with one column, intended for any center member attending, marked as "no." Rifat, who was paid a salary to support the iAgents, crossed out most of the "no" boxes and wrote in "yes."

Weekly iAgent meetings at the center resembled lectures about how to make money off the poor. iAgents sat on plastic chairs in classroom formation facing a large wooden table behind which ACRU staff members sat. Frequent power cuts kick-started the deafeningly loud generator, which could power only one fan in this room, the one directly over the staff table. The iAgents inched their chairs closer to be able to catch a breeze as well as the content of Sabbir's talk. Often the lecture focused on rural people, who are "like the disabled. They are not interested in their conscience or in taking responsibility. That is your job. You give suggestions to them, and that is how you will earn from these rural areas." When Sabbir discussed specific iAgent services, such as Aponjon, in which expectant and new mothers could receive health information, his lectures became more specific. "These rural women are giving birth every day! You should set your Aponjon targets very high!" Picking up momentum about how to target "types" of villagers for specific services, he continued,

> Our focus should be mainly on crops because this area is completely agriculture-based, so we need to identify demand for equipment and other inputs. But when you visit housewives' groups, if you try to tell them about agricultural matters, it will not be appropriate. You have to work in a different way to attract those housewives. Definitely a housewife wants to use some good shampoo or has received or is about to receive a family-planning method. In that case, you have to find out which method she has received or what she is doing for birth control. So please make a survey to find out how many members there are in each family and what people are using for birth control. I hope you understand the meaning of productive and unproductive couples. Don't you understand? Do you? Please speak up! Do you understand this? Those couples who have the fertility to give birth to a baby, this

is called a productive couple. A married couple that lacks capability to give birth, such as if they are over-aged, then you have no reason to talk about this issue with them, isn't that right? So you will observe that productive couples have adapted to different ways of controlling birth; some women prefer to take Femicon pill, some prefer to use condom, and some who are a little rich prefer taking a better one like . . . which one? [Rifat supplied the answer, "Nordet pill."] Soon we will make an agreement with Square Pharmaceuticals, and you will sell the Nordet pill to them. Understand? From Aponjon, from women giving birth, you get ten taka only one time and then you have to wait for her to get pregnant again one year later for another ten taka. But if you are selling her birth control, she needs it every month to avoid getting pregnant. So even if your commission is very low, your overall profit will be much higher.

In this speech, worth quoting at length, we see how customers and services were both "segmented" and gendered and also how the stereotyped behaviors and choices of poor people came to be analyzed in order for the wealthier (the rural NGO middle class) to benefit financially from them. Not unique to Bangladesh, "the management use of workers as 'instruments of labor' is paralleled by another set of ideologies, which regards women's bodies as the site of control where gender politics, health, and educational practices intersect" (Ong 1988, 35). We also glimpse the calculus of how local informal social policy is produced through NGO activities. To simplify the above reasoning, "Shall we support high birth rates or family planning? Well, family planning ultimately is more profitable for us, so . . ." In the local policy formation and implementation of the iAgent program, decisions are made by the positionality of an executive director, who asserts his class and gender superiority. He enacts the role of a patronizing, powerful leader despite official descriptors of the process as "empowering" for poor rural women. Development goals for achieving certain outcomes and impacts were often rendered not as goods in themselves at the level of implementation, but more cynically as vehicles of self-enrichment for the local NGO middle classes.

Evolution of a Model

Without Rohan, the TIE team embarked on building the next iAgent model to scale up its operations. Just before (and perhaps to justify) building this latest model, Adnan admitted to the flaws of the license model. "In the past, when we said that iAgents provided eighty-five services, that was unreasonable. They were only ever able to focus on five or six services, so we will choose ones that will be good for their incomes and only do those." He also recognized the faulty assumption that iAgents and information centers could reach sustainability without input from TIE. Centers, with their NGO mindsets, could not understand the model properly, reasoned Adnan, which is why "plug and play," an otherwise sound concept to him, failed.

To develop the new expansion model, TIE received "incubation" and funding from an internationally known network of social entrepreneurs based in the United States whose staff advised Adnan to make several significant changes. Although the license model was still running in nine locations, in 2014 TIE acknowledged its failure, abandoned it, and dissolved SSI. The new model meant eliminating the role of centers as well, with the management of new iAgents undertaken directly by TIE. In addition, in a reversal from the intellectual-property-protection philosophy of the license model, TIE formalized a manual about the iAgent program and decided to make it "open access" so that any other organization globally could replicate it. TIE would then offer "capacity building" to those organizations, for a hefty consultancy fee. iAgents would continue to take loans. TIE and National Bank in August 2014 signed a new Memorandum of Understanding with the ambitious goal of scaling up to 4,500 new iAgents by the end of 2016, by which time, according to *Al Jazeera* (in an article published in 2014), "there will be an iAgent at every rural doorstep in the country." While potential partners for this new model were shown the "success cases" of iAgents elsewhere in Bangladesh, they were not made aware that dramatically different business models underpinned their existence, nor were they told that cases of failure were as prevalent and destructive as the successes were celebrated and promoted.

Shortly before Adnan informed me of the new model, Atno Bishash received a shipment of new glossy flyers advertising the iAgent program. In the office attending their monthly meeting, iAgents pored over the pamphlets. Taking one too, I asked with surprise, "When did they send you new uniforms?" Instead of the iconic teal and mustard yellow, iAgents from this location were depicted sporting navy-blue, gray, and red outfits that I had never seen before. "We don't have new uniforms. This is Photoshop!" Rahela laughed, looking at a picture of herself wearing clothes that she did not own and enacting a "new" model she knew nothing about. Brishti and Nilufar grumbled about not being featured in any of the photographs, while several iAgents from previous generations, who quit years ago, were represented. "Maybe they are trying to sell the same project again in a new body?" speculated Zahir, who always marveled at the ability of the Dhaka elite to accumulate wealth seemingly out of nothing but its own set of representations, detached from reality.

This chapter demonstrates the extent to which the urban NGO elite, situated in privileged positions in office headquarters, remained largely disconnected from the everyday lives of people at the receiving end of their activities. Instead, as direct recipients of international funding and fame, they jockeyed over theoretical constructs about the characteristics of social enterprise models and they could easily pivot as fashions in global development changed. They waged subtle office wars with one another over the politics of recognition and their own self- and name-making endeavors. Anyone who held an agenda different from the aggrandizement of the organization was effectively pushed out. The aesthetic of the network was to mirror the properties of existing social and political relations. As an extension of middle-class exercises of personhood, the network also amplified the class ideologies of powerful individuals.

Meanwhile, at the middle level of the iAgent hierarchy, people had to implement these shifting projects. Rural NGO leaders struggled over an increasingly limited funding supply, one that now privileged "sustainable" and income-generating projects such as microcredit and the social enterprise models of iAgent involving bank loans. Their social positions and patronage roles were highly dependent on showing conformity to the trends and timelines of the international development community as well as on demonstrating their perceived compliance with their superiors in Dhaka.

Some local NGO leaders, such as Sabbir Hossain in Amirhat, viewed NGOs explicitly as a tool for their own self-making projects of social mobility. Other leaders found status, for a time, to be a feature of the ability to provide much-needed opportunities and resources to the community. Caught in the middle of the incompatibility between donor trends and villagers' expectations for NGOs, one leader, Shorif, decided to forego the profitable prospect of launching micro-credit, which thus subjected him to failure as a patron. Had he relented and begun implementing microfinance, the community would have judged him and his NGO for taking an exploitative turn. The alternative to business sustainability was to continue project cycles, which featured unstable jobs for staff lower down in the NGO employment chain (at a time when few projects could be secured). People in the community who praised Atno Bishash based their recollections on a past in which they too benefited alongside Shorif and his family. Yet the increasingly critical commentary about Shorif's activities reflected people's dissatisfaction with his present inability to conjure employment and resources for broader distribution, and thus his own consumption of development goods was labeled as corruption.

Facing these challenges, the NGO middle classes had to perform considerable relational work to maintain a foothold on increasingly scarce resources. A multi-perspectival and relational approach to class analysis reveals "the unremitting *work* associated with becoming and remaining middle class" (Jeffrey 2008, 533), work that was becoming ever unmanageable. Overall, what we witnessed was the slide from traditional models of social inequality and patron clientelism—in which the wealthy and the poor engaged in reciprocal relations—to ones of antisocial inequality—where the wealthy abandoned their support for the poor.

In the projects they were able to access (such as the iAgent model), local NGOs possessed little power or ability to shape the discourse of recognition and ownership, and their work was constantly vulnerable to appropriation by entities higher up the ladder. If contestation over credit for development models was a key feature of the urban NGO elites, then basic recognition and ability to direct the course of events in a project was a major concern for the rural, lower end of the NGO leadership hierarchy. All individuals in this chain struggled to maintain social respect among a network of friends and family members who enjoyed white-collar jobs in government or the big-business private sector. Their own claims to status were often tenable only when they were able to secure numerous projects with vast resources with which to cement their role as patrons among their social inferiors.

In sum, an examination of the players, personal projects, and class aspirations involved in the iAgent network tells the story of a changing development moral economy in rural Bangladesh. The class politics of the iAgent project network, haphazardly joined together, mediated seemingly well-prepared models and plans. This chapter engages with the ways in which models intimated coherence but instead contained considerable internal contestation, divergence, and continuous redefinition as employees and owners performed the relational work of representing the project in ways that better asserted their claims over future resources and over one another. A major factor that played a role in the shifting nature of models—and the practices that were meant to follow from them—was the instability of changing international development priorities. This context significantly affected the ability of players who occupied various points in the national development hierarchy to achieve their personal and class projects. In the early years of NGO involvement in Bangladesh, existing class relations were clearly inscribed in the politics of providing relief. By contrast, what does poverty capitalism do to class relations? A major effect has been to delink widely practiced notions of responsibility and unsettle patron-client ties between the poor and the rural middle class, which was no longer able to provide resources according to previous expectations.

The iAgents and NGO workers at each level experienced the contradictions and destabilizing effects of their organizations. The many complaints and criticisms people had of their superiors, read as relational acts of resistance, are a diagnostic of the intensifying power imbalance in place within the development moral economy. The shift from NGO to market-driven enterprise was part of a global movement. This chapter, adding the role of class politics to the analysis of such trends, speaks to this broader contemporary global phenomenon.[17]

THE AMBIGUOUS FIGURES
OF SOCIAL ENTERPRISE

People used to speak badly about Rahela for being a girl who wanted to go to school, and her own father used to curse her every day. But after she became an iAgent, everything changed. From a shy, scared little girl, she became a confident, independent, and empowered young woman. People who used to criticize her now looked at her with respect.

TIE's iAgent social enterprise is designed for creating more Rahelas with these stories full of achieved dreams. An iAgent's superpower is information. At every moment, an iAgent out there brings information services by riding her bicycle to people in villages who are deprived of opportunity.

—iAgent Facebook page, November 17, 2014

For the benefit of external audiences, TIE staff, under Kabir's leadership, wrote this version of Rahela's story about overcoming her struggles. As this book has demonstrated so far, representations of the iAgent abounded. Each of these representations was strategically narrated in specific ways by different actors in order to promote particular agendas. They each provided a partial picture that evoked certain types of relationships and possibilities to achieve desired effects. Anthropologists have shown how representations of charismatic characters and human-interest stories can be taken up as exemplars and embodiments of success, and the stories told about them can perform the relational work of attracting supporters. Such work is central to the way program "success" is produced (Gardner 2012; Karim 2011; Mosse 2005). Sometimes, people are able to advance multiple contradictory stories simultaneously, thus exploiting the convenient aspects of each one.

A fluid set of portrayals of the iAgent role enabled the social enterprise to manufacture success by controlling the narrative. While social enterprise staff were able to pivot easily and profitably between these different representations, iAgents struggled to handle a constantly shifting rules playbook. By emphasizing one or another set of these representations, iAgents could comply with or resist social enterprise logics, but ultimately these tactics were insufficient for reconciling the contradictions they faced.

The differences in the contrasting or contradictory portrayals of Bangladeshi women found in national and international circuits of representation "become not accidents or inadequacies, but an index to the political interests which the images represent" (White 1992, 1). We must apprehend such images through the social relations and discourses with which they were produced. To push this insight further, beyond the ways in which each representation encodes its own politics, we can observe what was achieved through the simultaneous advancement of multiple images. This chapter argues that market-driven development models created and extracted value in particular ways and that these two processes required separate relational economies and representations. The act of switching between these sets of relations and representations was work that was profitable for the enterprise but rested on unstable social relations.

This chapter focuses on the elements of structural inequality and hierarchical connection between TIE and iAgents. Because relationships within the social enterprise were constantly shifting and being represented in different ways, the links between TIE and iAgents were difficult to categorize and provoke reflection about the nature of power in this assemblage when different relational narratives were expressed or suppressed. I show that both parties took advantage of the ambiguity produced by the overlay of multiple relational models, but in the longer run it was to the benefit of the enterprise staff and to the detriment of the iAgents. This result stemmed from TIE's ability to control the overall narrative of what an iAgent was and what she could do. TIE also controlled mechanisms for co-opting the short-term interests of iAgents to align with dominant representations advanced by TIE. As a result, the agency and ability of iAgents to self-represent became considerably diminished and circumscribed within TIE leaders' opportunistic notions of the role.

The narrative at the head of this chapter illustrates the hidden politics behind representations and their interpretations. The image that accompanied this text on the iAgent Facebook page depicts a young woman who appears as the protagonist in a comic strip and is entitled "Our Superhero" (*amader superhero*, figure 13). The cartoon iAgent stands alone on a hill with a large setting sun framing her figure. Her eyes are closed, and her hands rest on her hips in a confident posture. She wears the iconic iAgent teal-and-mustard uniform, with the exaggerated superhero-like flourishes of tall black boots, a mustard-colored cape flowing behind her where the ends of her *urna* (a scarf draped around her shoulders) would dangle, and a large "i" for "iAgent" decorating the front of her *kameez* (tunic). Icons of a bicycle, laptop, mouse, modem, mobile phone, and camera shoot toward her from the sky. The caption reads, "Justice League of America has Wonder Woman, and Bangladesh has iAgent. iAgents are the Superheroes of Bangladesh."[1]

FIGURE 13. A sketch of a poster produced by TIE, entitled "Our Superhero," in which women's superpowers are depicted as deriving from digital technologies and physical mobility. Sketch by author, based on original image designed by TIE.

So, who is an iAgent? Is she a popular heroine or a destitute hawker? The people closest to the young women in question—parents, neighbors, and classmates—and even the iAgents themselves were the most unclear about the identity of the iAgent. "No idea. She's my cousin's daughter," was a common response, meaning an undefined distant relative. "She showed us videos about early marriage. Sometimes she makes the machine grab our arms so tightly that we can hear our hearts going *pshh, pshh* [from the blood-pressure cuff]. She should get married so she can stop this nonsense." "She works at that NGO," someone else chimed in. "They help us during the flood season."

People distant from the lives of actual iAgents held clear but differing notions about their role. According to a senior manager at Yamada Corporation, a major Japanese electronics giant, "iAgents are freelance consultants. They sell information and knowledge necessary for life in rural areas." The head of a prominent human-rights foundation asserted, "iAgents are one-hundred percent social workers. They selflessly look after the most marginalized people in society."

The sharp transition from undifferentiated village girl to independent and powerful young entrepreneur, which TIE asserted was the linear effect of its intervention, is significant. The definitiveness of this act of shape-shifting contrasted with actual iAgent experiences, which were marked by continual misunderstandings of their social role. It is precisely this ambiguity that enabled the enterprise to function. The uncertain nature of the iAgent's role in the community and her relationship to TIE allowed potential partners and resource-givers to hold such definitive and yet different ideas about the iAgent, ideas that TIE crucially needed to attract and retain their patronage.

Exploring the actual relations of hierarchy helps us to evaluate TIE's claims of endowing iAgents with the power to save people's lives and enact radical self-transformation, as suggested by the superhero imagery and accompanying descriptions. The relational work of insisting that iAgents achieved dramatic empowerment did more than attract external funders and supporters. It also served to obscure, under the guise of entrepreneurial independence, the vertical relations of domination and the structural ambiguity that were crucial to the survival of the model at its fundamental level.

The iAgent case allows me to propose a more general theoretical proposition, one that builds throughout the book. The political and ideological work of promoting entrepreneurship as a means of development and empowerment erodes the NGO-development moral economy—and consolidates more starkly unequal and coercive relations between patrons and clients. Market-driven development enterprises fail to achieve empowering outcomes for beneficiaries, but not because they were drawn into patron-client roles. Patron-clientage already characterized the contexts in which these new practices were installed. Rather, these enterprises failed because they sought to strip away the sociality and reciprocity from relationships to form a market society based on impersonal relations. They installed a new mode of antisocial inequality where previously relations of social inequality ensured mutuality and recognition. The new market space contained its own moralities of entrepreneurialism and self-help for the poor, but preexisting class relationships of dominance also remained. In the partial transition from an NGO-patronage moral economy to a market-based moral economy, the poor lost access to crucial resources of protection and support and were held responsible for their own survival, but they also remained beholden to domination by the NGO middle classes.

Mobilizing Multiple Representations

TIE established itself as intermediary between potential partner companies and rural villagers in order to connect services to service recipients. The organization did so via its control over the labor power of iAgents. It mediated products and services, such as Unilever's fast-moving consumer goods for iAgents to sell to villagers, Yamada's solar-powered-battery-recharging services that iAgents delivered weekly to off-grid areas, and the foundation's Right to Information Act (RTI) training. It also brokered the claim, to be asserted by those partner organizations, of achieving women's empowerment and poverty alleviation. Many companies found this aspect to be essential in fulfilling their social-responsibility mandates.

Yet the item most crucially mediated was the idea of the iAgent itself. The indefinite but malleable nature of the figure of the iAgent was a key factor in uniting and holding together the diverse players and interests in the assemblage. Actors were able to endow the iAgent idea with their own meanings, which generated discordance and confusion for iAgents but also enabled cooperation between TIE and its partners.

Maintaining the fluidity of the iAgent image was not an optional tactic for customizing a sales pitch. Rather, it was necessary for the model to function. In order to achieve the targets set by partners (such as enlisting two million SMS subscribers to the Aponjon program of USAID within three years of operation), TIE needed to ensure the participation of the entire network of iAgents across Bangladesh. While the primary selling point of the iAgent model was the transformation of poor but educated young women into independent entrepreneurs, TIE had to control their activities and monitor their outputs closely in order to achieve the partners' goals. This central contradiction formed the basis of representational flexibility and relational multiplicity in the link between TIE and iAgents. TIE needed to manage closely the narrative of the iAgent by juggling contradictory images of, on the one hand, women's empowerment through independent entrepreneurship and, on the other, a tightly managed rural distribution network of malleable workers. The first image sold the concept of social impact and thus moral legitimacy (in a process of strengthening values), while the second image sold the practical means of generating revenue (in a process of extracting value). TIE profited by flexibly manipulating the image of the iAgent according to context.

Katy Gardner (2012) analyzes a similar contradiction in the context of Chevron, a multinational energy company, and its relationship with people living in the Bangladesh villages surrounding its gas field. Despite the appropriation of agricultural plots for the purpose of building Chevron's infrastructure, non-landowning agricultural laborers were not given formal compensation for their loss of livelihood, nor were they able to become socially embedded in patronage relations with the company. Instead, the project was "located in moralities [of entrepreneurship and self-help] that deny both social connection and formal compensation" (Gardner 2012, 139). "The irony is striking: while local people are physically, culturally and economically disconnected from the gas field, Chevron must claim connection with them in order to promote its global reputation for 'partnership'" (Gardner 2012, 46). Chevron imagined and then performed a connection with the community, which it then converted into moral value that generated economic value for the company but not for the community. Rather, villagers were excluded from the value (in terms of ultimate profits) and values (in terms of patronage, help, and meaningful ties) produced by their enlistment in the company's corporate-social-responsibility programs. Such practice reveals the "ethic of detachment" (Cross 2011) exemplified in the "development gift" (Rajak 2011a, 2011b; Stirrat and Henkel 1997), or what Gardner (2012) calls "disconnected development."

The case of the iAgents (and similar social enterprises) differs from these other market-based practices in one key aspect. In development and corporate engagement with the community, brokering representations through one-off events and carefully curated ceremonies tends to be sufficient to achieve public-relations objectives. The semblance of connections claimed with participants can be performed while, in reality, actual disconnection can occur once events conclude. In the iAgent case, the organization needed also to broker the actual long-term compliance of the iAgents and harness their labor power to deliver tangible results for external partners into the future. Thus, the central contradiction of strengthening values while extracting value manifested more intensely and generated growing relational inconsistencies over time.

In addition to its deployment of multiple services offered to village clients that encoded different social and financial logics, the iAgent assemblage is an apt site for exploring the relational ambiguities produced by its internal structure and dynamics. If iAgents were meant to behave similarly to NGO workers who adhered to strict codes of regulated and controlled practice, if they were also represented as independent entrepreneurs engaging in free-choice market transactions with TIE, and if they were expected to behave as beneficiaries of patronage who showed their loyalty by obeying the directives of their superiors, then how did they navigate these competing logics?[2]

This chapter explores the mechanisms by which multiple representations and their relational economies were sustained and the strategies that people used to negotiate them. People sometimes invoked particular representations to achieve objectives within a certain context, but they did not stabilize them for all circumstances. Rather, the enterprise worked only through the ability of actors to switch among different positions flexibly. Representational flexibility was socially efficacious in holding assemblages together and in stabilizing relations of power. Three ethnographic cases offer insight into this process.

In the first ethnographic exploration, readers are reminded of the process by which TIE converted the iAgent project from an NGO-run donor-driven model to a market-driven, social enterprise structure. The relational work of disavowing sociality while also increasing control was central to this transition. Yet crucially, the conversion from dependence (on NGO as patron) to independence (as self-directing entrepreneur in business with the former patron) was never complete. TIE required aspects of both relational modes to exist simultaneously in order to hold together the assemblage. I outline the mechanisms by which TIE introduced a detached, impersonal relationship with iAgents in order to manage them.

The second case shows how the processes of adverse incorporation aligned the interests of iAgents with those of TIE. By enacting representations of themselves that they thought would attract the attentions of foreigners and powerful external others, iAgents lent legitimacy to TIE's dominant discourses. In this circumstance, it was the iAgents who stabilized TIE-generated narratives of themselves in pursuit of resources, but in the end it was TIE that appropriated the value produced by those narratives.

In the third account, I return to the story of the iAgents' RTI service introduced in chapter 4. iAgents used one of the program's own discursive framings against TIE as an act of resistance. By strictly performing according to the rules and expectations of a particular representation of themselves as self-maximizing independent entrepreneurs (as opposed to malleable employees or charitable social workers), iAgents built a compelling case to boycott participation in RTI work. Again, iAgents invoked a set of self-representations—with content and relational logics contradictory to those of their stories for foreigners—in order to derail the project and refuse the inadequate patronage of TIE's RTI-sponsoring partner. Due to TIE's ability to exert pressure on iAgents through the threat of complete abandonment, this act of rebellion resulted not in open negotiation of the terms of exchange but rather in more strict and oppressive terms.

These multiple angles show that the many representations of iAgents and their relationship with TIE were each unstable and incomplete. This overall ambiguity through multiplicity is what made the assemblage able to fulfill its responsibilities to partner organizations. Far from being the result of messy implementation, these structural and relational ambiguities, as well as moments of boundary delineation, were part of the fabric that held the iAgent program together under the control of TIE. The mechanisms by which TIE consolidated control over iAgents were devices of detachment, adverse incorporation, and threatened relationship closure.

Case One: Devices of Organizational Detachment

In engineering the shift from an NGO to a for-profit enterprise model, and to encourage iAgents to act like independent entrepreneurs rather than development-program beneficiaries, TIE staff needed to discipline the behavior and expectations of iAgents accordingly. The NGO–social enterprise shift was characterized by the changing priorities of international donors (now recast as "investors"), but it also occurred through a change in leadership from Rohan Alam (the sociology-trained project designer of the iAgent program) to Adnan Khan (the umbrella organization's economics-trained leader) and his supporters.

TIE used particular devices to install a rationalized market relationship while detaching from an affective one. As Jamie Cross notes, "Current trends in economic sociology approach the bracketing and ending of relationships between two parties in a transaction as crucial acts in the performance of a market, and seek to grasp how the terms of this 'detachment' are established and controlled" (Cross 2011, 35, drawing on Callon 1998). In the iAgent case, efforts to achieve relationship closure proved to be problematic, especially for TIE workers who had preexisting direct, often affective but hierarchical relationships with iAgents. Rather than a single act of severance, detachment—as a relational action—requires continuous effort and performance. To scale up the iAgent model—from two locations and twenty iAgents in 2012 (when it was possible to know all of the individuals) to a network of three hundred iAgents in 2013 and over eleven thousand planned for 2017 (when they would be reduced to abstract, numerical figures)—required Adnan's rationally efficient "plug-and-play" model to be automated to the greatest extent possible. "Detachment was seen as a precondition for the rational, market-oriented calculations and impartial decisions required of a modern professional, essential for achieving control and productivity" (Cross 2011, 39), especially to meet such ambitious goals.

As an informal broker of information between TIE and the iAgents, I was one conduit for TIE's procedures of detachment. After TIE moved me from Amirhat (so that I would not influence or witness the aftermath of the iAgents' group resignation from the program), I met with iAgent team leaders at TIE to discuss my possible research at Lalpur. Lalpur was their exemplary location, where all foreigners, news teams, and award evaluators were brought, and they agreed to my continued work. They were confident that Lalpur would restore my faith in the iAgent model, as it had inspired hundreds of foreigners before me.

Despite his confidence, the iAgent team leader at the time, Kabir, impressed upon me the importance of maintaining personal distance from center staff and iAgents alike. He assured me that my research project required that I follow only the official aspects of their work. "If the staff of Atno Bishash start to share internal or personal issues with you, you need to discourage them from doing so. In the beginning if you discourage them, they will not share with you again. You are not the problem solver for them. We are the best people to solve these issues, and there is a correct way that iAgents will share with the center, and the center will share with us." Other than being a treatise about how not to conduct anthropological research, Kabir's lecture signaled to me the deliberate and systematic changes TIE was making to put in place protocol-driven asocial market relationships. His orientation contrasted sharply with that of Rohan—the architect of the iAgent pilot model who was expelled from the organization—who phoned me regularly in Amirhat to understand my analysis of the situation and hear my suggestions for tackling deeply rooted problems in the model. I detail here some of the devices of detachment TIE employed to strip back iAgent relationships to transactional ones.

Detachment through Bureaucracy

Adnan's team introduced a regime of procedural rigidity to the iAgent model. Whereas previously iAgents communicated with the TIE employees they knew and trusted, now staff members were assigned as "designated responsible persons" for different locations of iAgents. Allocations were rotated in an attempt to eliminate the social relations of the previous era. Designated responsible persons, unfamiliar to iAgents, had often never visited the locations over which they now presided. When Taspia and her colleagues in Amirhat faced their most severe problems shortly before they resigned, they telephoned Shila to communicate their difficulties and ask for help. Shila no longer answered, but Fahim, a new team member, began taking their calls instead. He had never been to Amirhat, nor was he aware of the context of the difficult relations between the center and the iAgents. Crucial information about the state of affairs in Amirhat therefore failed to reach TIE.

Shila, who was in turn the new designated person for Lalpur, became angry in a meeting with the iAgents in that location for not communicating their problems directly to her. "If you go straight over my head to Jahid, you make it look as if I am not doing my job!" Jahid could have helped by forwarding the email to Shila, but he exonerated himself of the need to act citing the iAgents' failure to comply with protocol and correctly install the bureaucratic model. TIE staff pressured iAgents to use impersonal emails, rather than personal phone calls, as the primary medium of communication, and their messages needed to move along a predefined hierarchy of staff members.

Anthropologists have underscored the centrality of documents as artifacts of modern knowledge practices (Bear 2013; Cross 2011; Hull 2012; Riles 2006). TIE's digital documentary regimes achieved the work of temporal detachment and strategic ignorance through the manner in which they were created and handled. In the incorrect format, documents became delegitimized and rejected as carriers of inadmissible forms of information. Annelise Riles notes how "information" or "documents" are recognized as such only when they have traveled along official paths and have thus become formalized. Yet, "the very artifacts we imagine as being at the heart of 'information flows' may not partake in the aesthetic of flow at all" (Riles 2000, 113).

Linsey McGoey advances the study of what she calls "strategic unknowns" or "strategic ignorance," which is "the investigation of the multifaceted ways that ignorance can be harnessed as a resource, enabling knowledge to be deflected, obscured, concealed, or magnified in a way that increases the scope of what remains intelligible" (2012b, 1). Ignorance should not be assumed to impede power; it is not the failure to gain knowledge. Rather, non-knowledge, interpreted instead as a social fact that is itself productive, can be read as an advantage to be cultivated for various reasons, such as the management of risk, denial of responsibility, and exoneration of future blame. Each of these objectives was necessary for TIE to be able to scale up the iAgent model rapidly without being hindered by what it deemed to be extraneous or inefficient information. TIE needed to set the expectation that it would not solve or be responsible for iAgents' problems; all risk, responsibility, and consequences needed to be devolved downward.

Detachment through Language

Language is another important technology of detachment. A license model required iAgents to appear more like entrepreneurs than employees or dependent workers. Rather than signaling a change in the actual content of the relationship, the insistence on using a different set of vocabulary was itself performative: "Labels and institutional practices are issues of power; they are invented by institutions as part of an apparently rational process that is fundamentally political in nature" (Escobar 1991, 667). Changes in the particular kinds of transactions within a particular relation, including the terms used, are part of the relational work of exerting power. For instance, "to label a payment as a gift (tip, bribe, charity, expression of esteem) rather than an entitlement (pension, allowance, rightful share of gains) or compensation (wages, salary, bonus, commission) is to make claims about the relationship between payer and payee" (Zelizer 2011, 189). If Adnan's team wanted to implement a for-profit model, it needed to shift the expectations of iAgents away from continued patronage and support through grants. Before transitioning to the commercial loan structure, TIE experimented with the idea of requiring an informal investment from pilot-model iAgents for their own business start-up costs. Although TIE continued to operate in an NGO modality and was externally grant-funded itself, the organization decided that if iAgents put their own money into the project, they would be incentivized to work harder. TIE had initially issued equipment to the iAgents free of charge but later decided to treat the items as asset-based loans to be repaid. Gifts reinforce relationships; in contrast, institutional loans render them transactional and impersonal while retaining power over the recipients.

iAgents in the grant-based model began applying their incomes against repayment of the equipment they had received. Yet when they discovered that their laptops, medical equipment, bicycles, and other items had already been financed by a grant, they became complacent about their obligations to repay TIE. They knew the money was actually a gift disguised as a loan. TIE's support of them in the past had also set the precedent for continued gift-giving in the future. "It was a moral-hazard problem," explained Adnan. "We breached the model ourselves, and that was the beginning of the malfunctioning of our model." He assumed that a model of market relationships needed to be installed in a fresh domain that was not previously tainted by NGO-donation-type relations. He failed to realize that any context in rural Bangladesh where TIE could have operated would carry a legacy of an NGO-patronage moral economy, which shaped villagers' expectations of any institution establishing activities there.

Also, the failure to install a market logic of debt and detachment in the place of a patronage logic of gifts and connection was seen to arise when iAgents obtained the knowledge of the relational history of the equipment and the (grant) money with which it was purchased. For the detachment model to work, that history needed to be concealed, and thus strategic ignorance became a key mechanism of detachment in yet another way. Adnan began negotiating with commercial banks for the next batch of iAgents.

TIE employees endeavored to avoid this kind of "moral-hazard" mistake. Kabir chastised me over the phone for asking about new projects to be implemented for the iAgents. "Please be careful not to use the word 'project.' They are 'business opportunities.' The goal is to abandon the project mindset," he explained. "Rather than saying to them that 'a new project is coming from SAF or Yamada,' tell them, 'This is a new sales or service opportunity for you.' We are trying to communicate with the iAgents that our activity is 'business with partners,' instead of a 'project from donors.' When you speak with them, please take care to use the correct words." "Honorariums" were also removed as incentives for iAgents to run free educational sessions with their groups, but occasionally the women received "payments" from partners (even if the money was still donated to TIE by foundations) for distributing certain types of information. This watchful enforcement of language formed part of TIE's efforts to reframe information in order to manipulate iAgent behaviors and to change the appearance of the relationship for funders. Such exhortations evoke a particular type of relationship while obscuring the continued presence of others.

Case Two: Narrative Labor and Adverse Incorporation

This case and the next one explore the deliberate efforts of iAgents to negotiate their self-representations in orientation to outsiders. In both cases, pursuit of their interests led iAgents to align themselves with dominant but disparate representations advanced by TIE. Yet in the first, such alignment facilitated the efforts of their superiors to attract resources, while in the second, it marked a deliberate act of resistance against TIE.

As a broker, TIE need to appear as resource-giver from the perspective of the wider international development world in order to attract new projects. iAgents also learned which imagery and narratives appealed to certain kinds of people.

FIGURE 14.   Uniformed iAgents line up with their bicycles for a photo shoot requested by foreign visitors. Photo by author.

The representations they enacted, conjured in moments of performance, did not become fixed because they did not correspond to the everyday lives and work of these women.

The ways in which iAgents were aware of the benefits that publicity events and visitors could bring them, and the ways in which they took care to align themselves with the dominant external representations of themselves, incorporated them under TIE's authority and had an adverse effect on the iAgents themselves. In an appropriation of the value of the iAgents' affect-laden narratives, TIE was able to attract more funding and then deny the affective relation of patronage that infused the stories.[3]

Several forums designed by TIE enlisted iAgent performances and narratives for the explicit purpose of attracting potential partners and resource-givers. This particular set of representations took the common rhetorical form of personal-transformation and turning-point narratives, as exemplified by TIE's rendering of Rahela's journey in becoming an iAgent. In addition to Facebook pages, other spaces hosted stories using similar techniques, such as TIE's websites, annual reports, and applications for awards. While TIE edited the written media, iAgents could actively represent themselves, albeit under TIE influence, through radio interviews, documentary shoots, and field visits. I describe one such spectacle, a field visit by multiple groups of foreigners. The event was carefully curated to produce a particular set of effects for its participants, but the multiplicity of agendas and interests held by the different visitors complicated these efforts. Ultimately, it was the ambiguous nature of the iAgent idea that rendered the program into a script malleable by these diverse parties to insert their own text and interpretation.

The meeting room of Atno Bishash was packed. The temperature was a few degrees cooler inside the brick-and-mortar structure with dusty ceiling fans switched on at full power, but half the occupants of the room, sitting on wooden chairs around the periphery, still fanned themselves vigorously with NGO pamphlets. It was the first of September 2013, and fourteen foreigners had come to meet the iAgents of Lalpur. Rohan had managed to coordinate the visits of reporters from a Korean national news agency, documentary filmmakers from Switzerland, a delegation of executives from Japan's multinational electronics firm Yamada, and the resident anthropologist from London.[4] All four groups recorded, filmed, and photographed the event but for different preconceived purposes. The Korean news crew wanted to astound its viewers back home with stories of the hardship and perseverance of the young Bangladeshi village women. The Swiss documentary team aimed to capture the social complexities arising from a remote village's first interactions with the internet, via iAgents literally as its interface. Yamada sought to design and implement a feasibility study for distributing, through iAgents, its photovoltaic batteries in "base-of-the-pyramid" markets. And the anthropologist filmed both observers and performers to capture if and how these different interests—and their corresponding preconceived portrayals of iAgents—would be reconciled.

Six iAgents sat on chairs in an arc at the head of the room. They all wore teal-and-mustard uniforms but the different uniforms represented different eras of the iAgent model. The variations in their attire were subtle—a frilled collar on one, two green stripes around the ankles of the mustard *shalwar* of a second, and a longer coat of a third. Apart from style, the degree of the clothing's fading also indicated the amount of time that the young women had spent working as iAgents. Because they were required to wear them every day, the bright uniforms with neatly stenciled logos soon faded, and the detail work cracked under rough washing and sun exposure. Although none of the iAgents wore such modest coverings in everyday life, they perceived the uniforms—particularly the burqa (in the form of a knee-length smock resembling a colorful laboratory coat)—to be symbols of professionalism that commanded respect, similar to the outfits that BRAC health workers and female hospital staff wore.

Before this meeting took place, I overheard some iAgents requesting that TIE staff issue them new uniforms. If they were going to be filmed and shown across the world, it would be too embarrassing for them to wear old, faded clothes. Yet while iAgents wanted to be represented as respectable well-dressed experts, Rohan and his team, who controlled the distribution and use of new clothing, knew that there was more emotional (and therefore financial) purchase in the image of hard-working village girls who had accomplished so much with so little. Dress had become one more power-inflected struggle over the representation of iAgents.

TIE did decide to issue new uniforms, but not before the event. Instead, Rohan staged a "ceremony" at the end of the meeting so that foreigners could take photographs of TIE formally presenting new uniforms to the iAgents as if they were awards. Rohan lingered his grasp on the folded and plastic-encased material before the iAgent could take it, while he angled his body outward for the photos.[5]

By issuing uniforms, TIE deflected iAgent complaints by arguing that technically it had fulfilled their demands. Yet the organization also retained control of the narrative of threadbare young women who needed to be lifted out of poverty by engaging in entrepreneurship, with TIE as the benevolent activator of that process. TIE wanted to promote the extraordinariness of the iAgents, while making sure to assert its role in their creation (just as it had for the text on its Facebook page).

Rohan translated from Bangla to English the stilted and formulaic opening remarks by Shorif, the Atno Bishash executive director, before he launched into the background story of the origin and evolution of the iAgent program. iAgents sat quietly until Rohan asked them to introduce themselves one by one and down the line. Using the formula, "I am iAgent Dipa from Phulbari working area," they unsmilingly greeted the foreigners. Rohan then asked two iAgents to tell stories about their experience so far, as exemplars for the rest. Not surprisingly, the two he selected—Rahela and Dipa—sported the oldest-looking uniforms and were known by TIE to be the most articulate in ways favorable to the program. The visitors seemed not to notice that their attention was organized away from some iAgents and toward others, just as they were unaware that they had been brought deliberately to the oldest and best-functioning iAgent location.

The stories followed the familiar structure of the turning-point narrative, a technique common among social entrepreneurs to demonstrate simultaneously their troubled backgrounds and hence unwavering commitment to the social cause, the determination and persistence crucial for instilling trust in their ability to carry out the idea, and the emotional threads that enlist the sentiments and support of the listeners. The stories contained elements that Rahela and Dipa

FIGURE 15.   A foreign documentary filmmaker captures the process of TIE staff handing out new uniforms to iAgents (photo by author).

had been told that outsiders wanted to hear, such as encountering and debunking dangerous traditional practices and using the lifesaving role of "modern" knowledge to overcome archaic social values. Rohan used the process of interpreting as an editorial device by translating (from Bangla to English) the iAgents' words selectively, for example by differentiating implicitly between good and bad suffering and hardship. Good suffering, by Rohan's distinction, occurred before the program began and related to social problems in communities, thus rhetorically demonstrating the need for TIE to provide a solution. Bad suffering, meanwhile, occurred as a result of the program and was not meant for the audience's ears. From the iAgents' perspectives, hardship (or suffering, *kosto*) was an expression of the virtue, especially for women, of hard work sincerely performed. In italics I indicate speech glossed over or omitted in the English translation. My focus in presenting these two narratives is not on the facts of their content, but rather on their interpretation as scripts in the performance of enacting particular identities. Rahela spoke first:

> I arrived at my weekly housewife-group session and noticed that one woman, who had not been attending for three weeks, was again absent. After the session ended I visited her house. Her daughter was sick. Some people said that she was influenced by a ghost; others said that she had been affected by bad air. There were many superstitions like that. I informed the mother that we were hosting a health camp soon that would be aired on "Connecting Bangladesh."

Rohan interjected to explain that "Connecting Bangladesh" was a program TIE built to scale up the impact of the model by broadcasting iAgents' sessions, in which they facilitated and televised a live consultation with professional experts via videoconference. This way, villagers sitting in front of televisions around the country could benefit from the knowledge iAgents conveyed in sessions in their own villages. Rohan gestured for Rahela to continue.

> I enrolled the mother and daughter in the consultation with the doctor, who advised that the girl needed to come to Dhaka for a physical exam. The program agreed to fund the trip because the family could not afford it. The villagers discouraged us a lot. They told the mother that her daughter would be trafficked. *After arriving at the hospital, the mother saw that many children were dying and blamed me for sending her daughter to a place to die. Then the doctor needed to draw blood, which the mother thought would be sold to people in other countries.* After the procedures, the girl was sent back home. *My father forced me to stop working. He said, "You are doing something wrong with the community, and you are making people angry with our family."* But then the center staff told me, "If you become this weak under a challenge, you'll never be successful in life. You must be patient and do much more hard work." Later, the situation turned when the girl got better, and the man

who was threatening my father became shy with me, and later he sent another sick child to see me.

The foreigners clapped enthusiastically, which seemed to surprise the iAgents, who did not understand the translation or the visitors' backgrounds. Rahela had nearly caused her family to be alienated from the village, which was a source of great stress for her. She had taken a reputational and personal risk under the pressure of Shorif and his NGO team. What if the girl had died in the hospital in Dhaka? Regardless of the cause, people would always have blamed her, even her own family. The Koreans in the news team talked excitedly, and another layer of translation probably diluted her words further. Several of them nodded at Rahela and looked impressed. Rohan then invited Dipa to speak:

> A pregnant woman in my village was about to give birth. I went to her house and could hear her screaming inside. She was being treated by a traditional midwife who would not let me in, saying, "Who are you? You're just a young girl. You're not even married so what do you know about pregnancy?" But the pregnant woman's screams grew louder, and I pushed my way in. I saw that the birth was a difficult one and the baby was coming out heel-first. The midwife was only mas- saging the woman's stomach with oil. I pushed in and manipulated the baby around and then delivered it. The baby was not breathing, and I asked the midwife if she planned to do mouth-to-mouth, but she started burning the placenta. She said that the smoke from the burning placenta would make the baby start breathing. I knew that the smoke would prevent the baby from breathing so I did mouth-to- mouth myself, and after a short time the baby started crying. After that, people started to believe, Yes, maybe this girl does know some- thing after all!

Rohan did not censor any major components of Dipa's account. Dipa had already omitted any aspects that could be interpreted as the program's placing her in a vulnerable position in the community. (Not coincidentally, Dipa was selected to accompany Rohan on a fully funded trip to Germany to accept a corporate-sponsored award for information and communication technologies in develop-ment and online activism.) After another excited round of applause, the Korean and Swiss cameras moved in for close-up shots of the two women who had spo-ken. When Rohan invited the audience to ask questions, a Japanese man shot his hand up. Having worked in Bangladesh for several years, he positioned himself as a broker between Japanese companies and Bangladeshi NGOs to encourage social enterprise development. He had introduced Yamada's consultant to TIE to design the photovoltaic pilot program. He asked skeptically, "How are these stories connected either to ICT or the iAgent core business of making money?"

While the documentary and news teams were misty-eyed and emotionally affected by Rahela's and Dipa's narratives, the man from Japan focused on the technical aspects of the program and not on its sociopolitical content. Rohan responded that iAgents do not earn money from these types of incidents but that performing social work helps to establish their businesses. For Yamada's broker to understand the stories as meaningful for his own objectives, the narratives needed to be framed in terms of (and even subsumed under) economic goals.[6] (The deciding factor for Yamada to partner with TIE was not the visit to the countryside to meet off-grid villagers, nor was it hearing iAgent stories, but rather seeing, in TIE's head office in Dhaka, the detailed income and expense data that iAgents [supposedly] sent daily.)

While some Yamada delegation members stressed one type of representation of iAgents (as promoters and potential purveyors of technology), the iAgents asserted a different one. By emphasizing this particular style of narrative, with its focus on being empowered, overcoming obstacles, and saving lives through persistence in using "legitimate" forms of knowledge, iAgents attempted to conjure the type of money that such scenarios usually attracted. Their use of the drama-laden narrative, in their opinion and experience, was the most effective (and affective) way to generate revenue for TIE. Such stories had been the most potent form of account during the time that TIE had made money primarily through grants from foundations and charity from philanthropists. Now, with a new kind of potential patron to impress, iAgents needed to adapt their stories to focus on different registers. To secure the participation of actors such as Yamada, multiple other simultaneous representations had to be available for invocation (which TIE later accomplished, in the head office, by means of the income and expense data).

The encounter with Yamada shows how the agency of iAgents was circumscribed within the TIE-delineated iAgent persona, even when they spoke for themselves.[7] While young women accessed and forged new opportunities through their participation in the program, their repositioning as iAgents enhanced and restrained their capacity to act. Their visibility, power, and opportunities were contingent on remaining iAgents. Otherwise, they ceased being symbols and melted into the undifferentiated masses. While the speech acts of iAgents could be read as acts of agency in the localized sense that they chose to tell particular stories they thought might bring them benefit, TIE exerted a larger agenda-setting agency. iAgents' decisions were influenced by the ways in which TIE framed the encounter, which in turn tapped into enthusiasms currently active in the international development context.

While new projects did come, the hope of "trickle-down economics" (that is, of benefits awarded to TIE thus being distributed downward to iAgents) remained largely unrealized. iAgents were co-opted into implementing these new projects while TIE retained the vast majority of inflowing resources. Zahir often complained about the nature of TIE's partnership agreements whenever I asked why particular partners did not allocate higher levels of support directly to iAgents:

> Actually, it is TIE that completely makes this project. The organization writes the proposal and sends it to the partner. The partner knows only that, say, one hundred people will come to know about RTI, and fifty people will be habituated by receiving services through this act. The partner sees just the achievement, but how the plan will actually be implemented is hidden by TIE. When we received funding for the iAgent pilot, funds for only one and a half staff members were allocated to each of the two field sites. But twelve staff members were funded at the head level, and many of them were not directly related to the iAgent program.

Zahir worked on a plan to make the iAgents independent by forming an association that would be run by them and in which partnership agreements would be made directly without the exploitative brokerage role of TIE. His efforts were futile. TIE would not agree because the iAgents' independence would release them from TIE's claim to their productive and symbolic power.

The iAgents' performance in this gathering portrayed their empowerment and social impact through persistence and the power of "modern" information. They employed turning-point narratives as devices for cultivating an affect of empathy, admiration, and sentimentality in order to attract external resources. Yet the overall effect was to incorporate them more adversely with TIE. Although the iAgents exerted agency in choosing particular narratives and in speaking for themselves, the delivery of such narratives was curated by TIE, and any partnerships and resources resulting from this narrative labor were commandeered by the organization. iAgents further entrenched themselves as workers consigned to carry out projects whose terms were externally dictated. In the next section, I show how adherence to TIE's representations of them allowed iAgents to challenge the terms of the model.

Case Three: "Playing Along" as an Act of Resistance

In late October 2013 TIE asked Zahir to meet with all the iAgents in Lalpur to find out why they had stopped submitting reports on their work. Zahir had worked for many years at the iAgent center NGO and for nearly four of these he served as the primary person responsible for the iAgent program when external funding supported his salary. Now that the program had transitioned to a for-profit model, each entity in each tier in the license structure needed to fund itself. (The Atno Bishash executive director, not wanting to allocate his staff where no grant money existed, had reassigned Zahir to direct a recently acquired project funded by Oxfam Netherlands.) The relative success of the iAgents in Lalpur had been due in large part to the efforts of Zahir, who had spent each day with iAgents in the field, helping them to solve their problems, build their businesses, and assert their legitimacy among potential clients. Zahir had last met with these iAgents many months previously.

Entering the NGO meeting room where the nine iAgents sat in chairs in a semicircle, Zahir asked about their work. "Are your sessions running? How are you making an income?" All iAgents answered in the negative; they did not run sessions anymore but they still provided individual services: blood-pressure checks, diabetes tests, photographs, and product sales from their shops. Zahir expressed his disappointment. According to the plug-and-play model advanced by Adnan's new TIE team, after the iAgents were trained in all of the activities and able to demonstrate proficiency in conducting them, TIE could take a hands-off approach and manage the women from a distance. The iAgents would continue to work consistently, and in that way they, and therefore the centers and eventually SSI and TIE, would all become financially sustainable and profitable. So why did the iAgents' activity languish?

Zahir reasoned with them. "With NGO projects, you go out into the field for some time, the project finishes, and you stop. But you are entrepreneurs now. You are independent. You have to decide to do these things on your own, all of the time, and not just when a specific project comes from TIE. Remember how much higher your incomes were when you ran group sessions? Because then you had everyone in one place ready to buy products and get their pressure checked." Rahela and another iAgent asserted that they no longer received income from group sessions because the honoraria they had received for hosting such sessions had stopped along with the grant model, and therefore they could not continue to conduct them.

Rahela had ended her sessions before Ramadan, in June. While she enjoyed the four "free" months, she was not pleased that her income was so low. She had previously averaged 15,000 taka (192 USD) in income per month just from services, not including honoraria. Now, she was making only 7,000 taka (90 USD). Even without receiving honoraria, her income had been double just by conducting the sessions. But, she reasoned, "If there *are* no sessions, then how can I *go* to sessions?" Rahela demonstrated her knowledge of the NGO financial logic taught by her immediate superiors at the center as well as the TIE staff until that point. If no direct financial incentive or a project-oriented schedule existed to conduct the sessions, she would not do them. Rahela clarified the nuances of different types of money. "When you have income, you also have expenses. But when you have an honorarium, it comes, and it simply stays. I like that kind of money." That was the logic of NGO cash, received from above with loose expectations, no initial financial outlay necessary, and thus minimal risk.

iAgents did not act in ways that TIE would define as entrepreneurial, such as creating their own group meetings to attract customers and actively seeking out information gaps that they could fill for profit. Rather, the framework that seemed to guide their behavior was one of employeeship (*chakri*) and taking direction from above. They considered it possible to complete work as assigned to them in return for a consistent income. And employeeship, while not describing the financial relationship that linked them with TIE or the center, was what they aspired to attain. Even if they did not enact entrepreneurial behaviors, they were trained partially through the rhetoric of their independence in running profit-maximizing business ventures. Given a potential new activity in which they could engage, they looked for a direct relationship between the activity, its necessary outlay of time and expense, and its prospective financial benefit.

The work preferences of iAgents thus displayed a mixture of logics; they understood their interventions within the boundaries of project and funding cycles while they engaged in activities that enabled them to maximize their income-to-time-and-expense ratio. Both logics often served to the detriment of the empowerment that TIE claimed iAgents catalyzed in society. Yet this seemingly incompatible mixture of rationalities was necessary for the model (from its outward-facing perspective) to sustain itself. To illustrate this point, and to tie it to themes of relational work between iAgents and TIE, a description of the iAgents' fraught RTI work is useful. The circumstances exemplify the ways in which iAgents, to resist certain top-down imperatives from TIE, adhered to (or played along with) one particular set of logics and discourses advanced by TIE in order to facilitate the project's failure.

The Right to Information Act was passed in 2009 with the primary stated intention "to empower the citizens by promoting transparency and accountability . . . with the ultimate aim of decreasing corruption and establishing good governance" (Information Commission of Bangladesh n.d.). The act was based on the premise that information is a fundamental right rather than a resource differentially distributed at the discretion of the state. It also devolves some responsibility onto citizens for the conduct of the government: "An informed citizenry will be better equipped to keep necessary vigil over the instruments of government and make the government more accountable to the governed"

(Information Commission of Bangladesh n.d.). Yet the failure of the act to achieve a quick uptake was seen as a market problem on both the supply and the demand sides, according to Zahir and representatives of the Shabar Adhikar Foundation (SAF), which funded the iAgents' RTI project. Citizens, especially the poorest and most disenfranchised ones, needed to learn about their right to access information about the activities of state and non-state organizations. Similarly, these organizations, and the information officer appointed within each one, needed to learn their responsibilities to provide the requested information. By engaging iAgents as intermediaries, these gaps could be closed.

RTI was potentially one of the most important services that iAgents provided. It was the only one to engage with political and structural inequalities and to seek to shift power marginally to the poor by enhancing their voice. iAgents would help people to understand their rights as citizens and to make demands on the state for their entitled services by using the state's own mechanisms. Yet this model faced several conceptual challenges. This service converted information into a commodity when the point was to sanctify information as a right. Additionally, the purpose of the safety-net programs, which iAgents helped people to access through RTI, was to help desperate people to make ends meet during times of extreme hardship. Safety nets would not change the fundamental circumstances of poor people or militate against the causes and relations of their poverty, although poverty alleviation was a central claim of the iAgent program.

iAgent RTI work consisted of multiple activities: hosting sessions centered on the topic of RTI, making lists of people who did not receive their entitlements and collecting information from their identity cards, accompanying people individually to the appropriate local office to submit the question by paper application, returning for the answer, assisting clients in pressing their claims using the newly offered information, and writing reports about the outcomes of particular cases. iAgents would receive thirty taka (38 cents) from TIE for the completion of each case.

Yet a group of experienced iAgents in Lalpur decided collectively not to run the RTI program because of the antagonism they faced from their clients (as described in chapter 4). After receiving a three-day RTI training workshop, Rahela, Brishti, and three other iAgents sat together in Rahela's house. They jointly crafted a message, using a word processor on Brishti's laptop, to Amit, the Atno Bishash employee named at that time as "designated responsible person" for iAgents:

> Dear *Dada* ["elder brother," a respectful term of address for a Hindu man]. Please take my greetings. To do one RTI takes me at least three

days. Going to the office and taking the group member with me will incur expenses that will not be covered by the project. If I spend the time doing my usual work, then I will be able to earn a lot more money, so why wouldn't I do that? Working on the RTI project is not possible for me.

Rahela then circulated the text by USB drive to ten other iAgents, for each of them to email it to Amit. I asked Rahela what would happen next. "Nothing. *Dada* will read it and forget about it. He doesn't get paid to care about what we do or don't do. When someone from the TIE head office communicates with him later about how many RTIs we've done, then he will forward our email. By the time they want to do something about it, it will be too late, and we won't have to." By exploiting TIE's insistence that iAgents address their concerns formally by email to their local designated officer, who was supposed to move information up the chain in the proper way (rather than skipping the hierarchy and calling TIE directly), iAgents were able to take advantage of the elongated time that resulted in the bureaucratic process. By adhering to TIE's request that they submit individual demands, to avoid what Adnan feared would result in "group complaining sessions," iAgents bought themselves even more time. When Amit responded to management requests for updates by forwarding the email, it would appear as if only one iAgent had faced this problem, which might delay the response further.

In this context, iAgents embodied the independent entrepreneur empowered to speak from a strong position of bargaining for what was best for them, far different from image of the social worker freely giving community help that Rahela and Dipa had narrated previously. Profit-seeking trumped other subjectivities they were meant to display, such as community service, concern for the plight of fellow villagers, and the selfless heroism implied by the representations that begin this chapter. iAgents calculated cost-benefit as they had been trained to do, and they rationalized how they did and did not choose to spend their time. That iAgents had achieved "empowerment" through this model could be argued in this snapshot vignette. They had demonstrated the confidence, alternatives, and reasoning needed to stand up to their superiors and assert what they wanted.

Yet long-term ethnography reveals a perspective on power beyond momentary triumphs and defeats. Several weeks later, Jahid from TIE replied. In his email, following correct procedure, he addressed Shorif, the executive director, by saying, "We had an agreement between TIE and Atno Bishash, in which you came all the way to Dhaka to agree on all the points, to which you signed your name. So it is your responsibility to make the project happen. *You* solve it." He also included a message for Amit to convey to the iAgents. If they wanted to work as iAgents, they were obligated to implement all the projects TIE sent them. They could not pick and choose, as entrepreneurs might be able to do, but instead they needed to conform as dependent contract workers. Fearing the consequences of being cut off completely and lacking access to other, more profitable and aspirational jobs, the iAgents reluctantly agreed to continue RTI work.

Because ambiguity through flexible invocation of multiple relational logics was required for the system to work, the act of articulating just one logic proved to be effective in grinding the project to a halt, but only for a short time. Ultimately, given TIE's ability to coerce through the threat of disavowal, the iAgents' act of rebellion did not result in a better bargaining position but rather an even more oppressive one. The iAgent model—designed to ameliorate social inequalities—instead exhibited features of antisocial inequality in its own operations.

Superheroes and Contradictions

The more the iAgent social enterprise model moved away from a central commitment to social goals, the more emphatic its claims to positive impact became. This incongruity returns us to the cartoon image of the iAgent as the superhero of Bangladesh. As their control over the iAgents increasingly resembled coercive authority, members of the TIE staff promoted the opposite narrative of empowerment, which enabled them to attract external attention. The more iAgents were bound by TIE rules, the more TIE needed to insist on their empowerment, to the extent of representing them through dramatic metaphors of strength. On one level, I interpret such imagery as an attempt by its TIE authors to resolve in part the internal contradictions of the model.

Yet contradictions still appear. Stylistically, the iAgent superhero wears her *urna* (scarf) wrapped in the style of a schoolgirl, not in the style that would be worn in her real-life identity as a college student—a representation that infantilizes her. The iAgent-as-superhero derives her powers from the technologies that afford her access to information to distribute to people. Her powers come from devices that appear as icons, which are external to her and which are depicted as shooting toward her from the sky, as opposed to being generated from within herself or from her social milieu. Stripped of these technologies—such as when the social enterprise determines that an iAgent is no longer fit to participate (in Amirhat, where iAgents had to return their equipment), or when TIE provides her with faulty equipment (in Lalpur, where second-generation iAgents inherited the used instruments of women who had dropped out of the program)—she is no longer powerful. In this sense, the young woman's agency and empowerment are confined to the contours of the iAgent program and persona, which are controlled by other people. The superhero image belies the actual power dynamics embedded in the model, which real-life iAgents are unable to influence. The image is an accidental metaphor for the central contradiction of social entrepreneurship programs, in which representations of achieving empowerment (strengthening values) overlay models that necessitate the containment and restriction of the participants' agency (in order to extract value).

The casting of iAgent imagery as similar to Wonder Woman, an American comic-book superhero, directs the message to a Western audience. This particular style of iconography does not seem to resonate with local representations with which iAgents and their communities would be familiar, such as illustrations in schoolbooks, political pamphlets, or NGO posters. Rather, the image seems to invoke parallels with Wonder Woman's depiction as a feminist icon fighting for justice and gender equality, an association that Western and not necessarily Bangladeshi publics might draw. I suggest that such an image should be read less as an attempt to portray actual iAgents (or to recruit them) and more as an exercise in the self-expression of its makers. The previous chapter shows how particular narrative and representational forms are the currency with which the NGO middle classes in Bangladesh attract external resources and thus secure their middle-class livelihoods. This image similarly expresses a desired class identity made through associating one's name with the latest silver-bullet model for developing the country. Thus, the aesthetics of iAgent representations are revealed at once as a currency for attracting resources, as a platform for building status and claiming ethical merit, and as a meditation on the impossible contradictions of the model and efforts that aim partially to resolve them.

While the imagery and idea of iAgents attracted the interests of diverse actors, actual iAgents faced the contradictions of being represented and dealt with in different ways. In real life, these representations did not smoothly translate or transition from one to the next; rather, they clashed messily. By continuously moving between different relational forms—those of NGO patronage and market detachment—TIE increasingly denied the former, on which it based its implementation, and asserted the latter, on which it based symbolic representation. Without either relational mode, TIE would lose its claim of having access to a rural network of beneficiaries and the basis for mobilizing external resources.

iAgents tried to retain a grip on previous advantages of the NGO-patronage moral economy now being stripped away. Simultaneously, a discourse of their "independence" and "entrepreneurship," along with the devices of detachment that qualified the marketization of previously affective relations, rendered such claims impossible. Debunking the myth of the independent entrepreneur operating in the informal economy, romanticized in modern development narratives, "what is called self-employment is nothing other than a method of payment which forces the wage-dependent worker towards self-exploitation" (Breman 1996, 235). The case of the iAgent model suggests that the political work of promoting entrepreneurship for development and empowerment eroded the NGO-patronage moral economy in Bangladesh. It enabled the stripping back of support and obligation downward while existing forms of inequality and coercion remained. These processes were supported by the benevolent imagery of stimulating dignified empowerment. The iAgent project (and all other such projects) can be analyzed as a network of differently calibrated relationships in constant negotiation, an analysis that enables an examination of individual agency within the larger moving field of differential power relations. The book's conclusion brings together the multiple calculative and temporal regimes that structure the experiences of agency among actors in the iAgent network.

THE TIME OF SOCIAL ENTERPRISE

This book has detailed the properties and pursuits of a network of people who were linked together by the multivalent idea of the iAgent. These people were bound—sometimes tightly and sometimes loosely—by a set of activities and structures, bureaucratic procedures and market devices, personal projects and ideological notions, myriad ideas and ideals, and fervent aspirations and desperate efforts. Young women, labeled as the iAgents of Bangladesh, are the focal point of this network. Examining their relationships with kin and community and with staff members of Technological Innovation for Empowerment (TIE) and its organizational partners allows us to map the social, political, and economic features of the social enterprise.

This book has tracked the specific economic processes, innovative managerial-science approaches, and deliberate market techniques that produced the social enterprise in rural Bangladesh. It has revealed the intimate and complicit ways in which the subjectivities and identities of key actors were coproduced with these technical processes and were articulated across all levels of the development apparatus. Each of the six chapters explores a particular set of these devices, the ways in which iAgents and other actors sought to reconcile their contradictions, and the broader social effects these processes generated.

First, models of disruptive development asserted a singular vision of successful womanhood based on entrepreneurial success, expressed through generic stories of social transformation and through both fictional and real-life exemplars. Second, mobile telephones, other communication technologies, and the new modes of sociality and connectivity they implied formed the basis of the social enterprise's claims to broader social impact through women's digitally enabled entrepreneurial availability and doorstep service.

Third, the training protocol and its mechanisms of reformatting social identities and behaviors into digital entrepreneurial ones produced female workers as both agents and objects of development for the social enterprise. Fourth, the diversified basket of services delivered by iAgents—spanning public goods, private consumer goods, and development resources—enabled the social enterprise to accumulate capital both through direct-sales profits and by acting as an implementation partner for diverse organizations.

Fifth, public narratives in the form of websites, Wikipedia pages, annual reports, and social media postings reveal innovative development models to generate financial profits and also to serve as the currency of middle-class status in the development world. Sixth, the deliberately fluid portrayal of the entrepreneurs' roles—where public narratives and the internal dynamics of labor hierarchies intersect—was required for the social enterprise to produce social value and extract economic value for itself.

These multiple devices, procedures, and sets of values not only produced the social enterprise but also generated contradictory experiences for entrepreneurs and other development actors. They disrupted women's livelihoods in a context where women's work was already a field of cultural struggle; they generated moral anxiety about appropriate behavior for women; and they created conflicting socialities, temporalities, and relational obligations. The multiplicity of services, representations, and roles cast women as actors of ambiguous character; destabilized the class basis of the NGO-development moral economy; and skewed further the unequal balance of power between social enterprise practitioners and entrepreneur-beneficiaries.

Devices of Attachment and Detachment

The iAgent network, portrayed in formal representations and outward-facing narratives as a "social enterprise," was instantiated in the documents, procedures, legal instruments, and calculative devices that TIE used to install a particular set of market relationships among market actors. The central device employed to achieve market effects was the relationship of commercial debt, which generated detachment from personal relations and enabled TIE to exert ever-increasing coercive control. The iAgent social enterprise and the global and national institutions that contributed to its emergence in its then-present form thus unsettled existing social relations and produced alienated experiences of society for the many people drawn into its network. People struggled to shape their lives under the shadow of an increasingly unpredictable future.

The network, along with the relationships it encompassed, was fundamentally inflected by the existing dynamics of class, gender, and status ideologies and of kinship and patronage ties. These dynamics, specific to the then-current moment in Bangladesh's rapidly changing political economy of opportunity, were as much a constituting part of the network as were the documents and procedures—the formal devices—that represented it. Such formal devices became complicit in the relational work by which people exerted their social, economic, and political positions.

The network was thus Janus-faced. Looking outward were the formal representations of streamlined markets and market actors. Looking inward, these same individuals enacted their existing power inequalities through the social and material infrastructures of the network. This book has shown not only that official narratives and informal dynamics differed but also that the two faces of the social enterprise mutually constituted one another. I have illustrated how the current and rapid shifts toward market orthodoxy in "pro-poor" programs eroded the affective social relationships in the existing moral economy of access to resources and opportunities in rural Bangladesh. Such pro-poor programs include development NGOs seeking to build sustainable models; new hybrid entities or social enterprises pursuing multiple, simultaneous values; or corporations attempting to embed social-responsibility programs in their core business models. At the same time, hierarchical relations of power remained and grew increasingly extractive despite the semblance of their benevolent paternalism.

The Accelerated Time of Middle-Class Self-Making Projects

At the top of the NGO middle-class hierarchy, meeting in offices in Dhaka, organizational leaders and team members faced expanded agency as they conformed to global economic-development frameworks and thus unlocked new resources. Yet the conversion of NGOs to social enterprises, driven by the new time rhythms of national and international corporate and financial markets, conflicted with the time of local middle-class social reproduction through patronage politics and provisioning "one's own poor" (Gardner 1995). These lower-level development middle classes now faced a contradiction between the permanent paternalistic obligations that established their social status and the growing insecurity of a livelihood based on such relationships. Undergoing a hollowing-out of their patronage role, the middle classes attempted to reproduce their status through professional capacities and sought to make a name for themselves by experimenting with new development models. Their claims to ethical transformation—not only of their beneficiaries but also of themselves—grew stronger as they became increasingly detached from those beneficiaries. Yet as they accepted and accelerated the impersonal and financialized versions of their former work, they faced local accusations of predatory sociality and corruption, a discourse that undermined their authority. They faced a narrowing set of opportunities and a tradeoff between global expectations and local ones.

Procedures of detachment enabled power-holders the affective distance and the strategic ignorance (McGoey 2012a) that diminished their capacity to empathize with program participants. All of these factors constituted the struggle and relational work (Zelizer 2012) through which people sought to assert their particular personal projects and class positions. As market-driven development modalities increasingly eroded the NGO-development moral economy, three key shifts took place.

First, the close relationship of patronage and the ethical sense of responsibility of the local elite for one's own poor were replaced by detached coercion and control. While fictive kinship terms were still often employed between development workers and their beneficiaries, beneath the surface such utterances did not imply that the poor might actually expect support from their superiors. Development staff members were able to use the precarious positions of their inferiors to encourage compliance, at least to a degree (which the Amirhat iAgents showed).

Second, partnering organizations had previously been drawn into the network through notions of social justice, and their concern centered primarily on achieving particular outcomes within the communities where iAgents worked. As part of the new changes, however, partner entities remained at a distance, concerned primarily about the benefits they might derive through partnership with TIE and the iAgents. The intensity of relationships grew diffuse as partnerships were drawn from farther afield (such as Yamada, a Japanese multinational corporation) and from parties that were meant, by nature, to be detached from social relations (such as the National Bank).

Third, under TIE's NGO phase of piloting the iAgent model of social change, led by Rohan Alam, TIE's activities had focused primarily on establishing the reputation of iAgents among local religious, civic, and development leaders. Rohan frequently deployed his team to spend time with iAgents while they negotiated new relationships with members of their communities. Yet as TIE positioned itself to scale up the iAgent model under the leadership of Adnan Khan and Kabir Saadi, the organization remained primarily focused on establishing its own reputation in international social and business arenas.

The transformations that this set of processes implied did not bode well for the ability of the poor to navigate out of precariousness, despite the increasingly extravagant claims of local, regional, and global organizations to empower women, alleviate poverty, and generate positive "social impact."

The Precarious Social Reproductive Time of iAgents

In villages, families faced the diminishing horizon of lineage as a resource for security and support while extended kinship networks fragmented and nuclear families fended for themselves. Young women experienced keenly the time of social reproduction as they strove to fulfill expectations of domestic kin work, while responsibility for family subsistence and their own dowry payments increasingly pushed them into outside work.

Young women, now enfolded in the iAgent work that they hoped would yield stable employment, struggled to operationalize the debt relationships in which they found themselves. They attempted to produce more permanent social relationships, not only as providers for their families but also with their former NGO patrons. They undertook these risky projects in order to generate less precarious futures, but they consistently confronted clashes between the rhythms of debt obligations and the rhythms of village sociality. The time-regimented productivity imposed through the iAgent training regimen and exemplars such as iAgent Mita, as well as the time cycles of loan repayments and soap sales, conflicted with the social processes of young women who were swept into these projects of "emancipatory" outside labor.

Are young, unmarried women particularly suited to navigate and endure Bangladesh's own liminal state and atmosphere of perilous uncertainty? Perhaps they are. As I have demonstrated, these women are committed to family betterment and yet they lack a permanent attachment to a particular lineage, they tap into global enthusiasm about women's entrepreneurship, and they engage their moral resources while taking risks for socially generative ends. This book has highlighted the attempts of these women "to regain a sense of agency in settings of spatio-temporal inequality and conflictual experience" (Bear 2016, 20). To cope, iAgents drew on the mental and moral resources of *mon fres* and *mon bhalo* ("a fresh/good mind"), which spanned the temporalities of the everyday in the ethical actions of helping others and working hard as well as the long-term cycles of enduring extended hardship with patience, faith, and acceptance of divine judgment.

I have demonstrated the ways in which women acting as iAgents mediated between village timescapes and capitalist and nationalist timescapes by harnessing the one for the other and yet also being exploited by both (also Bear 2014c). Whereas historically many commercial transactions within kinship relations, such as dowry, have been about women, women more recently have moved to the forefront as actors and agents in such processes. By assuming an agentive role, women experienced new room to maneuver but they also remained bound by the social expectations and imaginations of their role held by men as fathers, uncles, husbands, loan officers, social enterprise managers, and foreign investors. I have shown the ways in which women exerted a sense of agency, for instance by exploiting the time stretch of bureaucratic regimes as subtle acts of protest and by invoking long-cycle ethical registers by acting virtuously in the present. I have illustrated how women's negotiations of social boundaries—for instance, regarding the role of men in their lives—were acts themselves agentive of change.

Yet the iAgents' acts of maneuvering called attention to themselves and often brought about increased coercive control by the organizational and familial patriarchy. Women found themselves co-opted into processes of their own exploitation. Thus, I critique the market-driven development "delusion that agency can be incentivized to operate independently of political economy" (Mosse 2011, 4). Instead, women must find the capacity to act within and through the various metaphors and representations that have historically linked them to broader processes of social, economic, political, and cultural change. As a political project, the idea of the Bangladeshi woman has invoked multiple images in the popular imagination, including Bengal as a maternal figure who protected her children against the masculine figure of the British in the late nineteenth and early twentieth centuries, and also including the wearing of saris as a political icon deployed to mobilize against Pakistan's dominance in the 1960s (White 1992, 11). More recently, textile-factory work, microcredit, and entrepreneurial labor have molded a new Bangladeshi feminine exemplar that serves as a clarion call, instrument, and celebration of domestic (household and national) economic growth.

Ambiguity as Network Adhesive

This book helps us to understand other social enterprise programs in the world by examining the deep ambiguities and contradictions they engender when they impose models of action that disrupt existing livelihoods, relationships, and values. Existing anthropological research and writing on poverty capitalism has focused on procedures of subjectivities formation, but I have shown that these particular subjectivities are problematic to inhabit because they rely on but also threaten social relationships. As networks such as the iAgent social enterprise are constructed and expand, what effects do these new relations and contradictions have on people's life rhythms and agency? What new patterns emerge, and in what ways are people able or unable to act within them?

Women participating in social enterprise programs are required to take on and switch among multiple roles. While the concepts of flexibility and relational work capture the positive (albeit labor-intensive) resources that enable people to assume different mantles and gain advantages, "ambiguity" expresses the morally perilous terrain onto which women entrepreneurs venture.

In this case, the experience of ambiguity appeared in multiple guises. First, iAgents were selected for their poverty and liminal state as young, mostly unmarried women. In a context where intense moral scrutiny was cast on women's propriety, the new activities of iAgents threw doubt on their social positions. Second, a deliberate lack of clarity regarding their working status (as employees or entrepreneurs?) secured acquiescence from young women and their families. Third, the services that iAgents provided to community members involved different and contradictory transactions, relations, and status markers and thus generated confusion regarding the type of figure that iAgents were meant to embody. Fourth, in its transition from NGO to social enterprise TIE alternately invoked its relationship with iAgents as patron to client, employer to employee, and contractor to entrepreneur according to organizational imperatives, even though these relational modes held disparate political implications. Overall, this book sheds light on the multiple contradictions that women entrepreneurs in Bangladesh faced, intertwined as they were among market, social-work, and community norms.

Women's intense efforts to navigate these ambiguities underwrote the ability of the social enterprise to function. The contradictory and competing forms of relational belonging mediated by financial products, communication technologies, and new measures and values often disadvantaged the entrepreneurs, who shouldered the risks when they could not manage to coordinate differing expectations about their economic and social roles. The case of the iAgents of Bangladesh gives texture to the social and political fabric of these "inclusive markets," which are built on the relational work and flexible subjectivities of young women. To analyze "social enterprise" through the contradictions between an emergent ethical discourse and its attendant business logics and through the morally perilous terrain of the invisible and gendered labor of reconciling multiple value systems reveals the ways in which poor women entrepreneurs are increasingly required to adopt subject positions that render them as ambiguous and shady figures in the cultural and institutional imagination.

Liminal Lifeworlds

This book tells the story of information innovation laminated onto development entrepreneurialism. It signals a new moment in economic development linked with the Silicon-Valley aesthetics of disruptive innovation and radical entrepreneurialism; the evolution of the Bangladesh NGO world; and the creation of new class dynamics surrounding the provision of key resources to the poor. Existing middle-class relations, created through Bangladesh's history of NGO structures, were fundamentally changed by enterprise-driven models. In shaping frontline service providers as digital entrepreneurial development subjects and recasting development patrons as entrepreneurial extractive business owners, disruptive development replaced a more balanced level of social inequality with an exacerbated level of antisocial inequality. Interclass solidarity and shared interests disintegrated into an exploitative race to the bottom. Yet the social enterprise model, as itself a technical device, rendered invisible these middle-class projects; the nature of relations of domination; and the sociocultural milieu of entrepreneurs. It also concealed the ethical labor of iAgents to mediate social enterprise–generated contradictions that subsidized the success of the program and formed the means and conditions of capital accumulation for the development elites.

Since its independence in 1971, Bangladesh has continuously undergone monumental change in its economy and society, recently exemplified by the summoning of iAgents as digital first responders to the site of a politically motivated railway tragedy. That generation of young women, more so than those of their mothers and grandmothers, was deeply implicated in processes of transformation. Young women epitomized the liminality, uncertainty, and ambiguity that has characterized the nation's experience with the conflicting times of speculative growth and blockaded mobility. As Bangladesh further liberalized its economy, decentralized its state functions, and submitted its poverty-alleviation plans to markets, the themes and trends identified in this book intensified. One such underlying theme, as shown, is a clash in the temporalities of social rhythms, political events, and economic imperatives that structure everyday life in contemporary Bangladesh. In a world fixated on boosting women's employment outside the home as a measure of both gender equity and national economic growth, this study illuminates the relationship between "the times of capitalist modernity and vectors of inequality" (Bear 2016, 2). iAgents were not alone in facing these challenges. In the accelerated time of Bangladesh's efforts to keep pace with the demands of fast fashion in Europe and North America, the export-oriented garment industry tapped into the liminal time in unmarried women's lifecycles as a source of docile, desperate labor.

The iAgent social enterprise assemblage is a particularly apt site to explore these transformations, fraught as they are with contradiction and ambiguity, because it is characteristic of an expanding series of such projects around the world. Poverty capitalism appears under the different guises of NGOs seeking to become "sustainable," governments outsourcing social services, corporations seeking new markets at the "base of the pyramid," and banks adopting "financial inclusion" policies. The more these various forms have moved away from a commitment to grassroots civic participation and social justice, the more insistent their claims of positive impact and individual empowerment seem to become. In a market society, relations of dependence often disappear from view, but they continue to order the realm of opportunity and possibility for people. Through the ethnographic case of the iAgents of Bangladesh, I have sought to explain the relational work that social enterprise participants and their managers perform to implement new kinds of market models. This process invokes multiple sets of representations as productive for their ability to extract benefits from the participants while at the same time celebrating and also dampening their agency.

Hope for the Future?

This book has shown the limitations of empowerment models that focus on individual autonomy and independence. Instead, we need empowerment models that recognize people's situatedness within social networks. Such models would enable people to become more active and powerful agents by making contributions to those networks rather than extracting themselves from webs of reciprocity.

People, including women, do need and want work. Development interventions need to spend time understanding what is or could be meaningful, dignified work that is recognized as contributing to the community.

People, including women, do want opportunities to engage with markets, and they also want to develop enduring connections while doing so. Development interventions should focus on enabling productive connectivity rather than encouraging a politics of disconnection (see also Gardner 2012).

People, including women, are willing to take on significant risks to move their families out of poverty. Development interventions should find innovative ways to help transfer these risk burdens away from already-vulnerable people.

Women's empowerment is an important and laudable goal. Development interventions need to pay careful attention to existing structures of power and the support that women need when they disrupt these dominant arrangements. Actions can include hiring more women for leadership, managerial, and frontline development work; highlighting realistic role models that acknowledge real challenges women in service roles face; and generating opportunities for career advancement through development infrastructures rather than dead-end roles. If social impact is an important organizational goal, then foregrounding locally determined social measures of success needs to be prioritized over profits for investors. Important experiments in social accounting are already taking place and represent a step in the right direction. Crucially, organizations need also to work with men and boys alongside women and girls to provide alternative models of workplace and domestic cooperation beyond patriarchy.

Finally, development organizations should recognize that many gains in development are unexpected, nonprogrammatic ones. If development leaders and staff spend more time on the front lines, they will be better equipped to identify what these gains are and help to amplify them. If people are modifying program processes, repurposing objects and technologies, or resisting project protocols, they may be indicating that the original model was inappropriate, awkward, stigmatizing, or otherwise undesirable. Rather than punishing vulnerable people, a closer and more respectful feedback loop would enhance the empowerment potential for those people.

Overall, this study shows the need for new development approaches and new kinds of social enterprises that reincorporate relational economies by recognizing the complexity of social life. Such a focus is important especially in the context of the wider capitalist project to frame the social out of the conversation and render it invisible.

Global Techno-Temporal Conjunctures

Young people type random digits into mobile-phone keypads to conjure new connections and cultivate aspirations. After cycling to remote, poverty-stricken areas and finding few people to register for a mobile-phone health project, iAgents complain that "even these people have become *digital*." Schoolchildren engage in nationalist dreams of modernity while they write about "Digital Bangladesh" for a final examination. Bangladesh abolishes paper applications under the Right to Information Act and celebrates transparent governance. Companies, development bodies, and NGOs around the world build social enterprise models to help farmers in checking market prices through village e-kiosks, to assist migrants in remitting money through their mobile phones, and to aid doctors in reaching patients via telemedicine.

Meanwhile, in Japan, fearing the loss of its global-market dominance in the ICT industry; seeking to reassert its role as a patron in the region; and hoping, at least symbolically, to offset the catastrophic setbacks to its carbon-emissions reduction plan following the earthquake and nuclear meltdown in 2011, the government develops a plan. It commissions Yamada, the Japanese multinational consumer electronics giant, to conduct a feasibility study of the carbon savings it could generate by repurposing its middle-class solar energy offerings to base-of-the-pyramid markets in Japan's partner countries for carbon-trading. In August and September 2013, executives from Yamada travel to Amirhat, Lalpur, and three other districts in Bangladesh to meet the iAgents and assess the feasibility of an exploratory project (Huang 2020).

This book concerns not only women in Bangladesh, ICT social entrepreneurship, and aspirations for technology-assisted development. It also examines the ways in which we understand economies and economic action in general. This particular case is not removed from the global economy writ large. It forms part of an extensive network that exhibits many of the same features, at a sweeping scale, as described in this study. The iAgents are part of a larger web of individual aspirations, national ideological projects, regional and global hierarchies of patronage, and clashes between nonhuman forces and the efforts of humans to control them. As the cycles of corporate strategies, carbon trading, and financial markets encounter and then run at variance to the cycles of social reproduction and structures of opportunity of life in villages in Bangladesh and in neighborhoods around the world, the people who most acutely bear the burden of their contradictory rhythms are figures exemplified by the iAgents.

iAgents at the Atno Bishash Information Center in Lalpur Subdistrict

Brishti, pilot-model iAgent (first cohort); we follow her through her working day

Dipa, pilot-model iAgent (first cohort) who was selected to represent iAgents in Germany; she provided financial support for her brother to find work abroad but he was scammed

Nilufar, pilot-model iAgent (second cohort); she is married and uses her work to escape her domestic situation

Rahela, pilot-model iAgent (first cohort); main interlocutor in Lalpur

Rajib, Rahela's younger brother

Rimi, pilot-model iAgent (first cohort)

Riya, pilot-model iAgent (third cohort) who dropped out because she could not afford the initial investment

Shanu, pilot-model iAgent (first cohort) who dropped out when she married; she continues to provide advice to fellow villagers

iAgents at the ACRU Information Center in Amirhat Subdistrict

Ayrin, license-model iAgent; her story appears at the beginning of part 3

Deepti, license-model iAgent; her story appears at the beginning of part 2

Jorina, Taspia's mother

Megh, license-model iAgent; her story appears at the beginning of part 1

Nilima, license-model iAgent

Rima, Taspia's cousin, who divorced and remarried

Sahara, Taspia's niece, who works in the Matador pen factory in Dhaka

Tamanna, Taspia's eldest sister, married to a corporate employee in Dhaka

Tanzila, Taspia's elder sister, married to a tractor driver in a neighboring village

Taspia, license-model iAgent; main interlocutor in Amirhat

Staff at Atno Bishash in Lalpur Subdistrict

Amit, designated responsible person for iAgent program 2013–15
Shoriful (Shorif) Islam, executive director
Sumaiya, iAgent monitoring officer 2009–12
Zahir Ahmed, iAgent field coordinator 2009–13

Staff at Akaas Center for Rural Upliftment (ACRU) in Amirhat Subdistrict

Rifat, iAgent field coordinator 2012–13
Sabbir Hossain, executive director

Staff at Technological Innovation for Empowerment (TIE)

Adnan Khan, CEO
Fahim, iAgent team member
Jahid, iAgent team member
Kabir Saadi, iAgent leader pre-2009, post-2013
Kanika, iAgent team member
Rasel, iAgent team member
Rohan Alam, iAgent leader 2009–13
Shila, iAgent team member

Glossary of Non-English Words

alosh lazy

amader our

apa elder sister, a term of respect when used for a non-kin woman

Aparajita rural saleswoman for Unilever; literally, "woman who cannot be defeated"

Aponjon health information program of USAID and the Bangladesh government

apu elder sister (informal), a term of respect when used for a non-kin woman

bari home

besi in excess; many; much

bhaggo fate

bhai elder brother (Muslim), a term of respect when used for a non-kin man

bhalamanush good people, referring to local elite classes

bhalo good

bideshi foreigner

biriyani rice cooked with spices and meat or vegetables

boro big

borolok big people, referring to local elite classes

boromanush big people, referring to local elite classes

burqa outer garment worn by women to cover their bodies when in public. The burqa included in iAgents' uniforms resembles a short lab coat or smock.

byebsha business

caci aunt, a term of respect when used for a non-kin woman

chakri salaried, formal-sector employment

char river island

chhoto small

chhotolok small people, referring to local lower classes

chhotomanush small people, referring to local lower classes

chilla volunteer traveling missionaries

dada elder brother (Hindu), a term of respect when used for a non-kin man

dal lentils

dhoni wealthy

doi yogurt

durneti corruption

Eid ul-fitr festival of breaking of the fast to mark the end of Ramadan, the Islamic holy month of fasting

feriwala hawker; peddler

fres fresh

ghar house

ghotok professional matchmaker in arranged marriages

gorib poor

gusthi patrilineal descent group

halim savory stew

hartal form of mass protest involving the shutdown of workplaces, offices, and roadways

hingsha envy

ichchha wish
izzat honor
jamai bridegroom
jhogra flight, quarrel
ji yes (honorific)
jomidar landowner
kacha made of mud, thatch, or other impermanent materials; literally, raw; deficient
kameez knee-length tunic
kosto suffering, struggle
jugaad improvised fix, often implying moral deficiency (Hindi)
lathi bamboo stick
lila ritual distribution at festivals
lobh greed
lobhi greedy
lojja shyness
lungi tube-shaped garment worn by men and tied around the waist
madrasa educational institution
mama mother's brother
mela festival or fair
mitha lie; falsehood
mon mind; heart
mon bhalo a good mind
mon fres a fresh mind
mukti juddha freedom fighter (man who fought in the Independence War)
oborodh form of mass protest involving the shutdown of workplaces, offices, and roadways
oshosheton unconscious; unsensitized; unaware
pandal bamboo-frame cloth-paneled tent to host events and festivals
pitha steamed rice cake
porisrom hard work
pukka built from permanent materials (describing a house); literally, cooked
pulao rice cooked in a seasoned broth
purdah seclusion of women for modesty and honor
Qurbani Eid festival of sacrifice during the twelfth month of the Islamic calendar
Ramadan ninth month of the Islamic calendar observed as a holy month of fasting
roti flat bread
sehri pre-dawn meal before a day of fasting
Shabe barat all-night Islamic holiday, in which Allah forgives sinners and determines people's fortunes for the upcoming year
shahaja help
shalwar loose cotton trousers
shartopor selfish
shorom shame; shyness
singara samosa; stuffed pastry
svopno dream
union parishad smallest rural-administration and local-government unit in Bangladesh
upazila subdistrict in Bangladesh
urna scarf draped over the shoulders and across the chest for modesty
zakat charitable contribution; one of the five pillars of Islam

Notes

INTRODUCTION

1. For aspects of these processes, see Cross and Street 2009; De Neve 2014; Dolan 2012; Elyachar 2005; Karim 2011; Mosse 2011; Redfield 2012; Roy 2010; Schwittay 2011b.

2. While SSI, which possessed its own nominal leadership structure, was the organization legally acting through the license model, the staff of the iAgent division at TIE made all the decisions and interacted with iAgents and partner organizations. Thus, I refer to TIE rather than SSI throughout the book, except where the legal distinction between the two sister entities is important.

3. For political analyses, see N. Chowdhury 2014; Harrison 2013; Mookherjee 2015; Riaz 2014; and Suykens and Islam 2013.

4. Many NGOs and microfinance institutions define poverty in Bangladesh as families living on less than half an acre of cultivable land or owning assets less than an acre of medium-quality land (Karim 2011, xvi).

5. For extended discussions of rural class structures, see Jahangir 1982; Jansen 1987; Lewis 2011; and van Schendel 1981, 2009.

6. Gardner (1995, 158); Lewis and Hossain (2008, 289); and van Schendel (2009, 134) discuss fictive kinship.

7. For extended analyses, see S. Grover 2009; Lamb 2000; and White 1992.

8. These terms are also found elsewhere in Bangladesh (Thorp 1978, 40; Rozario 1992, 6).

9. See also Lewis 2011, 22, on the decline in importance and role of *gusthi* and other residential communities.

10. Rather than referencing long-standing (or lacking) claims to social status and help, the use of these terms often accompanied behavioral descriptors. From the perspective of the poor, the rich were lazy and exploitative, "sitting and eating," while the poor labored for unfair wages and suffered. From the perspective of the rich, the poor were lazy and untrustworthy and apt to steal, cheat, and undermine employers' hard-built enterprises (Gardner 1995, 234; Scott 1985).

11. Batliwala (2011); Cornwall (2007); and Cornwall and Eade (2010) trace the history of the decontextualization of "empowerment."

12. Feldman (2003, 6–9) and Kabeer (2011, 505) trace the current status of these organizations.

13. The idea of NGOs as a shadow state is explored by Hussain (2014); Karim (2011); and Sobhan (1982) in Bangladesh, and by Shah (2010) in India.

14. Many scholars write about microfinance from anthropological perspectives; for instance: Goetz and Sen Gupta (1994); Kabeer (2001); Karim (2001; 2011); Lazar (2004); Morduch (1999); Otero and Rhyne (1994); Rahman (1999); Rankin (2001); Roy (2010); Schwittay (2011b); and Shakya and Rankin (2008).

15. See also Gardner 2012, 205; Lewis 2011, 125; and Scherz 2014 for moral critiques of development organizations that pursue new "sustainability" agendas.

16. The term "relational economy" is used in the social sciences to refer to a framework that "recognizes values, interpretive frameworks, and decision-making practices as

subject to the contextuality of the social institutions that characterize the relationships between the human agents" (Bathelt and Glückler 2011, n.p.).

17. See Dolan 2012 and 2014; Errington, Fujikura, and Gewertz 2012; Karim 2011; Redfield 2012; Roy 2012a, 2012b; Schwittay 2011a.

18. Chong (2012) demonstrates that external activities intentionally replicate internal practices, which allows these knowledge processes to become proprietary and thus sellable and scalable (also Mitchell 2007). This feature appears to be a driver of the license and consulting models of TIE's iAgent enterprise.

19. Anthropologists have demonstrated how exercises in extending liberal markets and market values have become vehicles for extending and reconfiguring patriarchal dominance (Elyachar 2002 and 2005; Karim 2011). Karim (2011) explains how microcredit practices in Bangladesh, purportedly to empower women borrowers by enhancing their economic power in household decision-making, merely layer organizational patriarchy over family patriarchy. Devices of "NGO governmentality" not only regulate the behavior of women but also keep women subservient to their male guardians. Yet by disguising these patriarchal relations beneath a veneer of technical processes and financial services delivery, existing relations of domination are amplified.

20. This insight resonates with other anthropological work that demonstrates a rich account of vehicles for status and self-fashioning beyond efforts of accumulation and consumption, such as particular practices of economic activity (Bear 2015b; Chong 2012; Ho 2009; Yanagisako 2002) and writing (Thomas and Eves 1999).

1. WOMEN'S WORK

1. By contrast, outside (often Western development) perceptions of the "authentic" Muslim female interpret the discourse of suffering as subjects who need to be saved (Shehabuddin 2011, 133).

2. In the South Asian literature, the unit of selfhood is described as "dividual," which conceptualizes persons as composite and having open boundaries through which they affect one another's natures. For discussion of dividual personhood, see Marriott 1976 and Marriott and Inden 1977. Yet, "though the ethnographic literature on South Asia shows a long tradition of research holding that Indians (in various ways) deemphasize individuality, anthropologists have also examined ways in which South Asians view persons in terms that we might consider 'individual'" (Lamb 2000, 40).

3. See also Borthwick 2015; Gardner 1995, 216; White 1992, 81.

4. Kin work is also described as "household service work" (Sharma 1985).

5. For descriptions of begging, see Gardner 1995, 71; Gardner 2012, 236; Kabeer 2011; and White 1992.

6. Shalini Grover shows that a woman's ability to seek refuge in her natal home rather than finding wage work is a point of leverage against an unemployed husband because otherwise she finds it difficult to negotiate while remaining in his home and performing the double duty of employment and housework (2009, 13). This insight contrasts with some feminist literature that reads women's earnings as the main determinant of bargaining power. Other scholars debunk assumptions that assets, land rights (Agarwal 1994), microcredit access (Kabeer 2001; Karim 2011), and labor-force participation (A. Sen 1990) are appropriate indicators of women's empowerment.

7. On educational prospects and opportunities for women, see Amin, Selim, and Waiz 2006, 18; Froerer 2015; Gardner 1995, 130, 180; Huda 2006, 255; and Rao and Hossain 2012, 424–26.

8. The emancipatory capacity of outside work is largely indirect and occurs in conjunction with other factors. Participation in additional institutional forms may provide the vantage point from which to evaluate "given" relationships; these may include

market-generated opportunities and public institutions for economic relationships (Dannecker 2002), local government and service-delivery opportunities (Goetz 2001), and NGO group-based approaches that create "communities of practice" and engage in dialogue about social hierarchy (Kabeer 2011). Some women find intrinsic positive value in the opportunity to move in public domains, which helps them discover new resources like courage (Kabeer 2001). Ultimately the relational factor is often the most important.

9. "The tendency to subtly combine coercion with the cultivation of certain moral strictures [is a form of structural violence]. . . . Decency thus becomes a weapon with which to attack women" (Guhathakurta 1985, 87). See also Lamb 2000 for further Foucauldian analysis of *purdah* norms.

10. Self-descriptions of "middle"-class status among rural villagers such as Taspia are not the same as the NGO middle classes discussed in chapter 5. Instead, Taspia and others are referencing their social, economic, and patronage position vis-à-vis members of their extended family and village. When discussing the wider global and Bangladesh context, they consider themselves to be "poor" (*gorib*) and "small people" (*chhotomanush*), compared with "rich" (*dhoni*) and "big people" (*boromanush*). The term resonates with studies in India; by the 1990s, many people called themselves "middle people" (Fuller and Narasimhan 2014).

11. See Gardner 1995; Lamb 2000; Vatuk 2004; White 1992.

12. Gardner (1997, 109–25) provides an extended narrative of the experience of being cheated by migration middlemen.

13. Anthropologists have documented the limits of treating only the household or the individual as a unit of analysis, and this chapter shows the dialectical nature of both units as drivers of decision-making. "Models that restrict analysis to household economic strategies and the pressures of rural poverty fail to account for the varied dynamics of migration [or other livelihood-related] decisions and practices in actual situations" (Mills 1997, 39). Gender studies, by contrast, are often limited by their focus on divisions among individuals, because they tend to overlook common membership and mutual concerns within households (White 1992, 120).

14. Lamb (2000) documents changing family moral systems and transactional modes in West Bengal, in particular the increasing perceived potential for the loosening of the bond between mother and son. This shift in relationship is experienced as a failure of resource flows among nuclear kin, which started in a downward direction from parents to children with the explicit expectation that children would support their elderly parents in the future. Conversely, "this kind of thinking—investing now for future family phases and reciprocated returns—was explicit in villagers' reasoning about why they provided care for their elders" (Lamb 2000, 51). This expectation was not handled transactionally or calculatingly per se; rather, it was the expected social order of life stages and part of ethical personhood vis-à-vis one's kin.

15. Such criticisms did not occur just within families; anthropological accounts about Bangladesh show general anxieties that young people no longer respected their elders and superiors (Devine and White 2013).

16. Narratives of the erosion of trust and help, which describe how the rich become greedy and selfish and how others must now cope on their own, are documented elsewhere (Huda, Rahman, and Guirguis 2008, 301; Rashid 2007, 117).

17. Her comments echoed those of other rural Bangladesh villagers who criticized the failure of wealthy persons to look after the poor while accumulating wealth at their exploitation: "The poor will not go to hell; hells are reserved for the rich people who have acted wrongly and who could have worked for the good of society" (Devine and White 2013, 141).

18. That the poor in Bangladesh are desperate to attach themselves to social structures of connection is a general theme explored by Gardner (2012).

2. DIGITAL TECHNOLOGY

1. Women's physical mobility serves as a medium for forging new relationships. In their studies of garment-factory and call-center workers, Naila Kabeer's (2000) and Rina Patel's (2010) discussions of male-female interaction focus on the negative stigma of alleged prostitution attached to such work. They do not discuss new kinds of relationships that are made possible by such circumstances. Mary Beth Mills (1997) argues that young women migrants are attracted to the idea of modern relationships, but they sometimes experience disappointment if young urban men prove to be disloyal and unreliable. See also Rashid 2007, 116.

2. Wrong-number relationships are described elsewhere as "random networking" (Kriem 2009) and "fishing" (J. Donner 2007).

3. Anthropological accounts set in other regions of the world describe the effects of new opportunities and technologies on the changing patterns of relationships. Communication technologies such as mobile phones and the internet can act as a new conduit to pursue long-standing values that are increasingly difficult to fulfill by "traditional" means. Nicole Constable (2009) examines the role of the internet in enabling businesses that facilitate introductions (to potential maids, brides, and employers); that allow intimate communications with family, spouses, and clients; and that ensure that intimate transactions reside in a more private and invisible "market." Jennifer Johnson-Hanks writes about Cameroonian women seeking European husbands through internet services: "E-mail-mediated marriage draws as much on local history as on global politics" (2007, 642), and these newly shaped aspirations are aligned with pursuing local ideals of successful womanhood and marriage. Sarah White urges scholars not to view technology as an external agent imposing new ways of being on people (1992, 4) and not to reduce the impact of people's use of new technologies to capitalism's victimizing effects at the margin. See also Ahearn 2003; H. Donner 2002 and 2008; S. Grover 2009; Jeffery and Jeffery 1996; Orsini 2007; Parry 2001; Raheja and Gold 1994; and Rozario 2012.

4. For India, a notable exception is S. Grover 2009.

5. Multiple people in a household often share devices, and individual phone users often have multiple subscriptions (SIM cards).

6. Bangladesh is not the only country to promote ICT-driven development strategies. "Digital India" is a campaign launched by the government to transform the country into a knowledge economy. With many state, corporate, and non-governmental e-services delivered across India (Mazzarella 2010; Schwittay 2008), the term "digital" may have gained local conceptual purchase there as well.

7. Others describe this phenomenon as "beeping," "flashing," "lost calls," and "pranking" (J. Donner 2007; Kriem 2009).

8. Even after "real" arranged-marriage agreements were settled, mobile phones facilitated the couple-to-be in getting acquainted, which had implications for the positioning of the two people within the joint family (Doron 2012). Katy Gardner (1995, 167) documents cases of "telephone marriage," in which the groom, living in London, required official marriage registration for the bride in Bangladesh to join him, so he tied the knot virtually.

9. Dan Jorgensen (2014, 11) suggests that the success of phone friendships depends on keeping them virtual.

10. Rising dowry payments, although forbidden by the Dowry Prohibition Act of 1980, rooted matchmaking primarily in finances (rather than in other markers of status) and put unprecedented pressure on the girl's family. Dowry was new in the postindependence era of the last several generations (1970s and '80s), as Jorina indicated. Previously a Muslim boy's family offered a religiously sanctioned dower or gift to the bride and her family, but people have nearly universally adopted the high-caste, urban Hindu practice of

dowry. Ahmed and Naher (1987); Alam and Matin (1984, 7); Bleie (1990, 505); Hartman and Boyce (1983, 83); Huda (2006, 249–51); Kabeer (2000, 60); Lindenbaum (1981); Rozario (1992, 131–34); and White (1992, 101–2) discuss the shift from dower to dowry.

11. Whereas dowry payments were historically tied to the woman's family's tangible assets (such as land they could mortgage), they have increasingly become tied to women's loan-generating and income-producing potential. This example reveals the ironic consequences of microcredit and other programs designed for "women's empowerment" when they do not consider the social situatedness of women. The availability of new forms of resources accessible primarily to women through the development apparatus seems to have regressive effects in which so-called "modernisation may accentuate and distort a traditional arrangement rather than eradicate it" (Tambiah 1973, 63). Scholars suggest that, rather than being related to religious beliefs, dowry is a modern secular economic issue favoring patriarchal society and is related to *nouveau riche* conspicuous consumption. For discussions of dowry and its relation to accumulation practices, see Gardner 1995, 180; Huda 2006, 253; Menski 1998.

12. See Wilce 1995 on styles of lament.

13. In other cases, especially in Sylhet in northeastern Bangladesh, if the bride's father was a migrant in London, he might request his son-in-law to manage the household in his absence (Gardner 1995, 167).

3. THE MAKING AND UNMAKING OF ENTREPRENEURS

1. For partial answers to this question, see Blowfield and Dolan 2008; Cross 2011; Dolan 2012, 2014; Dunn 2004, 2008. Nitya Rao and Munshi Israil Hossain (2012) emphasize the way in which training and learning are embedded in practice (Bourdieu 1984), change or reproduce structures of power (Street 1993), mediate relationships between local and global actants (Lave and Wenger 1991), and constitute gendered identities (Willis 1977). As Julia Elyachar (2005) also shows, new market-driven NGO initiatives were "designed to produce and maintain economic agents capable of having projects and taking responsibility for their debts and profits" (Çaliskan and Callon 2010, 14). Other projects of subjectivity-molding in rural Bangladesh inculcated different sets of modern norms. Joseph Devine and Sarah White (2013) show how volunteer traveling missionaries (*chillas*) visited local mosques to give training on Islamic practices and values such as embracing hard work and discipline, helping others, building truthful relations, prioritizing a life built around religious concerns, and implementing an austere lifestyle. Says a participant, "The *chilla* teaches us to be modern in the right way" (2013, 142).

2. Training regimes have long been used in development and in the public and private sectors, especially as Bangladesh increasingly fashions itself as a neoliberal state and franchises out state services (see Lewis 2011).

3. Meena is a cartoon character who stars in the UNICEF-produced South Asian children's television show by the same name and educates children about topics such as health, gender, and social inequality (UNICEF n.d.).

4. Catherine Dolan describes how entrepreneurial cultural repertoires are enforced similarly across contexts, including Avon ladies in South Africa, Catalyst commission agents in Kenya, and CARE/Unilever distributors in Bangladesh (Dolan 2012, 2014; Dolan and Johnstone-Louis 2011; Dolan, Johnstone-Lewis, and Scott 2012).

5. For other discussions about the temporalities of debt, see Bear 2014a, 2014b; De Neve 2014; James 2015; Kar 2018; Karim 2011; and Rankin 2004.

6. Laura Bear (2011) documents how new rationalities of time management were driven into place by the liberalized state in West Bengal in order to harness time and thereby set the conditions for profit.

7. This feature is not unique to market-driven development but is an ongoing practice within the history of development; see Mosse 2010.

8. Bruno Latour observes how, in development projects, failure is often presented as individual and is narrativized downward (e.g., these beneficiaries were too ungrateful to receive our services, that leader blocked our efforts to reach many people), and achievement is attributed to the soundness of the overall conceptual model. "While success buries the individual action or event and makes a project a unified source of intention and power [thus] directing attention to the transcendent agency of policy and expert design (and hence replicability), failure fragments into the dynamics of blame" (Latour 1996, 76).

4. A DIVERSIFIED BASKET OF SERVICES

1. For discussions about customer segmentation, see Applbaum 2003 and Dolan 2012.

2. See Gardner 2012; Jahangir 1982; Jansen 1987; Karim 2011; Lewis 2011; van Schendel 2009.

3. As Ara Wilson observes among Avon ladies in Thailand, who were door-to-door salespeople in a global multi-level marketing company, "Such selling mobilized, but was also contained by, social relationships" (1999, 410).

4. Brishti's "empowerment" as a successful iAgent necessitated her disavowal of the respectful aspects the program claimed to accord her. Instead of being the expert, she let the computer do the talking. Instead of being a successful woman shopkeeper, she let people think that the shop belonged to her male guardians.

5. Katy Gardner (1995, 216) and Sarah White (1992, 81) discuss women-operated markets such as door-to-door trading, share-tending of animals, and female moneylending.

6. These conflicts are explored in other studies (Grover 2009; Heath and Mobarak 2014; Kabeer 2001; Rinaldo 2014; Shehabuddin 2008; White 2012).

7. The fear was not unfounded. The poor were also often deceived through false medical information into selling their organs for a pittance; wealthy people in developed countries were the recipients. See Moniruzzaman 2012.

8. Gardner documents how conspicuous consumption (of electronic goods, clothing made of exotic materials, jewelry, wearing burqas for trips away from home, brick houses, furniture, photographs symbolizing cosmopolitanism, and feasts for festivals and rituals) marked economic success among migrants' families in Sylhet in northeastern Bangladesh (1995, 133–34). Elsewhere in South and Southeast Asia, Shakya and Rankin find "commoditised regimes of value growing increasingly salient as arbiters of status and opportunity—that is, how one is perceived, one's status and indeed honour, has increasingly more to do with the commodities one possesses and displays than with, say, one's caste or ethnic location" (2008, 1226). In some cases, consumption practices and financial wealth also transcend gender norms, such as when single daughters inherit their fathers' extensive property (Lamb 2000, 102).

9. Naila Kabeer (2000) finds similar contradictions among garment factory workers. Women's factory work did not lead to a renegotiation of domestic roles. Rather, women were expected to perform the dual labor of both productive and reproductive work.

5. MIDDLE-CLASS PROJECTS AND THE DEVELOPMENT MORAL ECONOMY

1. See De Neve 2014; Elyachar 2005; Karim 2011; Mosse 2011, 3; and Schwittay 2011a for observations of the ways in which credit accrues upward while risk devolves downward.

2. See Lewis and Mosse 2006; Mosse 2004; Mosse 2005; Mosse 2011; and Scherz 2014.

3. For discussions of the policy-practice relationship, see Lewis 2004 and Mosse 2004 and 2005.

4. Anthropologists have documented globally the shift from social development organizations to profit-making financial intermediaries (Otero 1994).

5. See also Rajak 2006; Stirrat and Henkel 1997.

6. See Alam 1995; Jeffrey 2008, 519; and Lewis 2011, 15–16. Craig Jeffrey (2008) discusses the historical process in the 1960s-80s in which rich farmers began intensifying, mechanizing, hiring in labor, sending children to private education and government jobs, and diversifying their income streams. He examines in North India the ways in which young men from wealthy rural farming families, unable to attain *chakri*, attempted to secure middle-class status alternatively through university politics and by employing social, symbolic, spatial, and cultural strategies to defend their position. For further discussions of *chakri*, see Gardner 1995, 132; Myrdal 1968, 1646; Rao and Hossain 2012, 415.

7. See also Lewis and Hossain 2008, 281; van Schendel 1981. Significant industries for middle-class prosperity include the ready-made garment sector in Bangladesh (Kabeer 2000), the engineering and IT related industries in South India (Fuller and Narasimhan 2014; Patel 2010; Upadhya 2009), and textile-industry enterprises in Tamil Nadu (Chari 2004; De Neve 2011). Jonathan Parry (2013) discusses how the distinction between secure employment and insecure wage labor marked a crucial boundary between the middle and working classes.

8. For other discussions of the new development middle classes, see Devine 1998; Karim 2009; and Lewis 1993.

9. See also Hussain 2014, 9; Mawdsley 2004; Mosse 2011, 9; Riles 2000, 58; and Robison and Goodman 1996.

10. Annelise Riles (2000, 61) documents the ways in which commenting on personal relations explicitly in the formal domain was a confrontational strategy among workers.

11. David Lewis and Abul Hossain (2008, 282) draw on personal communication with Imran Matin and Naomi Hossain to convey an account of BRAC's participation in similar programs involving local rich and poor families coordinating for village hygiene.

12. The inherent entrepreneurialism of the poor is a core assumption of the idea of poverty capitalism and also mirrors academic shifts in writing about entrepreneurs in the informal economy.

13. In other parts of Bangladesh, NGOs and microfinance institutions occasionally faced community accusations of immoral action. Some NGOs experienced fatwas (formal legal rulings by a qualified Islamic jurist) issued against them (Shehabuddin 1999; White 2012).

14. Eirik Jansen (1987) details the land transfers resulting from food-deficit families who entered credit relations with surplus households and lost possession of houses and assets to pay off debts.

15. Bilateral and multilateral development agencies pushed microcredit onto development projects by exerting pressure on NGOs (Rahman 1999; Wood and Sharif 1997).

16. Others have observed the conditional ethical critique of patrons elsewhere in Bangladesh: "Within the political economy of patronage, accusations of corruption made by ordinary people coexist with their expectations of benefits from patrons" (Gardner 2012, 205). People censured a landlord for not looking after them as an issue of moral deviance and did not raise the issue of the wealth he accumulated by exploiting them (Devine and White 2013, 141). Other anthropological research suggests that this trend more broadly characterizes international development. China Scherz (2014) observes that former recipients of development goods in rural Uganda criticized recent concepts of sustainability not as empowerment but as refusals to redistribute wealth. See also Shah 2010.

17. These observations are not confined to development networks. Entering the iAgent network first as a project evaluator (for a major award competition) and then as

an early-career researcher securing my own status within academia, I too occupy a class position linked to a distinct type of "knowledge" about the iAgent model. My position within global hierarchies dictates what "fields" I am able to access, the types of information available to me, and the ways my knowledge products will be received by different audiences. The particular representation of the iAgent network in this book moves in a circuit of value and knowledge implicated with the accrual of status and opportunity.

6. THE AMBIGUOUS FIGURES OF SOCIAL ENTERPRISE

1. The appeal of superhero imagery in development discourses in not unique to Bangladesh. The United Nations in 2016 briefly selected (and then dropped) Wonder Woman as "honorary ambassador" for women's empowerment. Critics focused attention on the irony that the United Nations was unable to name a real female human being who represented women's empowerment.

2. Researchers have observed that microfinance projects simultaneously push entrepreneurial and individual self-maximizing subjectivities, build behavioral sanctions into the mechanism of the financial tool to limit borrower behavior, and expect social and solidaristic relationality with other borrowers and with project staff (Karim 2011; Lazar 2004; Shakya and Rankin 2008, 1222).

3. Katy Gardner (2012) discusses how discourses of "partnership" with local communities performed similar work for multinational corporations, and David Mosse describes how "extreme vulnerability and the search for security allies the immediate interests of poor people to those of their exploiters" (2010, 1172).

4. See Huang 2020 for a discussion of Yamada's attempt to set up a solar social enterprise with the iAgents and an exploration of the multiple productive misunderstandings that characterized the encounter.

5. Gardner et al. describe such "handing-over ceremonies" as public and recorded celebrations of "success" and "partnership," intended for the primary audience of the project's external interpretive communities (2012; also Mosse 2005).

6. Julia Elyachar shows how aspiring receivers of development funds styled their presentations to powerful foreign donors as a personal lament and thus faced disappointment. Delivered using a wrong aesthetic form, "their tale could be taken either as a lament or as an easily solvable practical problem. It could not produce a research effect and become an artifact with quasi-magical powers of value transformation" (2006, 421).

7. In Soumhya Venkatesan's work among handloom weavers in South India, she asks, "Why and how are certain marginalized persons and things brought by powerful others to the centre of a framed social space?" (2009, 78).

References

Agarwal, Bina. 1994. *A Field of One's Own: Gender and Land Rights in South Asia*. New Delhi: Cambridge University Press.

Ahearn, Laura. 2003. "Writing Desire in Nepali Love Letters." *Language and Communication* 23 (2): 107–22. https://doi.org/10.1016/S0271-5309(02)00046-0.

Ahmed, Rahnuma, and Milu Shamsun Naher. 1987. *Brides and the Demand System in Bangladesh: A Study*. Dhaka: Centre for Social Studies.

Alam, S. M. Shamsul. 1995. *The State, Class Formation, and Development in Bangladesh*. Lanham, MD: University Press of America.

Alam, Sultana, and Nilufar Matin. 1984. "Limiting the Women's Issues in Bangladesh: The Western and Bangladesh Legacy." *South Asia Bulletin* 4 (2): 1–10. https://doi.org/10.1215/07323867-4-2-1.

Amin, Sajeda, Nasheeba Selim, and Nashid Kamal Waiz. 2006. *Causes and Consequences of Early Marriage in Bangladesh: A Background Report for Workshop on Programme and Policies to Prevent Early Marriage*. Dhaka: Population Council.

Anders, Gerhard. 2008. "The Normativity of Numbers: World Bank and IMF Conditionality." *Political and Legal Anthropology Review* 31 (2): 187–202. https://doi.org/10.1111/j.1555-2934.2008.00021.x.

——. 2015. "The Normativity of Numbers in Practice: Technologies of Counting, Accounting and Auditing in Malawi's Civil Service Reform." *Social Anthropology* 23 (1): 29–41. https://www.doi.org/10.1111/1469-8676.12101.

Andersen, Barbara. 2013. "Tricks, Lies, and Mobile Phones: 'Phone Friend' Stories in Papua New Guinea." *Culture, Theory and Critique* 54 (3): 318–34. https://doi.org/10.1080/14735784.2013.811886.

Appadurai, Arjun. 2004. "The Capacity to Aspire: Culture and the Terms of Recognition." In *Culture And Public Action: A Cross-Disciplinary Dialogue On Development Policy*, edited by V. Rao and M. Walton, 59–84. Stanford: Stanford University Press.

Applbaum, Kalman. 2003. *The Marketing Era: From Professional Practice to Global Provisioning*. New York: Routledge.

Arce, Alberto, and Norman Long. 2002. "Bridging Two Worlds: An Ethnography of Bureaucrat-Peasant Relations in Western Mexico." In *An Anthropological Critique of Development: The Growth of Ignorance*, edited by M. Hobart, 179–208. London: Routledge.

Archambault, Julie Soleil. 2013. "Cruising through Uncertainty: Cell Phones and the Politics of Display and Disguise in Inhambane, Mozambique." *American Ethnologist* 40 (1): 88–101. https://doi.org/10.1111/amet.12007.

Aretxaga, Begona. 2003. "Maddening States." *Annual Review of Anthropology* 32: 393–410. https://doi.org/10.1146/annurev.anthro.32.061002.093341.

Bangladesh Planning Commission. 2015. *Millennium Development Goals: Bangladesh Progress Report 2015*. Dhaka: General Economics Division, Bangladesh Planning Commission, Government of the People's Republic of Bangladesh. https://planipolis.iiep.unesco.org/en/2015/millennium-development-goals-bangladesh-progress-report-2015-6191.

Barry, Ellen. 2017. "India's 'Phone Romeos' Look for Ms. Right via Wrong Numbers." *New York Times*, March 22. https://www.nytimes.com/2017/03/22/world/asia/indias-phone-romeos-look-for-the-right-one-through-wrong-numbers.html?_r=0.

Bathelt, Harald, and Johannes Glückler. 2011. *The Relational Economy: Geographies of Knowing and Learning*. Oxford: Oxford University Press.

Batliwala, Srilatha. 2011. "Taking the Power Out of Empowerment: An Experiential Account." In *Deconstructing Development Discourse: Buzzwords and Fuzzwords*, edited by Andrea Cornwall and Deborah Eade, 111–21. Rugby, UK: Practical Action Publishing.

Bear, Laura. 2011. "Making a River of Gold: Speculative State Planning, Informality, and Neoliberal Governance on the Hooghly." *Focaal* 61): 46–60. https://doi.org/10.3167/fcl.2011.610104.

——. 2013. "'This Body is Our Body': *Vishwakarma Puja*, the Social Debts of Kinship, and Theologies of Materiality in a Neoliberal Shipyard." In *Vital Relations: Modernity And The Persistent Life Of Kinship*, edited by Susie McKinnon and Fenella Cannell, 155–78. Santa Fe, NM: School for Advanced Research Press.

——. 2014a. "Capital and Time: Uncertainty and Qualitative Measures of Inequality." *British Journal of Sociology* 65 (4): 639–49. https://doi.org/10.1111/1468-4446.12107.

——. 2014b. "Doubt, Conflict, Mediation: The Anthropology of Modern Time." *Journal of the Royal Anthropological Institute* 20 (S1): 3–30. https://doi.org/10.1111/1467-9655.12091.

——, ed. 2014c. "Special Issue: Doubt, Conflict, Mediation: The Anthropology of Modern Time." *Journal of the Royal Anthropological Institute* 20 (S1): vii–ix, 3–186. https://doi.org/10.1111/1467-9655.12091.

——. 2015b. *Navigating Austerity: Currents of Debt Along a South Asian River*. Stanford: Stanford University Press.

——. 2016. "Time as Technique." *Annual Review of Anthropology* 45: 487–502. https://doi.org/10.1146/annurev-anthro-102313-030159.

Benjamin, Walter. 1989. "On the Program of the Coming Philosophy." In *Benjamin: Philosophy, Aesthetics, History*, edited by G. Smith, 1–12. Chicago: University of Chicago Press.

Berlant, Lauren. 2011. *Cruel Optimism*. Durham, NC: Duke University Press.

Bhowmick, Nilanjana. 2013. "After Much Heartbreak, Some Good News at Last for Bangladesh." *Time*, July 18. http://world.time.com/2013/07/18/after-much-heartbreak-some-good-news-at-last-for-bangladesh.

Black, Annabel. 2004. "Ambiguity and Verbal Disguise within Diplomatic Culture." In *An Anthropology of Indirect Communication*, edited by Joy Hendry and C. W. Watson, 255–70. London: Routledge.

Bleie, Tone. 1990. "Dowry and Bridewealth Presentations in Rural Bangladesh: Commodities, Gifts or Hybrid Forms?" DERAP Working Paper 10. Bergen: Chr. Michelsen Institute.

Blowfield, Michael E., and Catherine S. Dolan. 2008. "Stewards of Virtue? The Ethical Dilemma of CSR in African Agriculture." *Development and Change* 39 (1): 1–23. https://doi.org/10.1111/j.1467-7660.2008.00465.x.

Bode, Brigitta, and Mick Howes. 2002. *The Northwest Institutional Analysis*. Dhaka: CARE Bangladesh.

Bornstein, David. 1996. *The Price of A Dream: The Story of the Grameen Bank*. Oxford: Oxford University Press.

Borthwick, Meredith. 2015. *The Changing Role of Women in Bengal, 1849–1905*. Princeton, NJ: Princeton University Press.

Bourdieu, Pierre. 1977. *Outline of a Theory of Practice*. Cambridge: Cambridge University Press.

———. 1983. "Forms of Capital." In *Handbook of Theory and Research for the Sociology of Education*, edited by John G. Richardson, 241–58. New York: Greenwood Press.

———. 1984. *Distinction*. Cambridge, MA: Harvard University Press.

———. 1998. "The Essence of Neo-Liberalism." *Le Monde Diplomatique*, December 8. http://mondediplo.com/1998/12/08bourdieu.

Breman, Jan. 1996. *Footloose Labour: Working in India's Informal Economy*. Cambridge: Cambridge University Press.

BTRC. 2016. "Mobile Phone Subscribers in Bangladesh October 2016." Bangladesh Telecommunication Regulatory Commission. http://www.btrc.gov.bd/content/mobile-phone-subscribers-bangladesh-october-2016.

Cain, Mead, Syeda Khanam, and Shamsun Nahar. 1979. "Class, Patriarchy and Women's Work in Bangladesh." *Population and Development Review* 5 (3): 405–38.

Çaliskan, Koray, and Michel Callon. 2009. "Economization, Part 1: Shifting Attention from the Economy Towards Processes of Economization." *Economy and Society* 38 (3): 369–98. https://doi.org/10.1080/03085140903020580.

Callan, Alyson. 2008. "Female Saints and the Practice of Islam in Sylhet, Bangladesh." *American Ethnologist* 35 (3): 396–412. https://doi.org/10.1111/j.1548-1425.2008.00042.x.

Callon, Michel. 1998. "An Essay on Framing and Overflowing: Economic Externalities Revisited by Sociology." In *Laws of the Markets*, edited by Michel Callon, 244–69. London: Blackwell.

Carey, Matthew. 2012. "'The Rules' in Morocco: Pragmatic Approaches to Flirtation and Lying." *HAU: Journal of Ethnographic Theory* 2 (2): 188–204.

Cattelino, Jessica. 2010. "The Double Bind of American Indian Need-Based Sovereignty." *Cultural Anthropology* 25 (2): 235–63. https://doi.org/10.1111/j.1548-1360.2010.01058.x.

Chari, Sharad. 2004. *Fraternal Capital: Peasant-Workers, Self-Made Men, and Globalization in Provincial India*. Stanford: Stanford University Press.

Chibber, Vivek. 2003. *Locked in Place: State-Building and Late Industrialization in India*. Princeton, NJ: Princeton University Press.

Chong, Kimberly. 2012. "The Work of Financialisation: An Ethnography of a Global Management Consultancy in Post-Mao China." PhD diss., London School of Economics and Political Science.

Chowdhury, M. Jashim Ali. 2015. "Elections in 'Democratic' Bangladesh." In *Unstable Constitutionalism: Law and Politics in South Asia*, edited by Mark Tushnet and Madhav Khosla, 192–230. Cambridge: Cambridge University Press.

Chowdhury, Nusrat S. 2014. "'Picture-Thinking': Sovereignty and Citizenship in Bangladesh." *Anthropological Quarterly* 87 (4): 1257–78.

Christensen, Clayton. 1997. *The Innovator's Dilemma: When New Technologies Cause Great Firms to Fail*. Boston: Harvard Business Review Press.

Constable, Nicole. 2009. "The Commodification of Intimacy: Marriage, Sex, and Reproductive Labor." *Annual Review of Anthropology* 38: 49–64. https://doi.org/10.1146/annurev.anthro.37.081407.085133.

Cornwall, Andrea. 2007. "Buzzwords and Fuzzwords: Deconstructing Development Discourse." *Development in Practice* 17 (4–5): 471–84. https://doi.org/10.1080/09614520701469302.

Cornwall, Andrea, and Deborah Eade, eds. 2010. *Deconstructing Development Discourse: Buzzwords and Fuzzwords*. Rugby, UK: Practical Action Publishing.

Cross, Jamie. 2011. "Detachment as a Corporate Ethic: Materializing CSR in the Diamond Supply Chain." *Focaal* 60: 34–46.

——. 2013. "The 100th Object: Solar Lighting Technology and Humanitarian Goods." *Journal of Material Culture* 18 (4): 367–87. https://doi.org/10.1177/135918351 3498959.

——. 2019. "Selling with Prejudice: Social Enterprise and Caste at the Bottom of the Pyramid in India." *Ethnos* 84 (3): 458–79. https://doi.org/10.1080/00141844.2018 .1561487.

Cross, Jamie, and Alice Street. 2009. "Anthropology at the Bottom of the Pyramid." *Anthropology Today* 25 (4): 4–9. https://doi.org/10.1111/j.1467-8322.2009.00675.x.

Dannecker, Petra. 2002. *Between Conformity and Resistance: Women Garment Workers in Bangladesh.* Dhaka: The University Press Limited.

De Neve, Geert. 2011. "'Keeping It in the Family': Work, Education, and Gender Hierarchies among Tiruppur's Industrial Capitalists." In *Being Middle-Class in India: A Way of Life,* edited by Henrike Donner, 73–99. London: Routledge.

——. 2014. "Fordism, Flexible Specialization and CSR: How Indian Garment Workers Critique Neoliberal Labour Regimes." *Ethnography* 15 (2): 184–207. https://doi.org/10.1177/1466138112463801.

Devine, Joseph. 1998. "Empowerment and the Spiritual Economy of NGOs in Bangladesh." Paper presented at the European Network of Bangladesh Studies, Fifth Workshop, University of Bath. April 16–18.

Devine, Joseph, and Sarah White. 2013. "Religion, Politics and the Everyday Moral Order in Bangladesh." *Journal of Contemporary Asia* 43 (1): 127–41. https://doi.org/10.10 80/00472336.2012.735544.

Di Leonardo, Michaela. 1987. "The Female World of Cards and Holidays: Women, Families, and the Work of Kinship." *Signs* 12 (3): 440–53.

Dobush, Grace. 2015. "How Mobile Phones are Changing the Developing World." Consumer Technology Association, July 27. https://www.cta.tech/News/Blog/Articles/2015/July/How-Mobile-Phones-Are-Changing-the-Developing-Worl.aspx.

Dolan, Catherine. 2007. "Market Affections: Moral Encounters with Kenyan Fairtrade Flowers." *Ethnos* 72 (2): 239–61. https://doi.org/10.1080/00141840701396573.

——. 2012. "The New Face of Development: The 'Bottom of the Pyramid' Entrepreneurs." *Anthropology Today* 28 (4): 3–7. https://doi.org/10.1111/j.1467-8322.2012.00883.x.

——. 2014. "Crossing the Line: Youth and Economies of Distinction at the 'Bottom of the Pyramid' in Kenya." Paper presented at Department of Anthropology, London School of Economics and Political Science, May 2.

Dolan, Catherine, Julia Huang, and Claire Gordon. 2019. "The Ambiguity of Mutuality: Discourse and Power in Corporate Value Regimes." *Dialectical Anthropology,* online first.

Dolan, Catherine, and Mary Johnstone-Louis. 2011. "Re-Siting Corporate Responsibility: The Making of South Africa's Avon Entrepreneurs." *Focaal* 60: 21–33. https://doi.org/10.3167/fcl.2011.600103.

Dolan, Catherine, Mary Johnstone-Louis, and Linda Scott. 2012. "CARE Bangladesh Rural Sales Programme (RSP)." Saïd Business School Cases.

Dolan, Catherine, and Dinah Rajak. 2016. *The Anthropology of Corporate Social Responsibility.* New York: Berghahn.

Dominguez, Gabriel. 2015. "US Blogger's Killing 'Exposes Level of Political Volatility' in Bangladesh." *Deutsche Welle,* March 5. http://www.dw.com/en/us-bloggers-killing-exposes-level-of-political-volatility-in-bangladesh/a-18294948.

Donner, Henrike. 2002. "'One's Own Marriage': Love Marriages in a Calcutta Neighbourhood." *South Asia Research* 22 (1): 79–94. https://doi.org/http://10.1177/02627 2800202200104.

———. 2008. *Domestic Goddesses: Maternity, Globalization and Middle-Class Identity in Contemporary India*. Aldershot: Ashgate.

———. 2012. "Whose City is it Anyway? Middle Class Imagination and Urban Restructuring in Twenty-First Century Kolkata." *New Perspectives on Turkey* 46 (Spring): 129–55.

Donner, Jonathan. 2007. "The Rules of Beeping: Exchanging Messages Via Intentional 'Missed Calls' on Mobile Phones." *Journal of Computer-Mediated Communication* 13 (1): 1–22. https://doi.org/10.1111/j.1083-6101.2007.00383.x.

Doron, Assa. 2012. "Mobile Persons: Cell Phones, Gender and the Self in North India." *Asia Pacific Journal of Anthropology* 13 (5): 414–33. https://doi.org/10.1080/14442 213.2012.726253.

Drèze, Jean, and Amartya Sen, eds. 1990. *The Political Economy of Hunger, Volume 1: Entitlement and Well-Being*. Oxford: Clarendon Press.

Dunn, Elizabeth. 2004. *Privatizing Poland: Baby Food, Big Business and the Remaking of Labor*. New York: Cornell University Press.

———. 2008. "Standards and Person-Making in East Central Europe." In *Global Assemblages: Technology, Politics and Ethics as Anthropological Problems*, edited by Aihwa Ong and Stephen Collier, 173–193. Oxford: Wiley Blackwell.

Eisenberg, Eric M. 1984. "Ambiguity as Strategy in Organizational Communication." *Communication Monographs* 51 (3): 227–42.

Elkington, John, Alejandro Litovsky, and Charmian Love. 2009. *The Phoenix Economy: 50 Pioneers in the Business of Social Innovation*. London: Volans Ventures Ltd.

Elyachar, Julia. 2002. "Empowerment Money: The World Bank, Non-Governmental Organizations, and the Value of Culture in Egypt". *Public Culture* 14 (3): 493–513. https://doi.org/10.1215/08992363-14-3-493.

———. 2005. *Markets of Dispossession: NGOs, Economic Development, and the State in Cairo*. Durham, NC: Duke University Press.

———. 2006. "Best Practices: Research, Finance, and NGOs in Cairo." *American Ethnologist* 33 (3): 413–26. https://doi.org/10.1525/ae.2006.33.3.413.

Errington, Frederick, Tatsuro Fujikura, and Deborah Gewertz. 2012. "Instant Noodles as an Antifriction Device: Making the BOP with PPP in PNG." *American Anthropologist* 114 (1): 19–31. https://doi.org/10.1111/j.1548-1433.2011.01394.x.

Escobar, Arturo. 1991. "Anthropology and the Development Encounter: The Making and Marketing of Development Anthropology." *American Ethnologist* 18 (4): 658–82.

Faaland, Just, and Jack R. Parkinson. 1976. *Bangladesh. The Test Case for Development*. London: Hurst.

Feldman, Shelley. 2003. "Paradoxes of Institutionalism: The Depoliticisation of Bangladeshi NGOs." *Development in Practice* 13 (1): 5–26. https://doi.org/10.1080/09614 52022000037955.

Ferguson, James. 2013. "Declarations of Dependence: Labour, Personhood, and Welfare in Southern Africa." *Journal of the Royal Anthropological Institute* 19 (2): 223–42. https://doi.org/10.1111/1467-9655.12023.

Foucault, Michel. 1977. *Discipline and Punish: The Birth of the Prison*. New York: Random House.

———. 1980. *An Introduction. History of Sexuality, vol. 1*. Translated by Robert Hurley. New York: Vintage.

Freeman, Carla. 2007. "The 'Reputation' of Neoliberalism." *American Ethnologist* 34 (2): 252–67.

Froerer, Peggy. 2015. "Young People and the Risk of Education in Rural Chhattisgarh." *South Asian History and Culture* 6 (3): 365–79. https://doi.org/10.1080/19472498. 2015.1030873.

Fuller, C. J., and Haripriya Narasimhan. 2014. *Tamil Brahmans: The Making of a Middle-Class Caste*. Chicago: University of Chicago Press.

Gardner, Katy, Zahir Ahmed, Fatema Bashir, and Masud Rana. 2012. "Elusive Partnerships: Gas Extraction and CSR in Bangladesh." *Resources Policy* 37 (2): 168–74. https://doi.org/10.1016/j.resourpol.2012.01.001.

Gardner, Katy. 1995. *Global Migrants, Local Lives: Travel and Transformation in Rural Bangladesh*. Oxford: Oxford University Press.

——. 1997. *Songs at the River's Edge: Stories from a Bangladeshi Village*. London: Pluto Press.

——. 2012. *Discordant Development: Global Capitalism and the Struggle for Connection in Bangladesh*. London: Pluto Press.

——. 2015. "Chevron's Gift of CSR: Moral Economies of Connection and Disconnection in a Transnational Bangladeshi Village." *Economy and Society* 44 (4): 495–518. https://doi.org/10.1080/03085147.2015.1087750.

Gershon, Ilana. 2017. *Down and Out in the New Economy: How People Find (or Don't Find) Work Today*. Chicago: University of Chicago Press.

Gilligan, Carol. 1982. *In a Different Voice*. Cambridge, MA: Harvard University Press.

Goetz, Anne Marie. 2001. *Women Development Workers: Implementing Rural Credit Programs in Bangladesh*. New Delhi: Sage Publications.

Goetz, Anne Marie, and Rina Sen Gupta. 1994. "Who Takes the Credit? Gender, Power, and Control Over Loan Use in Rural Credit Programmes in Bangladesh." IDS Working Paper 8. Brighton: IDS.

Grover, Shalini. 2009. "Lived Experiences: Marriage, Notions of Love, and Kinship Support amongst Poor Women in Delhi." *Contributions to Indian Sociology* 43 (1): 1–33. https://doi.org/10.1177/006996670904300101.

GSMA Intelligence. 2014. "Country Overview: Bangladesh." https://www.gsmaintelligence.com/research/?file=140820-bangladesh.pdf&download.

Guérin, Isabelle. 2017. "Female Market Makers and the Forced March of Social Capitalism." Working Paper, 2017–2, Microfinance in Crisis Working Paper Series.

Guhathakurta, Meghna. 1985. "Gender Violence in Bangladesh: The Role of the State." *Journal of Social Studies* 30: 77–90.

Hardt, Michael, and Antonio Negri. 2000. *Empire*. Cambridge, MA: Harvard University Press.

Harrison, Frances. 2013. *Political Islam and the Elections in Bangladesh*. London: New Millennium.

Hartmann, Betsy, and James Boyce. 1983. *A Quiet Violence: View from a Bangladesh Village*. London: Zed Books.

Heath, Rachel, and A. Mushfiq Mobarak. 2014. "Manufacturing Growth and the Lives of Bangladeshi Women." *The National Bureau of Economic Research* Working Paper No. 20385. https://doi.org/10.3386/w20383.

Hilhorst, Dorothea. 2003. *The Real World of NGOs: Discourses, Diversity and Development*. London: Zed Books.

Hirschkind, Charles. 2006. *The Ethical Soundscape: Cassette Sermons and Islamic Counterpublics*. New York: Columbia University Press.

Ho, Karen. 2009. *Liquidated: An Ethnography of Wall Street*. Durham, NC: Duke University Press.

Horst, Heather, and Daniel Miller. 2005. "From Kinship to Link-Up: Cell Phones and Social Networking in Jamaica." *Current Anthropology* 46 (5): 755–78.

Huang, Julia Qermezi. 2020. "Transient Assemblages, Ephemeral Encounters, and the 'Beautiful Story' of a Japanese Social Enterprise in Rural Bangladesh." *Critique of Anthropology* 40 (3).

Huda, Karishma, Sabeel Rahman, and Catherine Guirguis. 2008. "Social Capital and What it Represents: The Experience of the Ultra-Poor in Bangladesh." *Journal of Power* 1 (3): 295–315. https://doi.org/10.1080/17540290802479210.

Huda, Shahnaz. 2006. "Dowry in Bangladesh: Compromizing Women's Rights." *South Asia Research* 26 (3): 249–68. https://doi.org/10.1177/0262728006071707.

Hull, Matthew. 2012. *Government of Paper: The Materiality of Bureaucracy in Urban Pakistan*. Berkeley: University of California Press.

Hussain, Delwar. 2013. *Boundaries Undermined: The Ruins of Progress on the Bangladeshi-India Border*. London: Hurst.

———. 2014. "The State of Relief on the Bangladesh-India Border." *South Asia Multidisciplinary Academic Journal* 9: 2–14. https://doi.org/10.4000/samaj.3728.

Inda, Jonathan Xavier. 2005. *Anthropologies of Modernity: Foucault, Governmentality, and Life Politics*. Malden, MA: Blackwell.

Information Commission of Bangladesh. n.d. Home page. http://www.infocom.gov.bd, accessed April 23, 2015.

Islam, Mohammad Mozahidul. 2015. "Electoral Violence in Bangladesh: Does a Confrontational Bipolar Political System Matter?" *Commonwealth & Comparative Politics* 53 (4): 359–80. https://doi.org/10.1080/14662043.2015.1089001.

J.P. Morgan and Rockefeller Foundation. 2010. Impact Investments: An Emerging Asset Class. November 29. https://thegiin.org/knowledge/publication/impact-investments-an-emerging-asset-class.

Jackson, Michael. 2005. "Storytelling Events, Violence, and the Appearance of the Past." *Anthropological Quarterly* 78 (2): 355–75. https://doi.org/10.1353/anq.2005.0020.

Jahan, Rounaq. 1972. *Pakistan: Failure in National Integration*. New York: Columbia University Press.

Jahangir, B. K. 1982. *Rural Society: Power Structure and Class Practice*. Dhaka: Dhaka University Press.

James, Deborah. 2015. "Indebtedness in South Africa: Mediated Capitalism." Paper presented at DME Final Conference, The Quest for the Good Life in Precarious Times: Grassroots Perspectives on the Value Question in the 21st Century, University of Manchester. March 22–26.

Jansen, Eirik. 1987. *Rural Bangladesh: Competition for Scarce Resources*. Dhaka: Dhaka University Press.

Jeffery, Patricia. 1979. *Frogs in a Well: Indian Women in Purdah*. London: Zed Press.

Jeffery, Patricia, and Amrita Basu, eds. 1998. *Appropriating Gender: Women's Activism and Politicized Religion in South Asia*. New York: Routledge.

Jeffery, Patricia, and Roger Jeffery. 1996. *Don't Marry Me to a Plowman! Women's Everyday Lives in Rural North India*. Boulder: Westview Press.

Jeffrey, Craig. 2008. "Kicking Away the Ladder: Student Politics and the Making of an Indian Middle Class." *Environment and Planning D: Society and Space* 26 (3): 517–36. https://doi.org/10.1068/dcos4.

———. 2010. *Timepass: Youth, Class, and the Politics of Waiting in India*. Stanford: Stanford University Press.

Jita Bangladesh. n.d. Home page. www.jitabangladesh.com, accessed April 5, 2015.

Johnson-Hanks, Jennifer. 2007. "Women on the Market: Marriage, Consumption, and the Internet in Urban Cameroon." *American Ethnologist* 34 (4): 642–58. https://doi.org/10.1525/ae.2007.34.4.642.

Jorgensen, Dan. 2014. "*Gesfaia*: Mobile Phones and Anonymous Intimacy in Papua New Guinea." Paper given at the meetings of the Canadian Anthropological Society, Toronto, April 30.

Juris, Jeffrey S. 2012. "Reflections on #Occupy Everywhere: Social Media, Public Space, and Emerging Logics Of Aggregation." *American Ethnologist* 39 (2): 259–79. https://doi.org/10.1111/j.1548-1425.2012.01362.x.

Kabeer, Naila. 2000. *The Power to Choose: Bangladeshi Women and Labour Market Decisions in London and Dhaka.* London: Verso.

——. 2001. "Conflicts Over Credit: Re-Evaluating the Empowerment Potential of Loans to Women in Rural Bangladesh." *World Development* 29 (1): 63–84. https://doi.org/10.1016/S0305-750X(00)00081-4.

——. 2011. "Between Affiliation and Autonomy: Navigating Pathways of Women's Empowerment and Gender Justice in Rural Bangladesh." *Development and Change* 42 (2): 499–528.

Kar, Sohini. 2013. "Recovering Debts: Microfinance Loan Officers and the Work of 'Proxy-Creditors' in India." *American Ethnologist* 40 (3): 480–93. https://doi.org/10.1111/amet.12034.

——. 2018. *Financializing Poverty: Microfinance, Development and Financial Risk in India.* Stanford: Stanford University Press.

Karim, Lamia. 2001. "Politics of the Poor? NGOs and Grass-Roots Political Mobilization in Bangladesh." *Political and Legal Anthropology Review* 24 (1): 92–107. https://doi.org/10.1525/pol.2001.24.1.92.

——. 2009. "Democratising Bangladesh: State, NGOs and Militant Islam." In *Recreating the Commons? NGOs in Bangladesh*, edited by Farida Chowdhury Khan, Ahrar Ahmad, and Munir Quddus, 149–81. Dhaka: The University Press.

——. 2011. *Microfinance and its Discontents: Women in Debt in Bangladesh.* Minneapolis: University of Minnesota Press.

Khan, Akhter Hameed. 1983. *The Works of Akhter Hameed Khan: Rural Development Approaches and the Comilla Model.* Comilla: The Bangladesh Academy for Rural Development.

Khilnani, Sunil. 1997. *The Idea of India.* London: Hamish Hamilton.

Kielmann, Karina. 2002. "Gender, Well-Being and the Quality of Life." Paper presented at the Gender, Health and Politics Workshop in South Asia, University of Heidelberg, July 18–19.

Klein, Naomi. 2005. "The Rise of Disaster Capitalism." *Nation* 280 (17): 9–11.

Kriem, Maya S. 2009. "Mobile Telephony in Morocco: A Changing Sociality." *Media, Culture & Society* 31 (4): 617–32. https://doi.org/10.1177/0163443709335729.

Lamb, Sarah. 2000. *White Saris and Sweet Mangoes: Aging, Gender, and Body in North India.* Berkeley: University of California Press.

Lambek, Michael, ed. 2010. *Ordinary Ethics: Anthropology, Language, and Action.* New York: Fordham University Press.

Latour, Bruno. 1996. *Aramis, or the Love of Technology.* Translated by Catherine Porter. Cambridge, MA: Harvard University Press.

Lazar, Sian. 2004. "Education for Credit: Development as Citizenship Project in Bolivia." *Critique of Anthropology* 24 (3): 301–19. https://doi.org/10.1177/0308275X04045423.

Lewis, David. 1993. "Bangladesh Overview." In *NGOs and the State in Asia: Rethinking Roles in Sustainable Agricultural Development*, edited by John Farrington and David Lewis, 47–58. London: Routledge.

——. 2004. "On the Difficulty of Studying 'Civil Society': Reflections on NGOs, State and Democracy in Bangladesh." *Contributions to Indian Sociology.* 38 (3): 299–322. https://doi.org/10.1177/006996670403800301.

——. 2011. *Bangladesh: Politics, Economy and Civil Society.* Cambridge: Cambridge University Press.

Lewis, David, and Abul Hossain. 2008. "Beyond 'The Net'? Institutions, Elites, and the Changing Power Structure in Rural Bangladesh." In *Local Democracy in South Asia: Microprocesses of Democratization in Nepal and its Neighbours*, edited by David Gellner and Krishna Hachhethu, 279–300. New Delhi: Sage Publications India.

Lewis, David, and David Mosse, eds. 2006. *Development Brokers and Translators: The Ethnography of Aid and Agencies*. Bloomfield, CT: Kumarian Press.

Lewis, David, Dennis Rogers, and Michael Woolcock. 2008. "The Fiction of Development: Literary Representation as a Source of Authoritative Knowledge." *Journal of Development Studies* 44 (2): 198–216. https://doi.org/10.1080/00220380701789828.

Li, Tania Murray. 2009. "To Make Live or Let Die? Rural Dispossession and the Protection of Surplus Populations." *Antipode* 41 (S1): 66–93. https://doi.org/10.1111/j.1467-8330.2009.00717.x.

Lin, Angel. 2005. "Gendered, Bilingual Communication Practices: Mobile Text-Messaging among Hong Kong College Students." *Fibreculture* 6 (January): n.p.

Lindenbaum, Shirley. 1981. "Implications for Women of Changing Marriage Transactions in Bangladesh." *Studies in Family Planning* 12 (11): 394–401.

Ling, Richard Seyler. 2008. *New Tech, New Ties: How Mobile Communication is Reshaping Social Cohesion*. Cambridge, MA: MIT Press.

Lipset, David. 2013. "Mobail: Moral Ambivalence and the Domestication of Mobile Telephones in Peri-Urban Papua New Guinea." *Culture, Theory and Critique* 54 (3): 335–54. https://doi.org/10.1080/14735784.2013.826501.

Luetchford, Peter. 2007. "Hidden Hands in Fair Trade: Nicaraguan Migrants and the Labour Process in the Costa Rican Coffee Harvest." Sussex Migration Working Paper No. 44.

Mahmood, Saba. 2005. *The Politics of Piety: The Islamic Revival and the Feminist Subject*. Princeton, NJ: Princeton University Press.

Marriott, McKim. 1976. "Hindu Transactions: Diversity Without Dualism." In *Transaction and Meaning: Directions in the Anthropology of Exchange and Symbolic Behavior*, edited by Bruce Kapferer, 109–42. Philadelphia: Institute for the Study of Human Issues.

Marriott, McKim, and Ronald Inden. 1977. "Toward an Ethnosociology of South Asian Caste Systems." In *The New Wind: Changing Identities in South Asia*, edited by Kenneth H. David, 227–38. The Hague: Mouton Publishers.

Martin, Emily. 1994. *Flexible Bodies: Tracking Immunity in American Culture from the Days of Polio to the Age of AIDS*. Boston: Beacon Press.

Matador Ball Pen Industries. n.d. "About us." http://www.matador.com.bd/mbi.php, accessed January 9, 2015.

Maurer, Bill, Taylor C. Nelms, and Stephen C. Rea. 2013. "'Bridges to Cash': Channelling Agency in Mobile Money." *Journal of the Royal Anthropological Institute* 19 (1): 52–74. https://doi.org/10.1111/1467-9655.12003.

Mawdsley, Emma. 2004. "India's Middle Classes and the Environment." *Development and Change* 35 (1): 79–103. https://doi.org/10.1111/j.1467-7660.2004.00343.x.

Mazzarella, William. 2010. "Beautiful Balloon: The Digital Divide and the Charisma of New Media in India." *American Ethnologist* 37 (4): 783–804. https://doi.org/10.1111/j.1548-1425.2010.01285.x.

Menski, Werner, ed. 1998. *South Asians and the Dowry Problem*. Stoke-on-Trent: Trentham Books.

McCarthy, Florence. 1977. "Bengali Village Women as Mediators of Social Change." *Human Organization* 36 (4): 363–70.

McGoey, Linsey. 2012a. "Strategic Unknowns: Towards a Sociology of Ignorance." *Economy and Society* 41 (1): 1–16. https://doi.org/10.1080/03085147.2011.637330.

——. 2012b. "The Logic of Strategic Ignorance." *British Journal of Sociology.* 63 (3): 553–76. https://doi.org/10.1111/j.1468-4446.2012.01424.x.

Mills, Mary Beth. 1997. "Contesting the Margins of Modernity: Women, Migration, and Consumption in Thailand." *American Ethnologist* 24 (1): 37–61. https://doi.org/10.1525/ae.1997.24.1.37.

Mitchell, Timothy. 2007. "The Properties of Markets." In *Do Economists Make Markets?: On the Performativity of Economics*, edited by Donald MacKenzie, Fabian Muniesa, and Lucia Siu, 244–75. Princeton, NJ: Princeton University Press.

Moniruzzaman, Monir. 2012. "'Living Cadavers' in Bangladesh: Bioviolence in the Human Organ Bazaar." *Medical Anthropology Quarterly* 26 (1): 69–91.

Mookherjee, Nayanika. 2015. *The Spectral Wound: Sexual Violence, Public Memories, and the Bangladesh War of 1971.* Durham, NC: Duke University Press.

Moore, Sally Falk. 1987. "Explaining the Present: Theoretical Dilemmas in Processual Ethnography." *American Ethnologist* 14 (4): 727–36. https://doi.org/10.1525/ae.1987.14.4.02a00080.

Morduch, Jonathan. 1999. "The Role of Subsidies in Microfinance: Evidence from the Grameen Bank." *Journal of Development Economics* 60 (1): 229–48. https://doi.org/10.1016/S0304-3878(99)00042-5.

Mosse, David. 2004. "Is Good Policy Unimplementable? Reflections on the Ethnography of Aid Policy and Practice." *Development and Change* 35 (4): 639–71. https://doi.org/10.1111/j.0012-155X.2004.00374.x.

——. 2005. *Cultivating Development: An Ethnography of Aid Policy and Practice.* London: Pluto Press.

——. 2010. "A Relational Approach to Durable Poverty, Inequality and Power." *Journal of Development Studies* 46 (7): 1156–78. https://doi.org/10.1080/00220388.2010.487095.

——. 2011. "Introduction: The Anthropology of Expertise and Professionals in International Development." In *Adventures in Aidland: The Anthropology of Professionals in International Development*, edited by David Mosse, 1–31. New York: Berghahn.

——. 2013. "The Anthropology of International Development." *Annual Review of Anthropology* 42: 227–46.

Muniesa, Fabian, Yuval Millo, and Michel Callon. 2007. "An Introduction to Market Devices." *Sociological Review* 55 (S2): 1–12. https://doi.org/10.1111/j.1467-954X.2007.00727.x.

Myrdal, Gunnar. 1968. *Asian Drama: An Inquiry into the Poverty of Nations, Volume III.* London: Penguin Press.

Ong, Aihwa. 1988. "The Production of Possession: Spirits and the Multinational Corporation in Malaysia." *American Ethnologist* 15 (1): 28–42. https://doi.org/10.1525/ae.1988.15.1.02a00030.

——. 1991. "The Gender and Labor Politics of Postmodernity." *Annual Review of Anthropology* 20: 279–301.

——. 1999. *Flexible Citizenship: The Cultural Logics of Transnationality.* Durham, NC: Duke University Press.

Ong, Aihwa, and Stephen Collier, eds. 2005. *Global Assemblages: Technology, Politics, and Ethics as Anthropological Problems.* Malden, MA: Blackwell Publishing.

Orsini, Francesca, ed. 2007. *Love in South Asia: A Cultural History.* New Delhi: Cambridge University Press.

Otero, Maria. 1994. "The Evolution of Nongovernmental Organizations toward Financial Intermediation." In *The New World of Microenterprise Finance: Building*

Healthy Financial Institutions for the Poor, edited by Maria Otero and Elizabeth Rhyne, 94–104. West Hartford, CT: Kumarian Press.

Otero, Maria, and Elizabeth Rhyne, eds. 1994. *The New World of Microenterprise Finance: Building Healthy Financial Institutions for the Poor.* West Hartford, CT: Kumarian Press.

Parry, Jonathan. 2001. "Ankalu's Errant Wife: Sex, Marriage and Industry in Contemporary Chhattisgarh." *Modern Asian Studies* 35 (4): 783–820.

——. 2013. "Company and Contract Labour in a Central Indian Steel Plant." *Economy and Society* 42 (3): 348–74. https://doi.org/10.1080/03085147.2013.772761.

——. 2014. "Sex, Bricks and Mortar: Constructing Class in a Central Indian Steel Town." *Modern Asian Studies* 48 (5): 1242–75. https://doi.org/10.1017/S0026749X1400002X.

Patel, Rina. 2010. *Working the Night Shift: Women in India's Call Center Industry.* Stanford: Stanford University Press.

"The Path through the Fields." 2012. *The Economist*, November 3. http://www.economist.com/news/briefing/21565617-bangladesh-has-dysfunctional-politics-and-stunted-private-sector-yet-it-has-been-surprisingly.

Pattenden, Jonathan. 2011. "Gatekeeping as Accumulation and Domination: Decentralization and Class Relations in Rural South India." *Journal of Agrarian Change* 11 (2): 164–94. https://doi.org/10.1111/j.1471-0366.2010.00300.x.

Petras, James. 1997. "Imperialism and NGOs in Latin America." *Monthly Review* 49 (7). http://monthlyreview.org/1997/12/01/imperialism-and-ngos-in-latin-america/.

Povinelli, Elizabeth. 2011. *Economies of Abandonment: Social Belonging and Endurance in Late Liberalism.* Durham, NC: Duke University Press.

——. 2012. "The Will to be Otherwise/The Effort of Endurance." *South Atlantic Quarterly* 111 (3): 453–75. https://doi.org/10.1215/00382876-1596236.

Prahalad, C. K. 2006. *The Fortune at the Bottom of the Pyramid: Eradicating Poverty through Profits.* Upper Saddle River, NJ: Wharton School Publishing.

Raheja, Gloria Goodwin, and Ann Gold. 1994. *Listen to the Heron's Words: Reimagining Gender and Kinship in North India.* Berkeley: University of California Press.

Rahman, Aminur. 1999. "Micro-Credit Initiatives for Equitable and Sustainable Development: Who Pays?" *World Development* 27 (1): 67–82. https://doi.org/10.1016/S0305-750X(98)00105-3.

Rajak, Dinah. 2006. "The Gift of CSR: Power and the Pursuit of Responsibility in the Mining Industry." In *Corporate Citizenship in Africa: Lessons from the Past; Paths to the Future*, edited by Wayne Visser, Malcolm McIntosh, and Charlotte Middleton, 190–200. Sheffield: Greenleaf Publishing.

——. 2011a. *In Good Company: An Anatomy of Corporate Social Responsibility.* Stanford: Stanford University Press.

——. 2011b. "Theatres of Virtue: Collaboration, Consensus and the Social Life of Corporate Social Responsibility." *Focaal* 60 (Summer): 9–20.

Rankin, Katharine N. 2001. "Governing Development: Neoliberalism, Microcredit, and Rational Economic Woman." *Economy and Society* 30 (1): 18–37. https://doi.org/10.1080/03085140020019070.

——. 2004. *The Cultural Politics of Markets: Economic Liberalization and Social Change in Nepal.* Toronto: University of Toronto Press.

Rao, Nitya, and Munshi Israil Hossain. 2012. "'I Want to be Respected': Migration, Mobility, and the Construction of Alternate Educational Discourses in Rural Bangladesh." *Anthropology & Education Quarterly* 43 (4): 415–28. https://doi.org/10.1111/j.1548-1492.2012.01194.x.

Rashid, Sabina Faiz. 2007. "*Durbolota* (Weakness), *Chinta Rog* (Worry Illness), and Poverty: Explanations of White Discharge among Married Adolescent Women in an Urban Slum in Dhaka, Bangladesh." *Medical Anthropology Quarterly* 21 (1): 108–32. https://doi.org/10.1525/maq.2007.21.1.108.

Rashid, Saif. 2014. "JITA Social Business Bangladesh Limited: Reaching the Unreachable in Bangladesh." *Field Actions Science Reports* 12. https://journals.openedition.org/factsreports/3704.

Redfield, Peter. 2012. "Bioexpectations: Life Technologies as Humanitarian Goods." *Public Culture* 24 (1): 157–84. https://doi.org/10.1215/08992363-1443592.

Riaz, Ali. 2014. "Bangladesh's Failed Election." *Journal of Democracy* 25 (2): 119–30.

Riles, Annelise. 2000. *The Network Inside Out*. Ann Arbor: University of Michigan Press.

Rinaldo, Rachel. 2014. "Pious and Critical: Muslim Women Activists and the Question of Agency." *Gender & Society* 28 (6): 824–46. https://doi.org/10.1177/0891243214549352.

Robison, Richard, and David S. G. Goodman, eds. 1996. *The New Rich in Asia: Mobile Phones, McDonald's and Middle-Class Revolution*. London: Routledge.

Roosevelt, Franklin D. 1938. "The Forgotten Man." Radio address, April 7, 1932. Reprinted in *The Public Papers and Addresses of Franklin D. Roosevelt, Vol. 1, The Genesis of the New Deal, 1928–32*, edited by S. Rosenman. New York: Random House.

Roy, Ananya. 2010. *Poverty Capital: Microfinance and the Making of Development*. New York: Routledge.

——. 2012a. "Ethical Subjects: Market Rule in an Age of Poverty." *Public Culture* 24 (1): 105–8. https://doi.org/10.1215/08992363-1443574.

——. 2012b. "Subjects of Risk: Technologies of Gender in the Making of Millennial Modernity." *Public Culture* 24 (1): 131–55. https://doi.org/10.1215/08992363-1498001.

Rozario, Santi. 1992. *Purity and Communal Boundaries: Women and Social Change in a Bangladeshi Village*. London: Zed Press.

——. 2012. "Islamic Marriage: A Haven in an Uncertain World." *Culture and Religion* 13 (2): 159–75. https://doi.org/10.1080/14755610.2012.674955.

Scherz, China. 2014. *Having People, Having Heart: Charity, Sustainable Development, and Problems of Dependence in Central Uganda*. Chicago: University of Chicago Press.

Schuller, Mark, and Julie K. Maldonado. 2016. "Disaster Capitalism." *Annals of Anthropological Practice* 40 (1): 61–72. https://doi.org/10.1111/napa.12088.

Schuster, Caroline. 2014. "The Social Unit of Debt: Gender and Creditworthiness in Paraguayan Microfinance." *American Ethnologist* 41 (3): 563–78. https://doi.org/10.1111/amet.12095.

——. 2015. *Social Collateral: Women and Microfinance in Paraguay's Smuggling Economy*. Berkeley: University of California Press.

Schwittay, Anke. 2008. "'A Living Lab': Corporate Delivery of ICTs in Rural India." *Science Technology and Society* 13 (2): 175–209.

——. 2011a. "The Financial Inclusion Assemblage: Subjects, Technics, Rationalities." *Critique of Anthropology* 31 (4): 381–401. https://doi.org/10.1177/0308275X11420117.

——. 2011b. "The Marketization of Poverty." *Current Anthropology* 52 (S3): S71–S82

Scott, James. 1972. "The Erosion of Patron-Client Bonds and Social Change in Rural Southeast Asia." *Journal of Asian Studies* 32 (1): 5–37. https://doi.org/10.2307/2053176.

——. 1977. *The Moral Economy of the Peasant: Rebellion and Subsistence in Southeast Asia*. New Haven, CT: Yale University Press.

———. 1985. *Weapons of the Weak*. New Haven, CT: Yale University Press.

Sen, Amartya. 1990. "Gender and Cooperative Conflicts." In *Persistent Inequalities: Women And World Development*, edited by Irene Tinker, 123–49. Oxford: Oxford University Press.

Sen, Samita. 1999. "Beyond the 'Working Class'; Women's Role in Indian Industrialisation." *South Asia* 22 (2): 95–117. https://doi.org/10.1080/00856409908723367.

Shah, Alpa. 2010. *In the Shadows of the State: Indigenous Politics, Environmentalism, and Insurgency in Jharkhand, India*. Durham, NC: Duke University Press.

Shakya, Yogendra B., and Katharine N. Rankin. 2008. "The Politics of Subversion in Development Practice: An Exploration of Microfinance in Nepal and Vietnam." *Journal of Development Studies* 44 (8): 1214–35. https://doi.org/10.1080/00220380802242461.

Sharma, Ursula. 1985. *Women's Work, Class, and the Urban Household: A Study of Shimla, North India*. London: Tavistock.

Shehabuddin, Elora. 1999. "Contesting the Illicit: Gender and the Politics of Fatwas in Bangladesh." *Signs* 24 (4): 1011–44.

———. 2008. "Jamaat-i-Islami in Bangladesh: Women, Democracy and the Transformation of Islamist Politics." *Modern Asian Studies* 42 (2–3): 577–603. https://doi.org/10.1017/S0026749X07003204.

———. 2011. "Gender and the Figure of the "Moderate Muslim": Feminism in the Twenty-First Century." In *The Question of Gender: Joan W. Scott's Critical Feminism*, edited by Judith Butler and Elizabeth Weed, 102–42. Bloomington: Indiana University Press.

Simmons, Ruth, Rezina Mita, and Michael A. Koenig 1992. "Employment in Family Planning and Women's Status in Bangladesh." *Studies in Family Planning* 23 (2): 97–109. https://doi.org/10.2307/1966539.

Snyder, Benjamin. 2016. *The Disrupted Workplace: Time and the Moral Order of Flexible Capitalism*. New York: Oxford University Press.

Sobhan, Rehman. 1982. *The Crisis of External Dependence: The Political Economy of Foreign Aid to Bangladesh*. Dhaka: The University Press.

Stacey, Judith. 1990. *Brave New Families: Domestic Upheaval in Late Twentieth Century America*. New York: Basic Books.

Stirrat, R. L., and Heiko Henkel. 1997. "The Development Gift: The Problem of Reciprocity in the NGO World." *Annals of the American Academy of Political and Social Science* 554 (November): 66–80.

Street, Alice. 2015. "Caring by Numbers: Humanitarian Management in a Global Health Crisis." Paper presented at the Department of Anthropology, London School of Economics and Political Science, May 29.

Street, Brian V. 1993. *Cross-Cultural Approaches to Literacy*. Cambridge: Cambridge University Press.

Suykens, Bert, and Aynul Islam. 2013. "*Hartal* as a Complex Political Performance: General Strikes and the Organisation of (Local) Power in Bangladesh." *Contributions to Indian Sociology* 47 (1): 61–83. https://doi.org/10.1177/006996671204700103.

Tambiah, Stanley Jeyaraja. 1973. "Dowry and Bridewealth, and the Property Rights of Women in South Asia." In *Bridewealth and Dowry*, edited by Jack Goody and Stanley Jeyaraja Tambiah, 59–169. London: Cambridge University Press.

Tenhunen, Sirpa. 2008. "Mobile Technology in the Village: ICTs, Culture, and Social Logistics in India." *Journal of the Royal Anthropological Institute* 14 (3): 515–34. https://doi.org/10.1111/j.1467-9655.2008.00515.x.

Thomas, Nicholas, and Richard Eves. 1999. *Bad Colonists: The South Seas Letters of Vernon Lee Walker and Louis Becke*. Durham, NC: Duke University Press.

Thorp, John P. 1978. *Power among the Farmers of Daripalla: A Bangladesh Village Study.* Chicago: Caritas.

UNDP. n.d. "Eight Goals for 2015: Bangladesh's Progress on the MDGs." http://www.bd.undp.org/content/bangladesh/en/home/post-2015/millennium-development-goals.html, accessed March 31, 2016.

UNICEF. n.d. "Meena." http://www.unicef.org/meena/, accessed November 1, 2014.

Upadhya, Carol. 2009. "India's 'New Middle Class' and the Globalising City: Software Professionals in Bangalore, India." In *The New Middle Classes: Globalizing Lifestyles, Consumerism and Environmental Concern*, edited by Hellmuth Lange and Lars Meier, 253–68. Dordrecht: Springer.

Urciuoli, Bonnie. 2008. "Skills and Selves in the New Workplace." *American Ethnologist* 35 (2): 211–28. https://doi.org/10.1111/j.1548-1425.2008.00031.x.

van Schendel, Willem. 1981. *Peasant Mobility: The Odds of Life in Rural Bangladesh.* Assen: Van Gorcum.

——. 2009. *A History of Bangladesh.* Cambridge: Cambridge University Press.

Vatuk, Sylvia. 2004. "*Hamara Daur-i Hayat*: An Indian Muslim Woman Writes Her Life." In *Telling Lives in India: Biography, Autobiography, and Life History*, edited by David Arnold and Stuart H. Blackburn, 144–74. Bloomington: Indiana University Press.

Venkatesan, Soumhya. 2009. "Rethinking Agency: Persons and Things in the Heterotopia of 'Traditional Indian Craft'." *Journal of the Royal Anthropological Institute* 15 (1): 78–95. https://doi.org/10.1111/j.1467-9655.2008.01531.x.

Wassener, Bettina. 2012. "Success in a Land Known for Disasters." *New York Times*, April 09. http://www.nytimes.com/2012/04/10/world/asia/success-in-a-land-known-for-disasters.html.

Wedel, Janine. 2004. "'Studying Through' a Globalizing World: Building Method through Aidnographies." In *Ethnographies of Aid: Exploring Development Texts and Encounters*, edited by Jeremy Gould and Henrik Secher Marcussen, 149–74. International Development Studies, Occasional Papers No. 24. Roskilde: Roskilde University Press.

Weber, Max. 1930. *The Protestant Ethic and the Spirit of Capitalism*, translated by T. Parsons. London: Allen and Unwin.

White, Sarah. 1992. *Arguing with the Crocodile: Gender and Class in Bangladesh.* London: Zed Books.

——. 1999. "NGOs, Civil Society, and the State in Bangladesh: The Politics of Representing the Poor." *Development and Change* 30 (2): 307–26. https://doi.org/10.1111/1467-7660.00119.

——. 2012. "Beyond the Paradox: Religion, Family and Modernity in Contemporary Bangladesh." *Modern Asian Studies* 46 (5): 1429–52. https://doi.org/10.1017/S0026749X12000133.

Wilce, Jim. 1995. "'I Can't Tell You All My Troubles': Conflict, Resistance, and Metacommunication in Bangladeshi Illness Interactions." *American Ethnologist* 22 (4): 927–52.

Wilson, Ara. 1999. "The Empire of Direct Sales and the Making of Thai Entrepreneurs." *Critique of Anthropology* 19 (4): 401–22. https://doi.org/10.1177/0308275X9901900406.

Wood, Geoffrey. 1994. *Bangladesh: Whose Ideas, Whose Interests?* London: Intermediate Technology Publications.

Wood, Geoffrey D., and Iffath Sharif. 1997. *Who Needs Credit? Poverty and Finance in Bangladesh.* Dhaka: University Press.

The World Bank. 2014. "Bangladesh: Safety Nets to Protect the Poor." March 27. http://www.worldbank.org/en/news/feature/2014/03/27/bangladesh-safety-nets-to-protect-the-poor.

The World Bank. 2016. "Bangladesh Development Update: Economy Moving Forward Despite Internal and External Challenges." April. http://www.worldbank.org/en/country/bangladesh/publication/bangladesh-development-update-economy-moving-forward-despite-challenges.

World Bank Report. 1996. *Pursuing Common Goals*. Dhaka: World Bank Publications.

Yanagisako, Sylvia. 2002. *Producing Culture and Capital: Family Firms in Italy*. Princeton, NJ: Princeton University Press.

Yardley, Jim. 2012. "Made in Bangladesh: Export Powerhouse Feels Pangs of Labor Strife." *New York Times*, August 23. http://www.nytimes.com/2012/08/24/world/asia/as-bangladesh-becomes-export-powerhouse-labor-strife-erupts.html?smid=pl-share.

Zelizer, Viviana. 2011. *Economic Lives: How Culture Shapes the Economy*. Princeton, NJ: Princeton University Press.

——. 2012. "How I Became a Relational Economic Sociologist and What Does That Mean?" *Politics & Society* 40 (2): 145–74. https://doi.org/10.1177/0032329212441591.

Index

Page numbers in italics refer to figures.

CPSIA information can be obtained
at www.ICGtesting.com
Printed in the USA
LVHW091955020420
652036LV00002B/75

9 781501 749551